KEATON HENSON
INSIDE VOICE

Sketchbooks 2011-2022

These books have been with me in every bus, train, plane, hotel room, hospital waiting room and park bench I have ever inhabited.
 Since childhood I have had one at my side at most hours of most days, catching whatever falls from my withering head, keeping me company.

 They are as close to a glimpse inside my brain as I can offer. messy, unsettling and strange as they may be.
 Yours earnestly,
 Keaton H

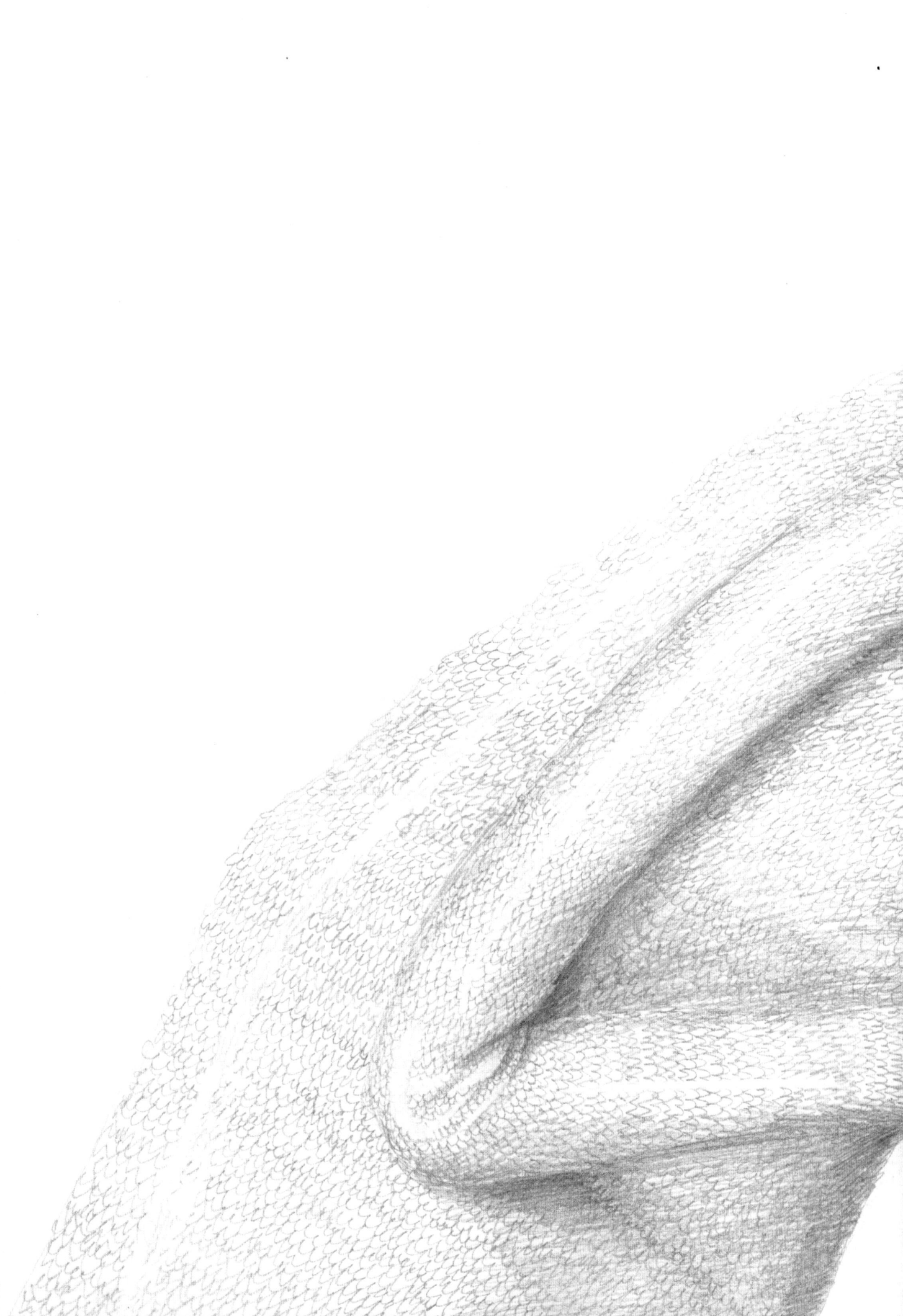

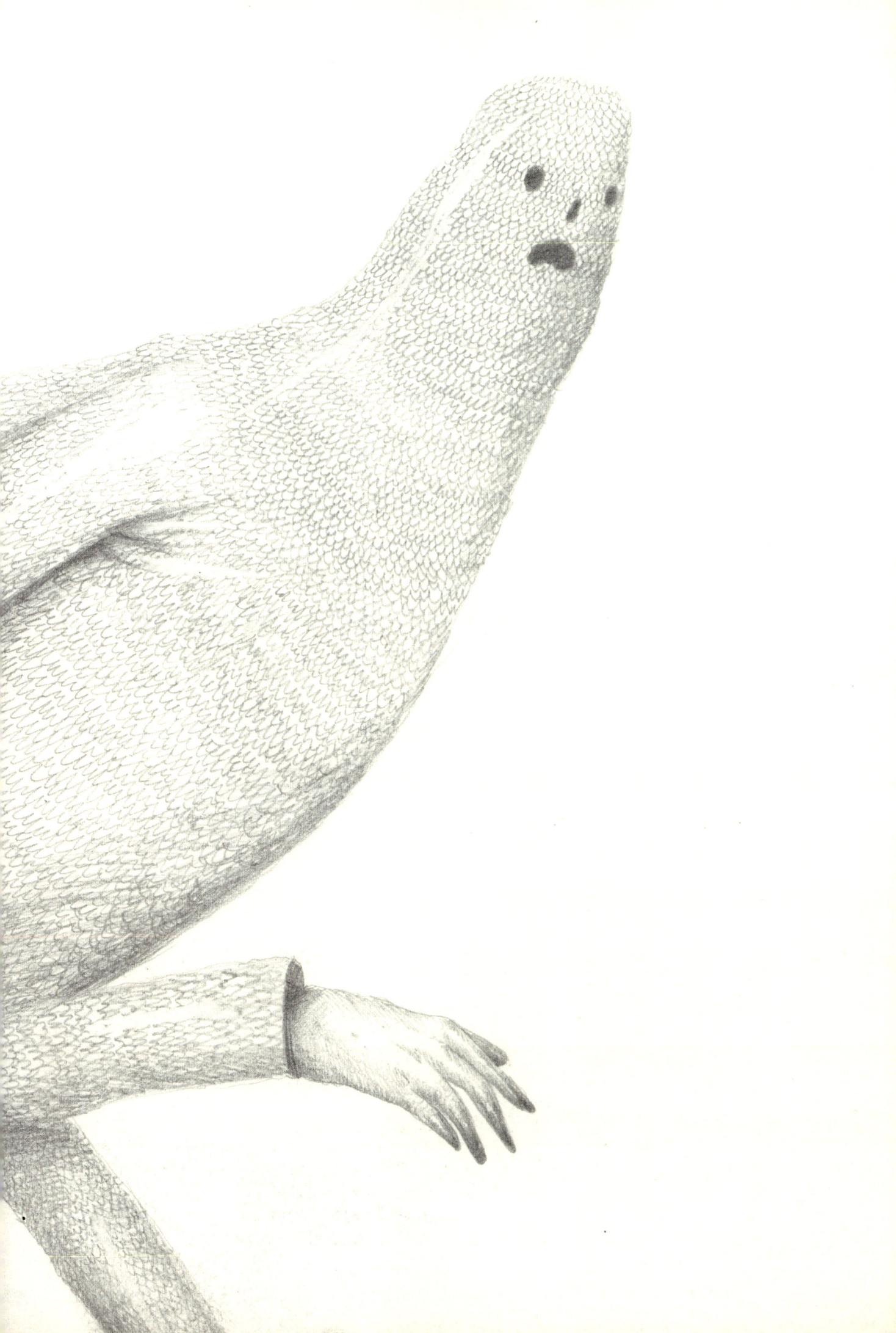

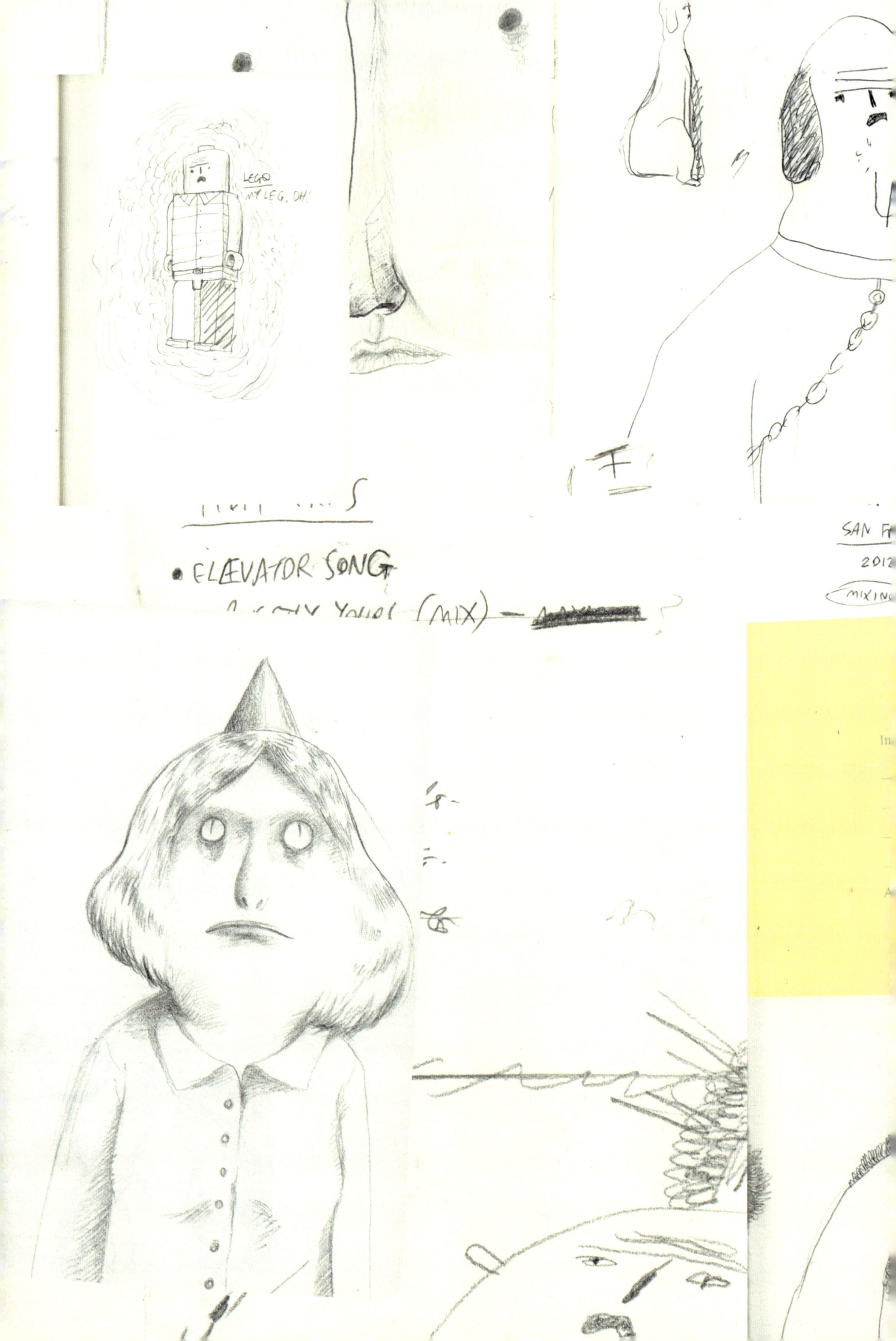

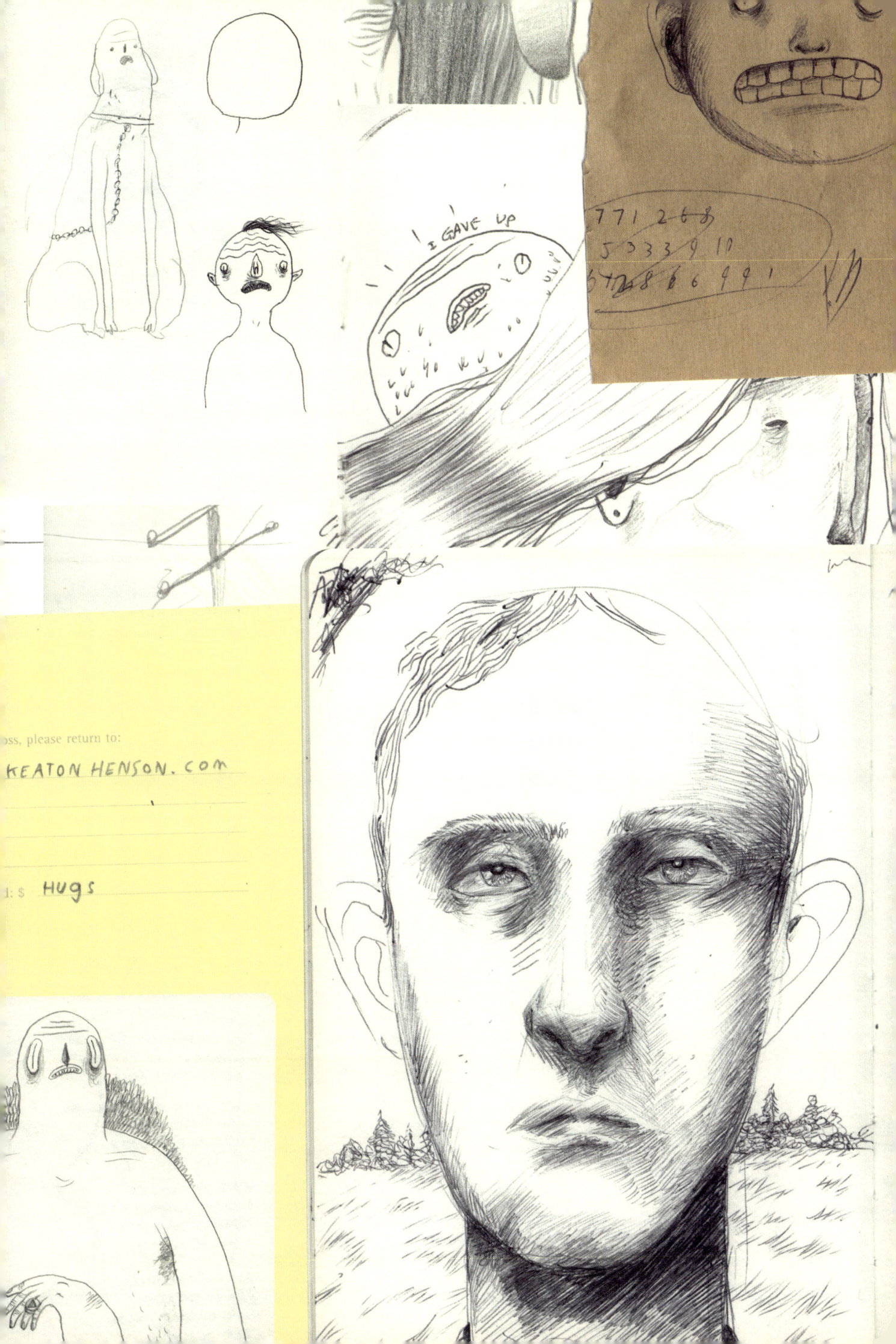

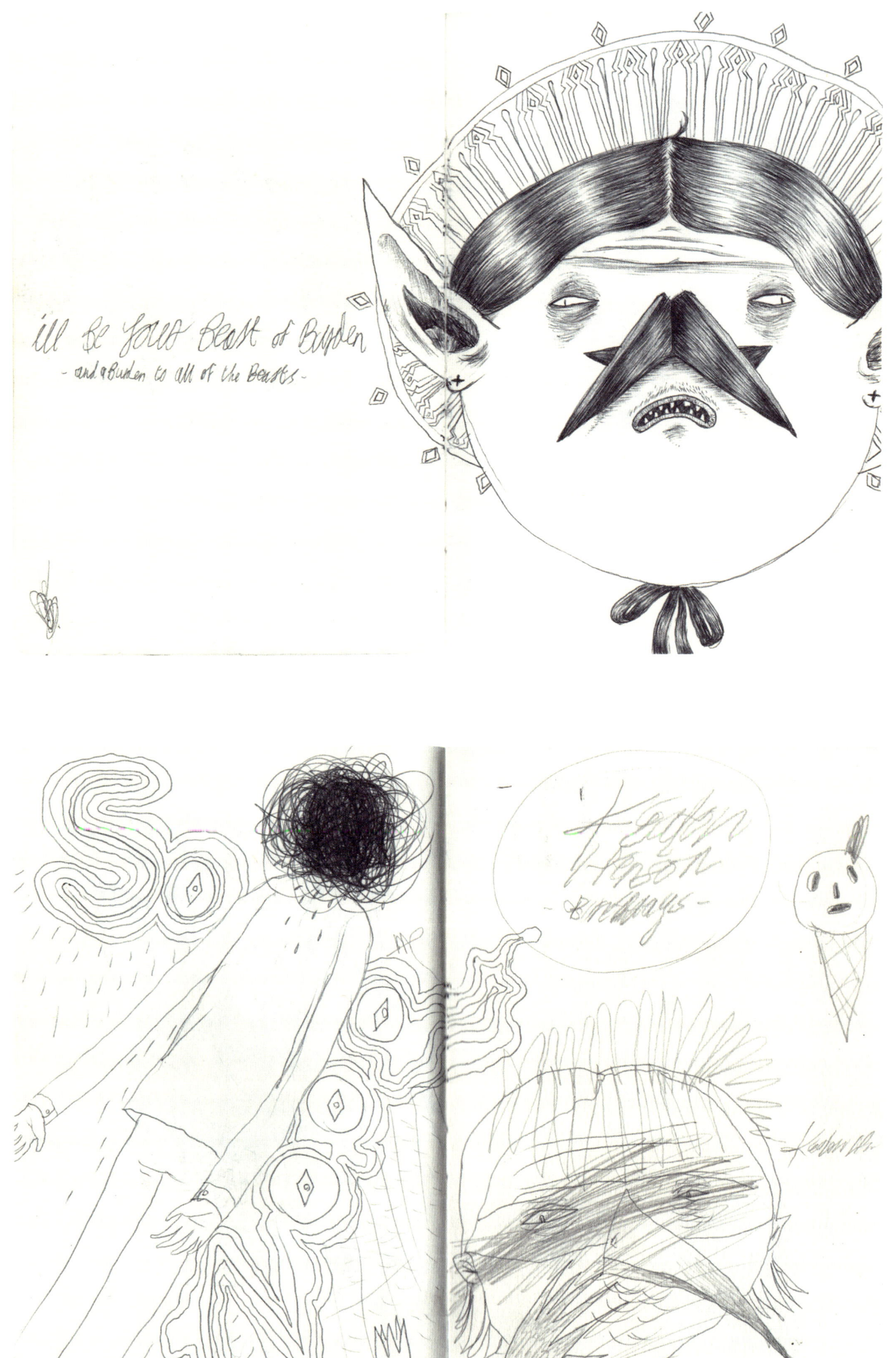

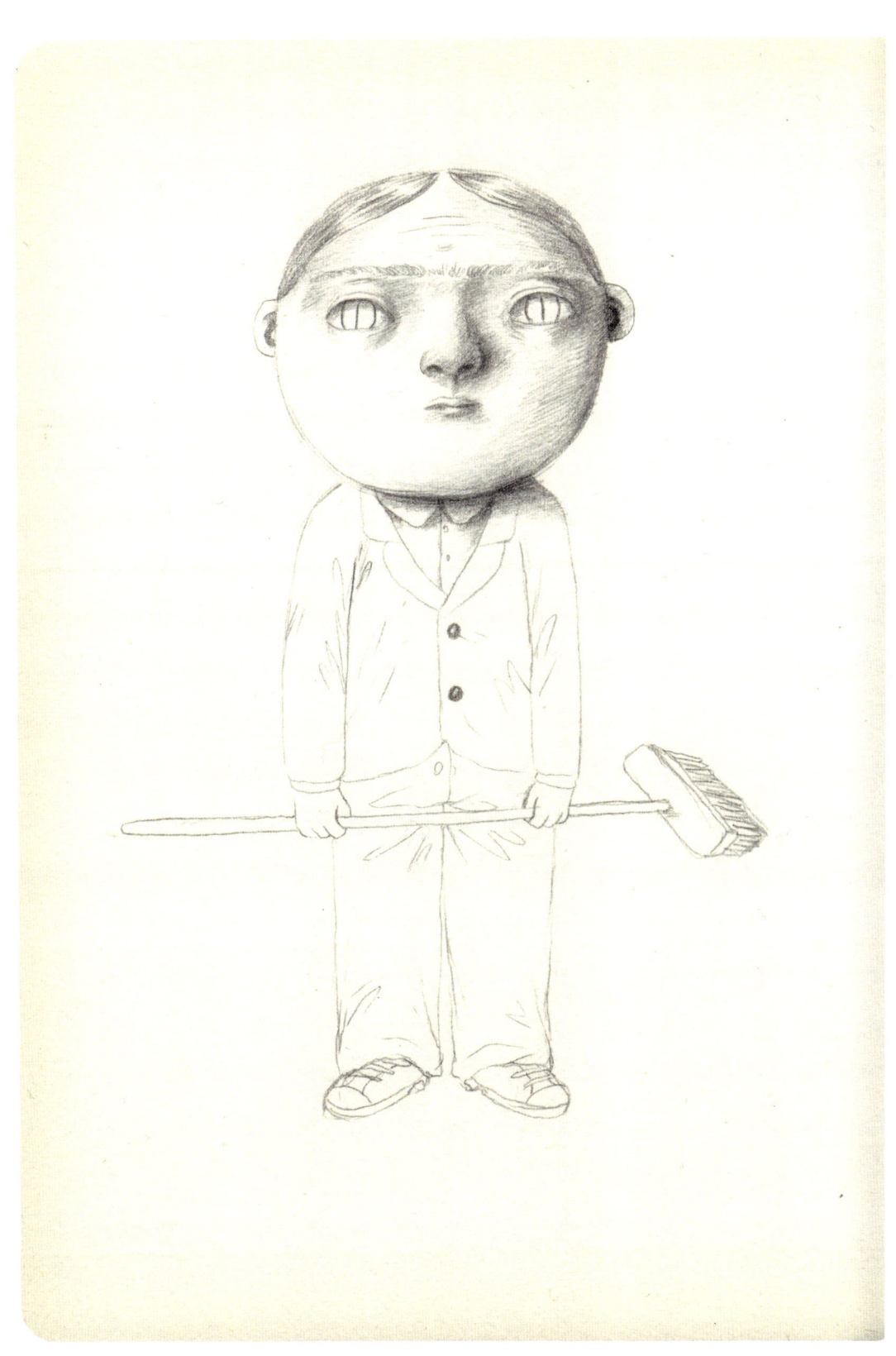

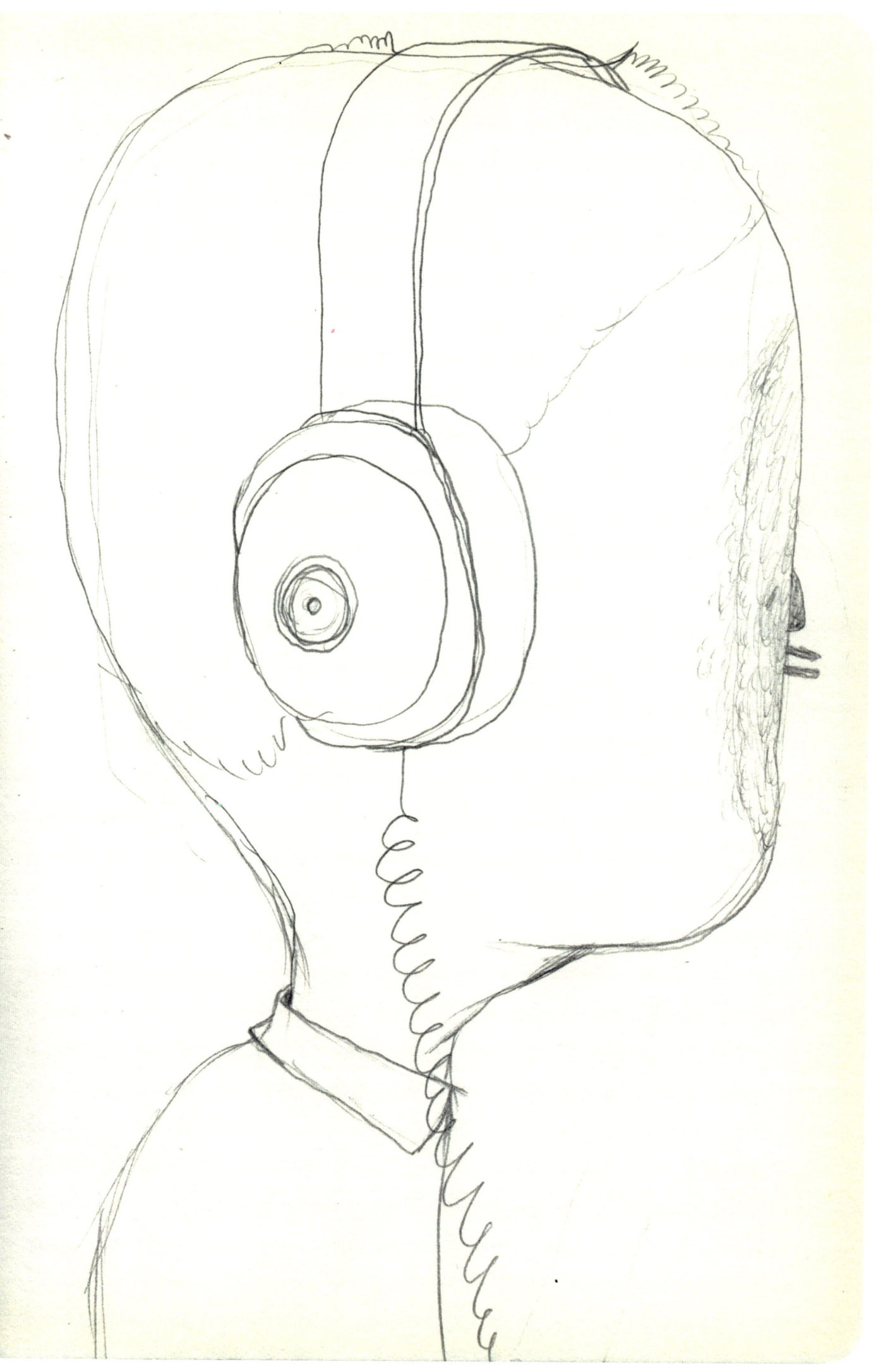

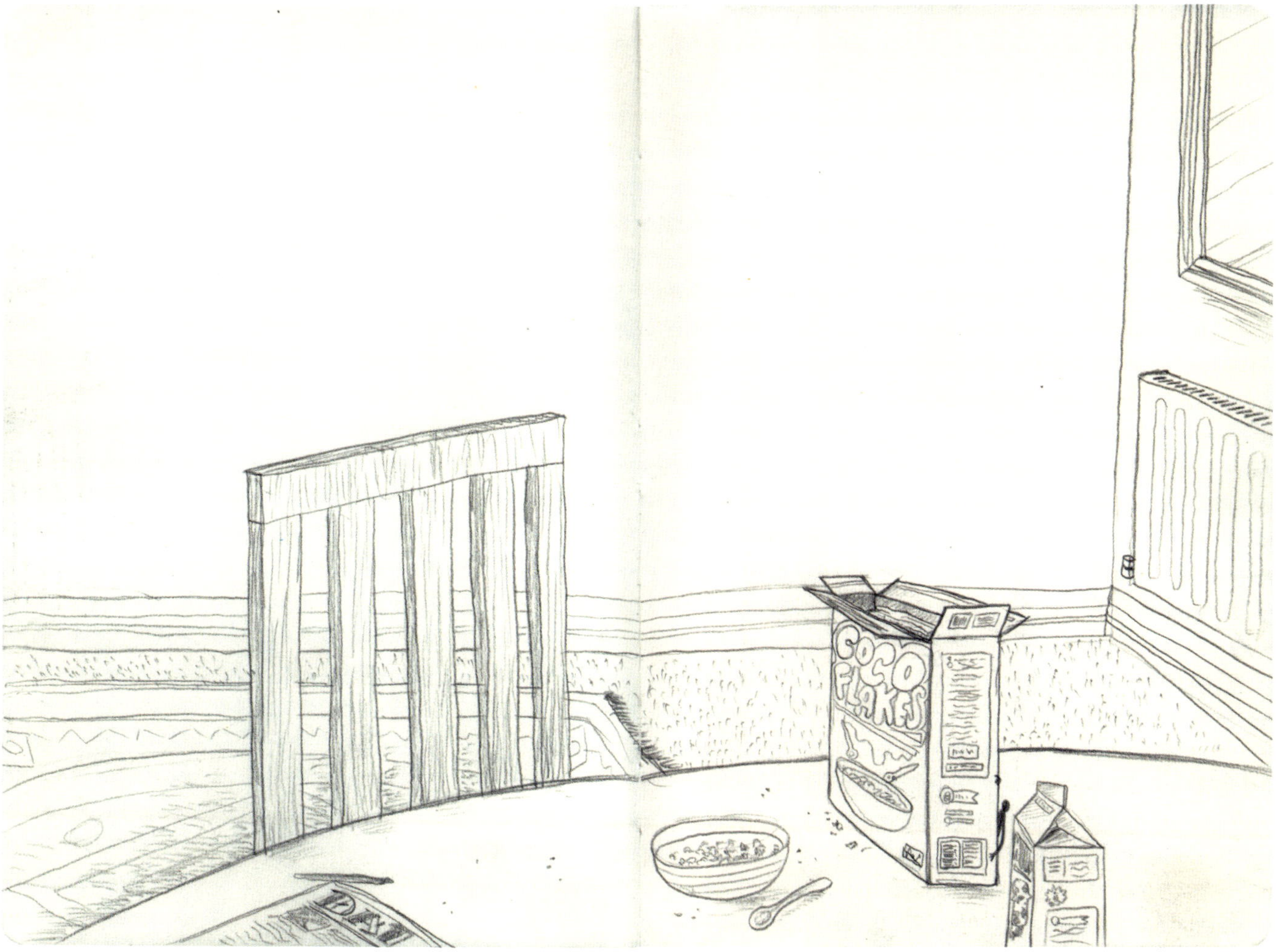

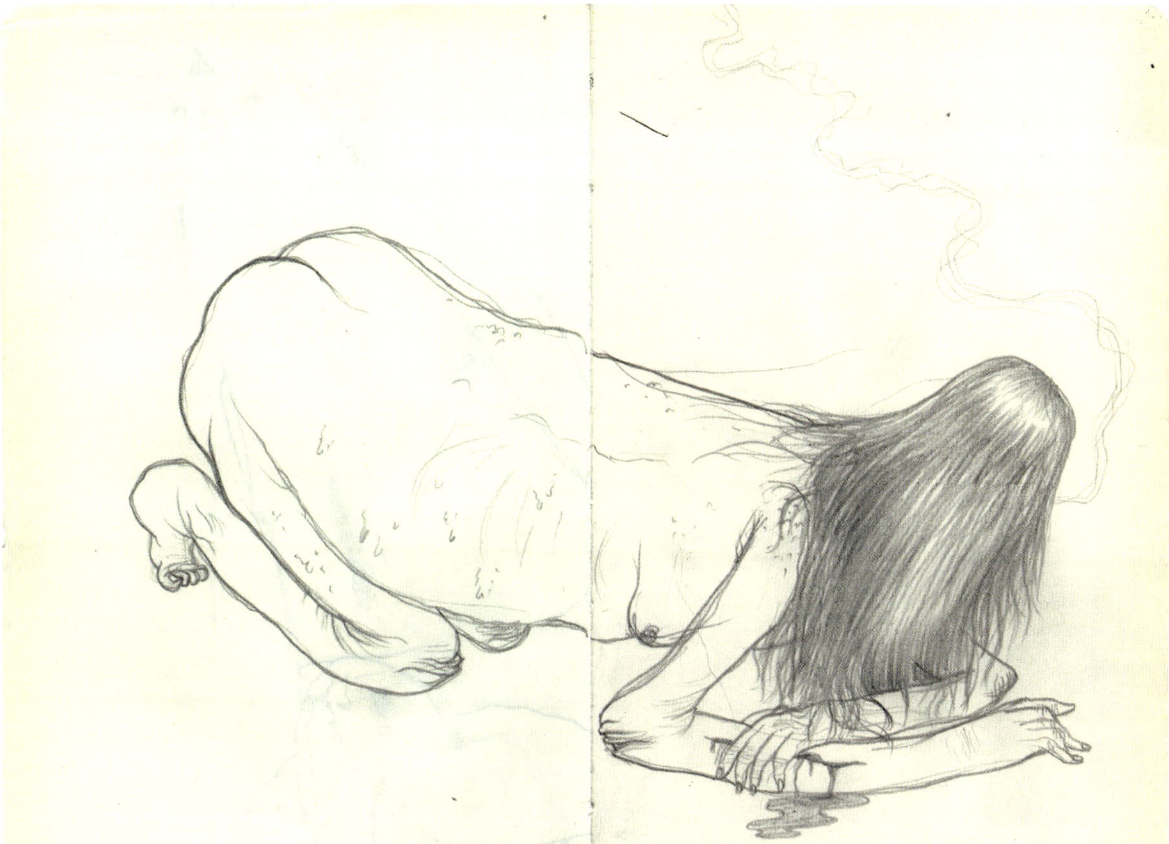

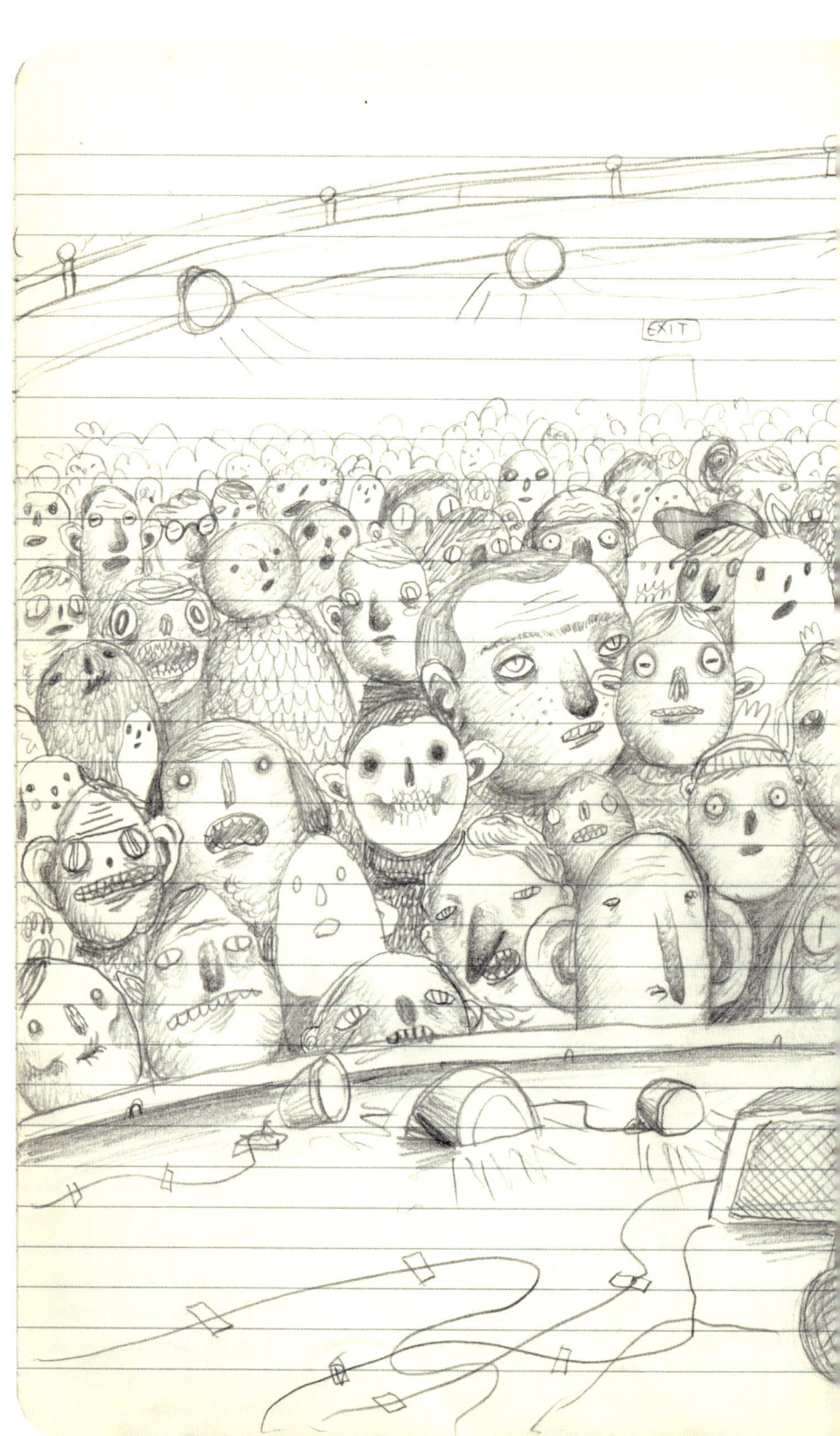

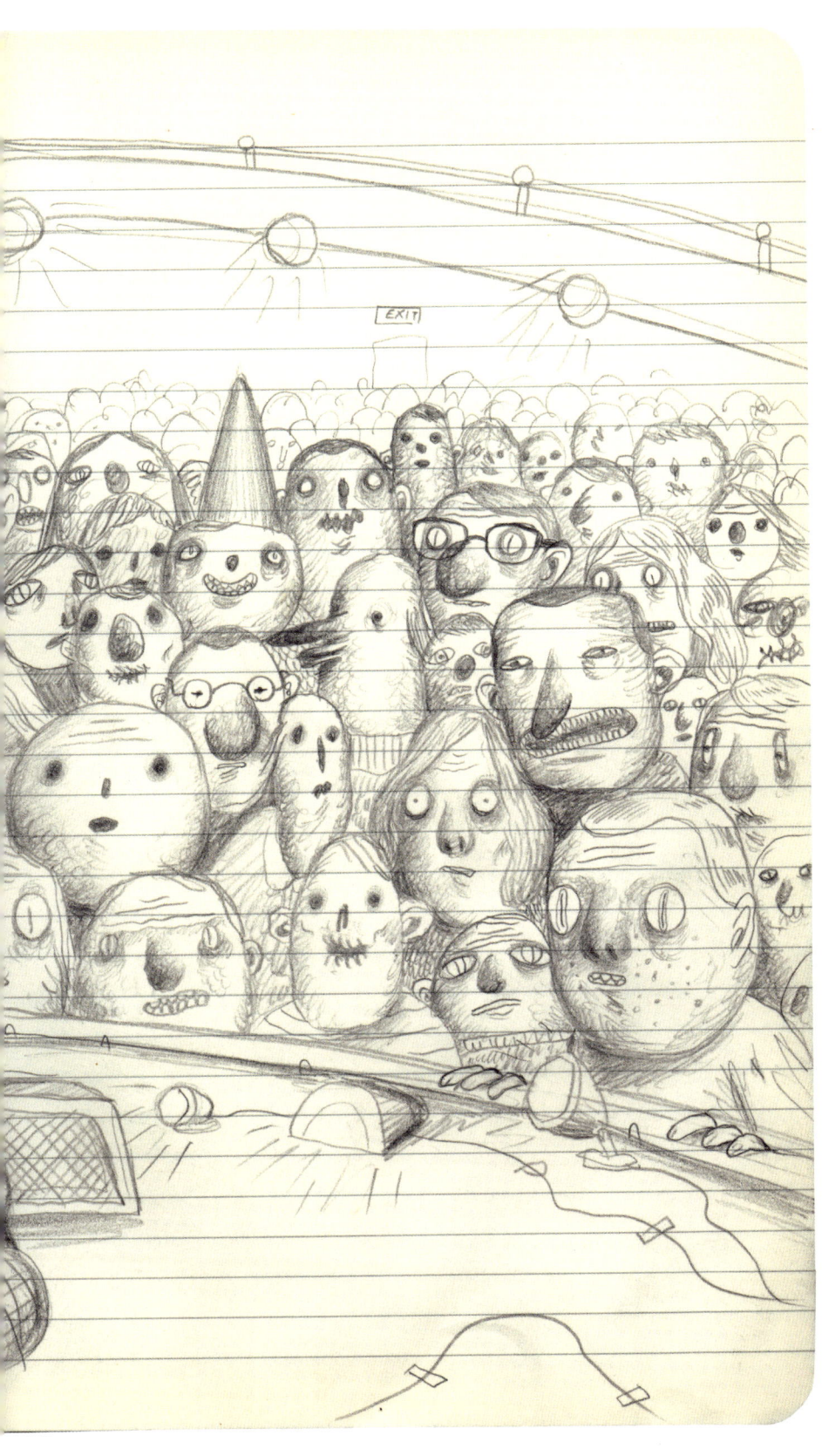

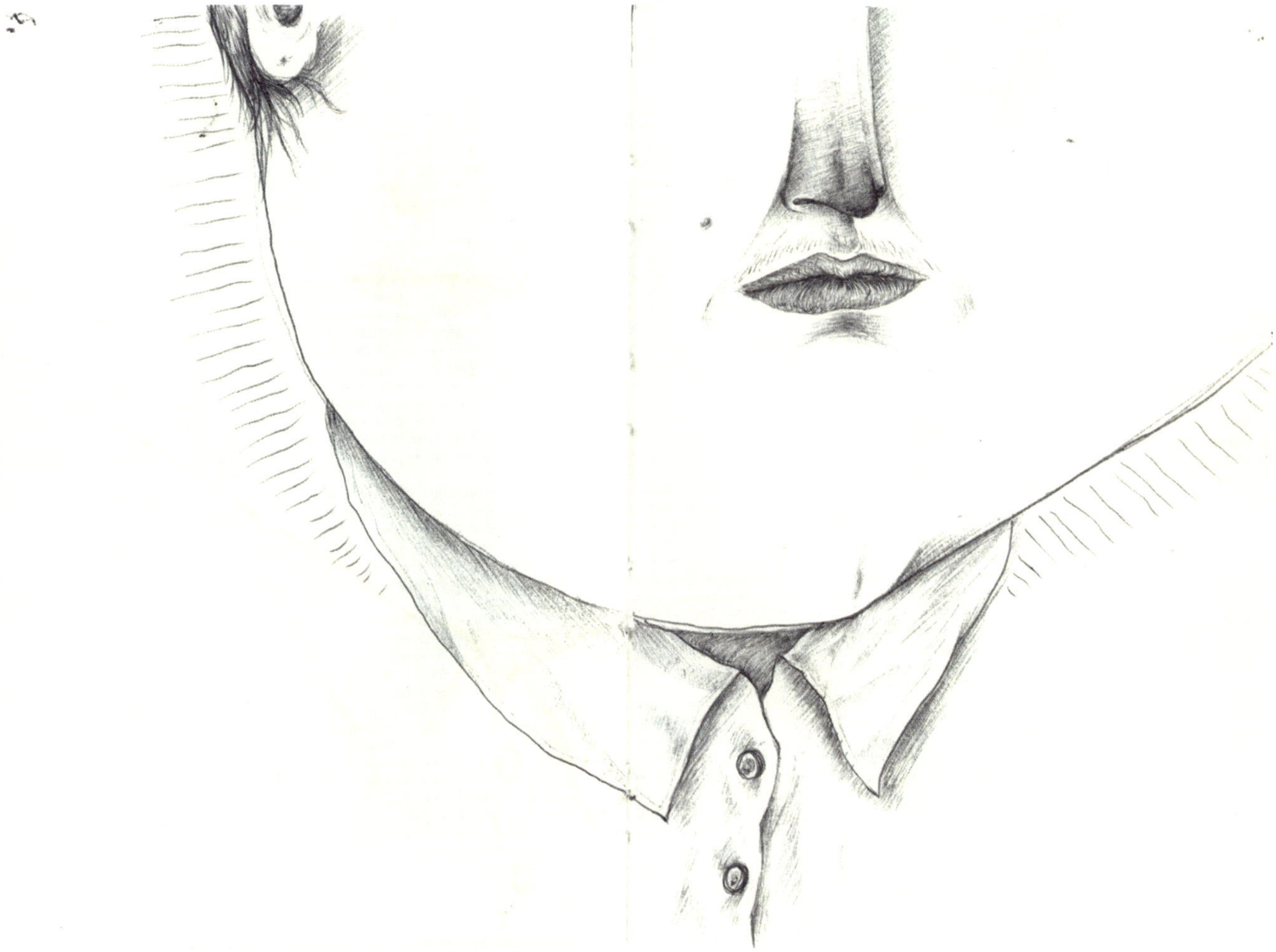

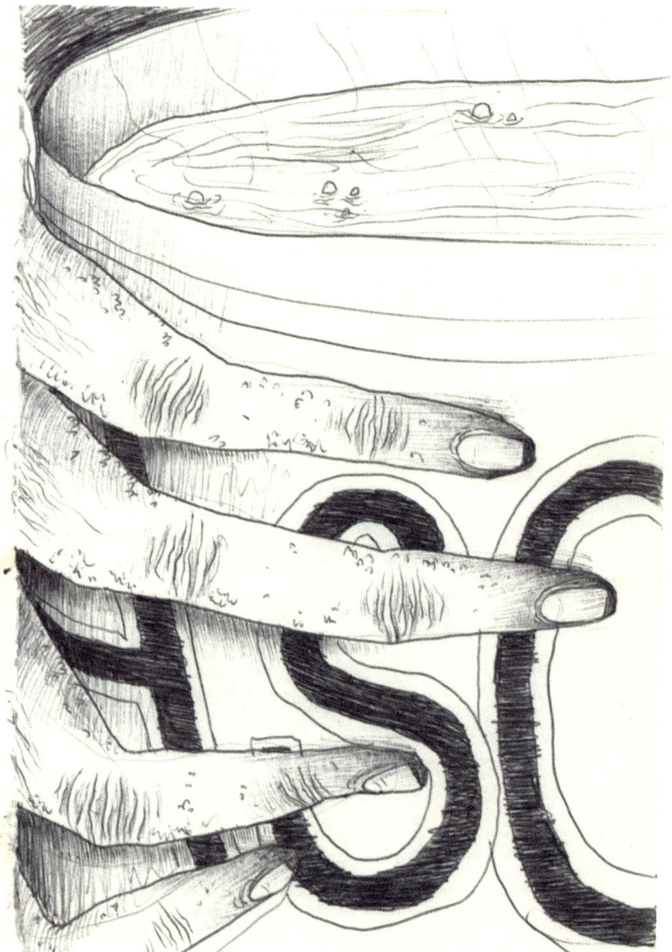

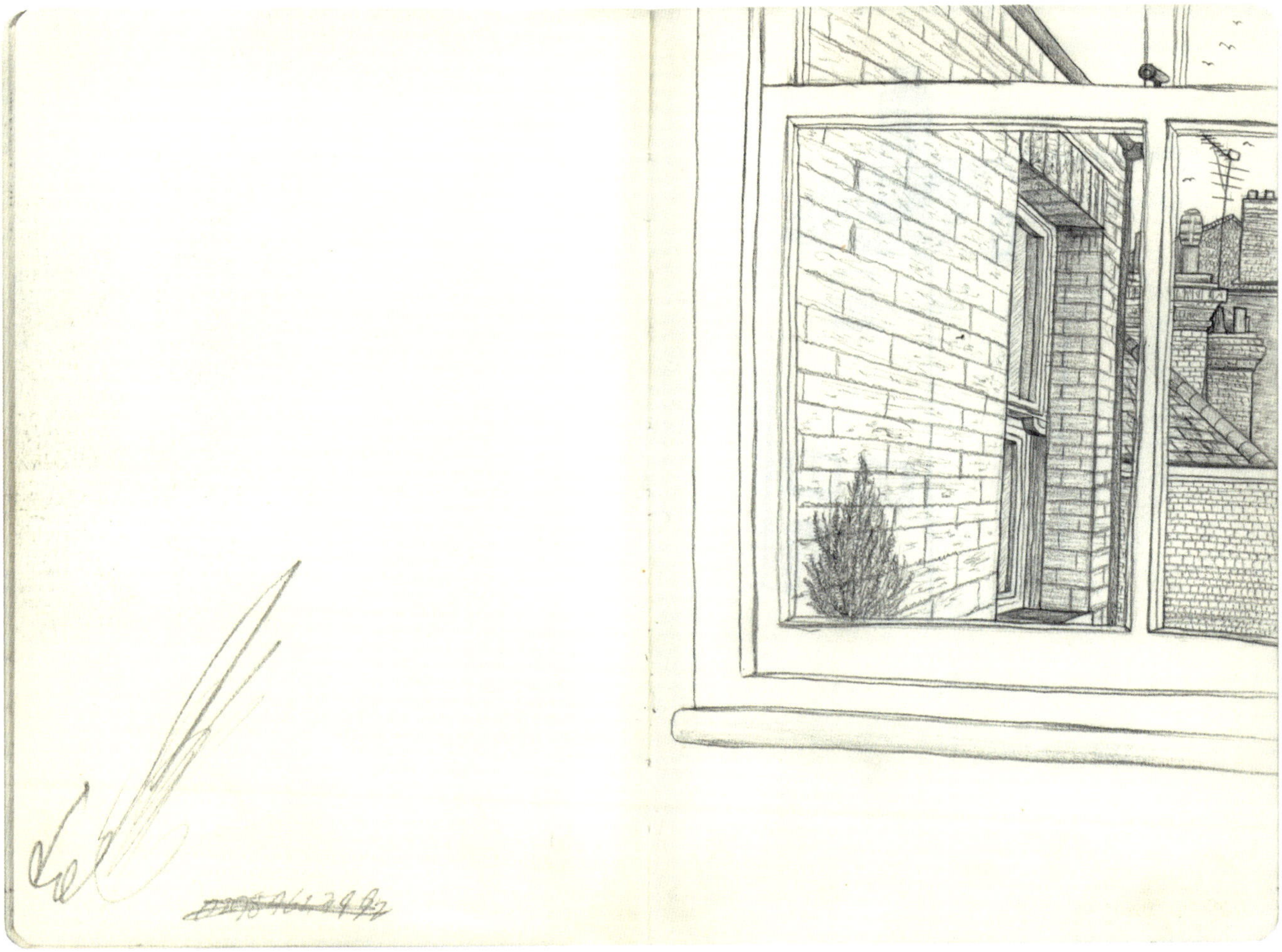

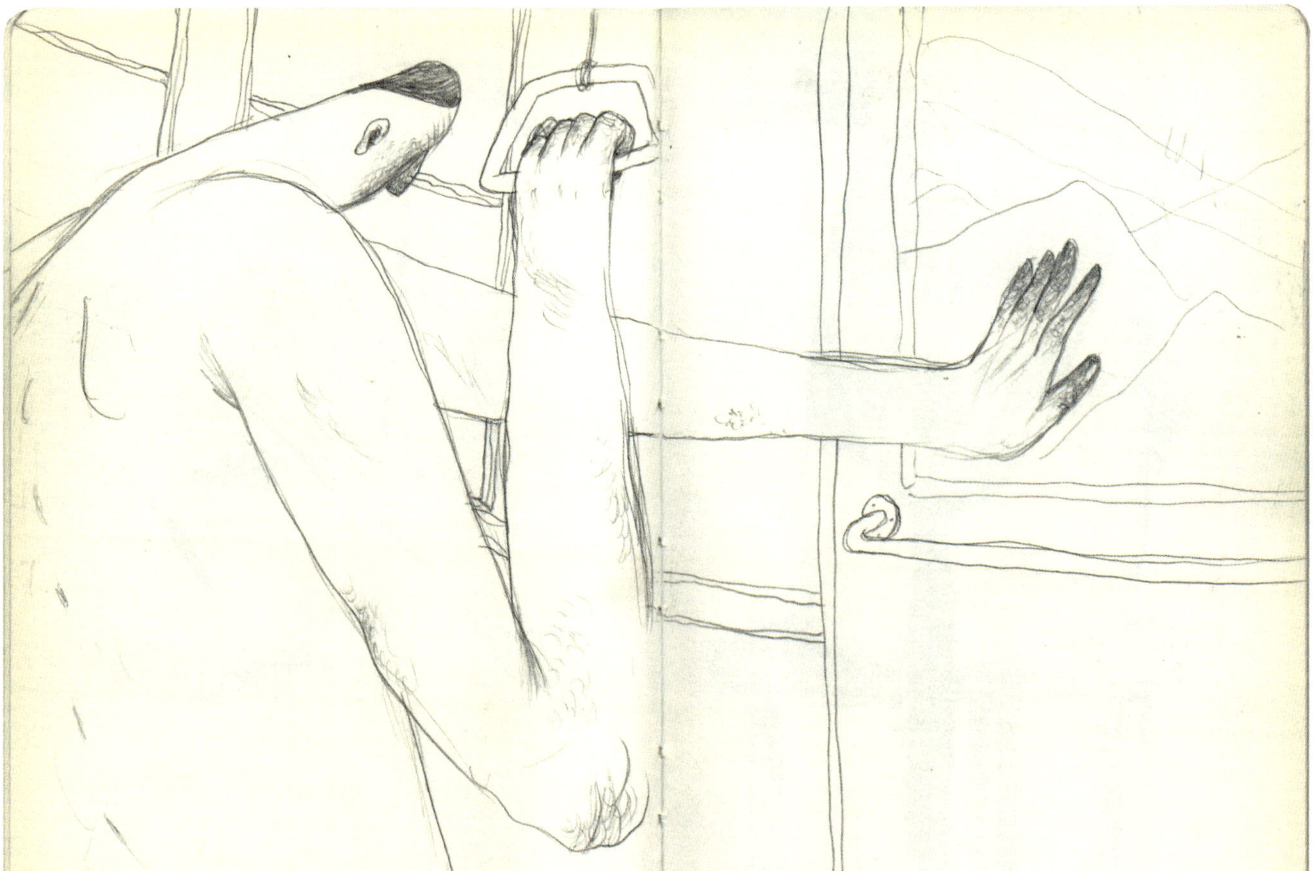

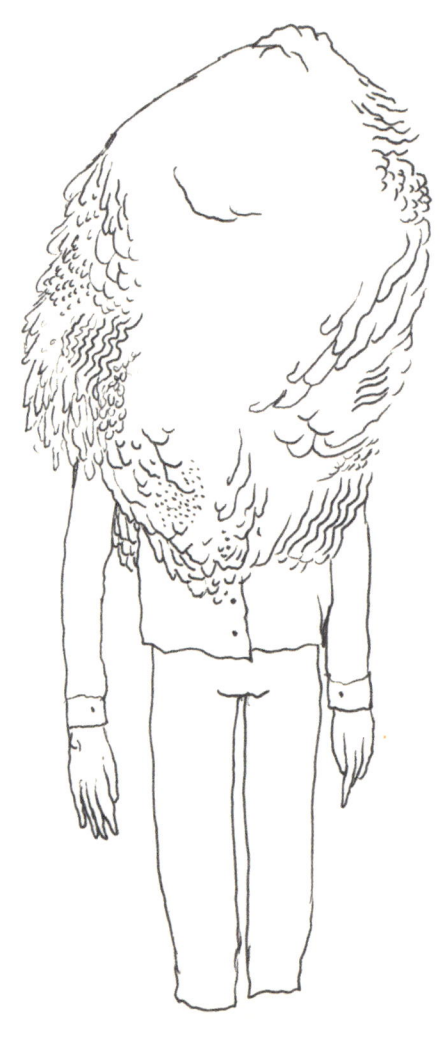

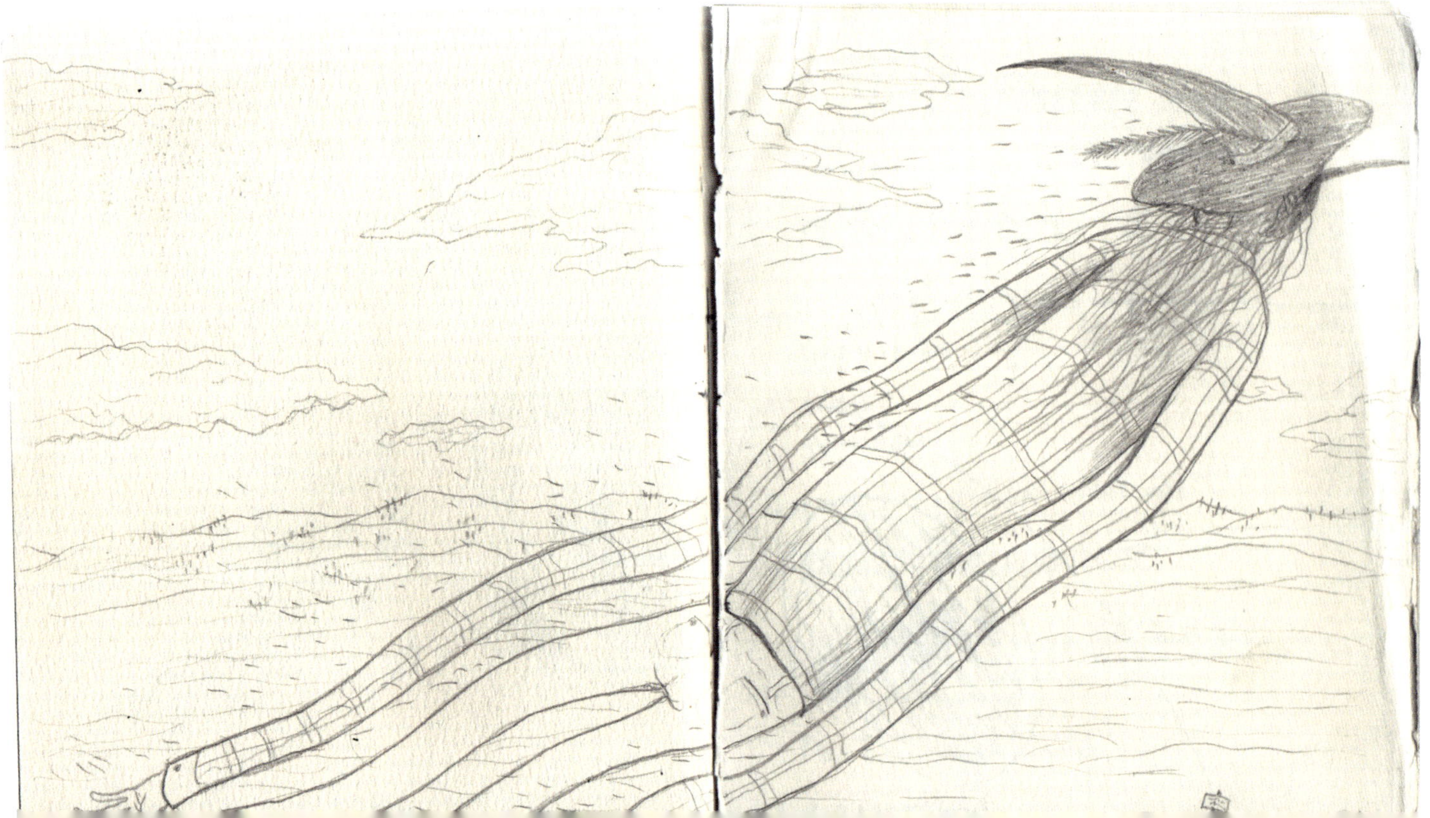

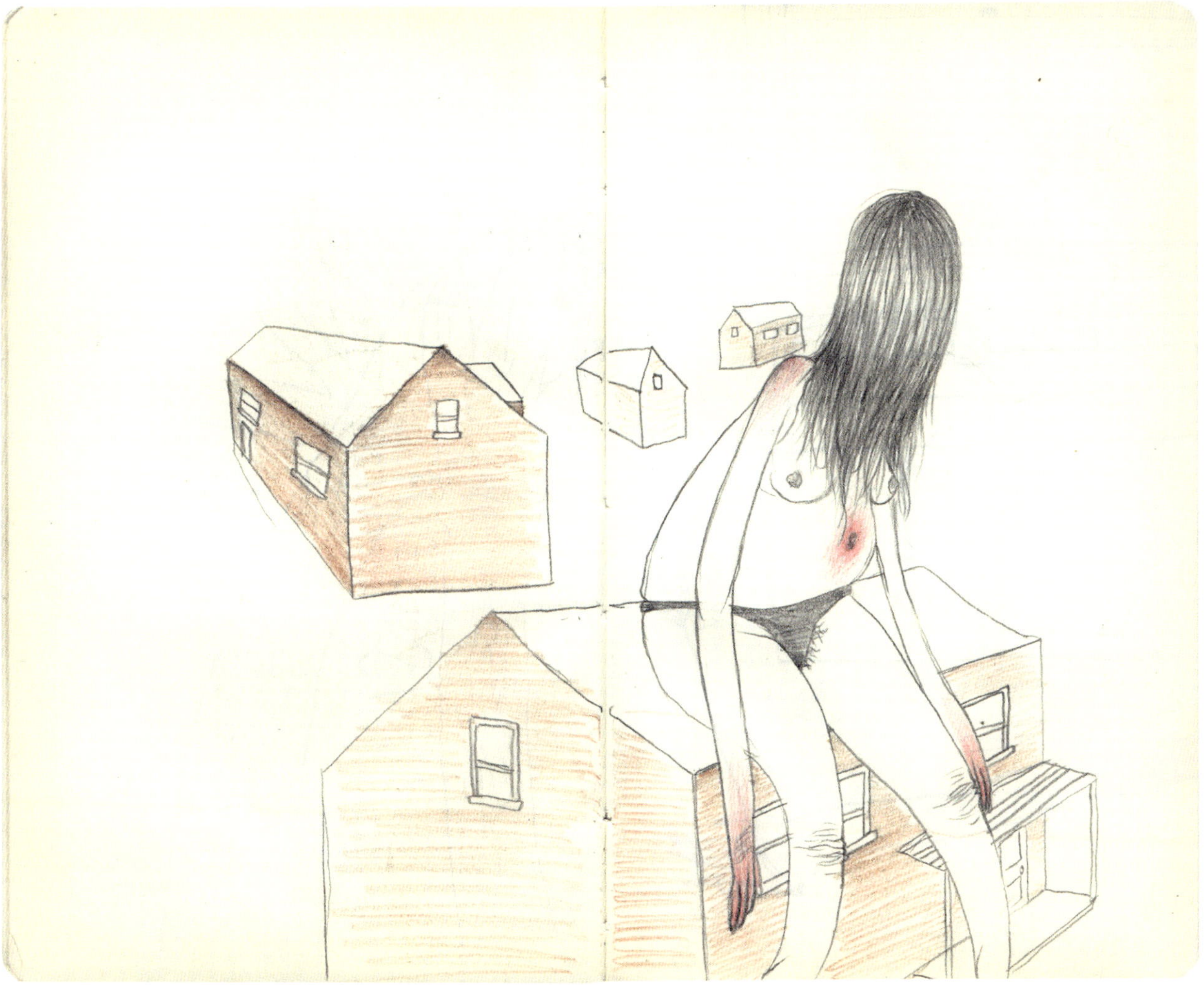

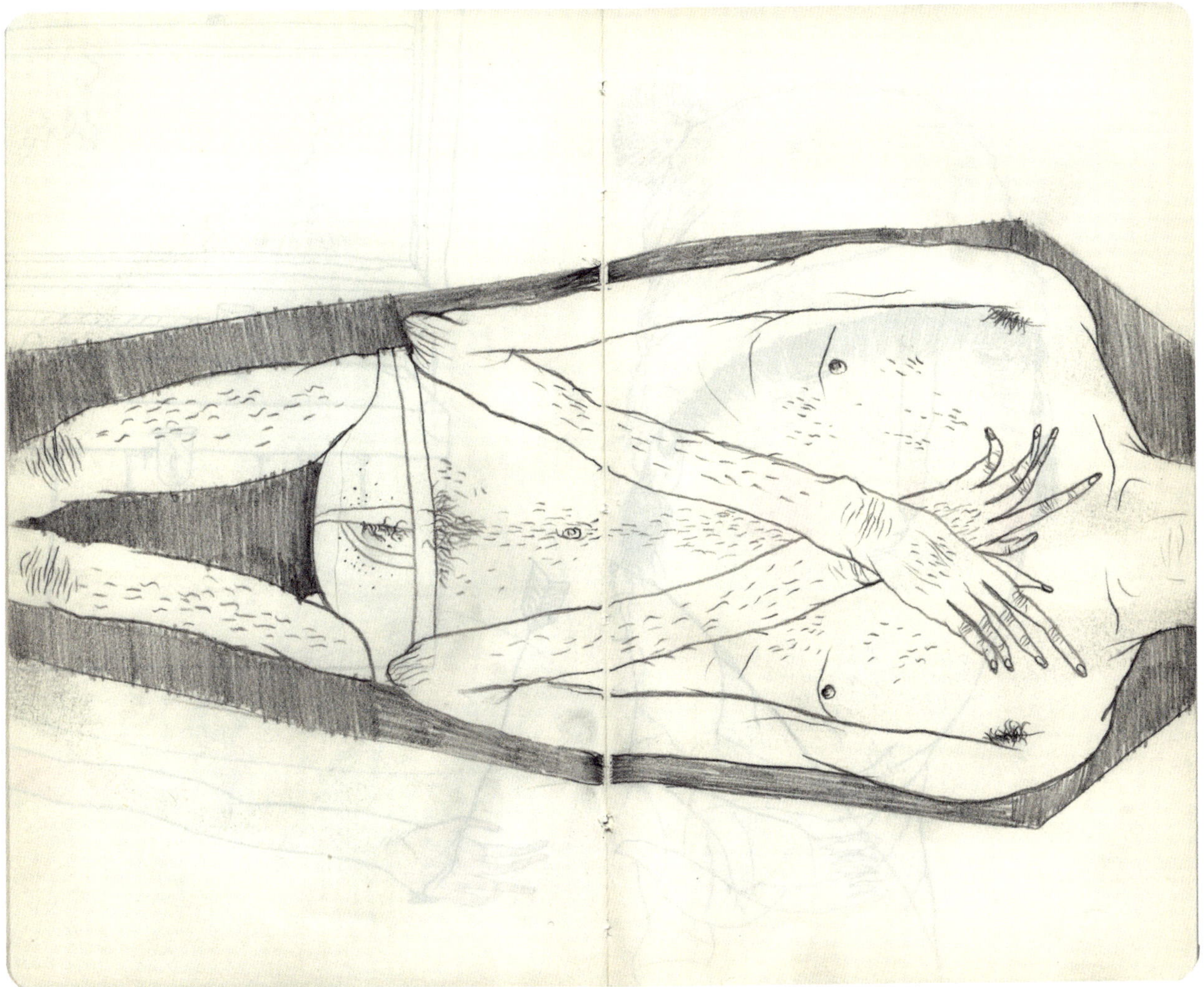

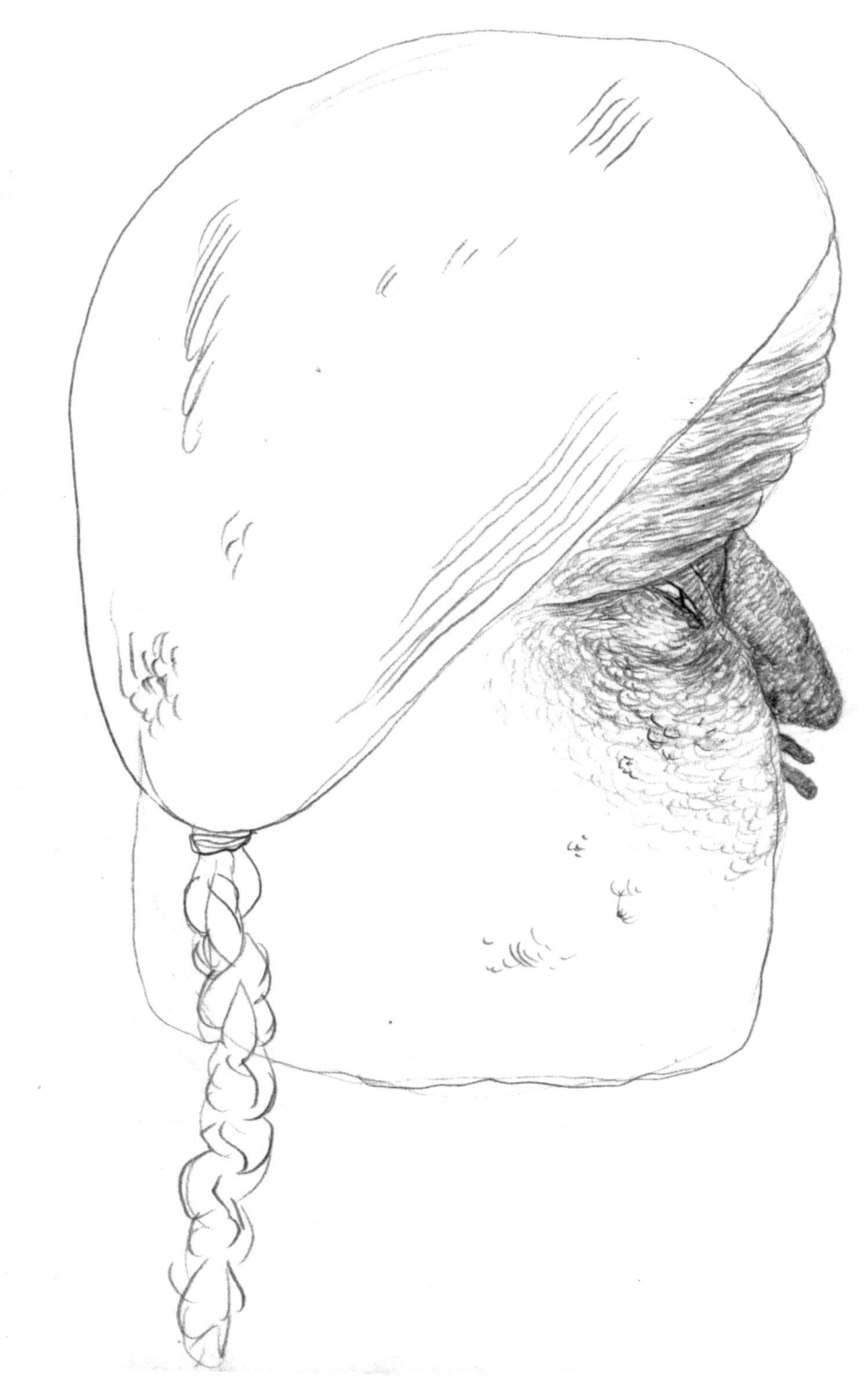

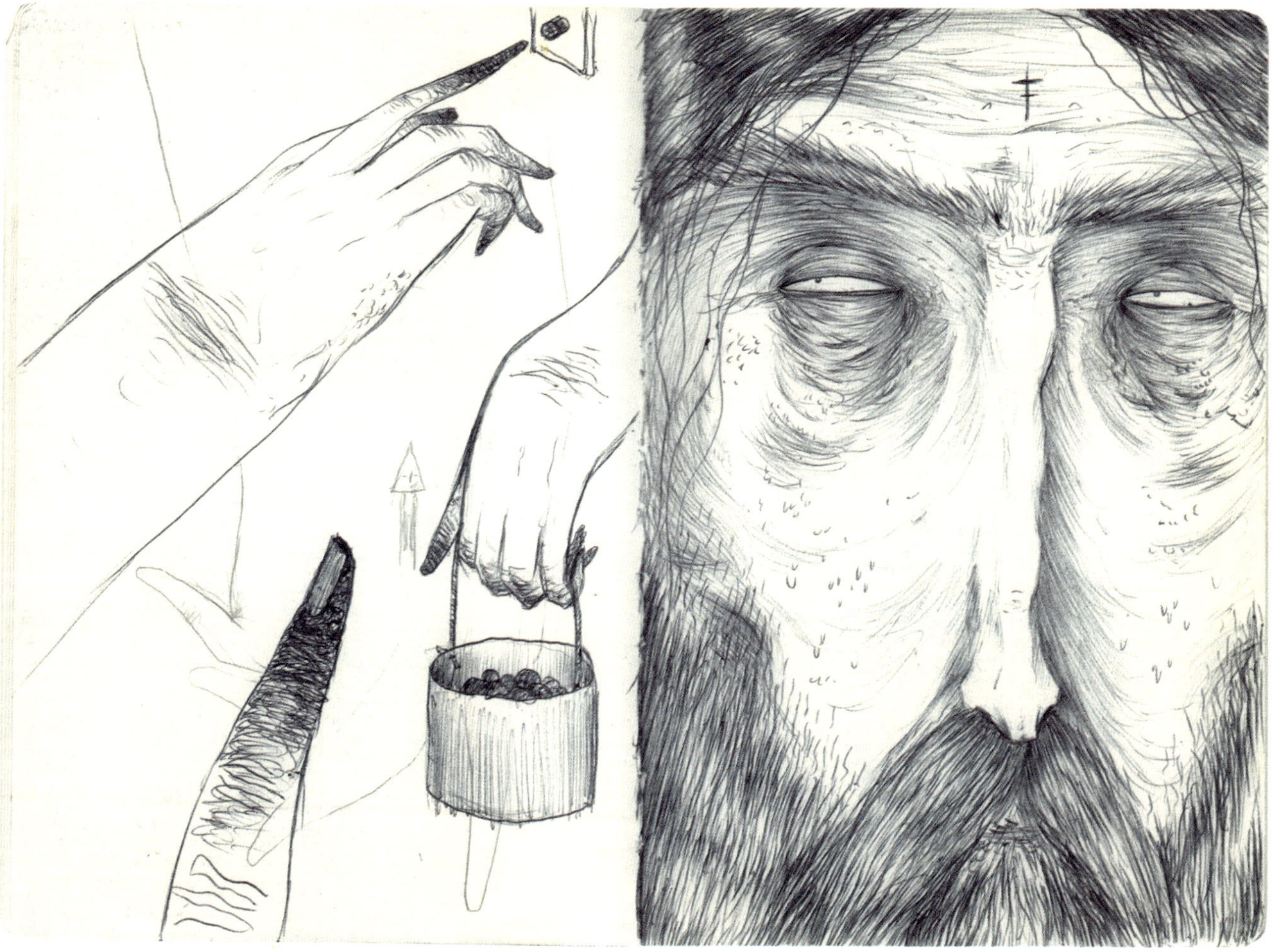

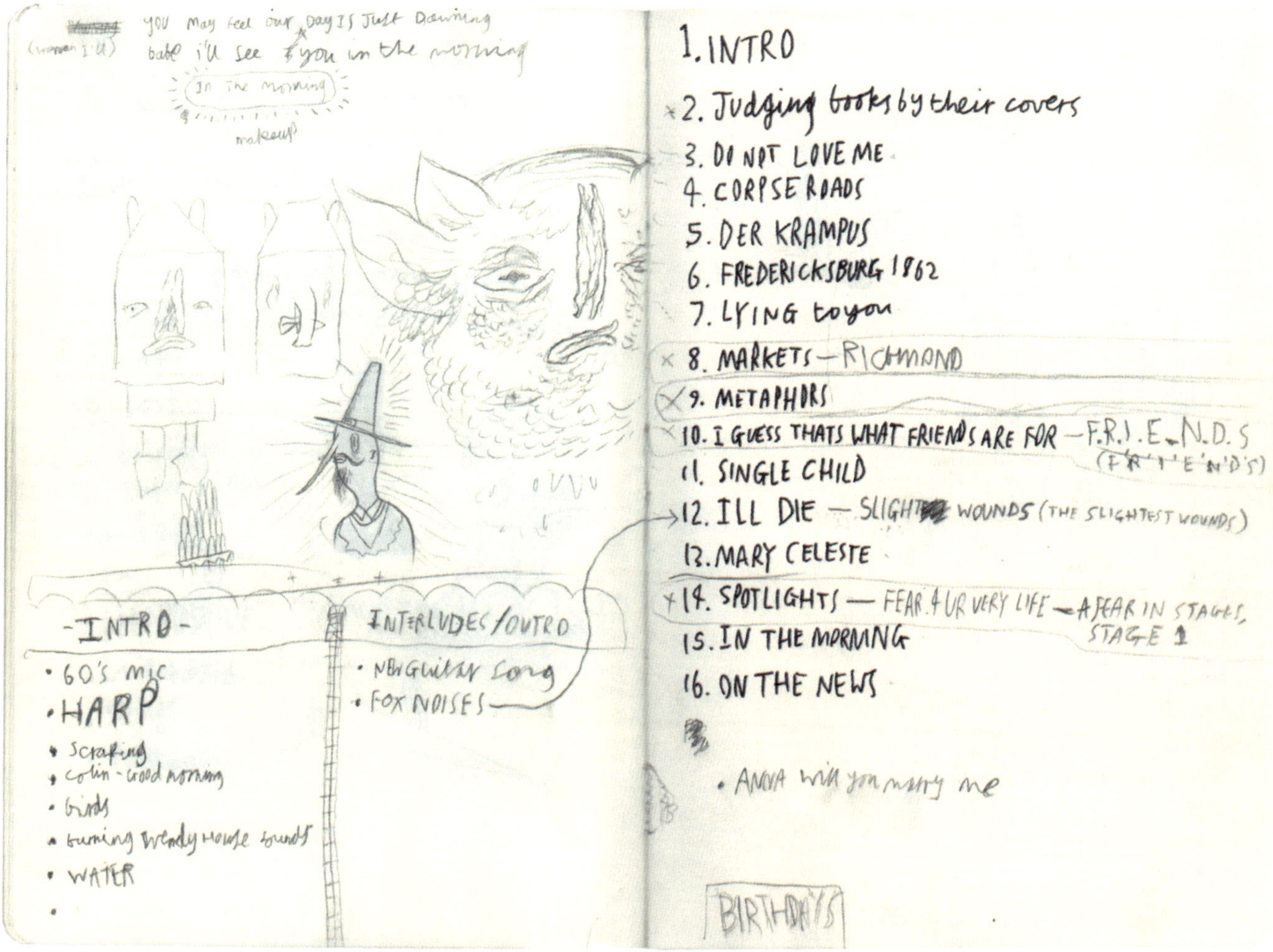

You may feel our day is just dawning
babe i'll see you in the morning
(In the morning)
makeup

-INTRO-
- 60's mic
- **HARP**
- scraping
- colin - good morning
- birds
- burning wendy house sounds
- WATER

INTERLUDES/OUTRO
- New Guitar song
- FOX NOISES

1. INTRO
2. Judging books by their covers
3. DO NOT LOVE ME
4. CORPSE ROADS
5. DER KRAMPUS
6. FREDERICKSBURG 1862
7. LYING to you
8. MARKETS — RICHMOND
9. METAPHORS
10. I GUESS THATS WHAT FRIENDS ARE FOR — F.R.I.E.N.D.S (FR'IE'N'D'S)
11. SINGLE CHILD
12. ILL DIE — SLIGHT WOUNDS (THE SLIGHTEST WOUNDS)
13. MARY CELESTE
14. SPOTLIGHTS — FEAR 4 UR VERY LIFE — A FEAR IN STAGES, STAGE 1
15. IN THE MORNING
16. ON THE NEWS

- ANNA will you marry me

BIRTHDAYS

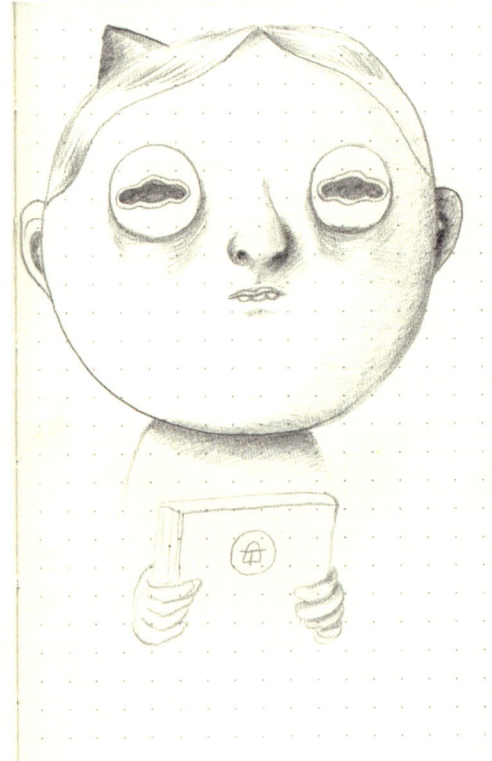

// THE SUN DRAGS THE DAY WITH IT
STUBBORN AS THE SEA
HE EASES ME
INTO ~~MY~~ MY EVENING

HERE HE COMES AGAIN TO SHOW
THAT NOTHING LASTS FOREVER
NOT EVEN THE NOTHING OF SLEEP

THE suddenly deep
deep in my feelings

OUR FEARLESS HERO

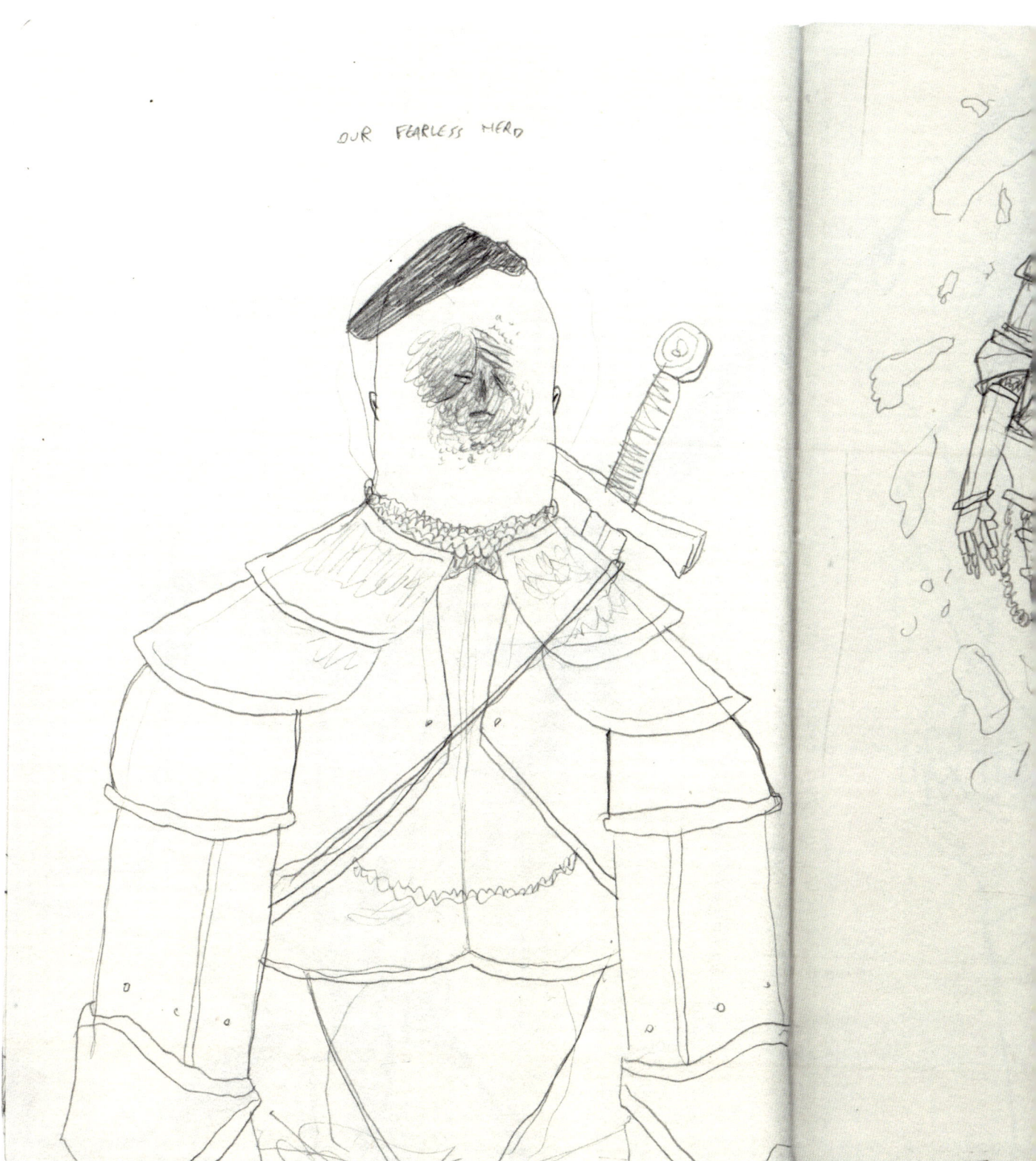

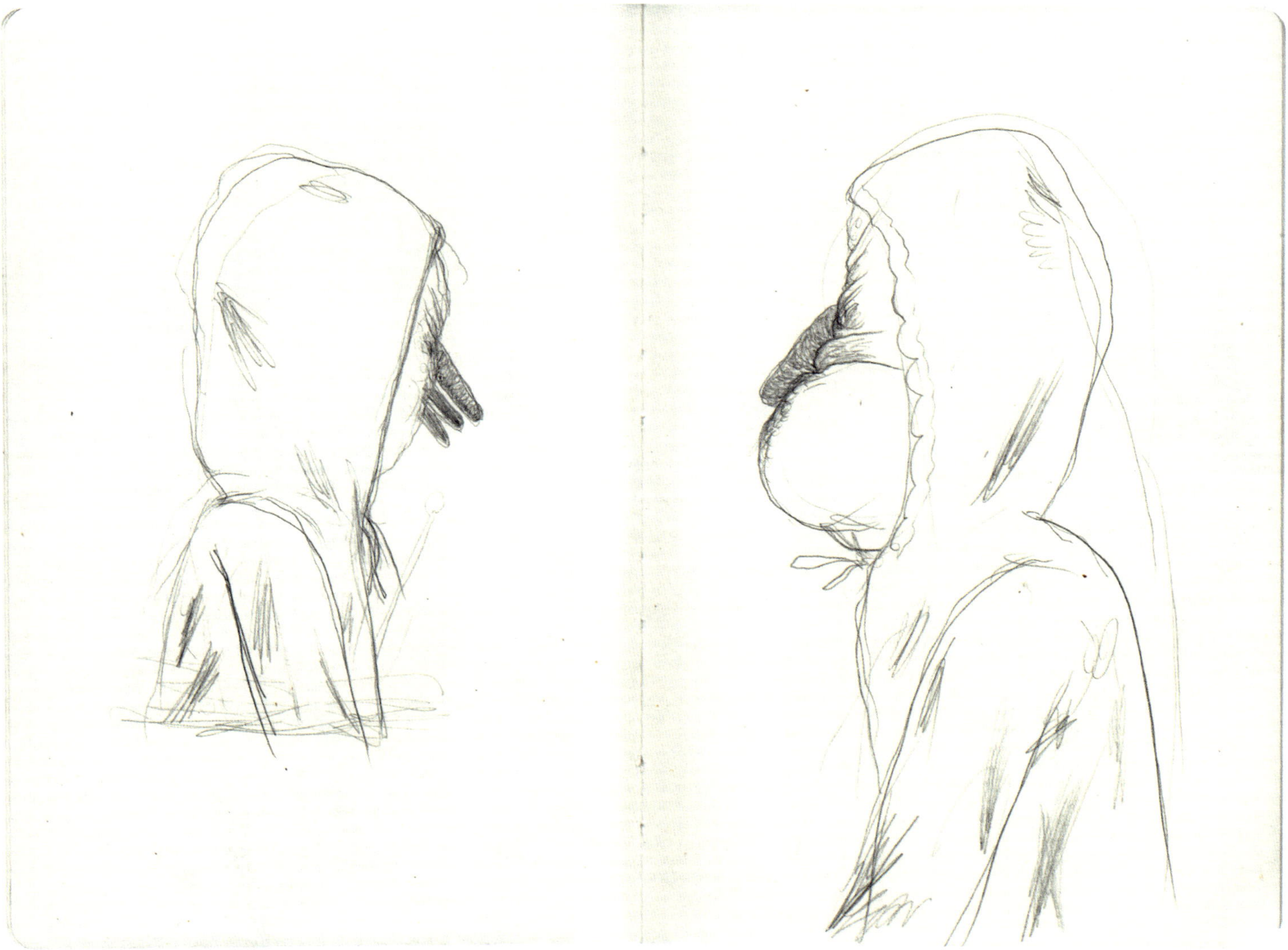

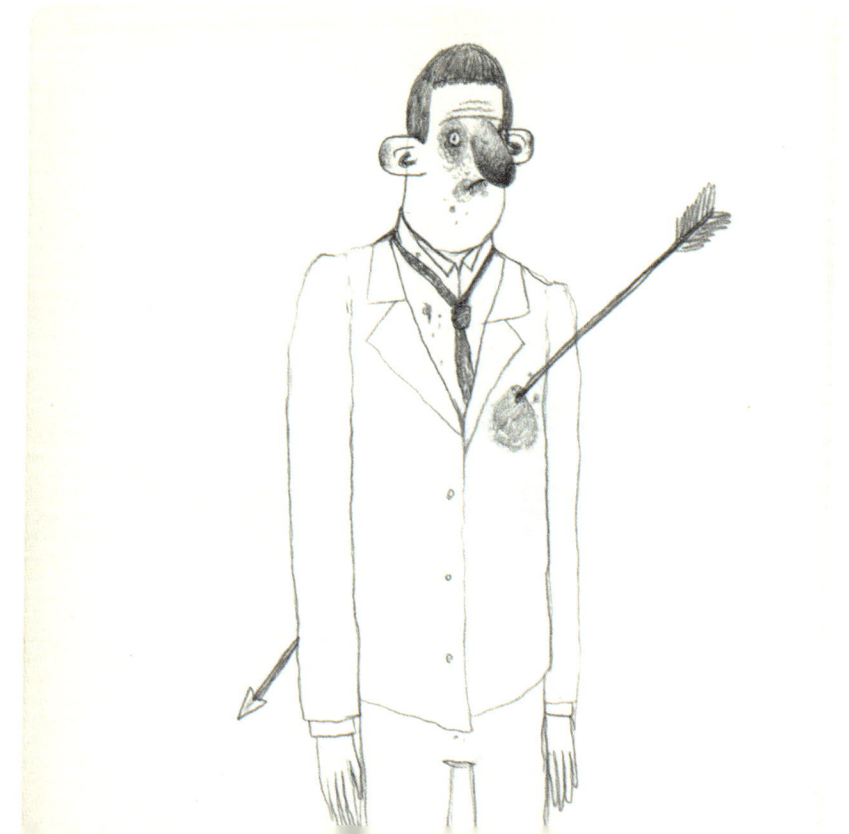

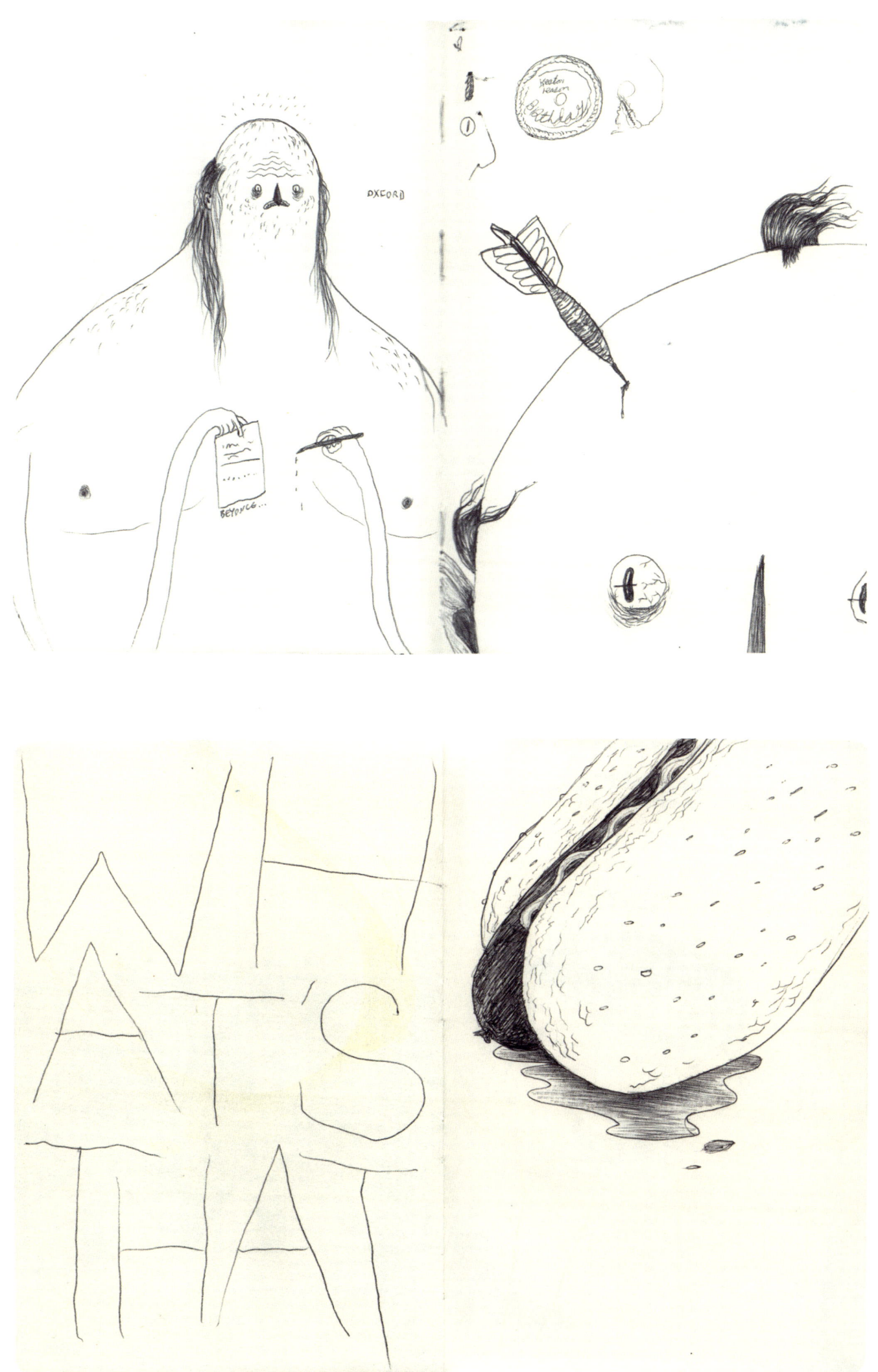

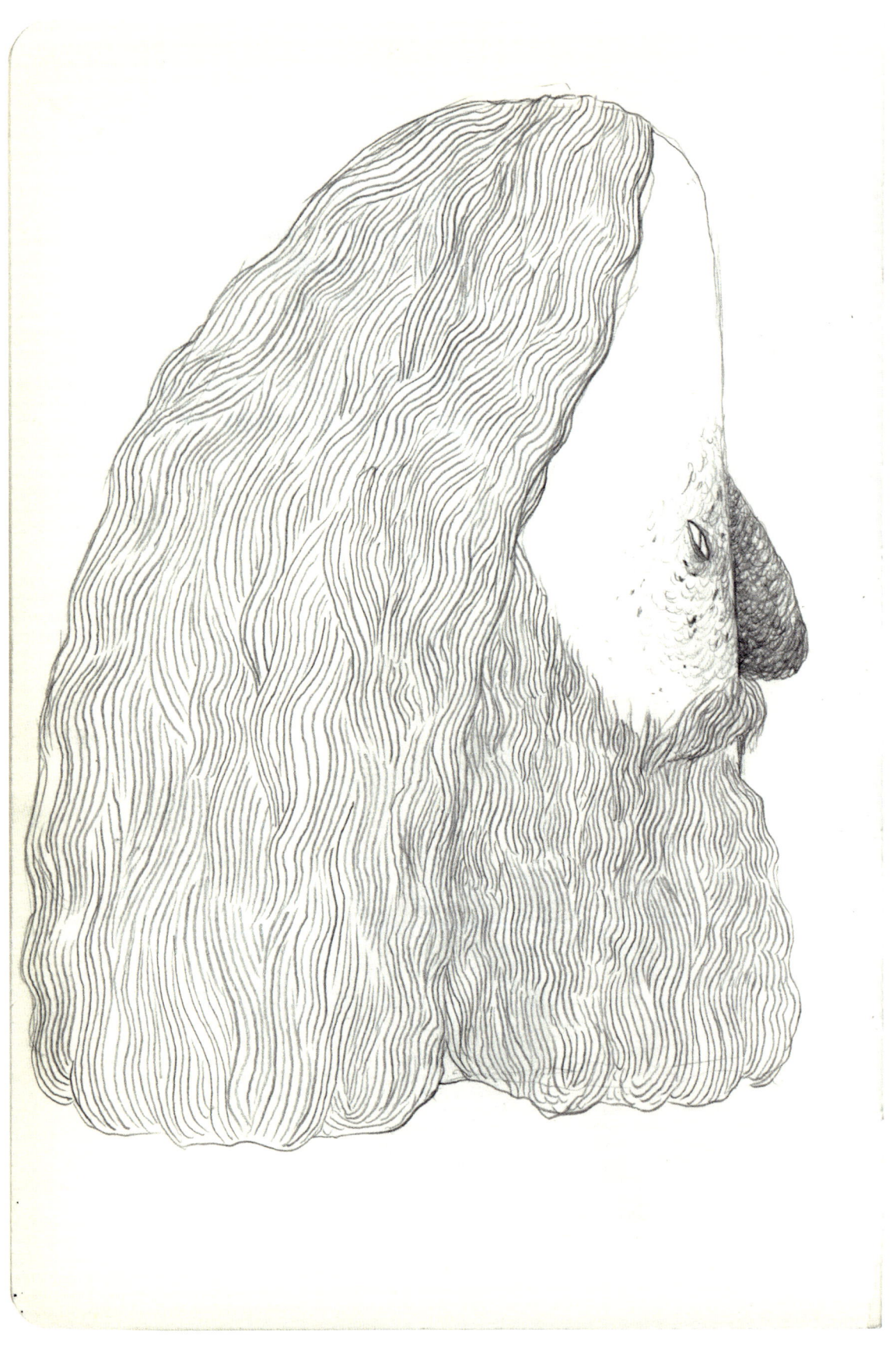

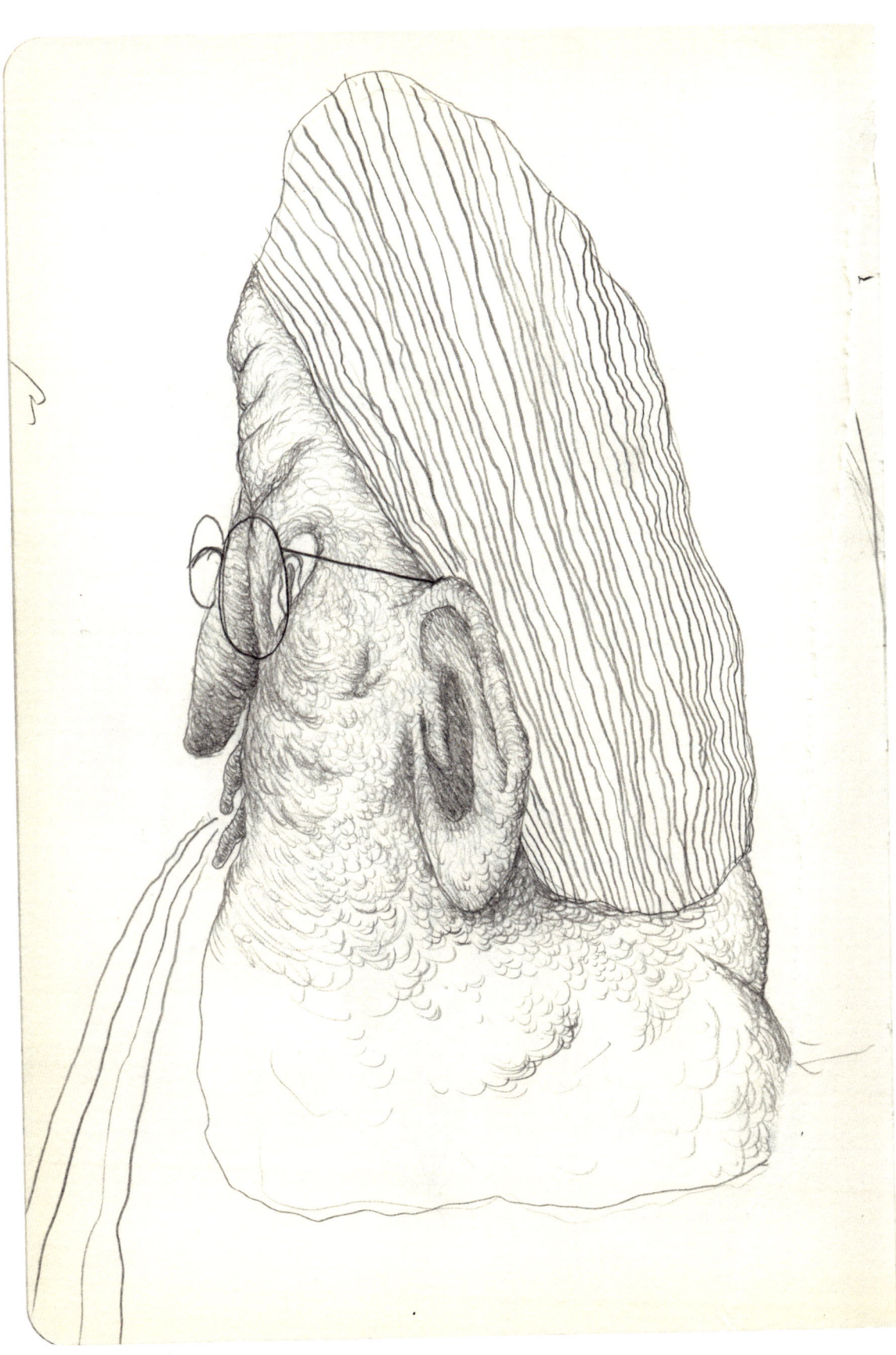

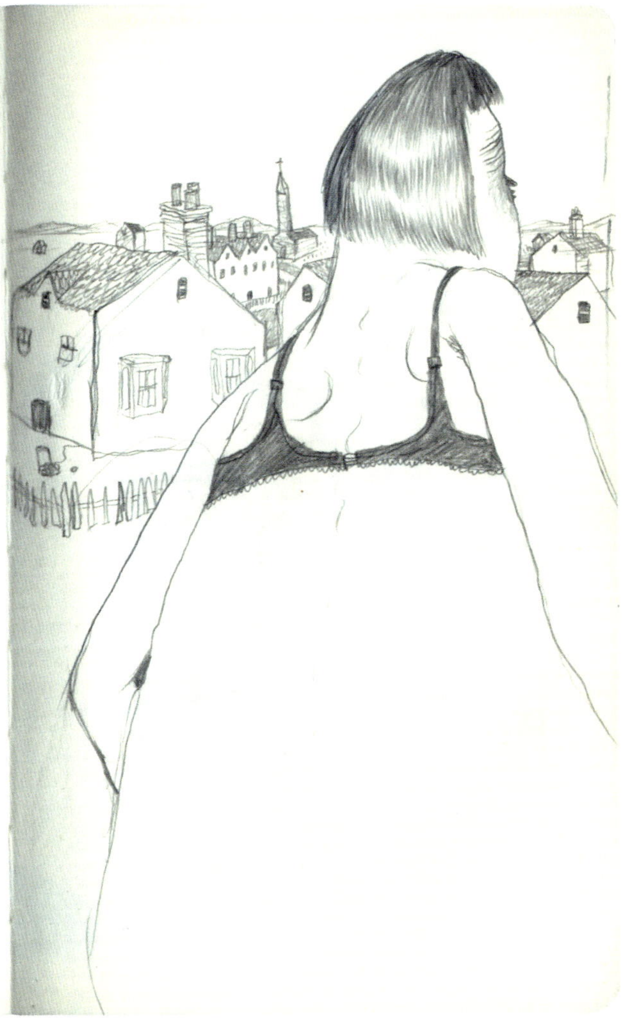

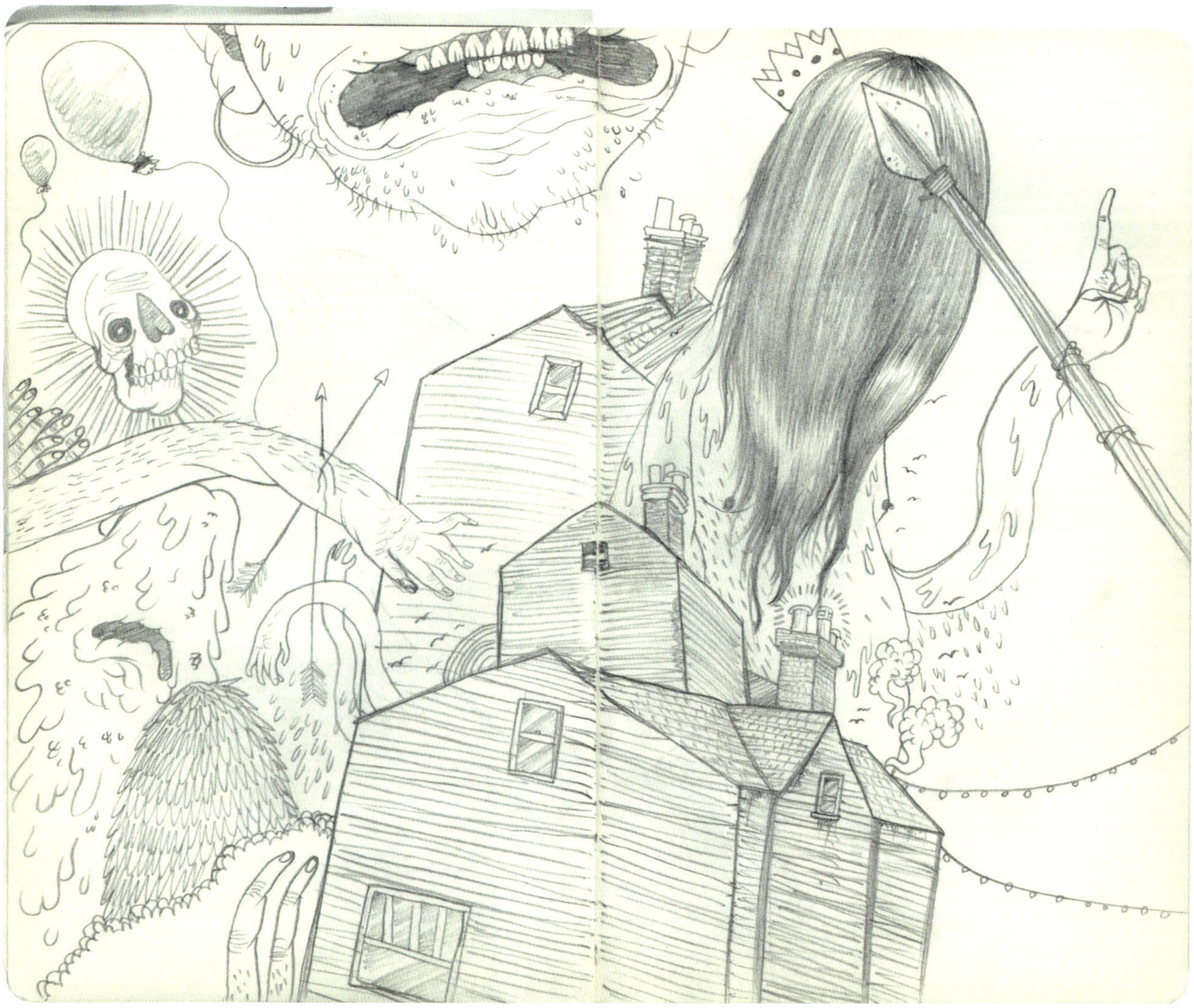

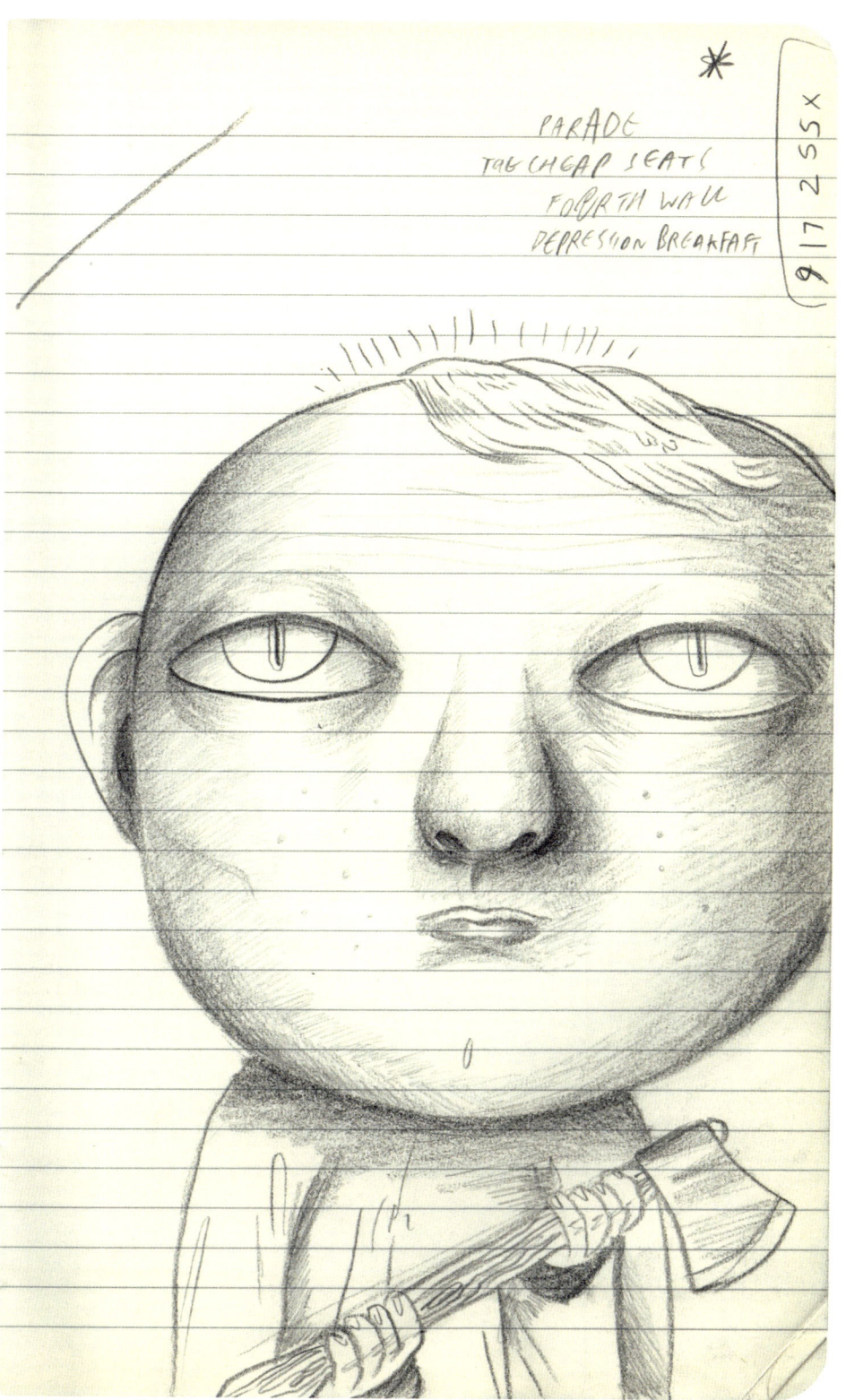

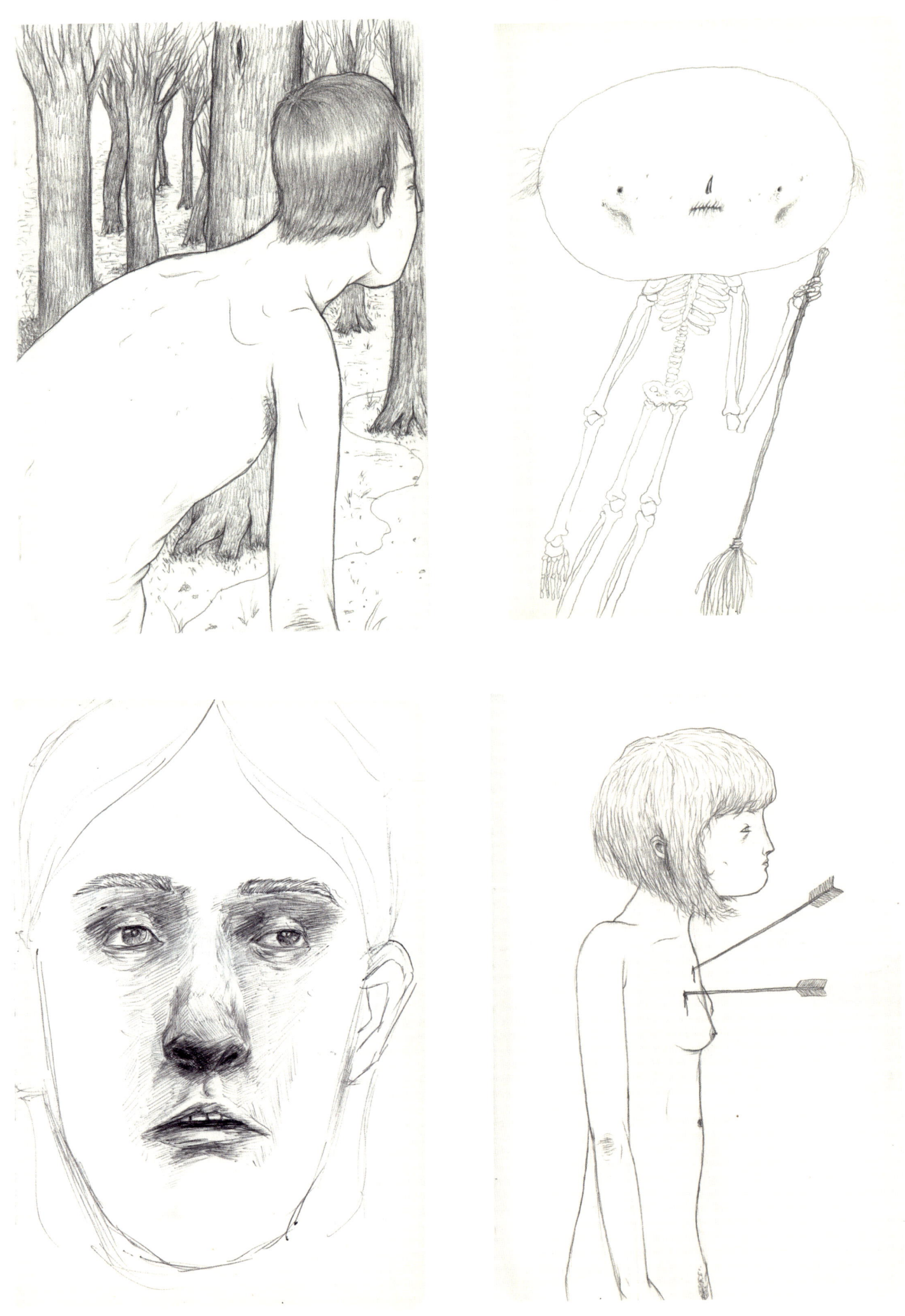

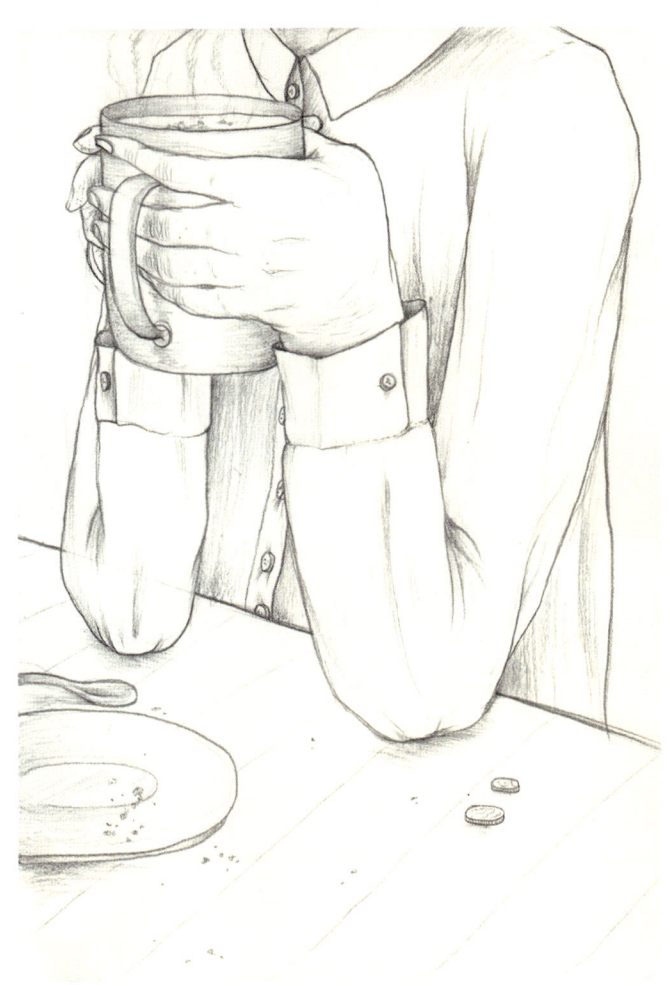
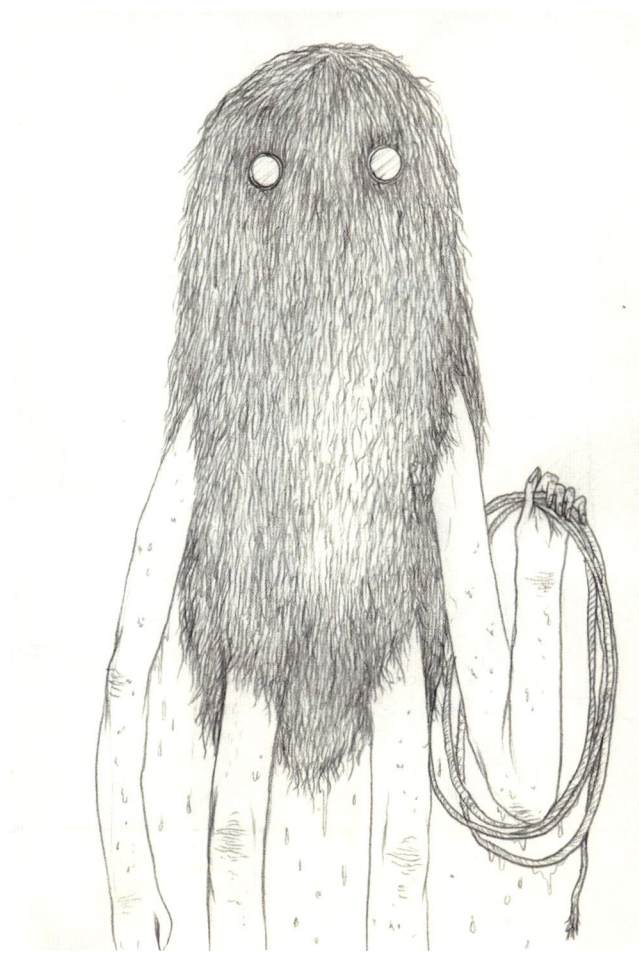
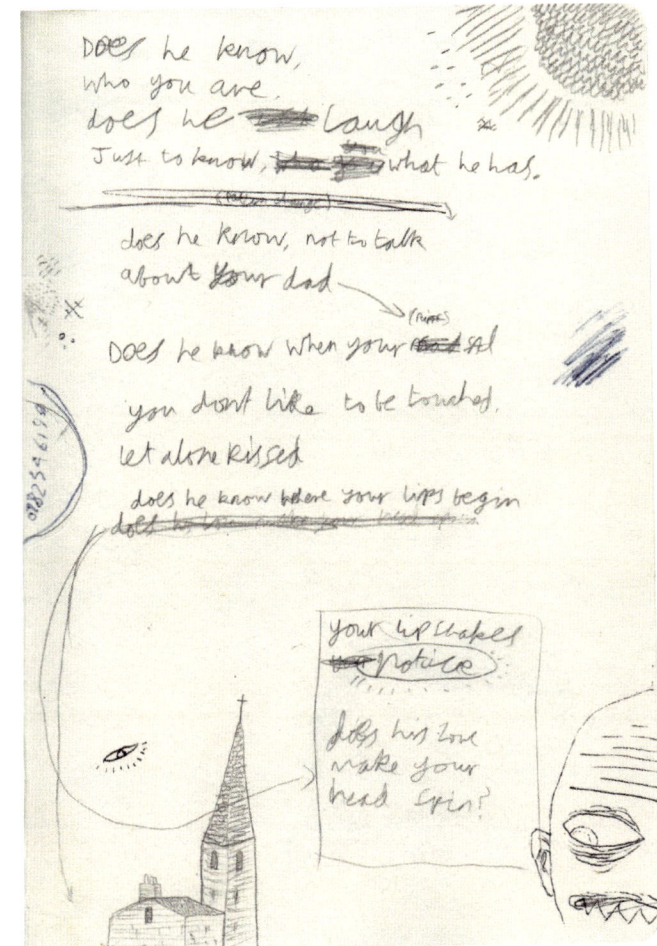
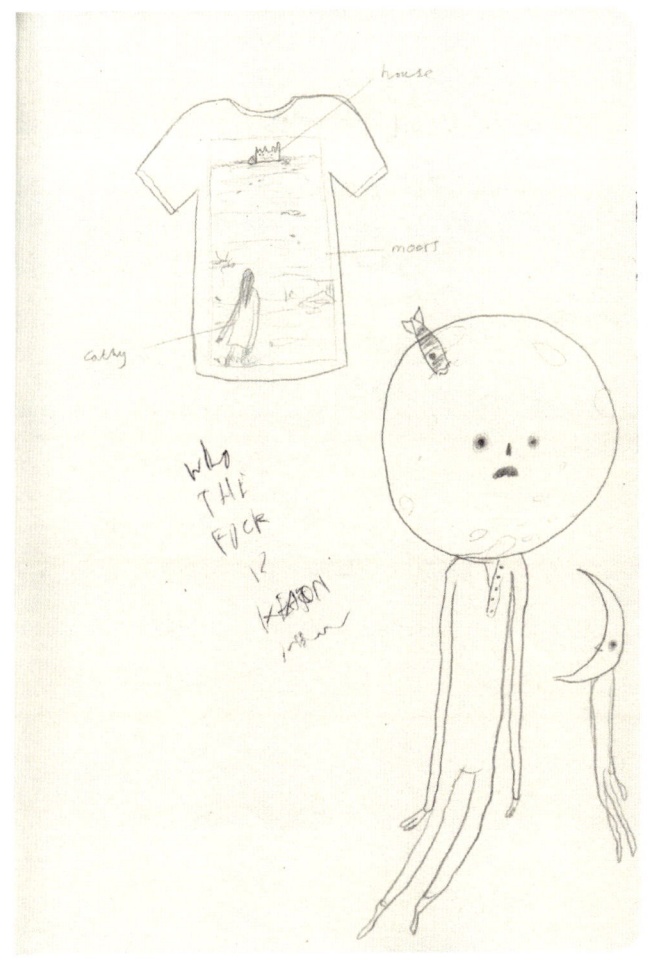

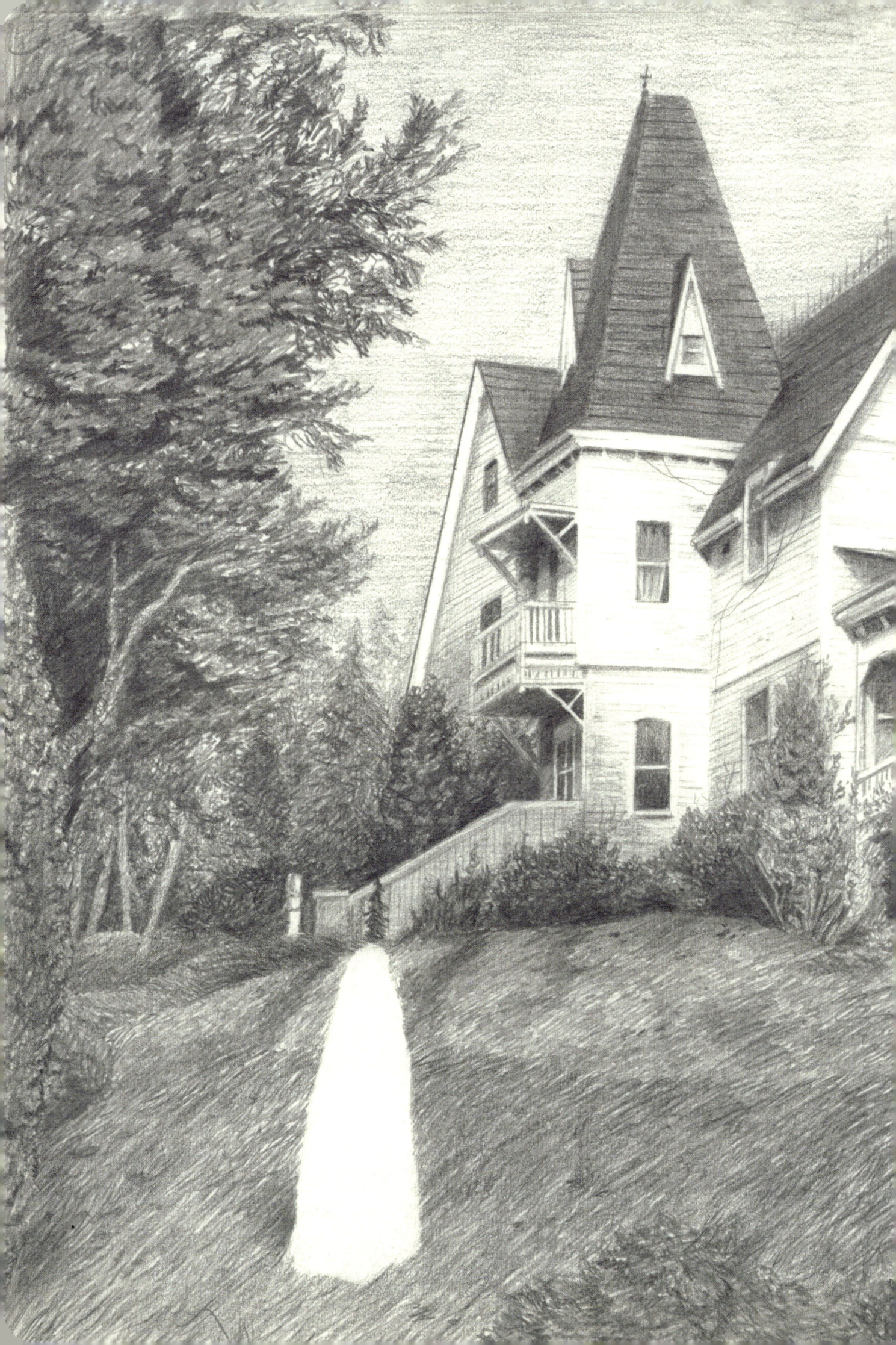

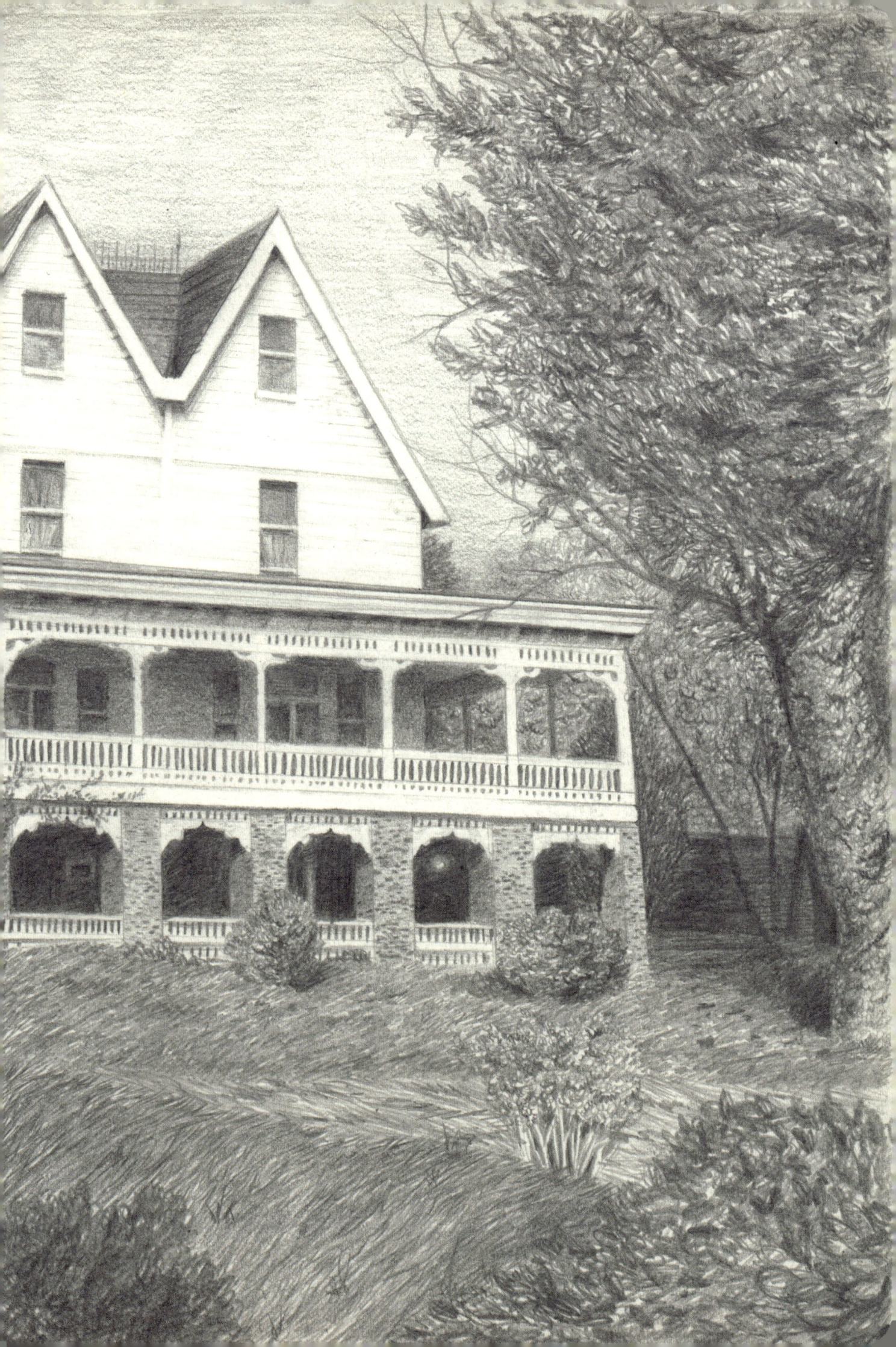

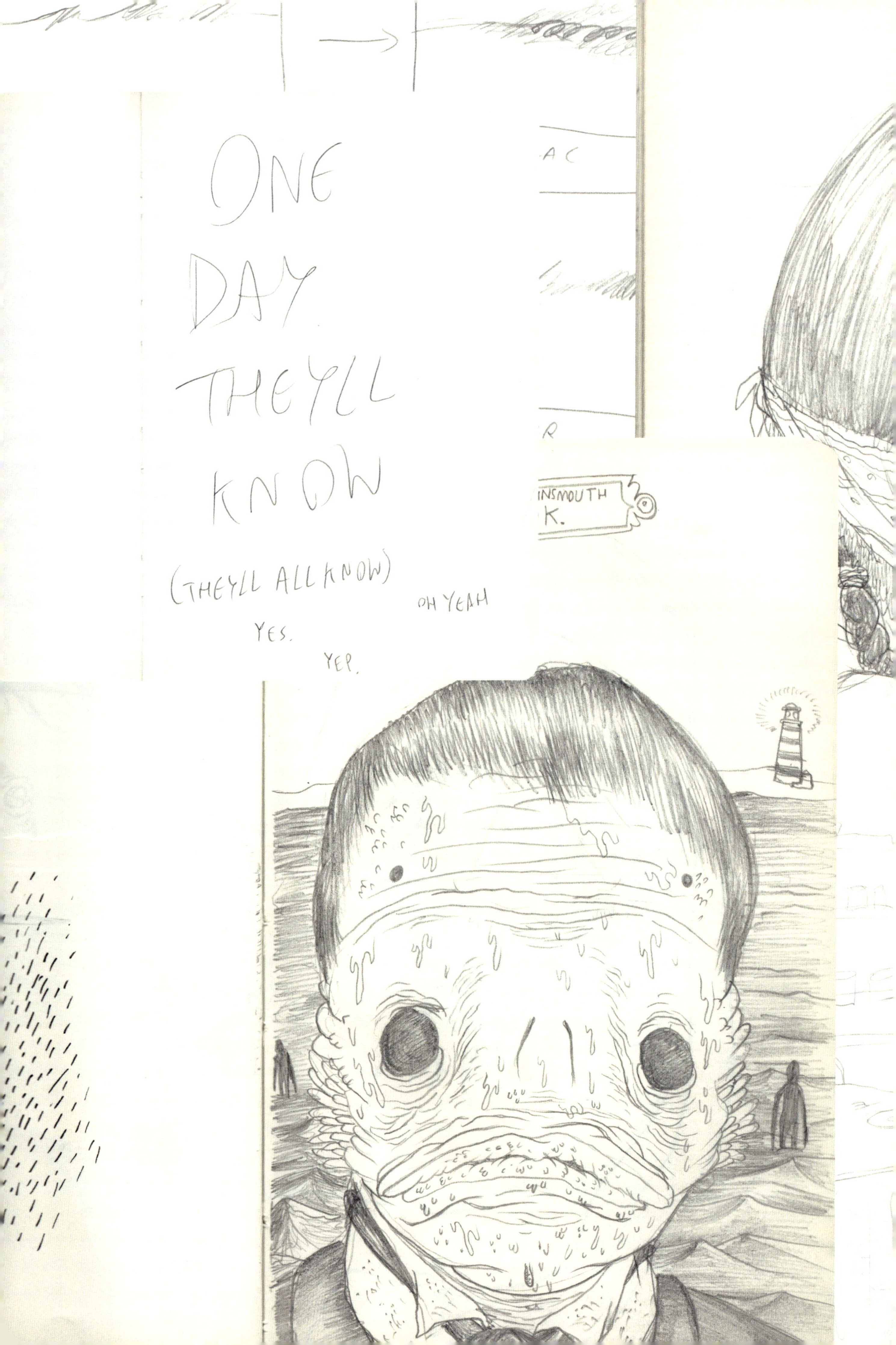

ONE DAY THEY'LL KNOW

(THEY'LL ALL KNOW)

YES.   OH YEAH
   YEP.

INSMOUTH
K.

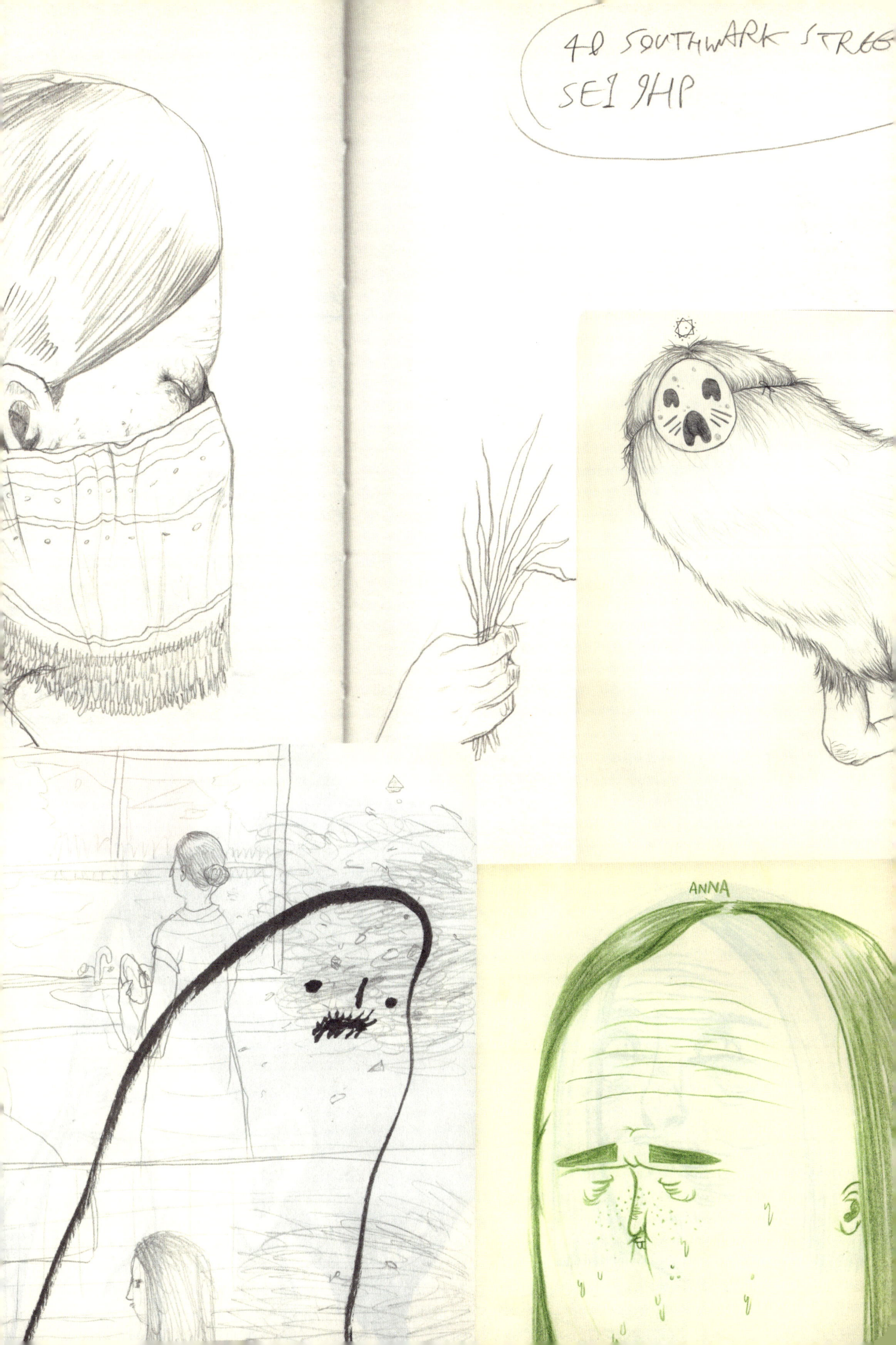

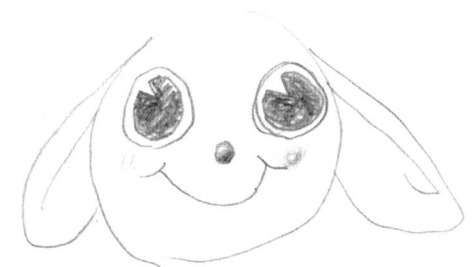

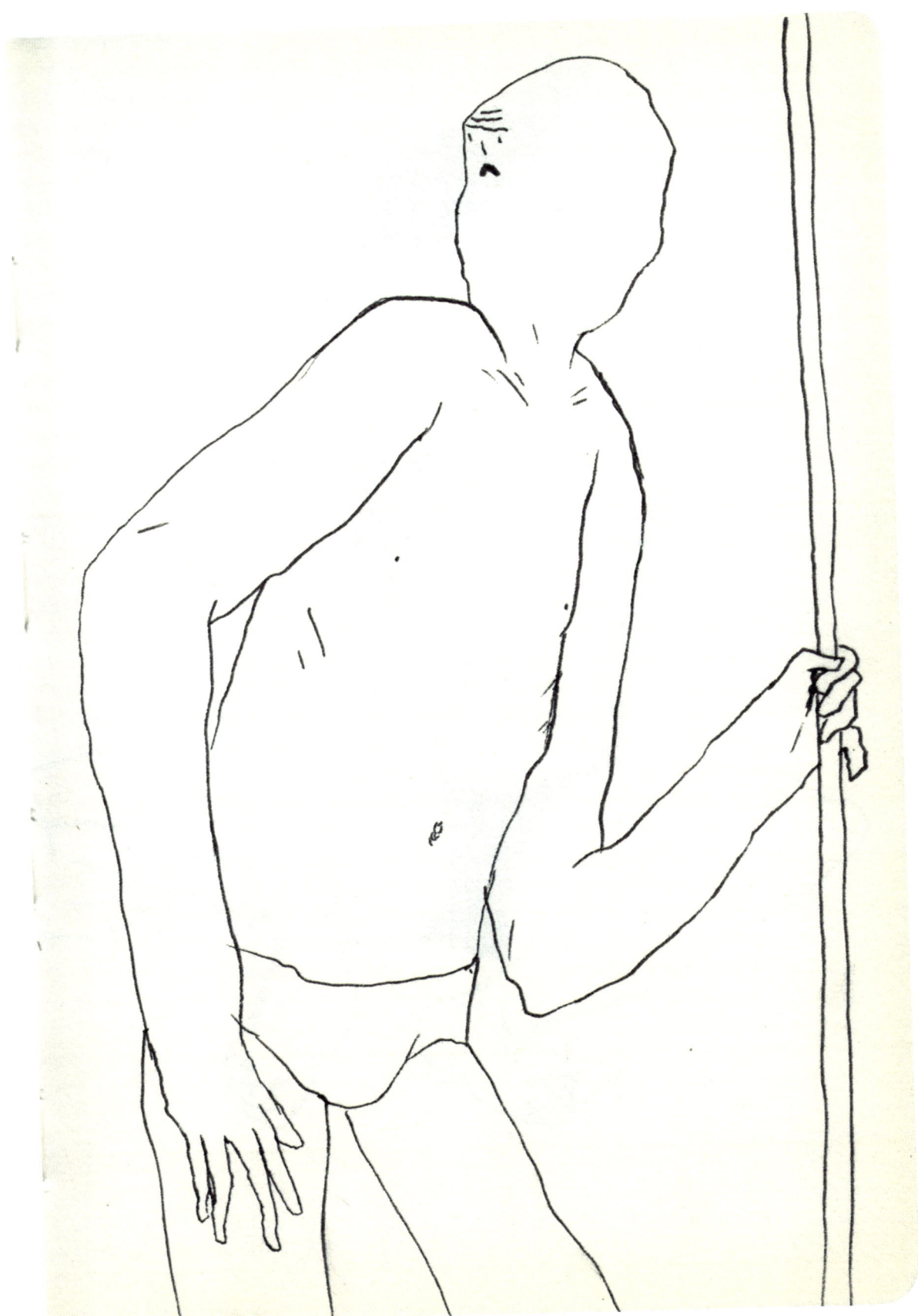

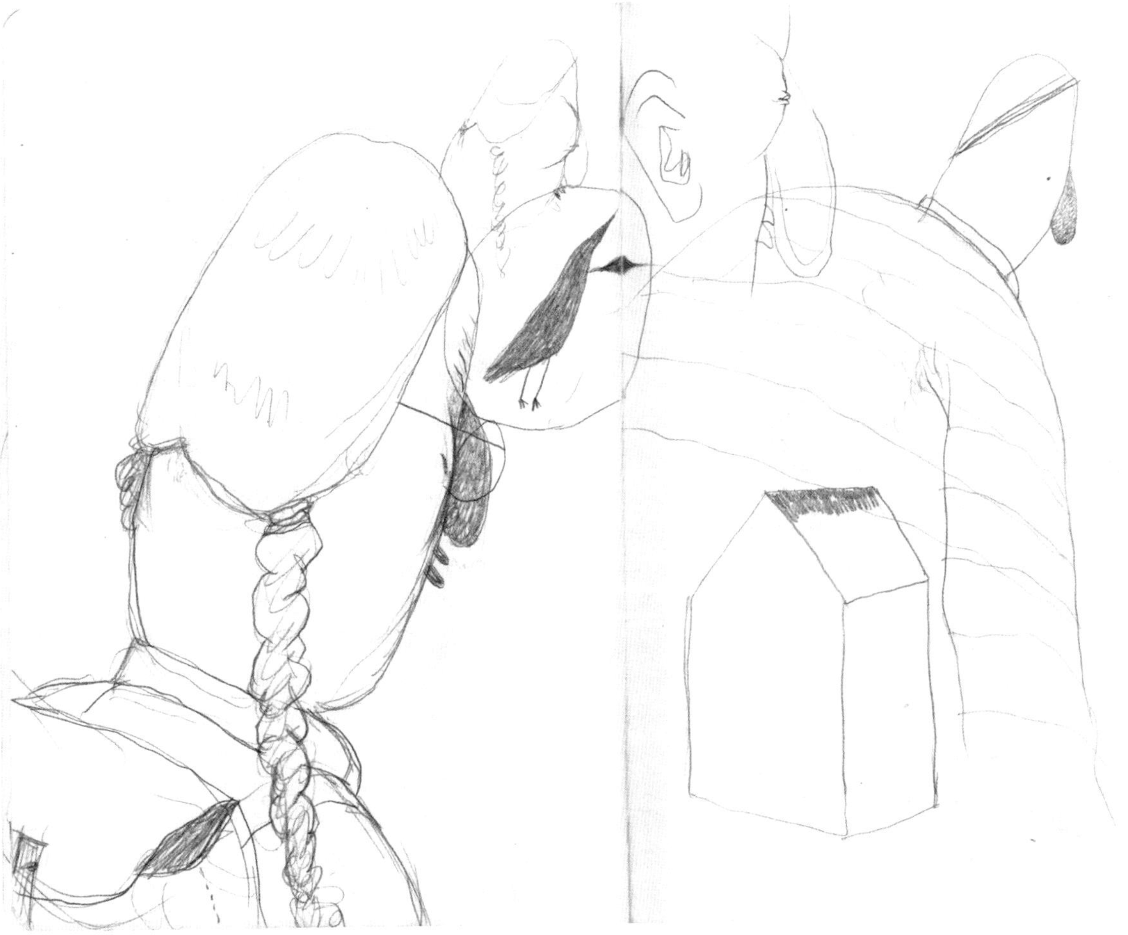

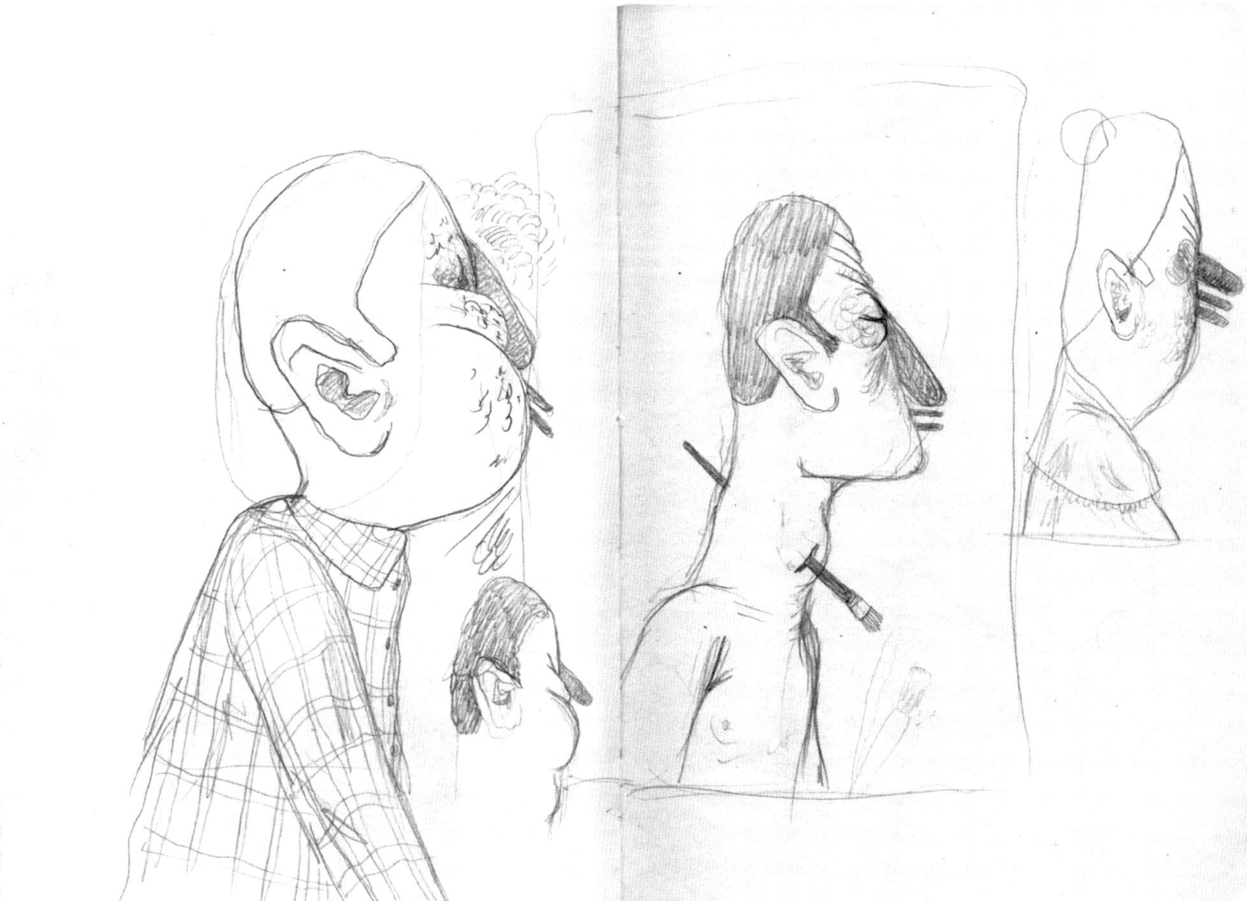

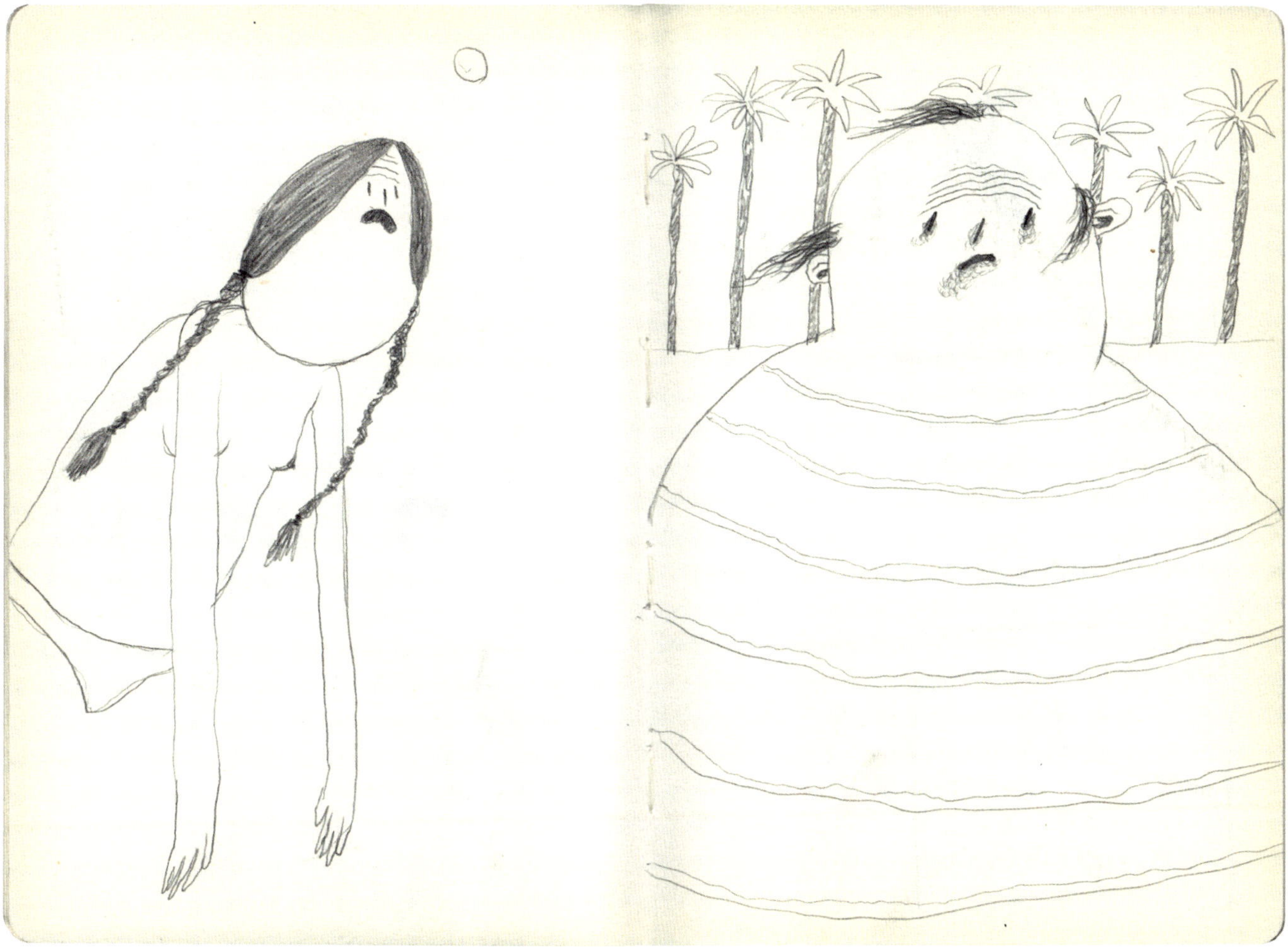

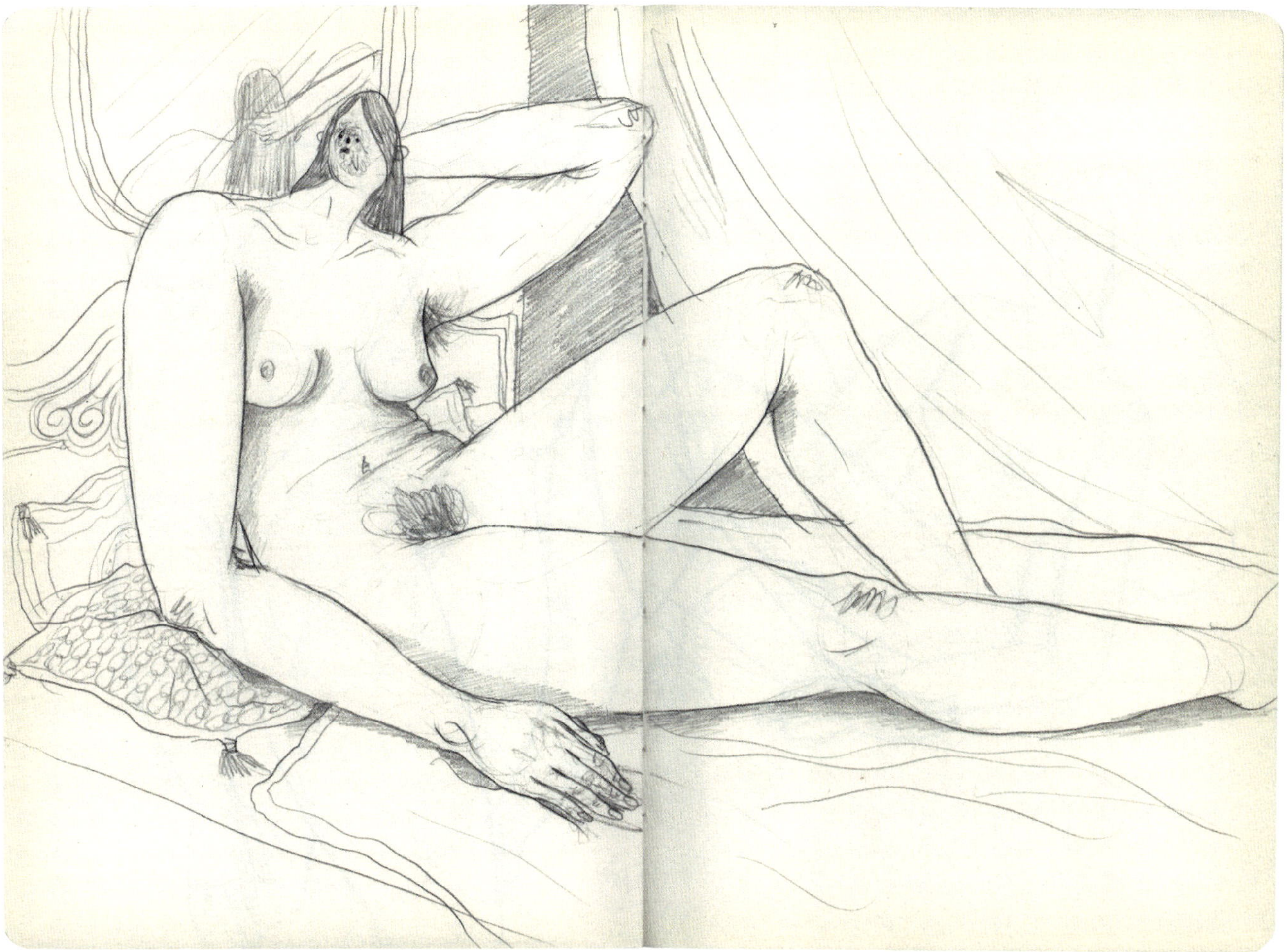

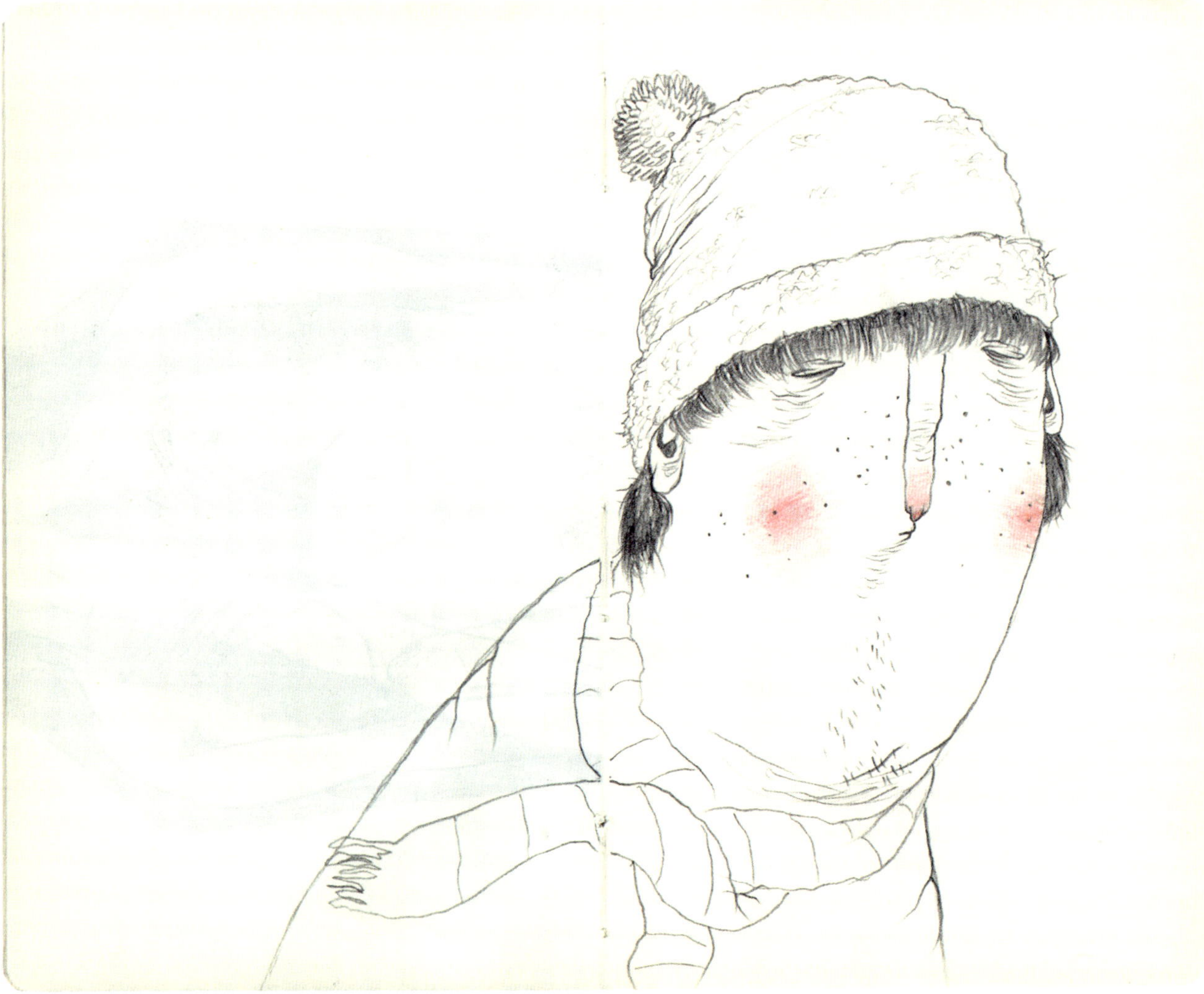

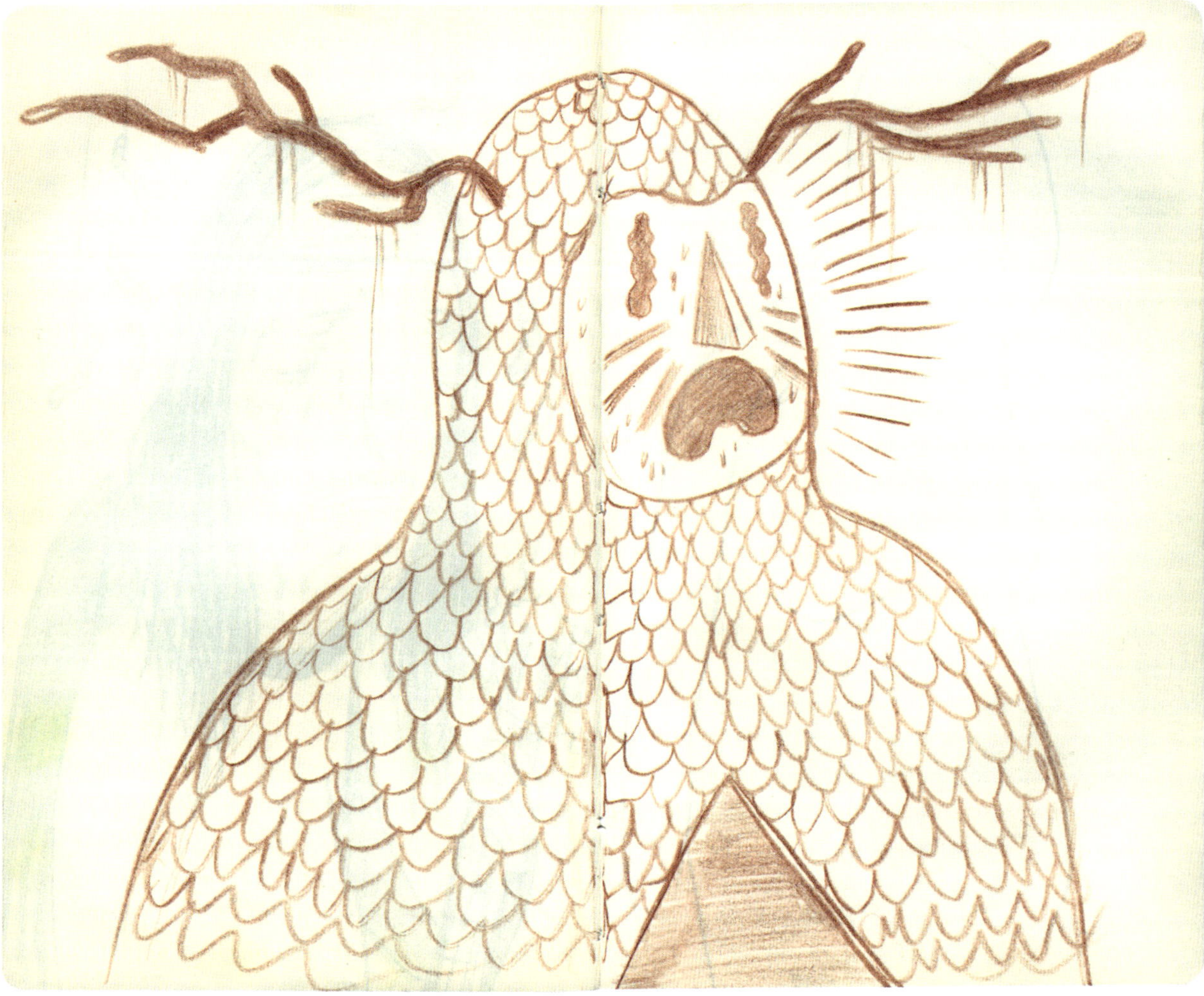

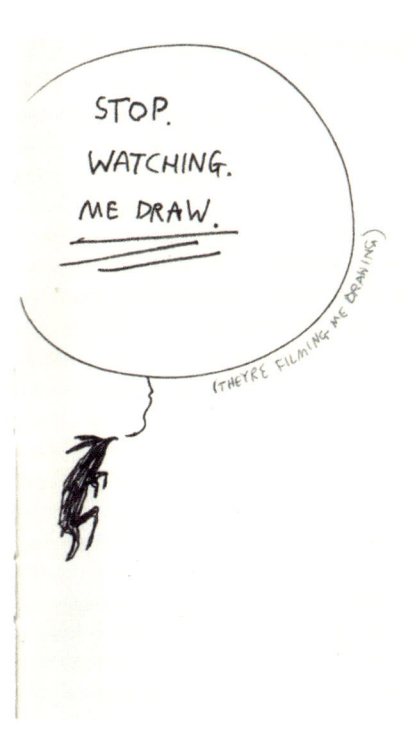
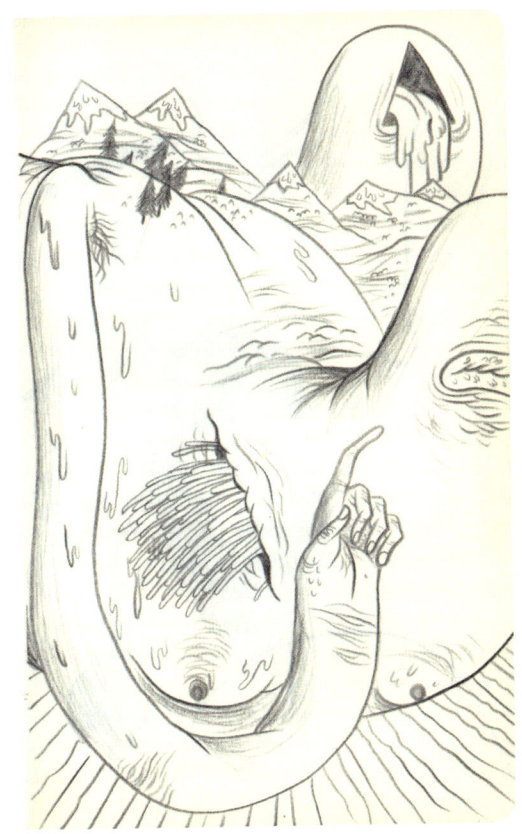

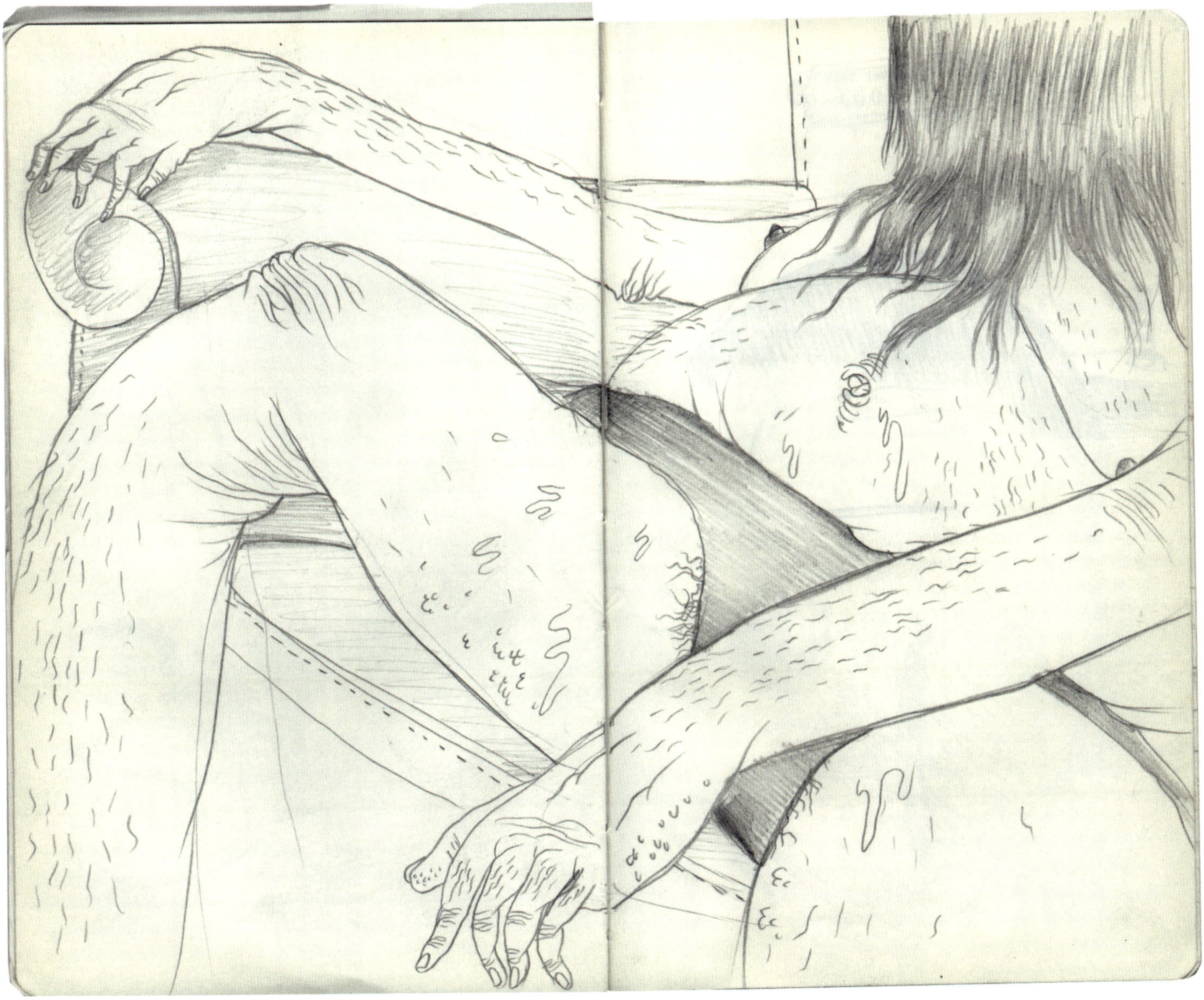

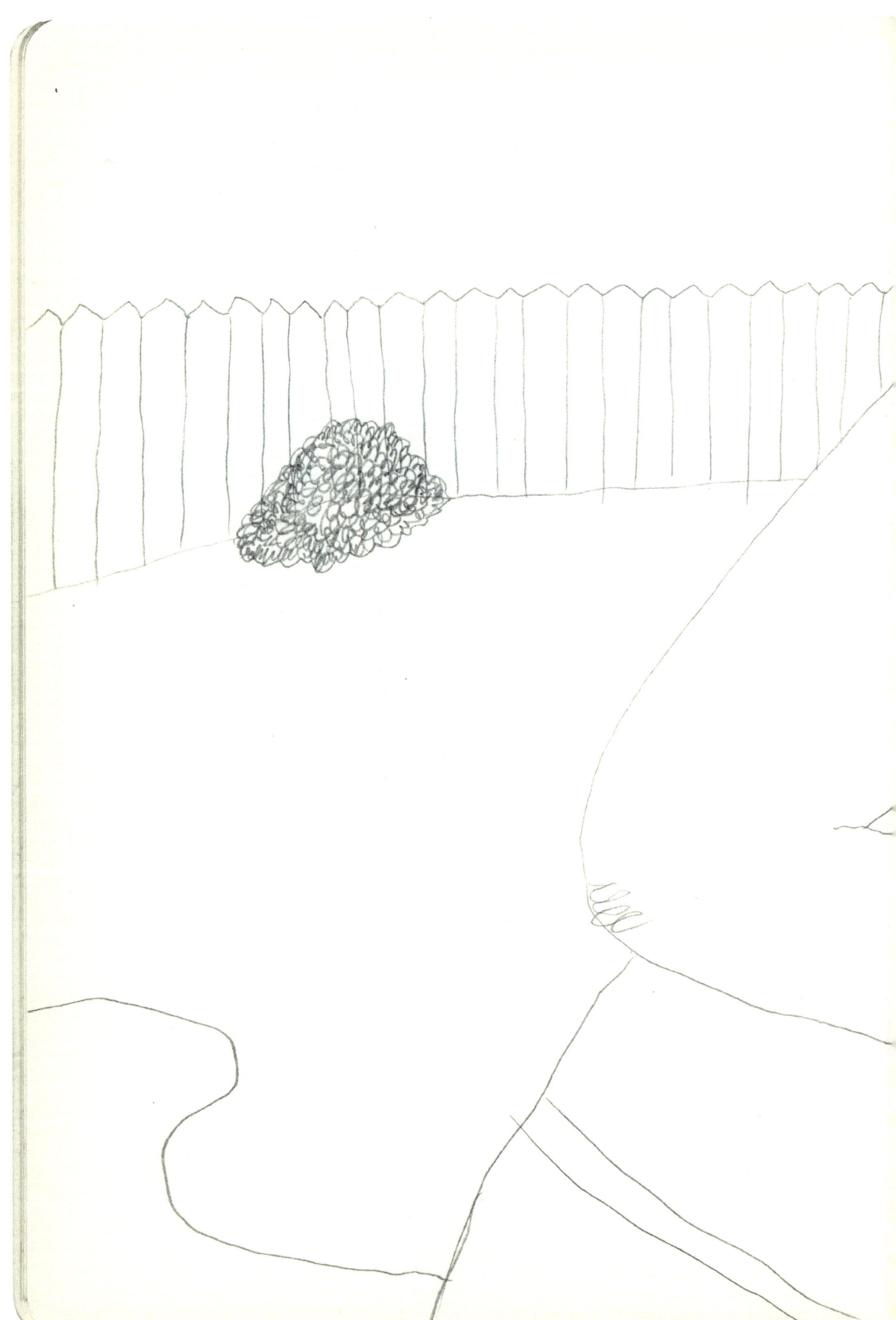

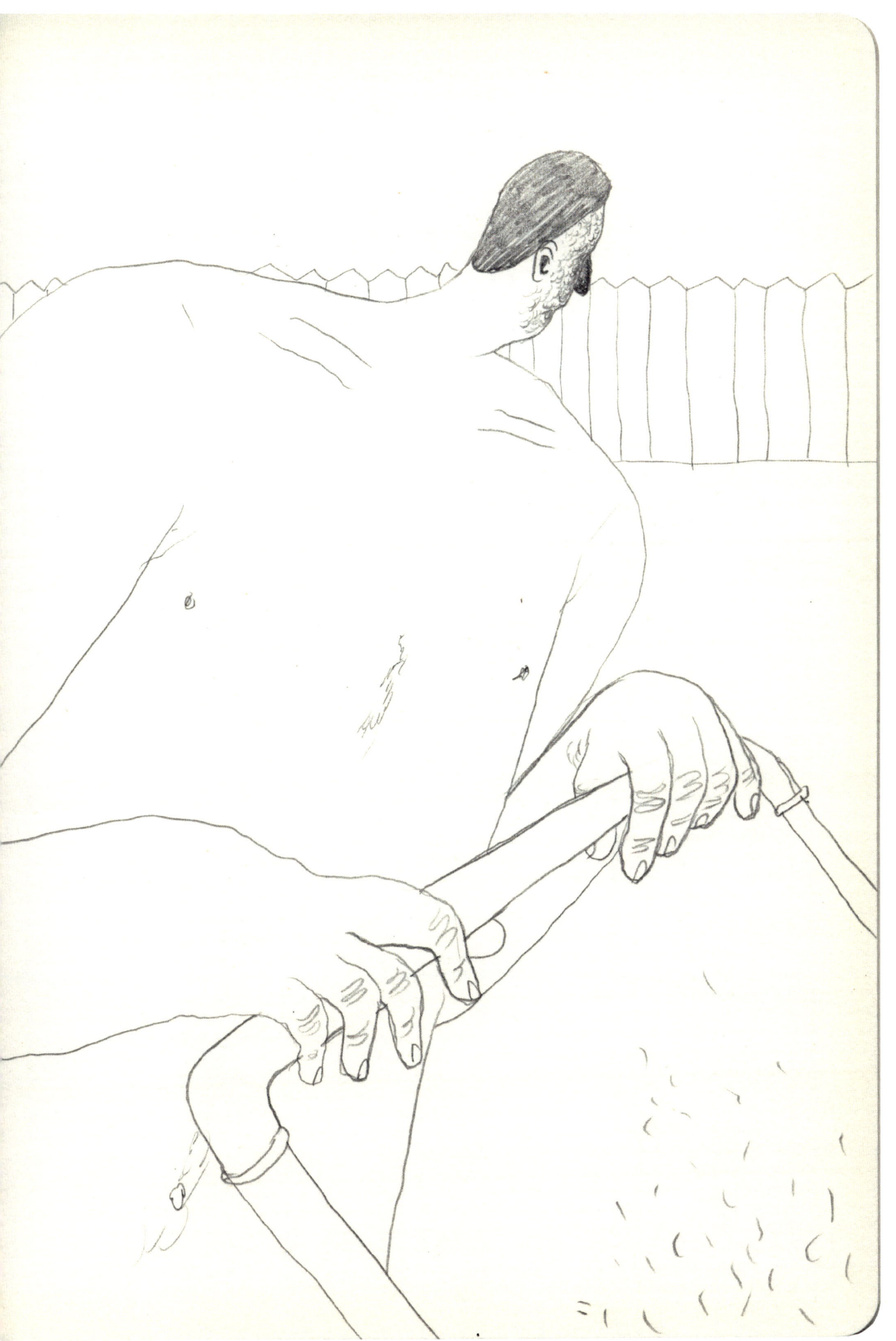

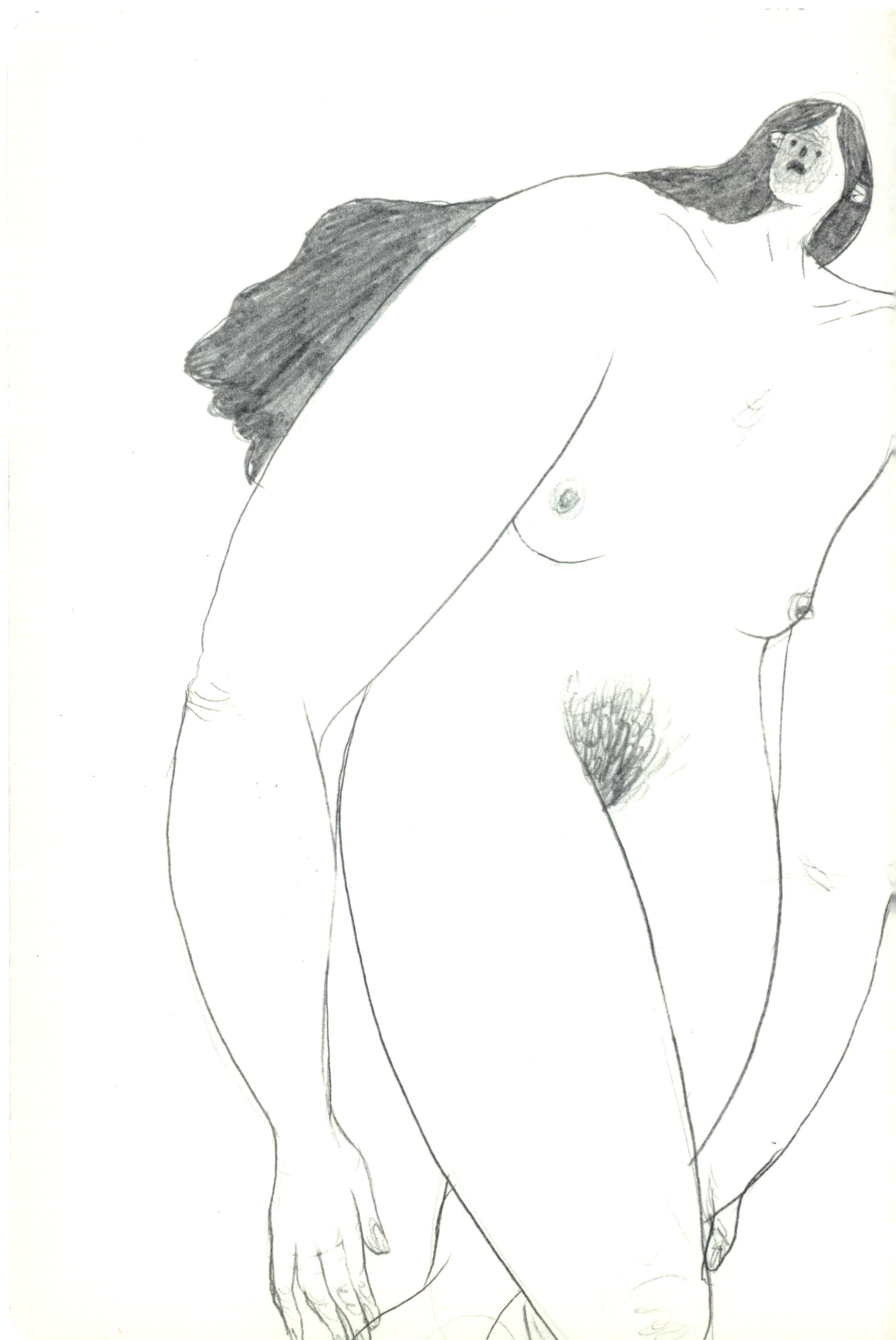

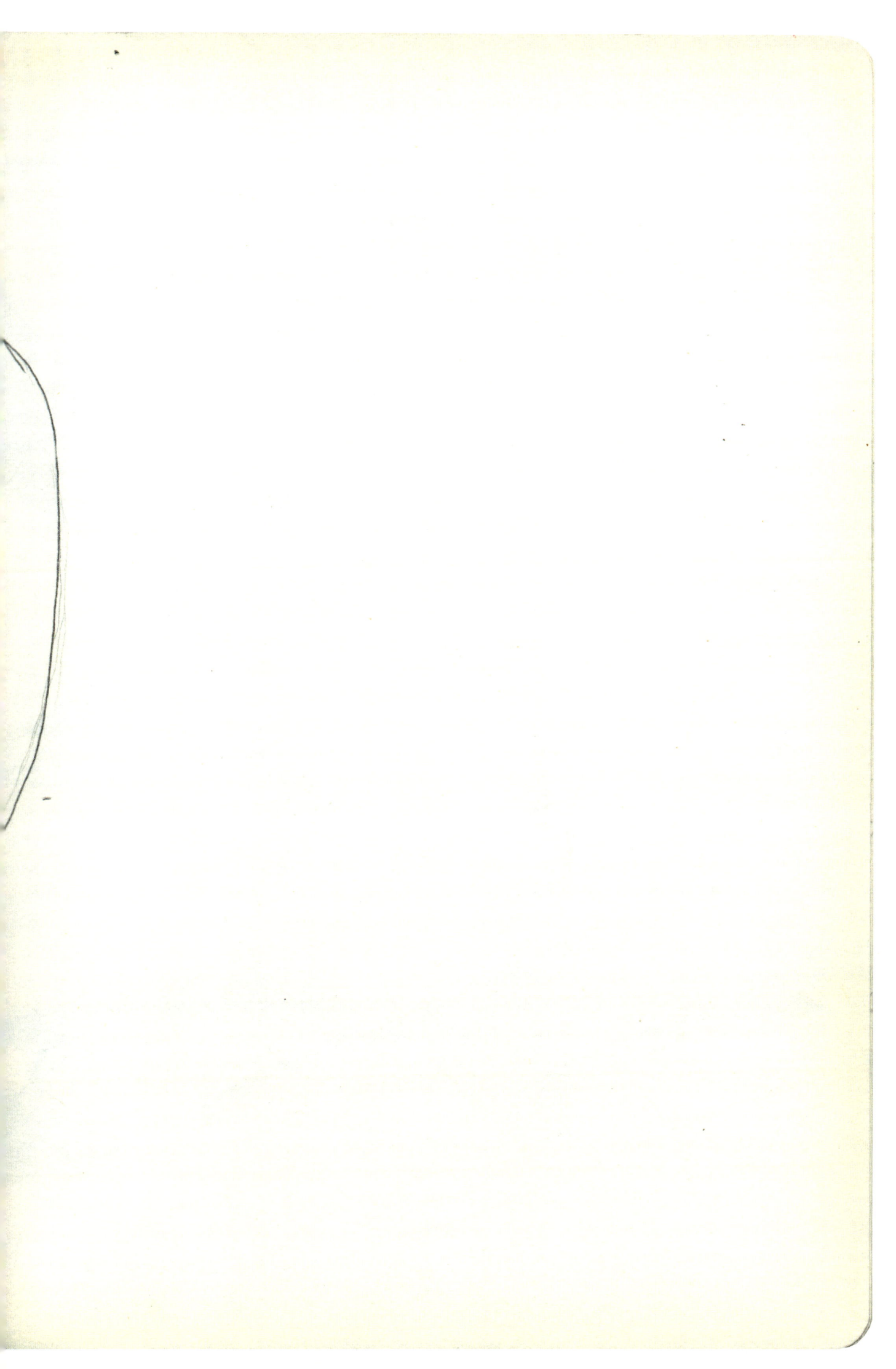

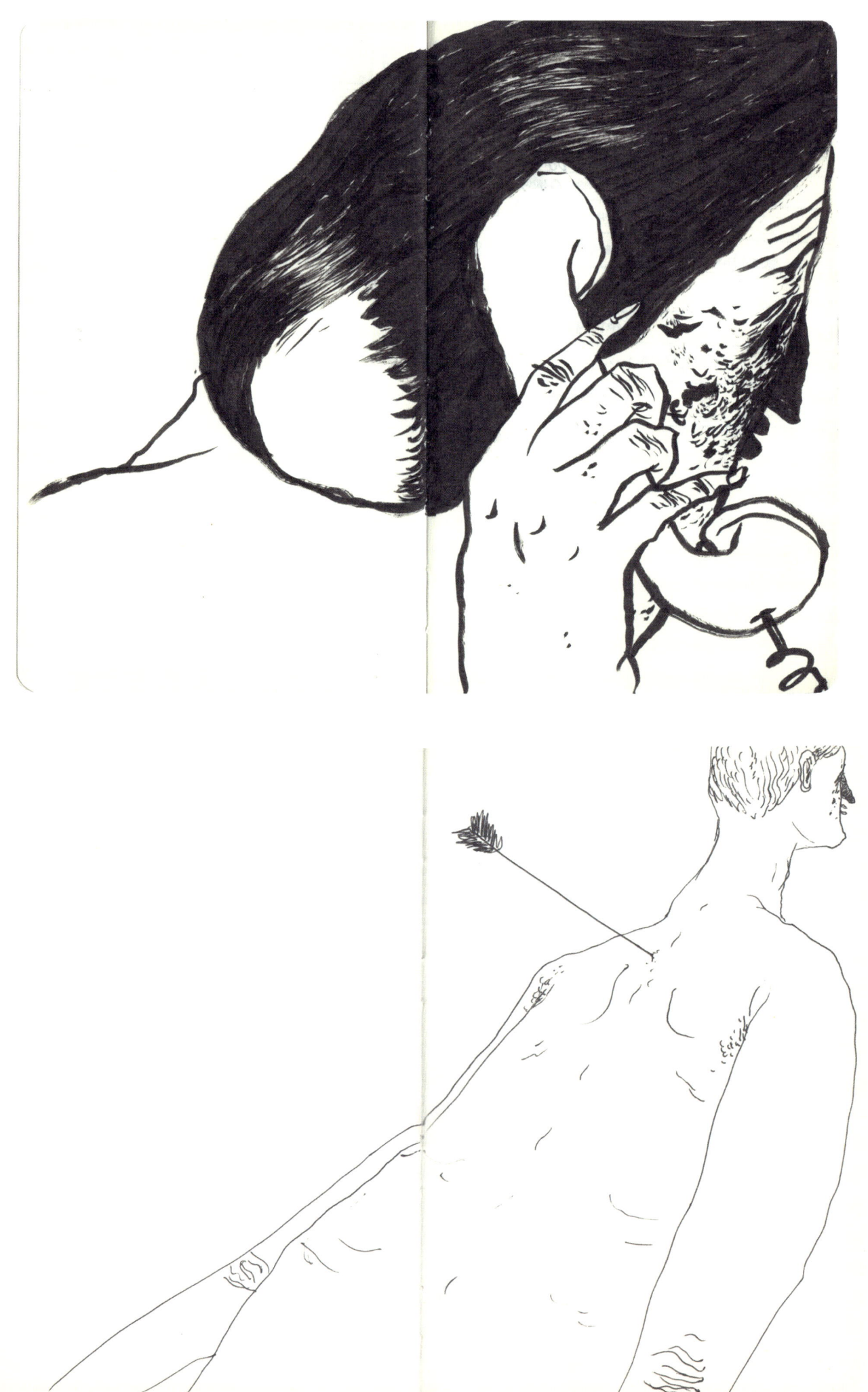

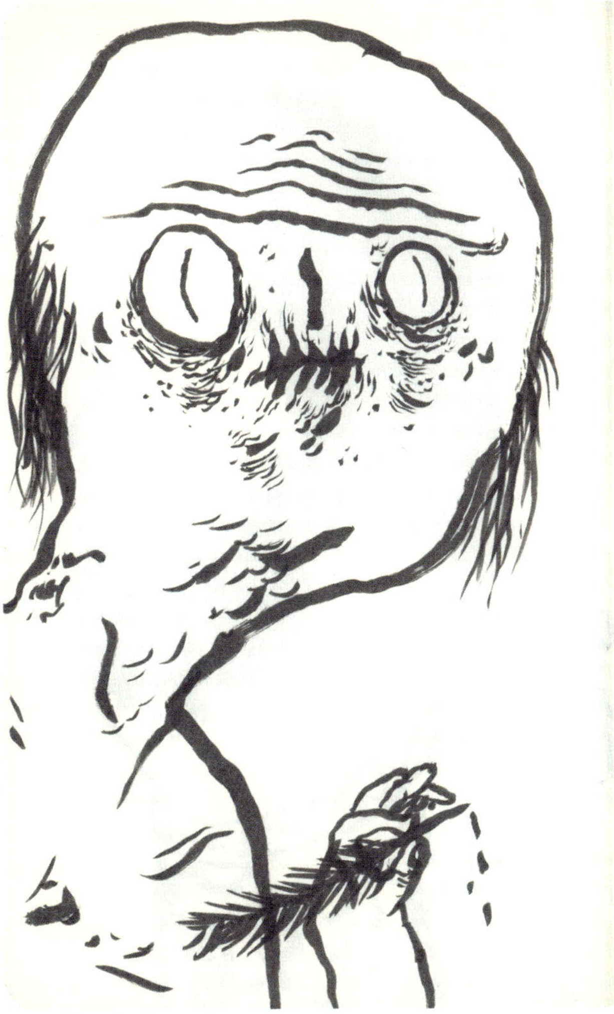

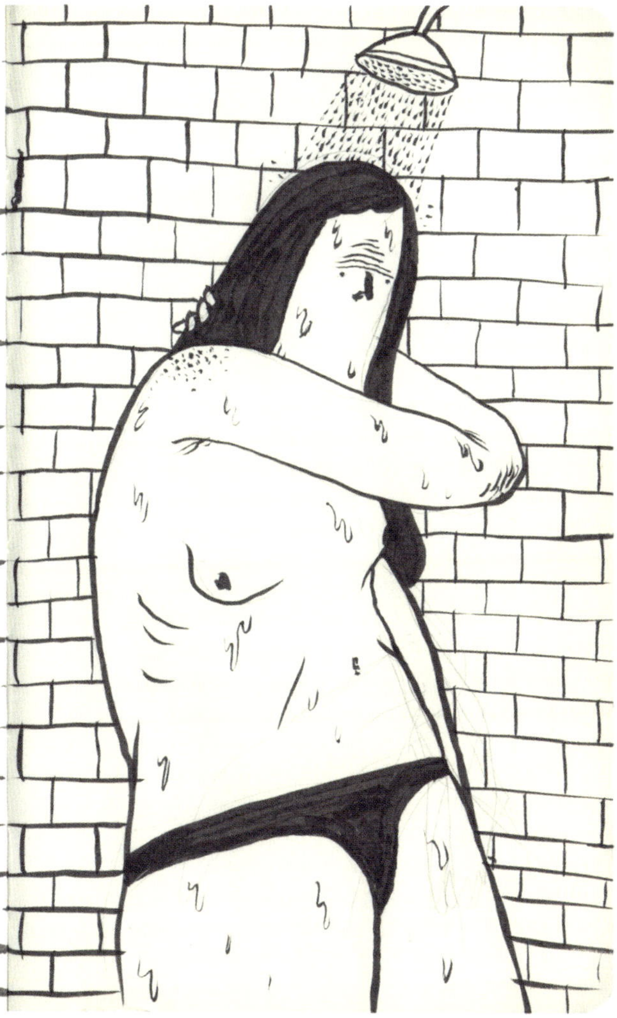

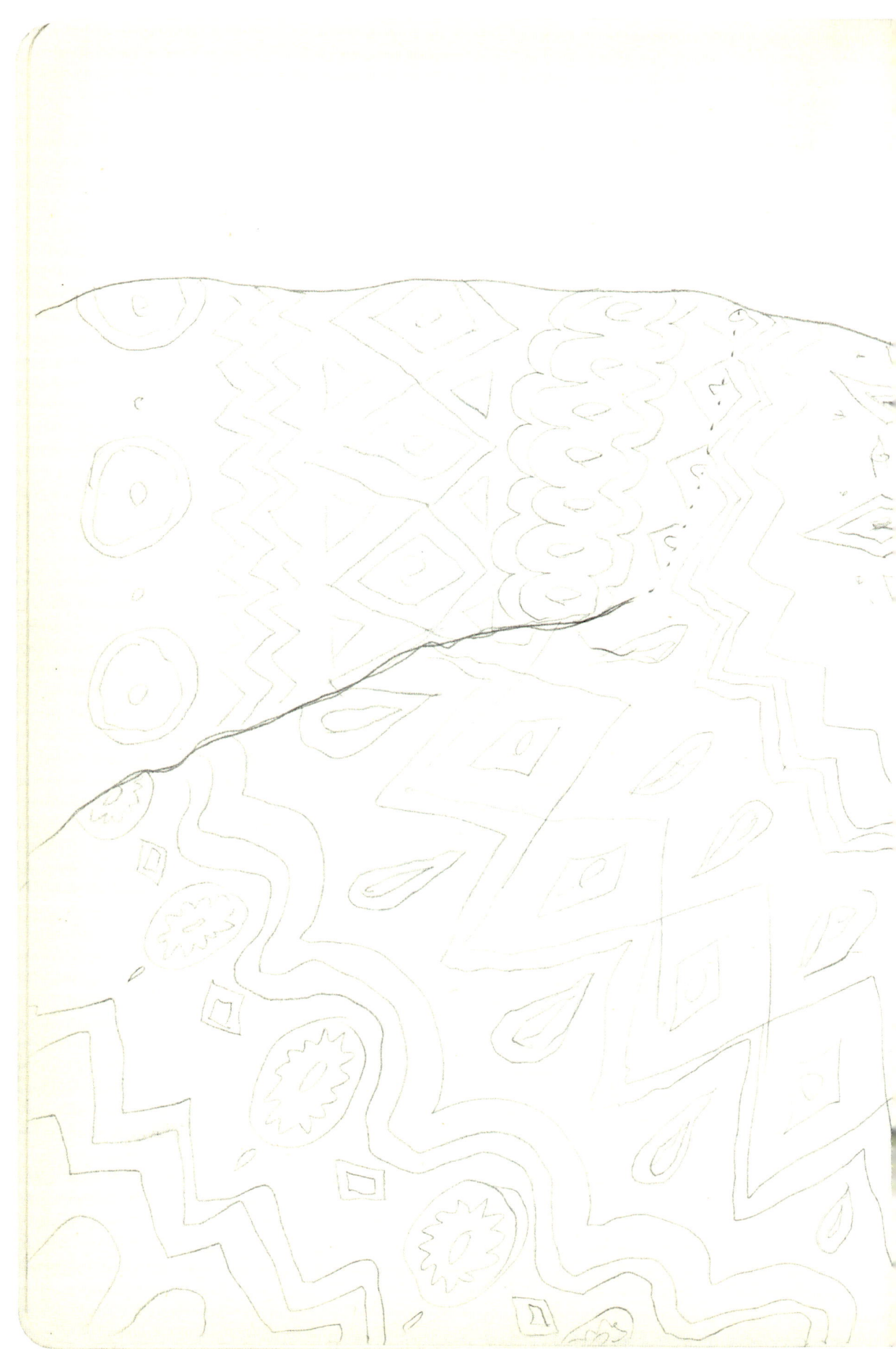

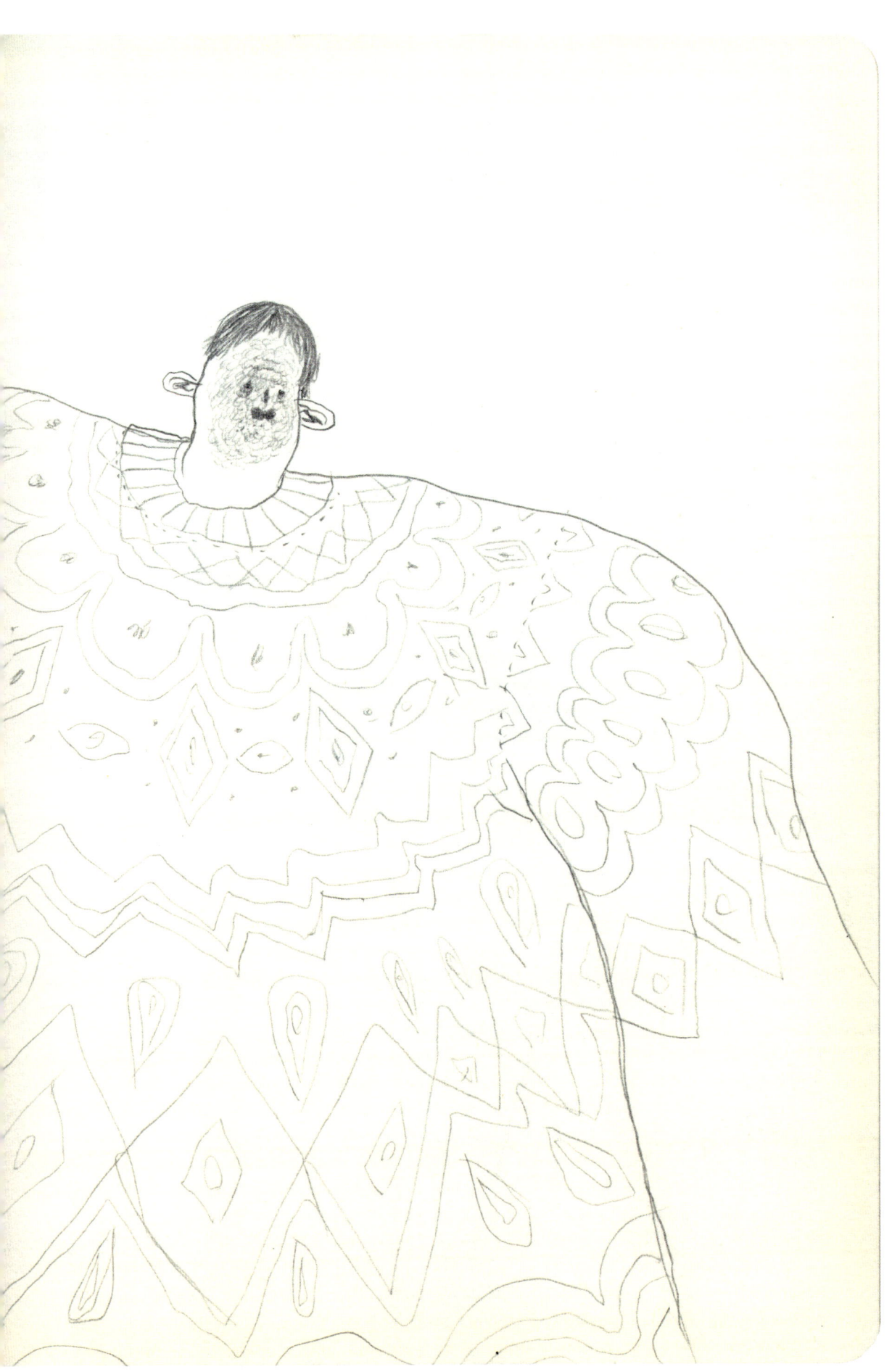

OD
CHORUS

HOORAY
HIDE THOSE FEELS ⇐ ??
I'M NOT THERE

RAIN
HOLIDAY

PUNCTUATE
"WEAR THEM LIKE
SIGNS (INTO CH2)

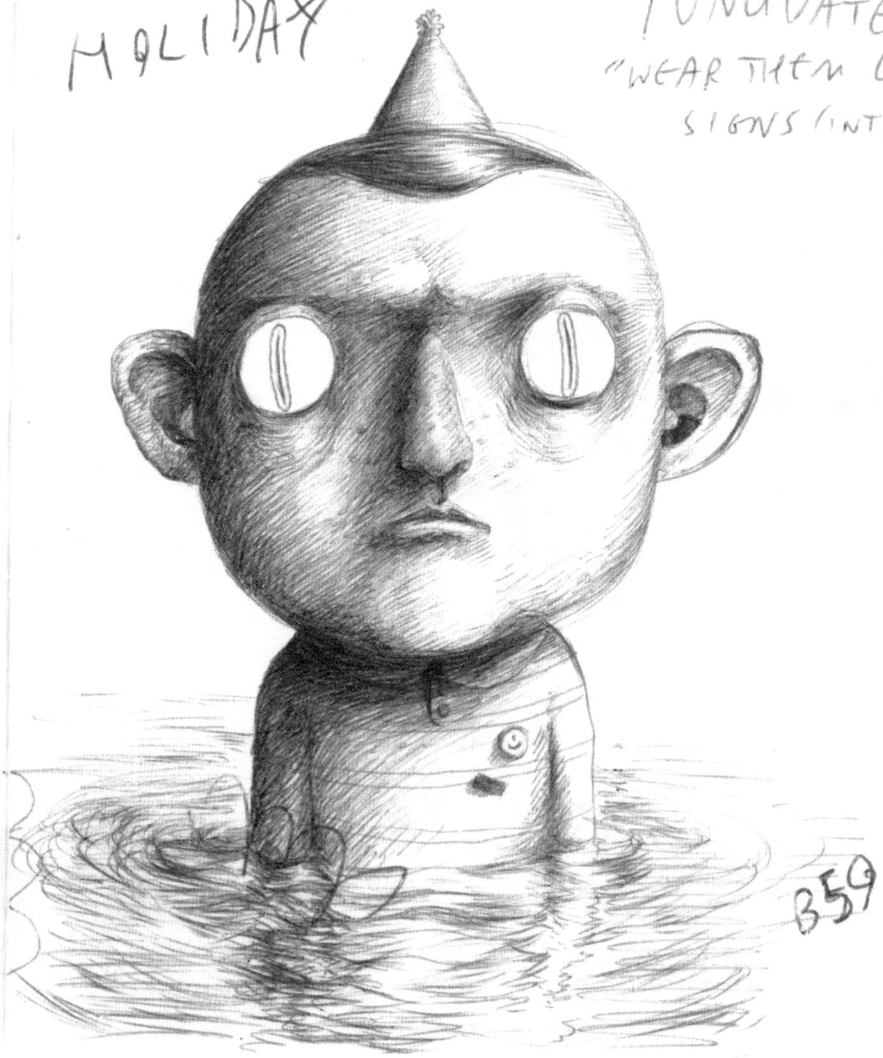

B59

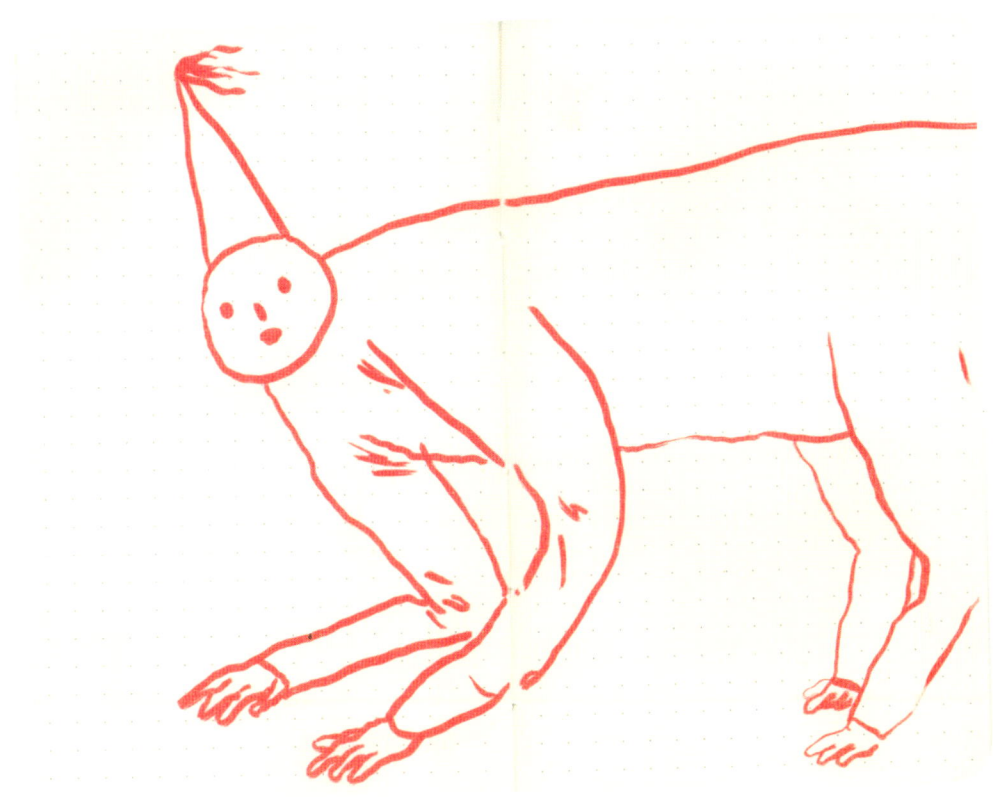

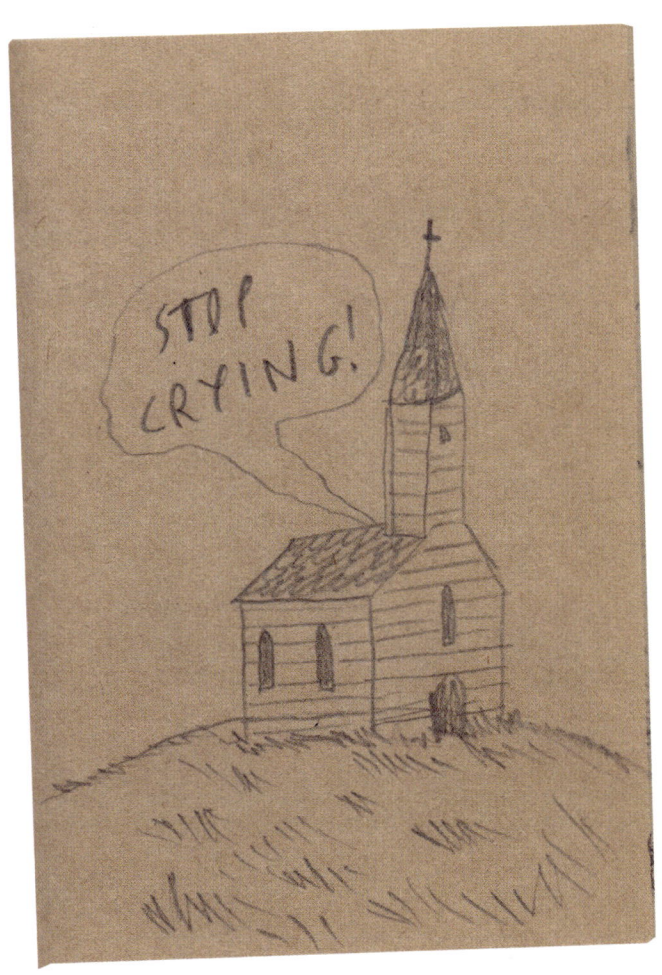

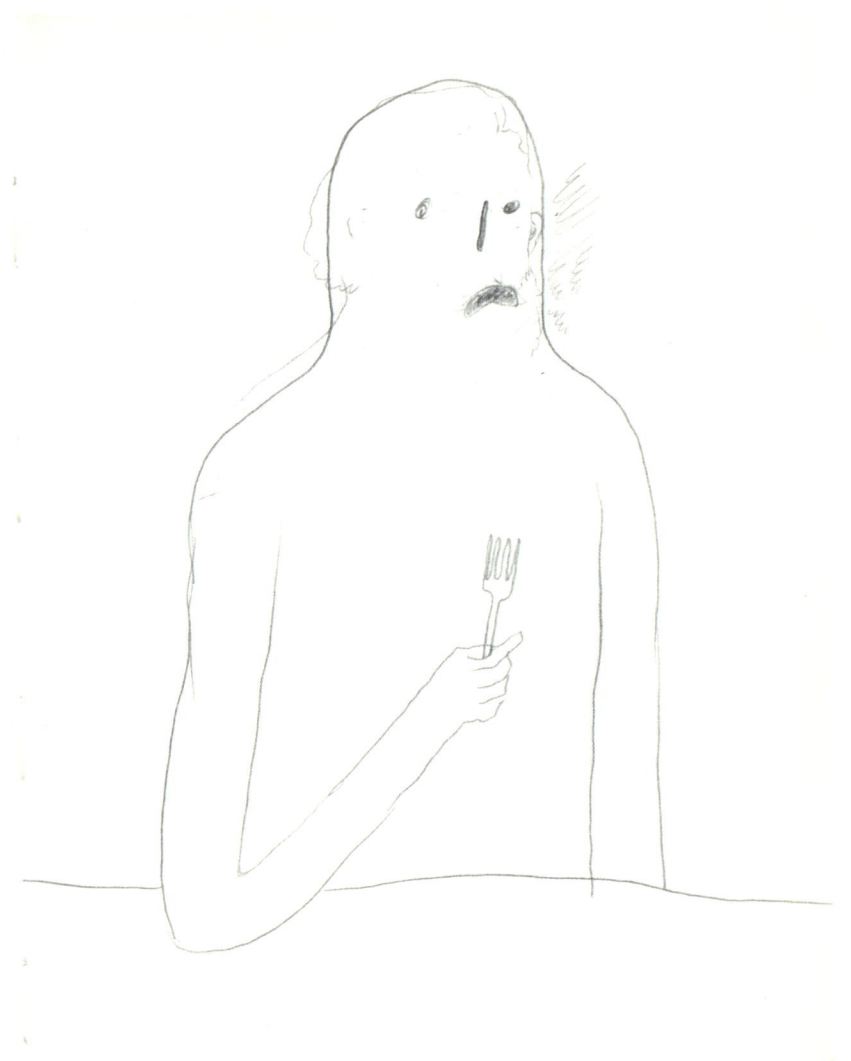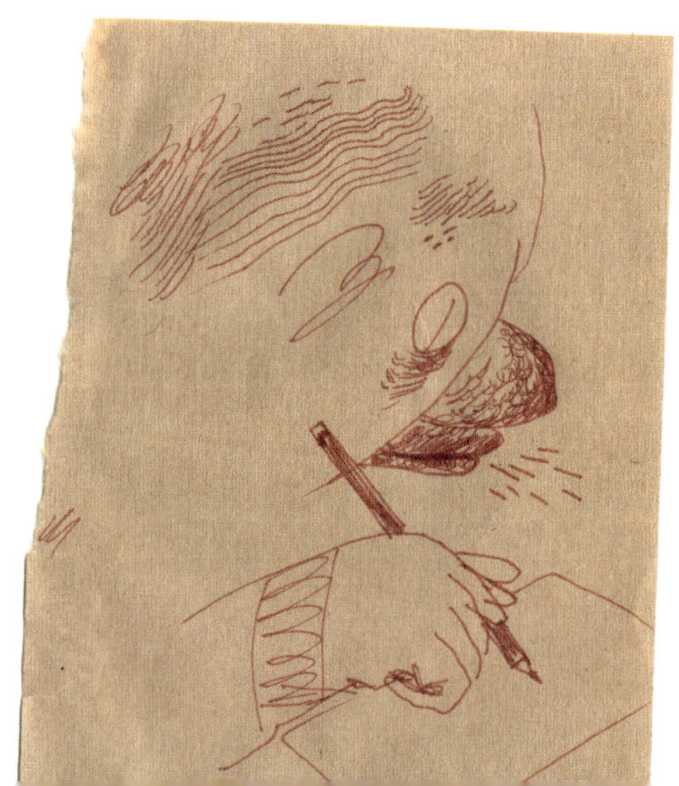

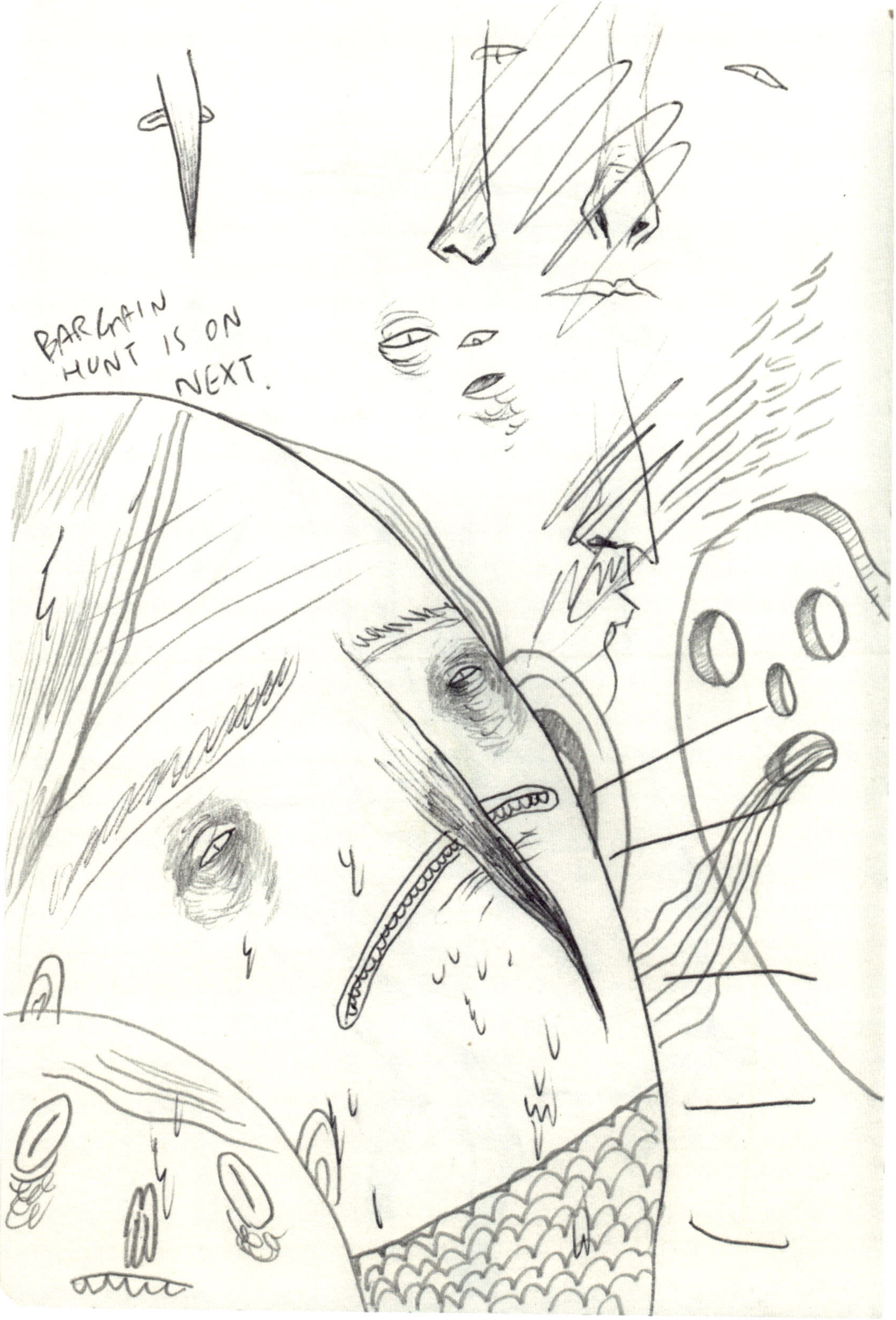

BARGAIN HUNT IS ON NEXT.

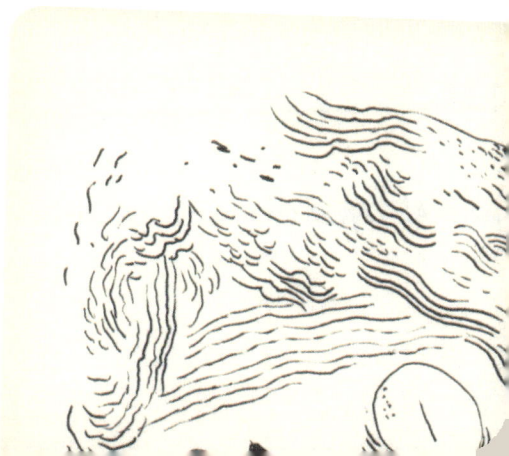

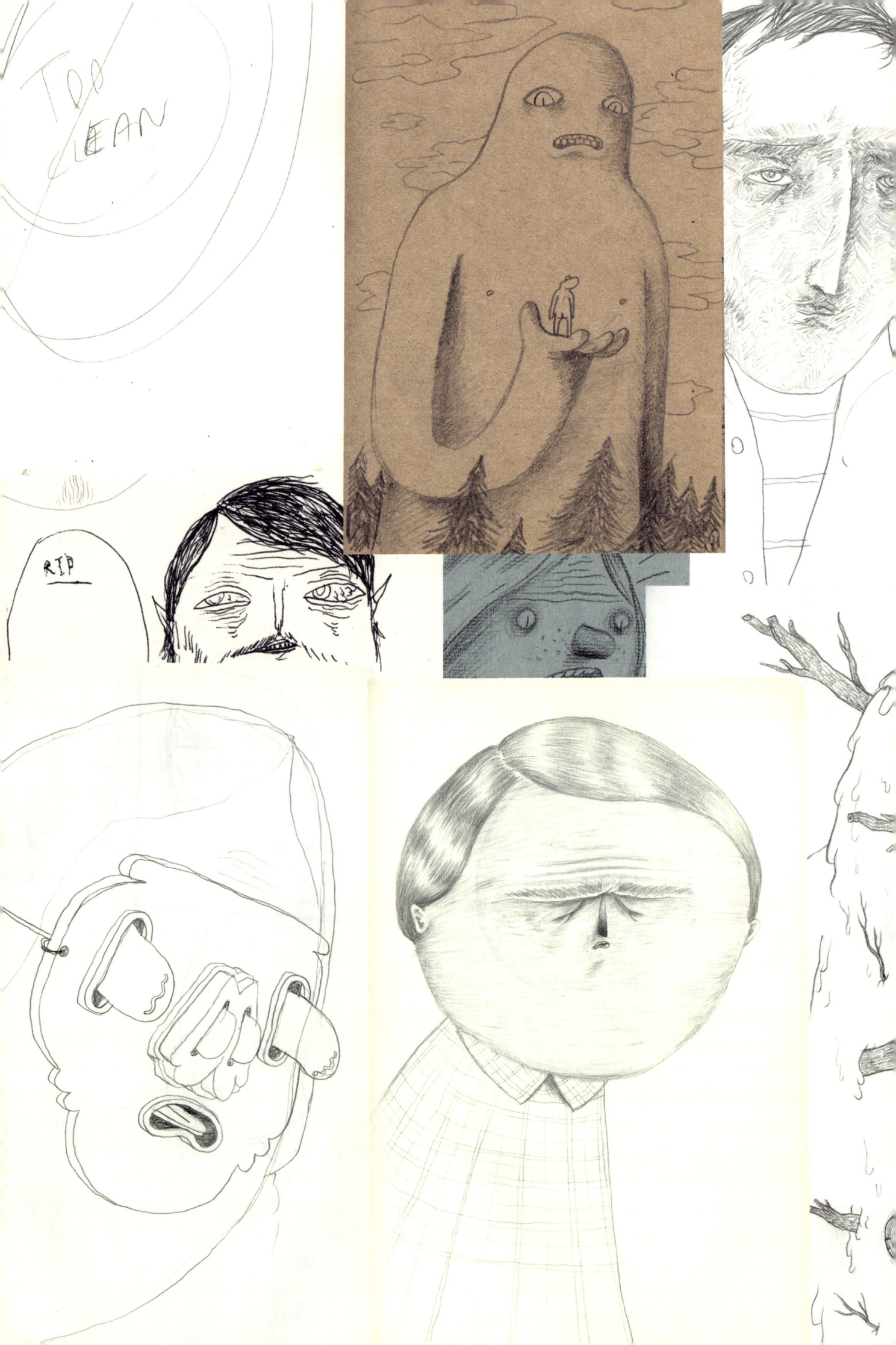

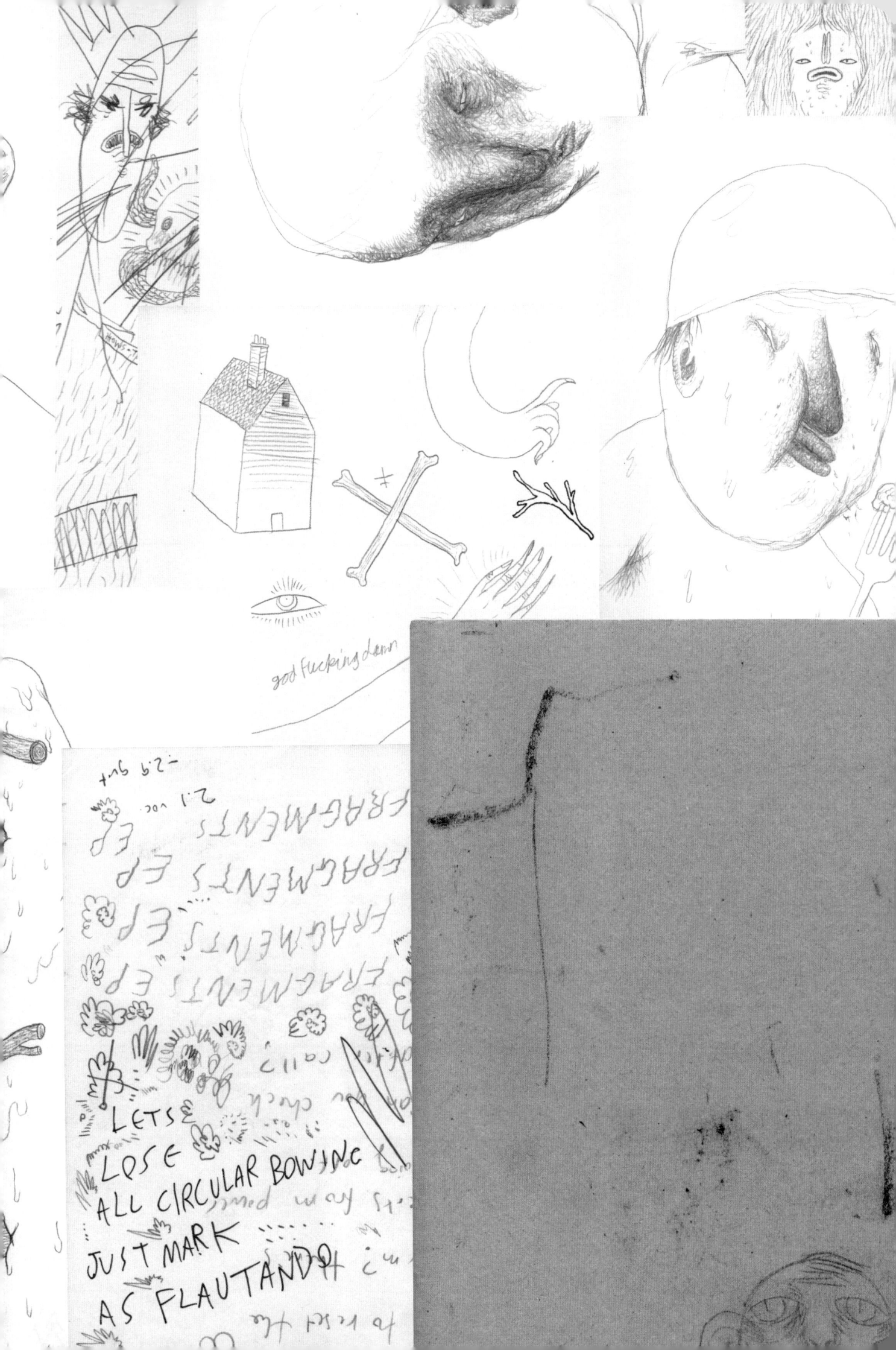

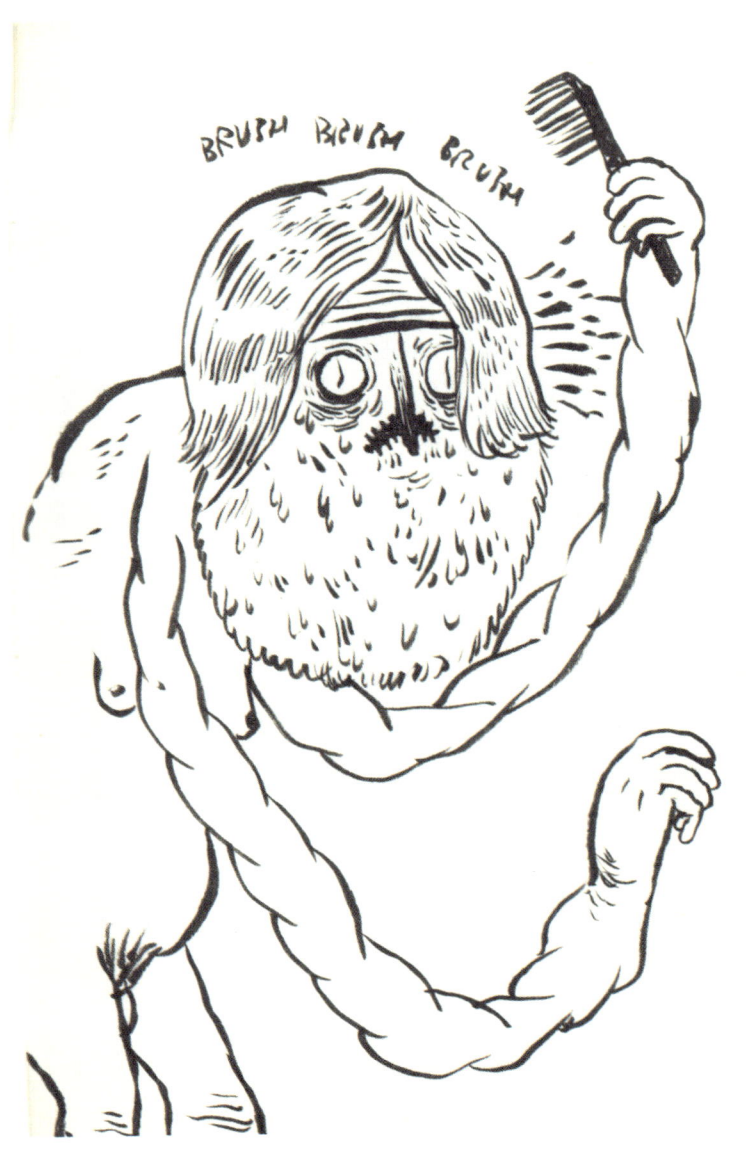

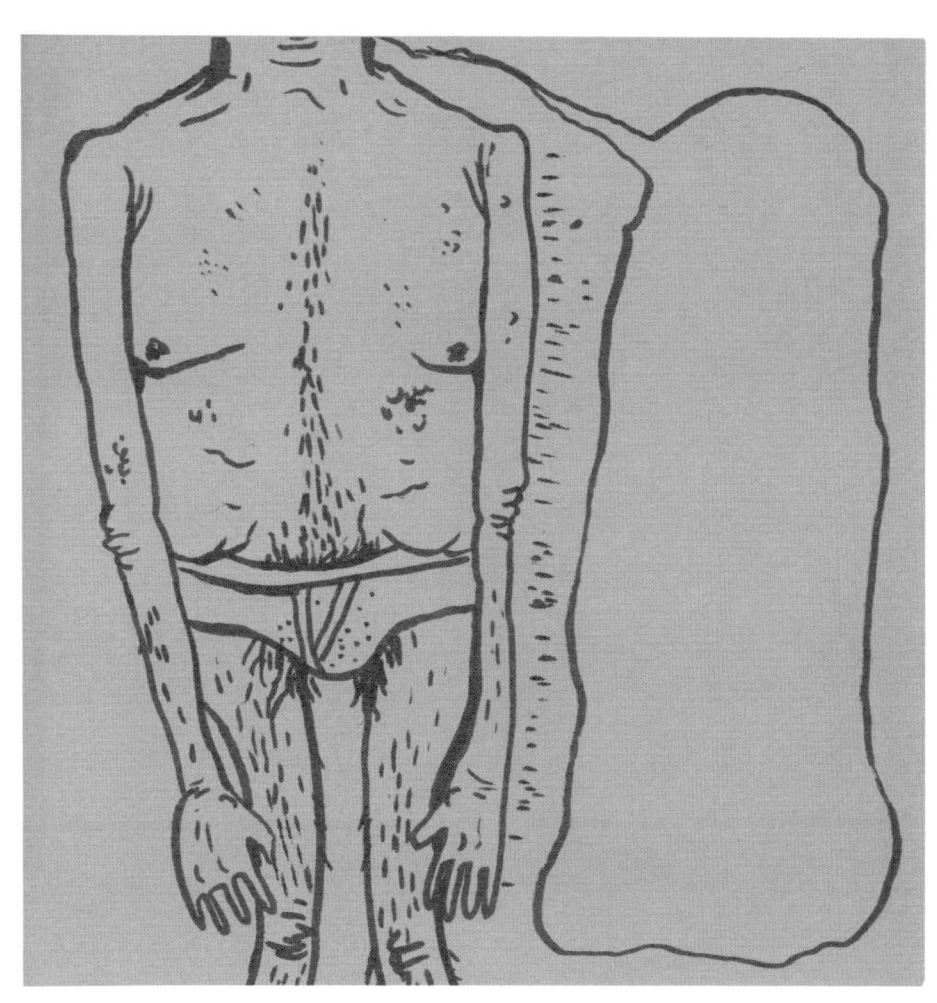

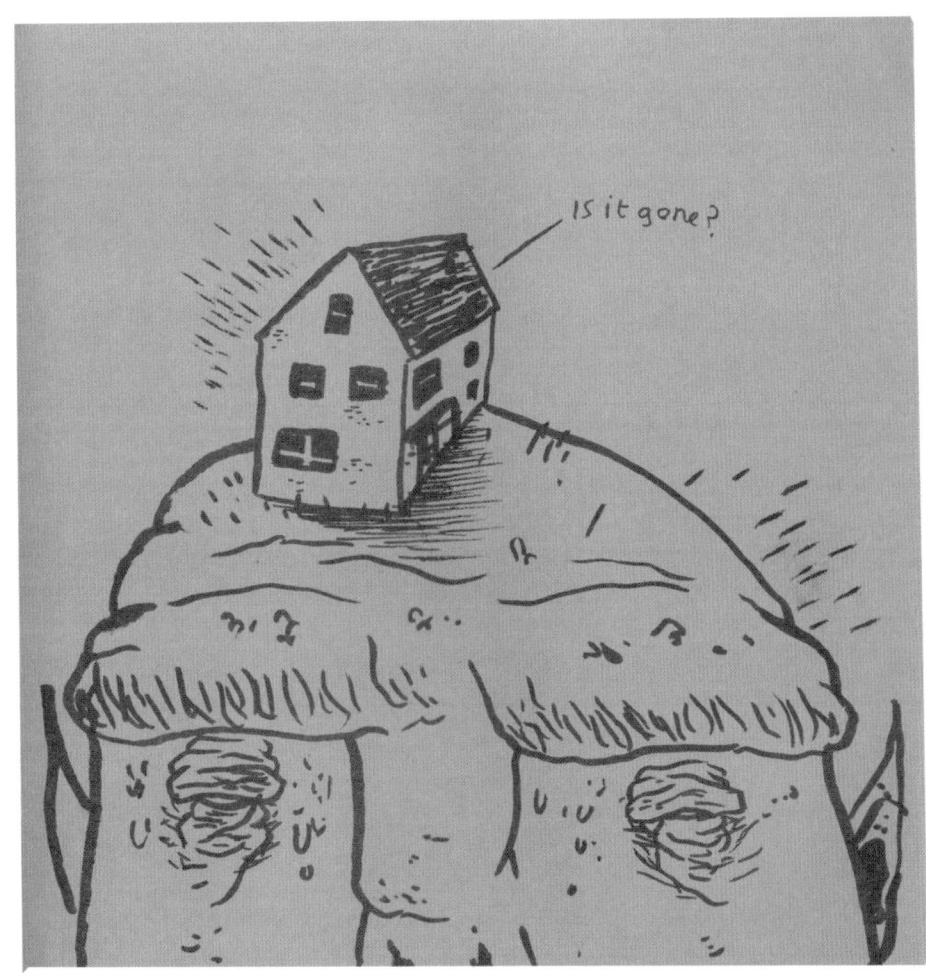

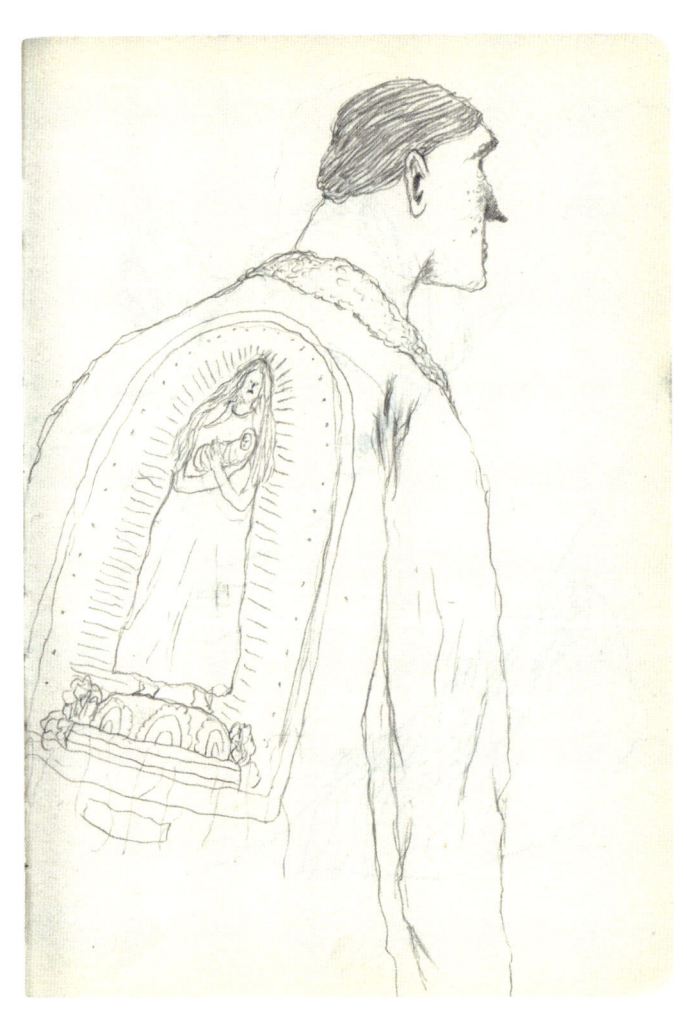
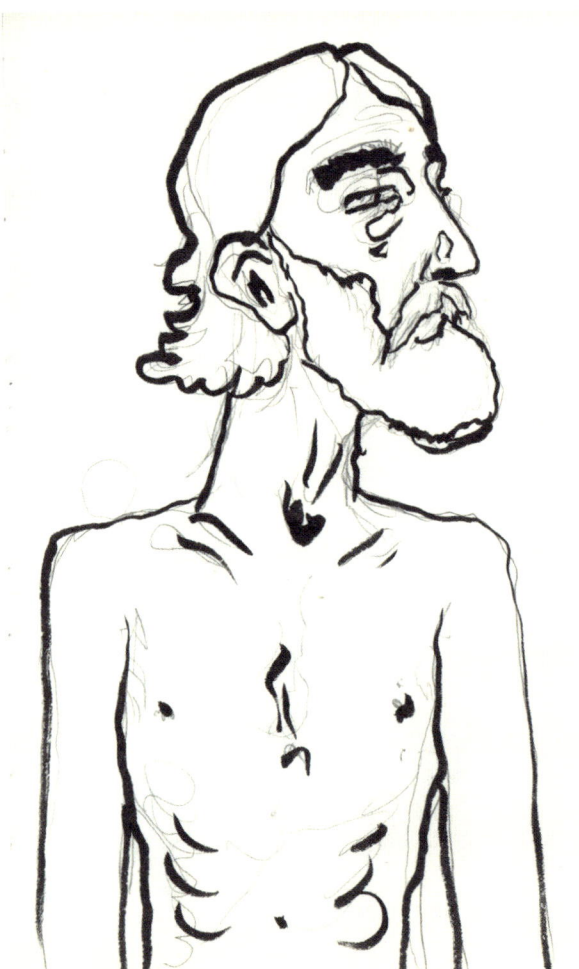

YOU
ARE
ALL ~~EVERYTHING~~

TU
ES
TOUT

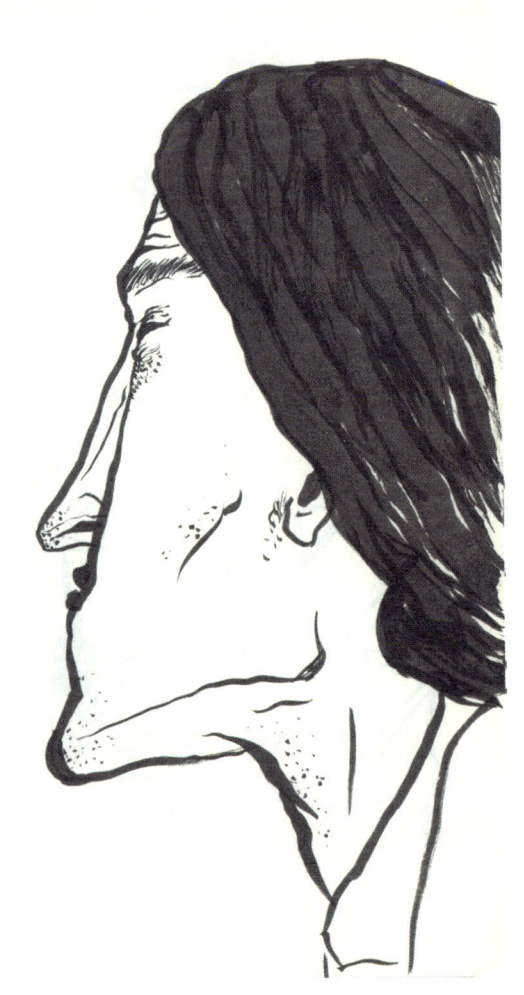

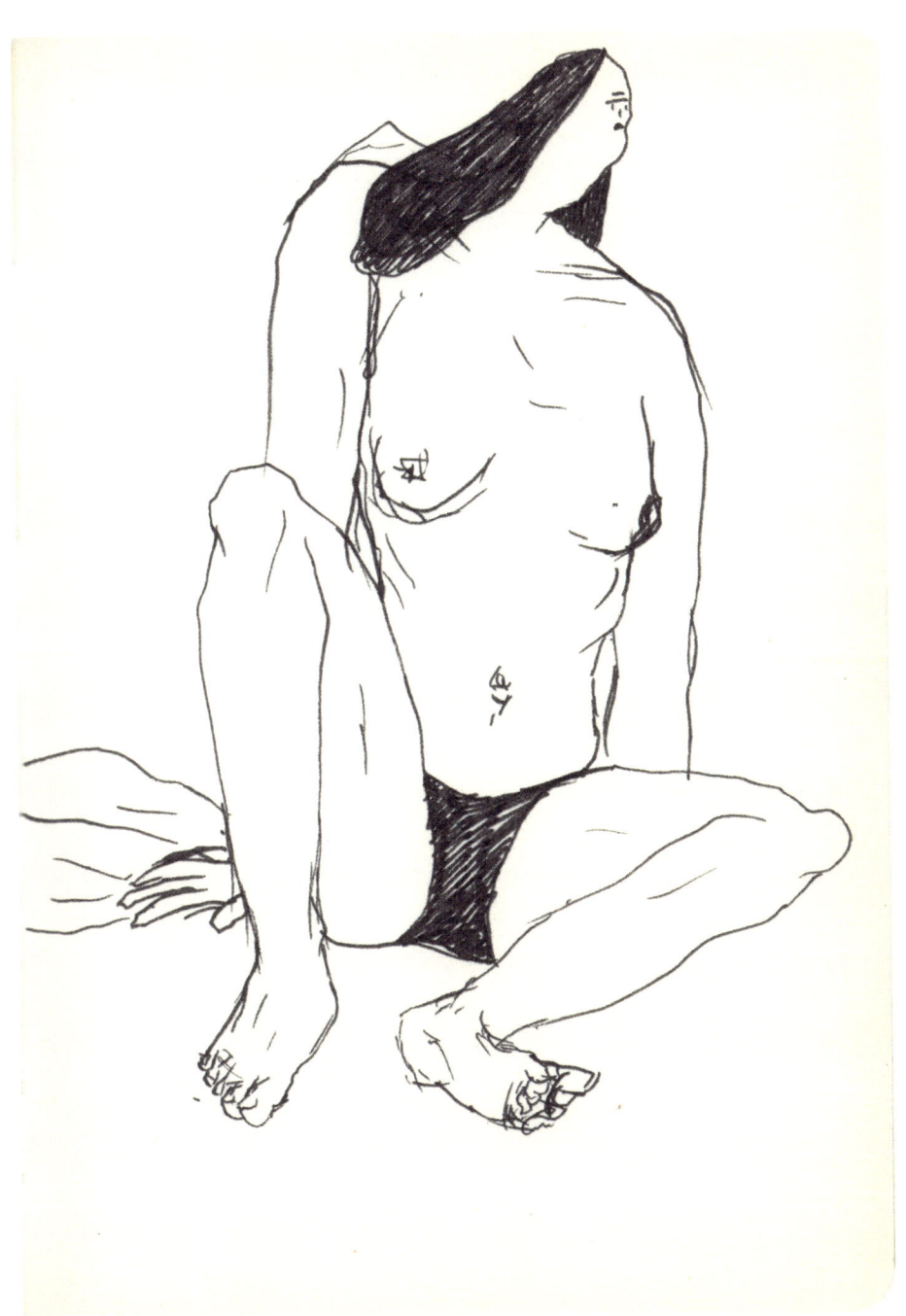

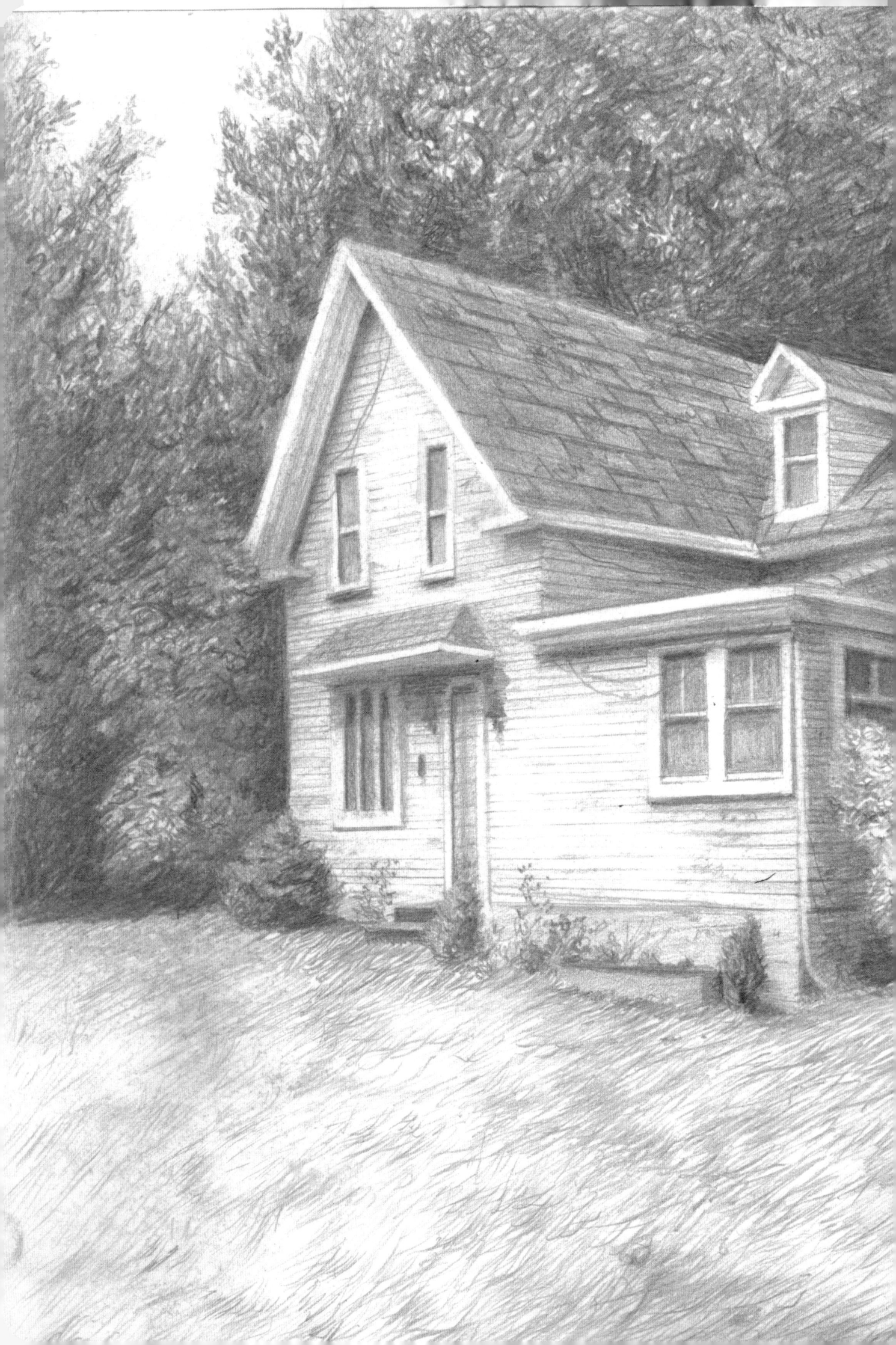

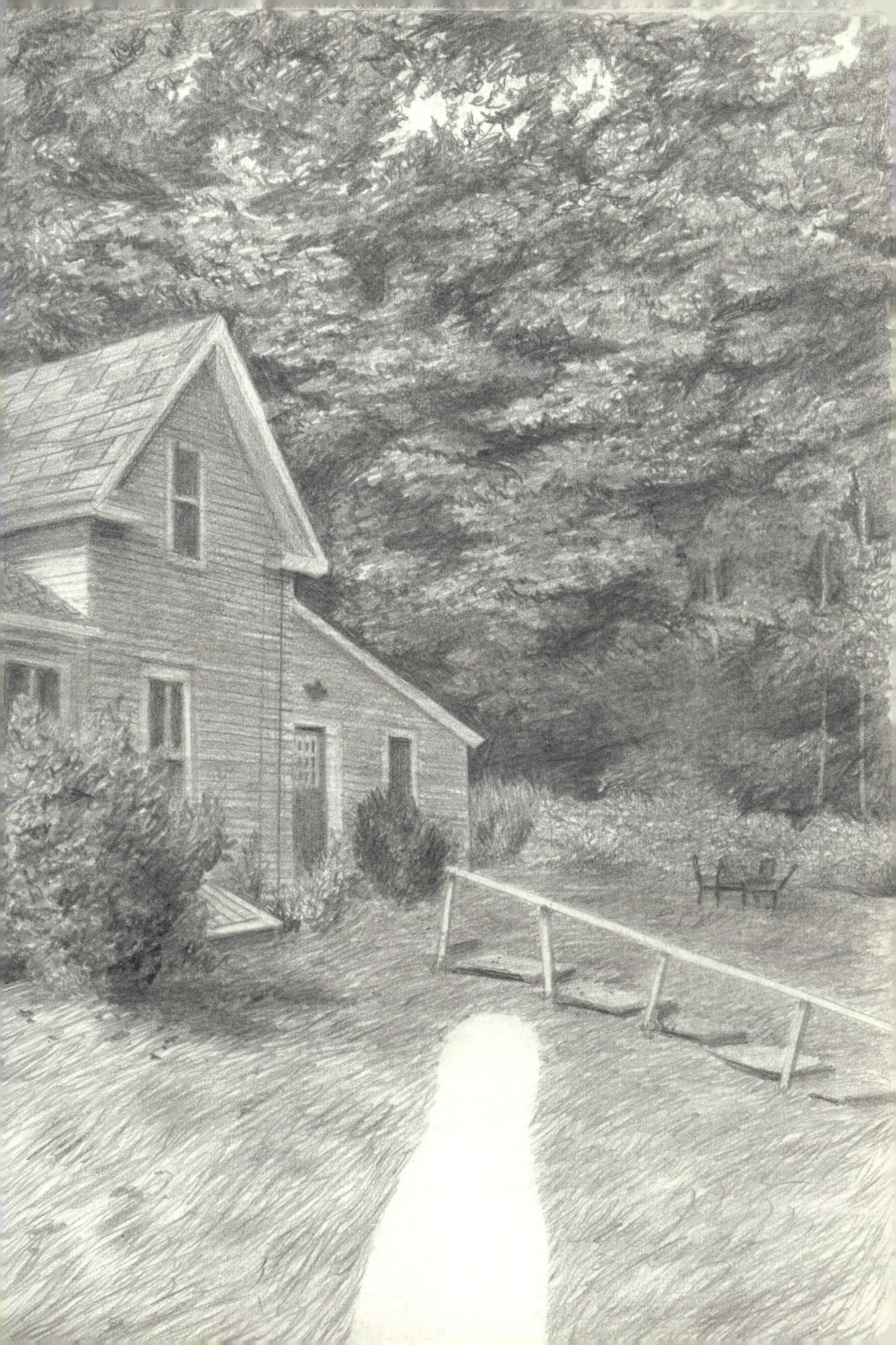

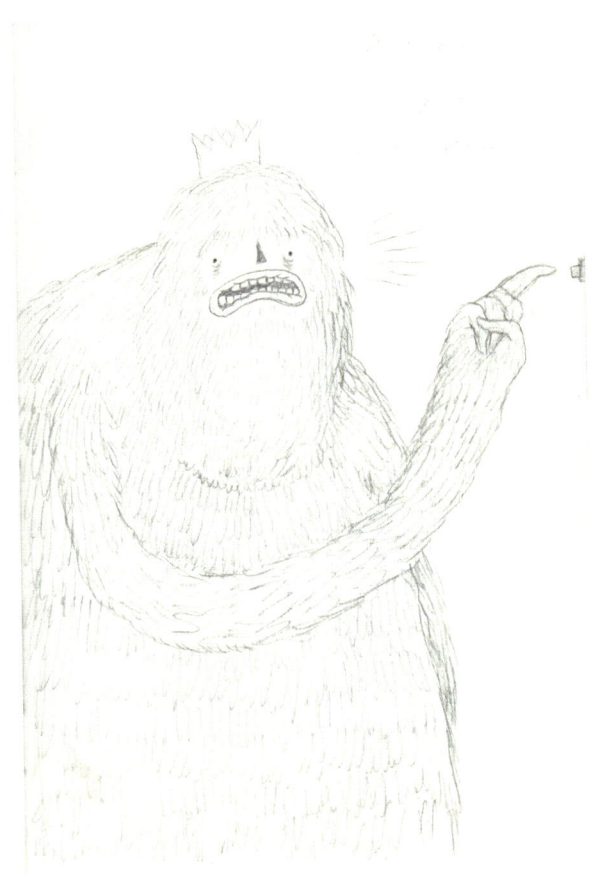

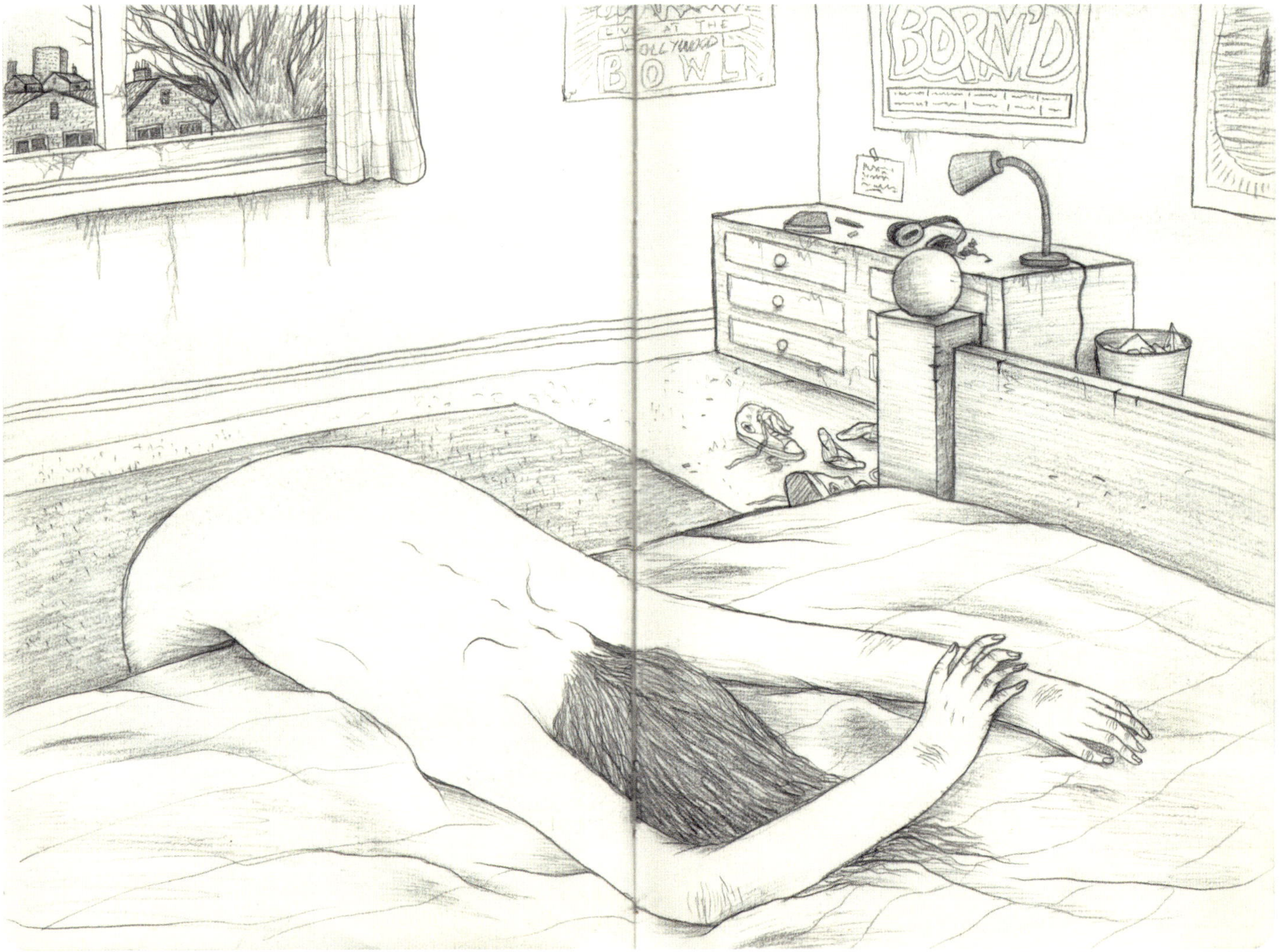

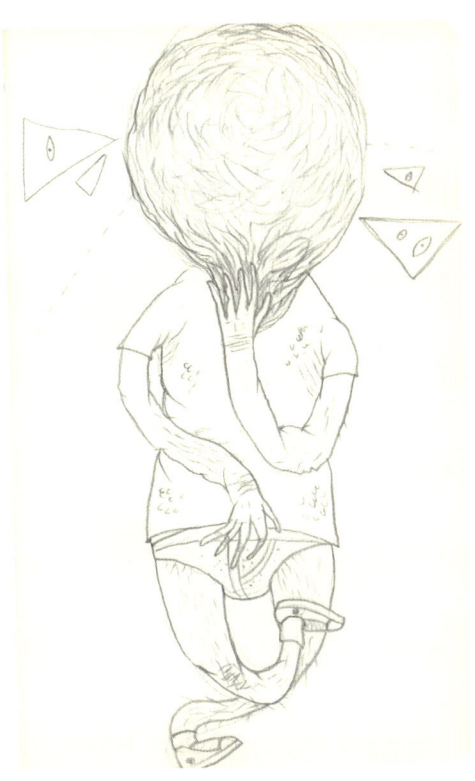
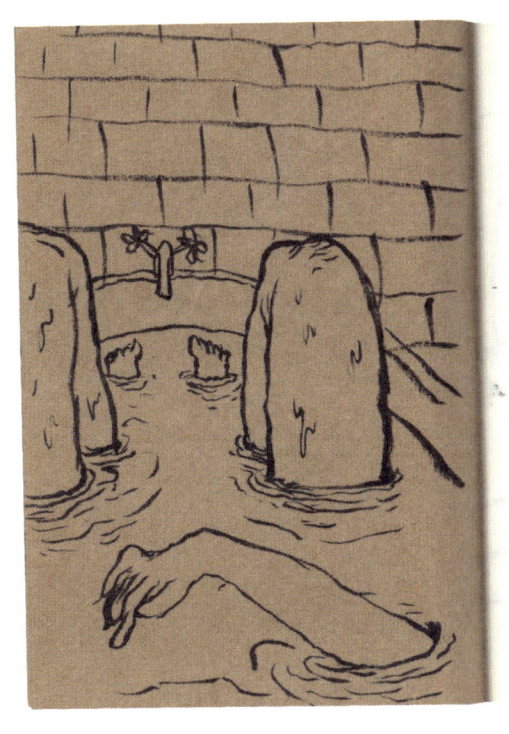
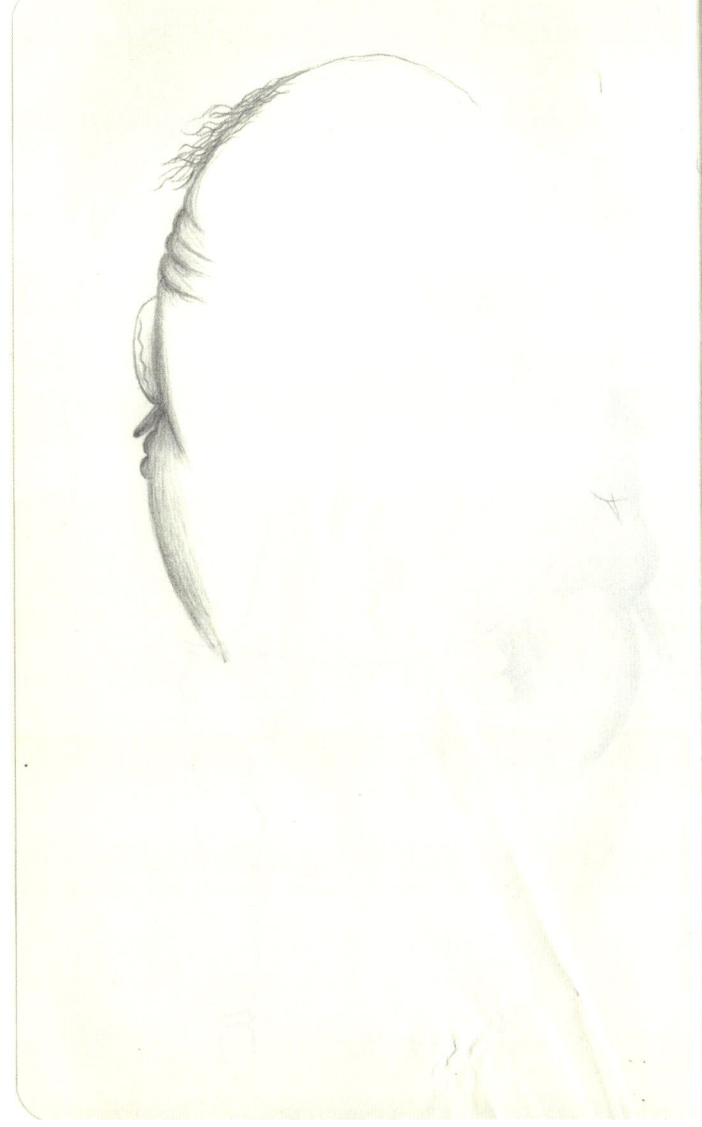

HEALAH ~~ARRIVES~~ DREAMS

meeting

PUB, PARK, TUBE
HE WALKS THROUGH the crowd and
MJ DANCE THROUGH environment,

MONTAGE,
AMBIENT (PEDALS ETC) OF Lala h

~~APARTMENT~~
~~HEALAH~~ WINDOWBIRDS
APARTMENT, DINNER DANCE THRO

Montage

HEALAH DEPARTING

APARTMENT, PRYING ARGUE, L
LEAVES

Camera reveals me & Ren

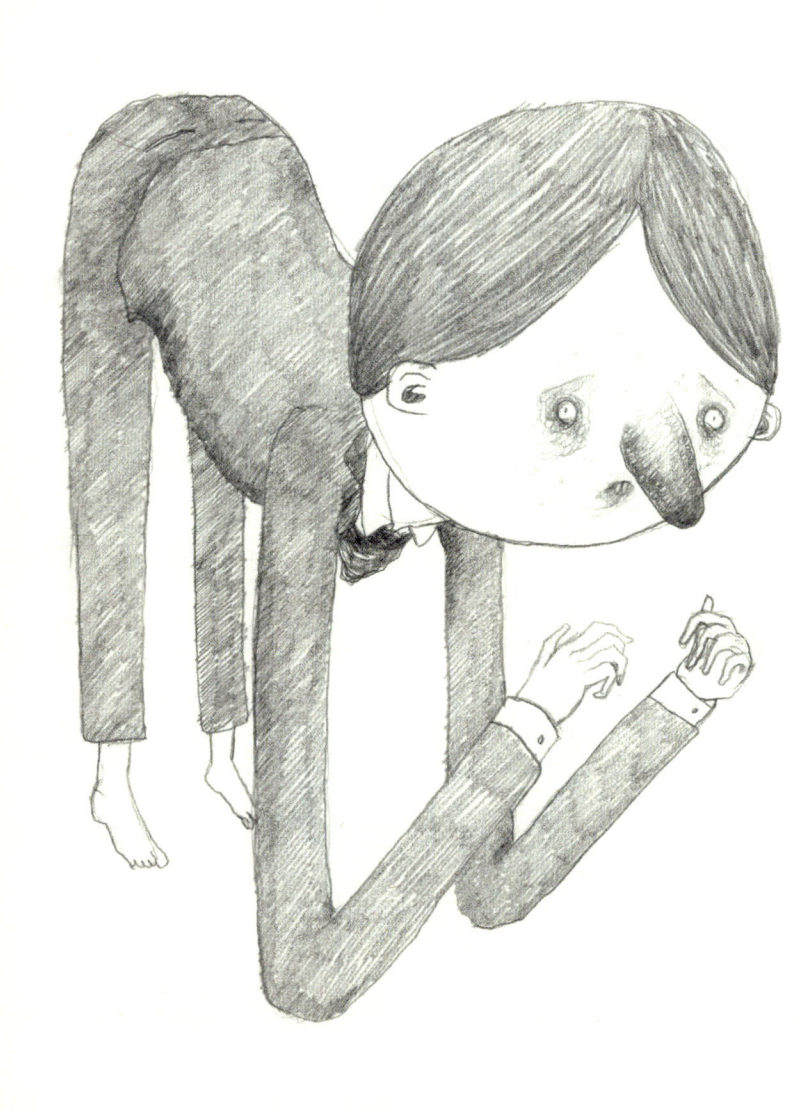

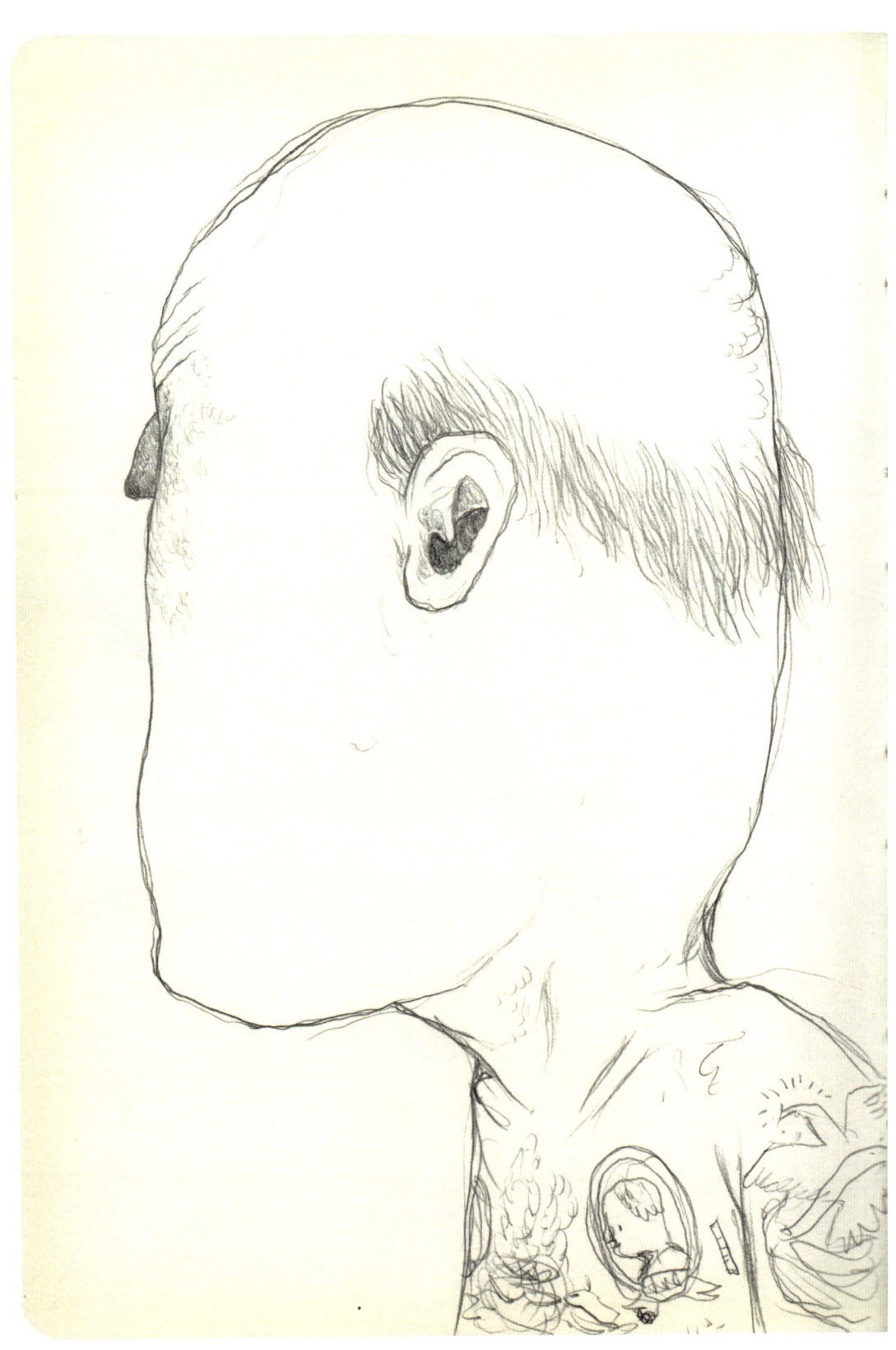

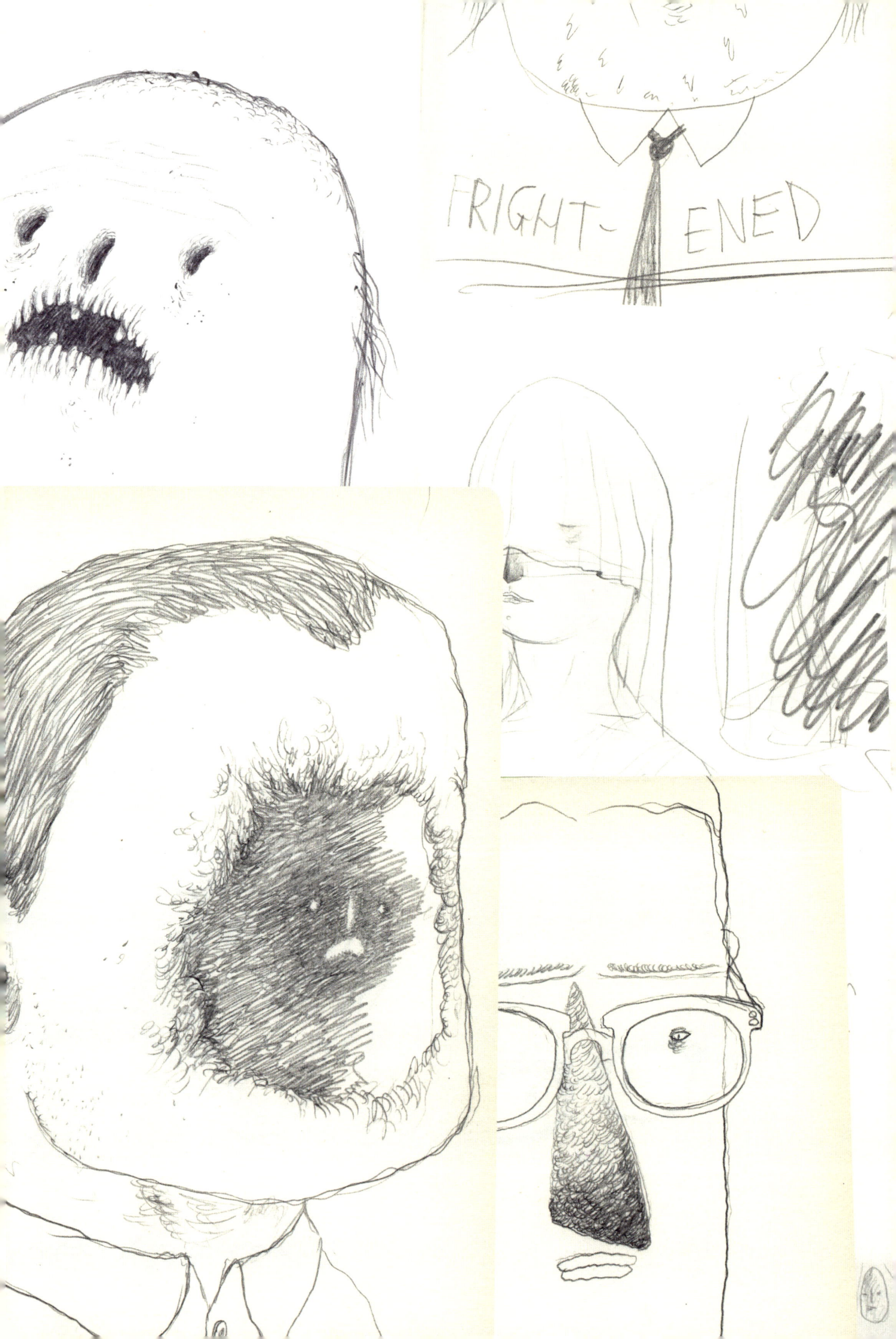

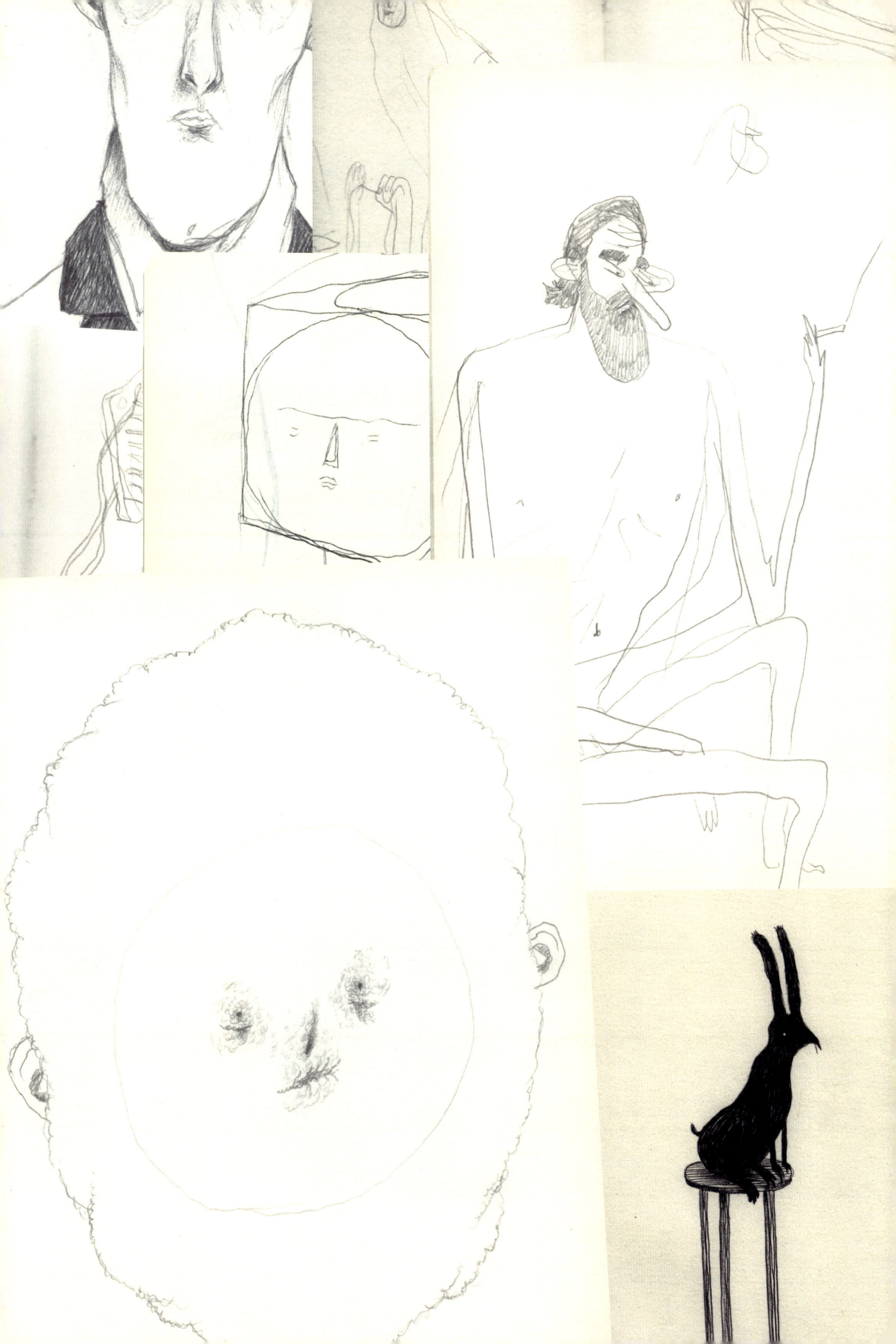

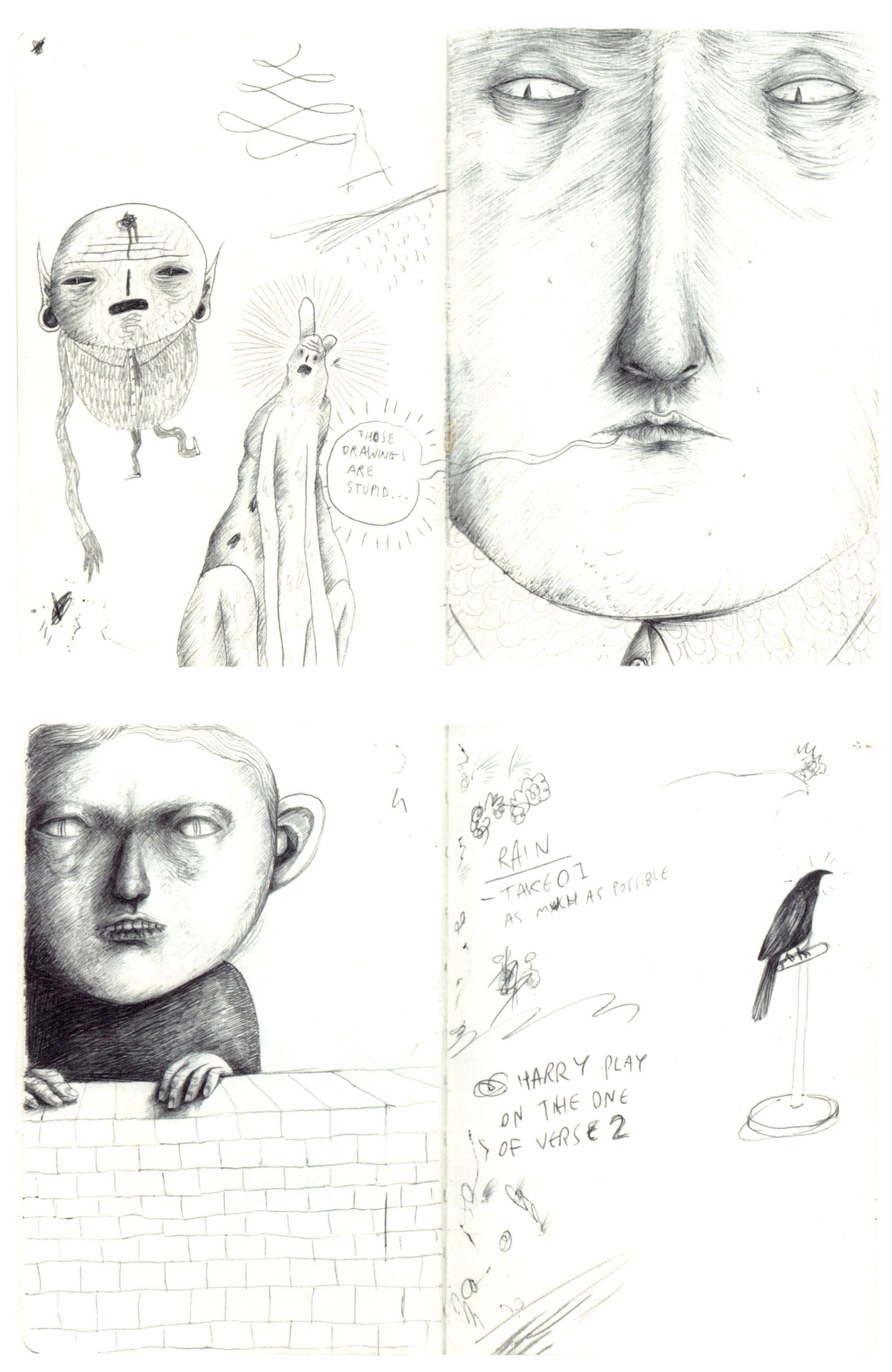

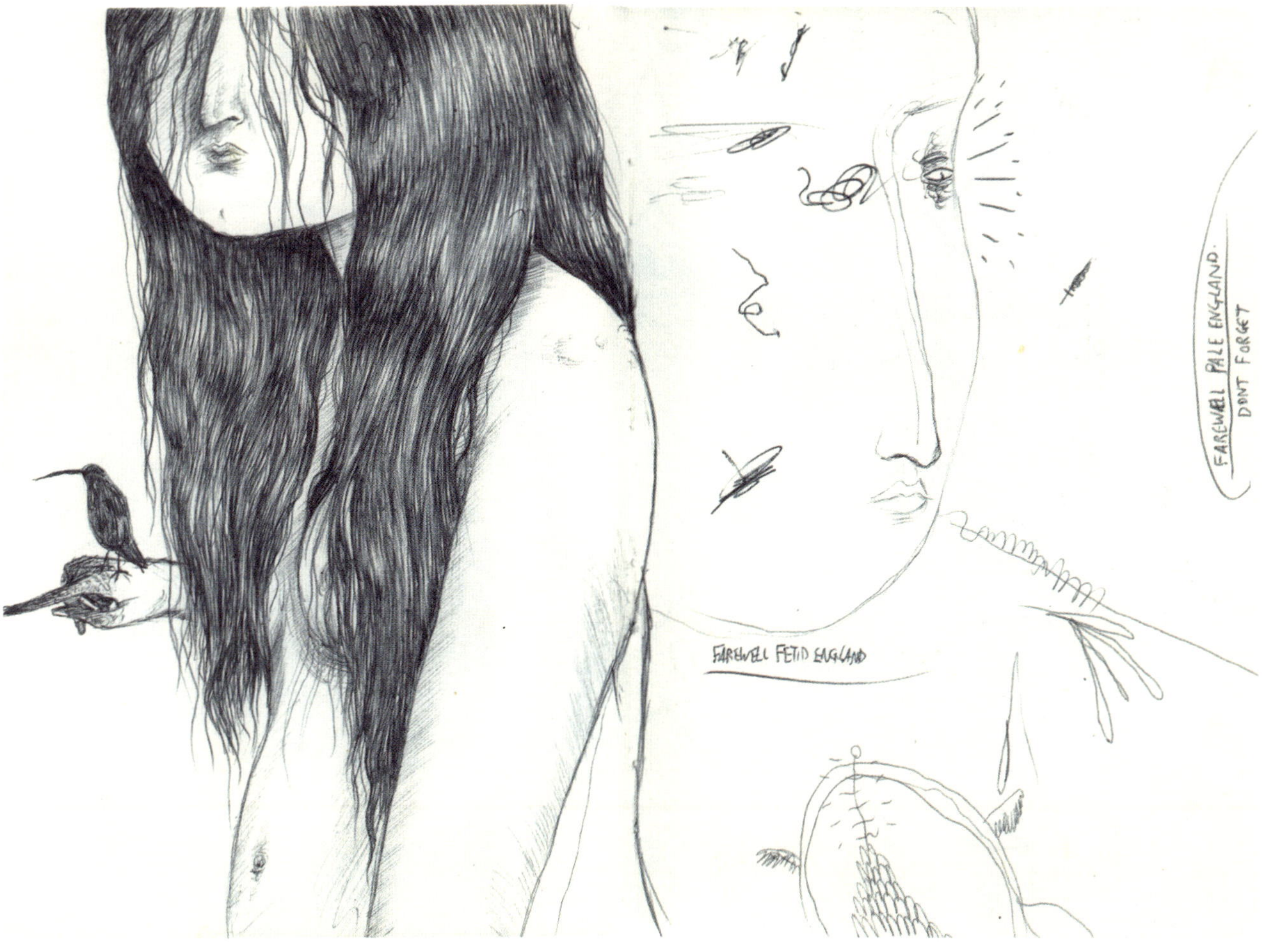

FAREWELL PALE ENGLAND.
DON'T FORGET

FAREWELL FETID ENGLAND

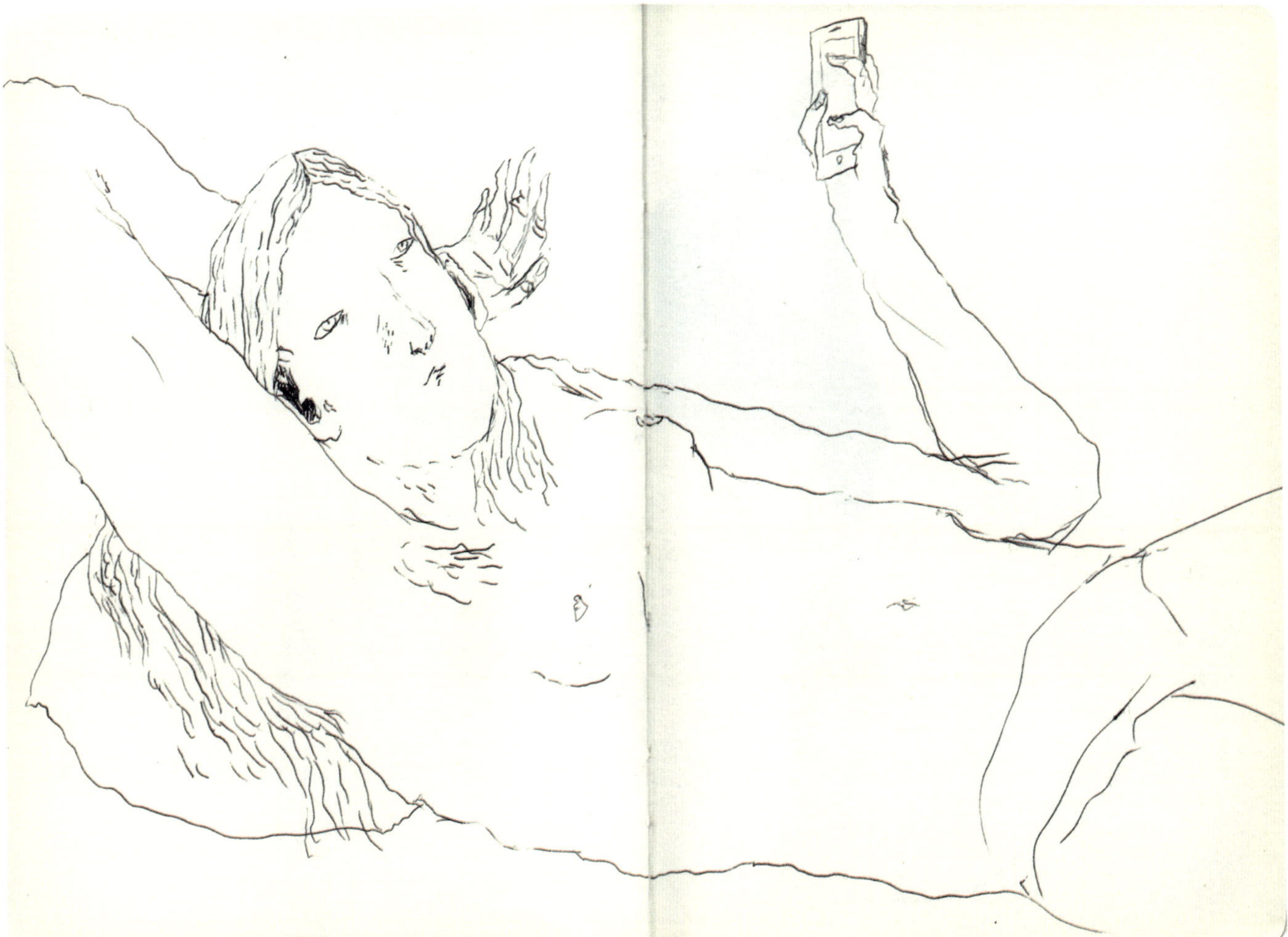

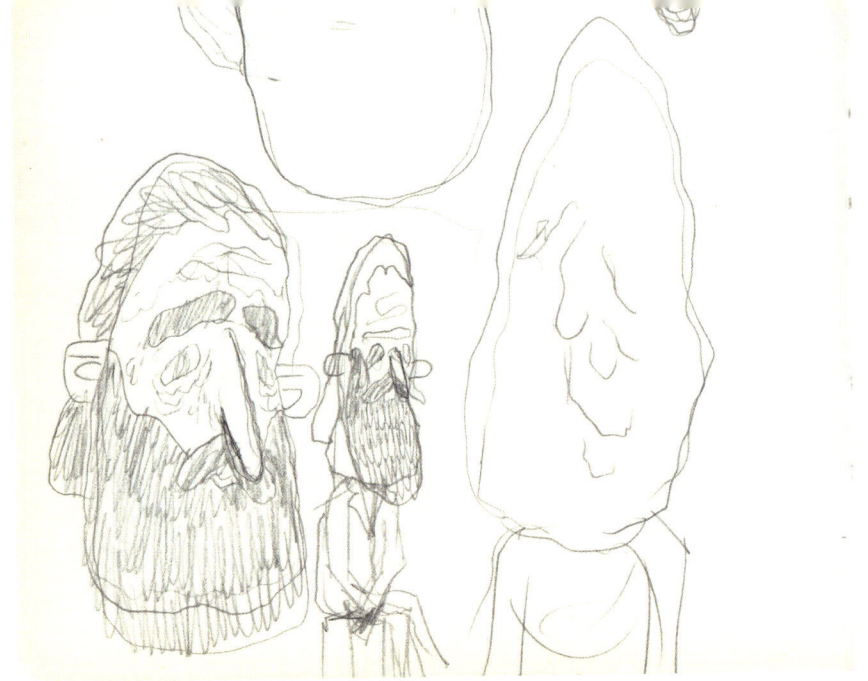

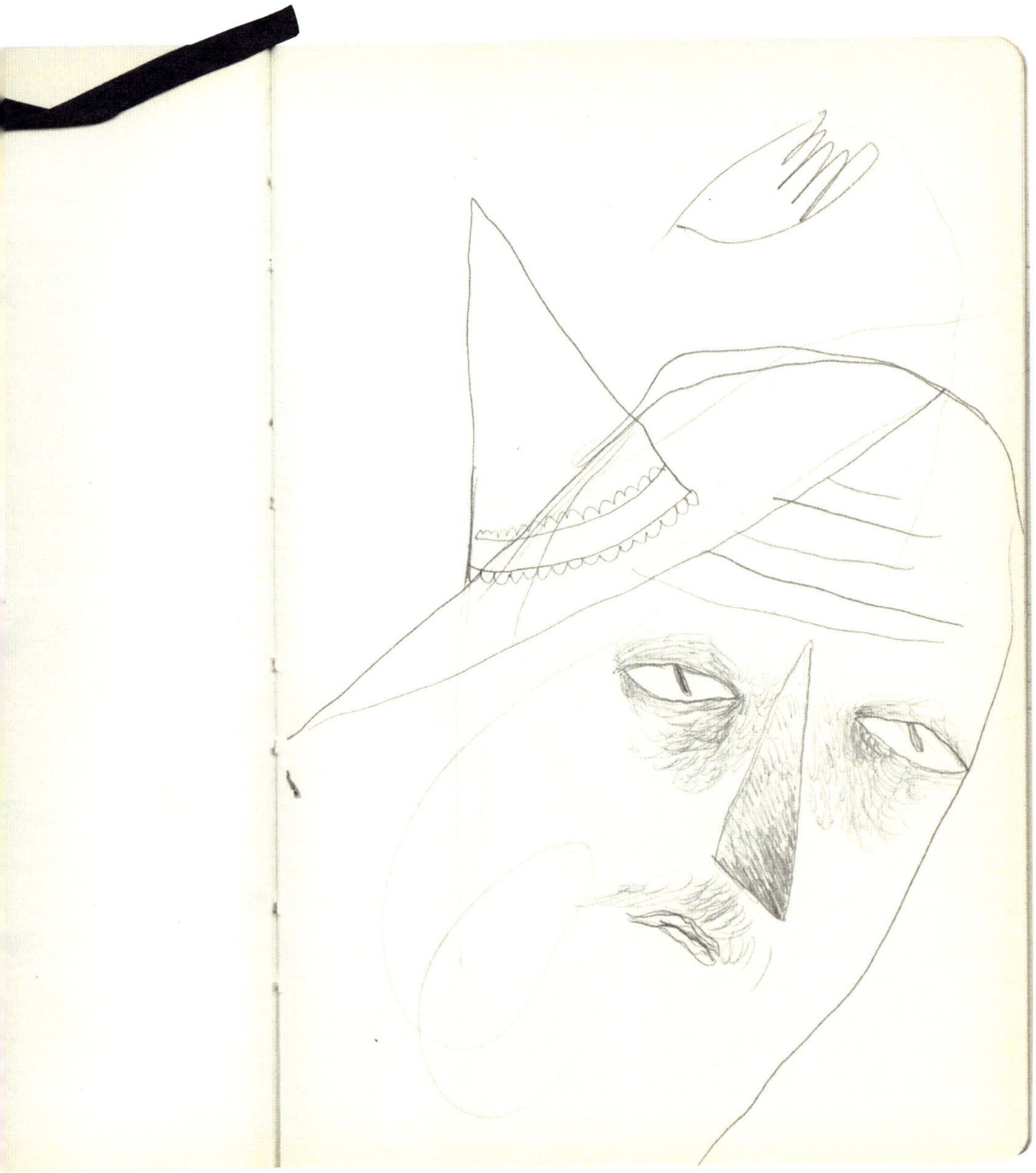

Its not like riding a bike
OH my god, I think she's right

But I don't mind, I won't fight
as long as you promise to stay the
whole night.

~~But but what I had in mind~~

Though you are smart
Though you are kind
~~A~~ Woman your not
what I had in mind

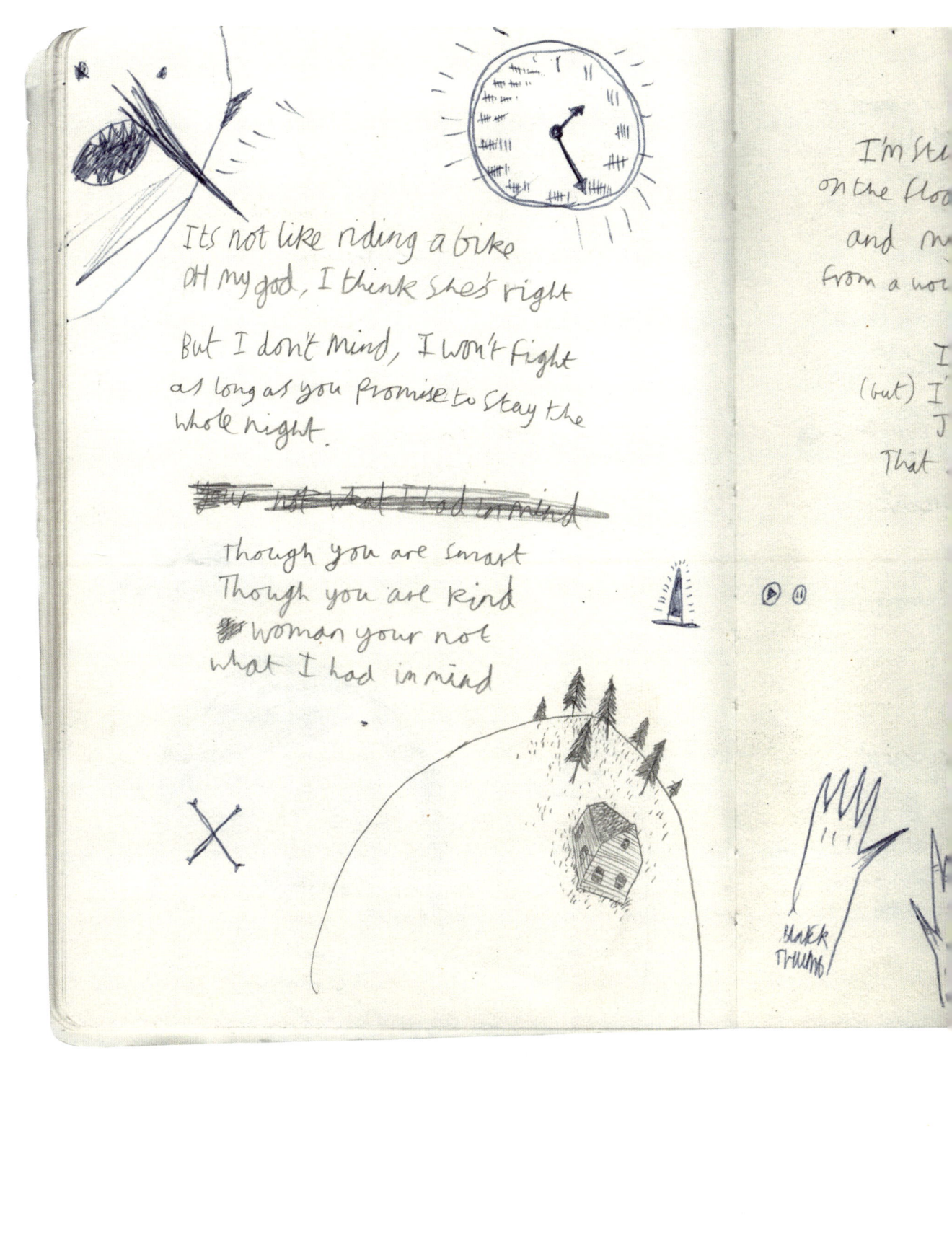

I'm st
on the flo
and m
from a no

I
(but) I
J
That

BLACK
THUMB

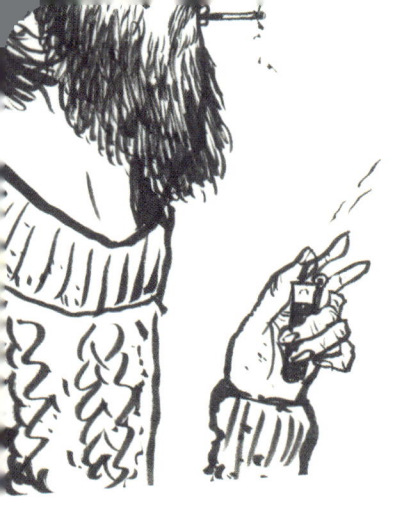
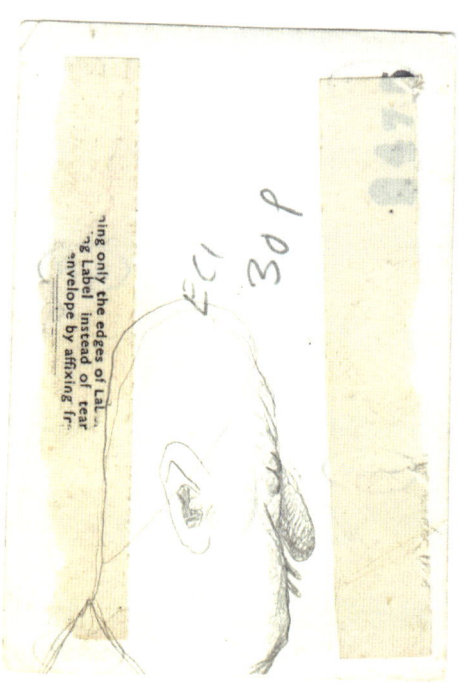

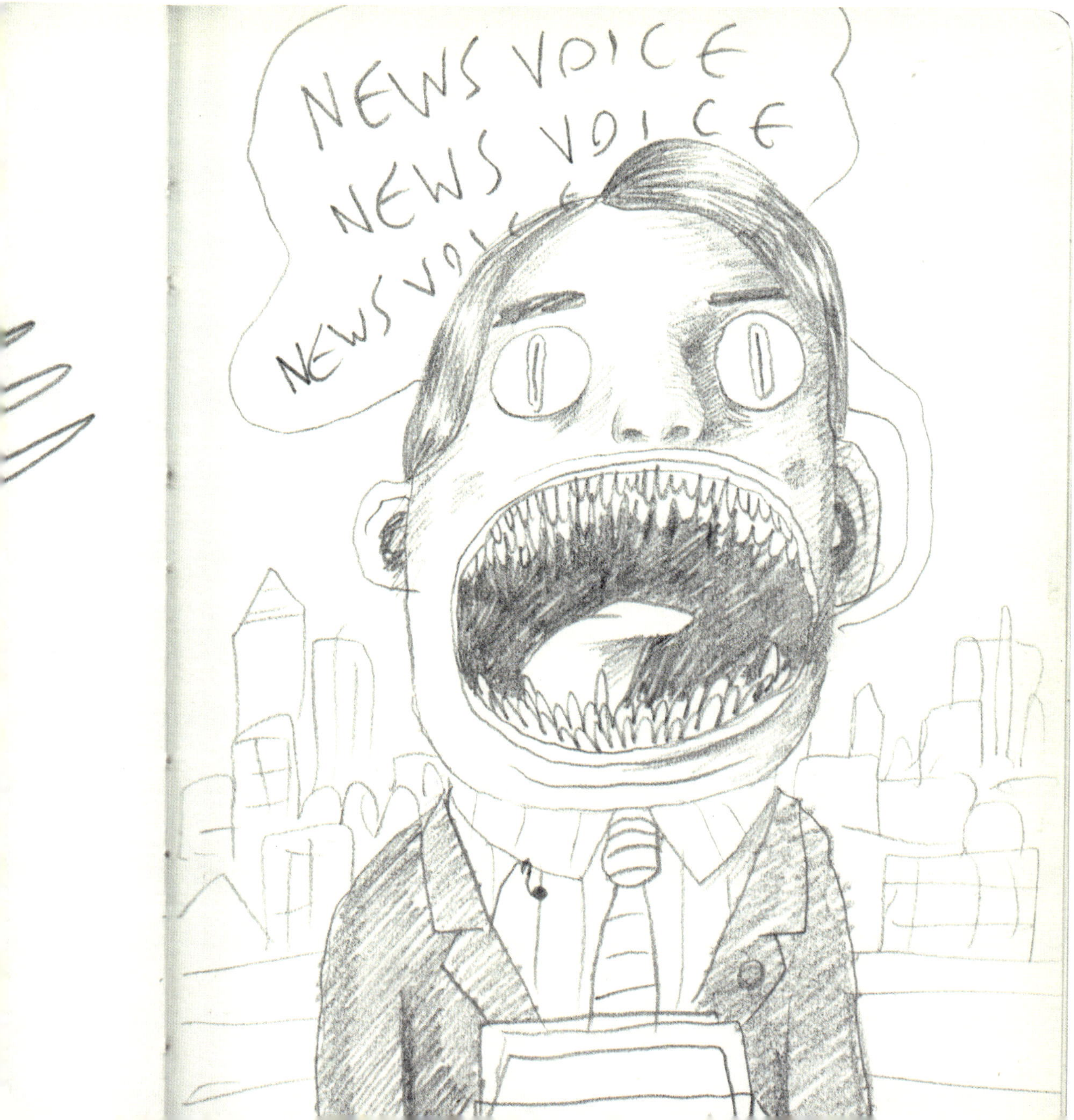

IN AN AIRPORT BATHROOM
WASHING ENGLAND OFF MY HANDS

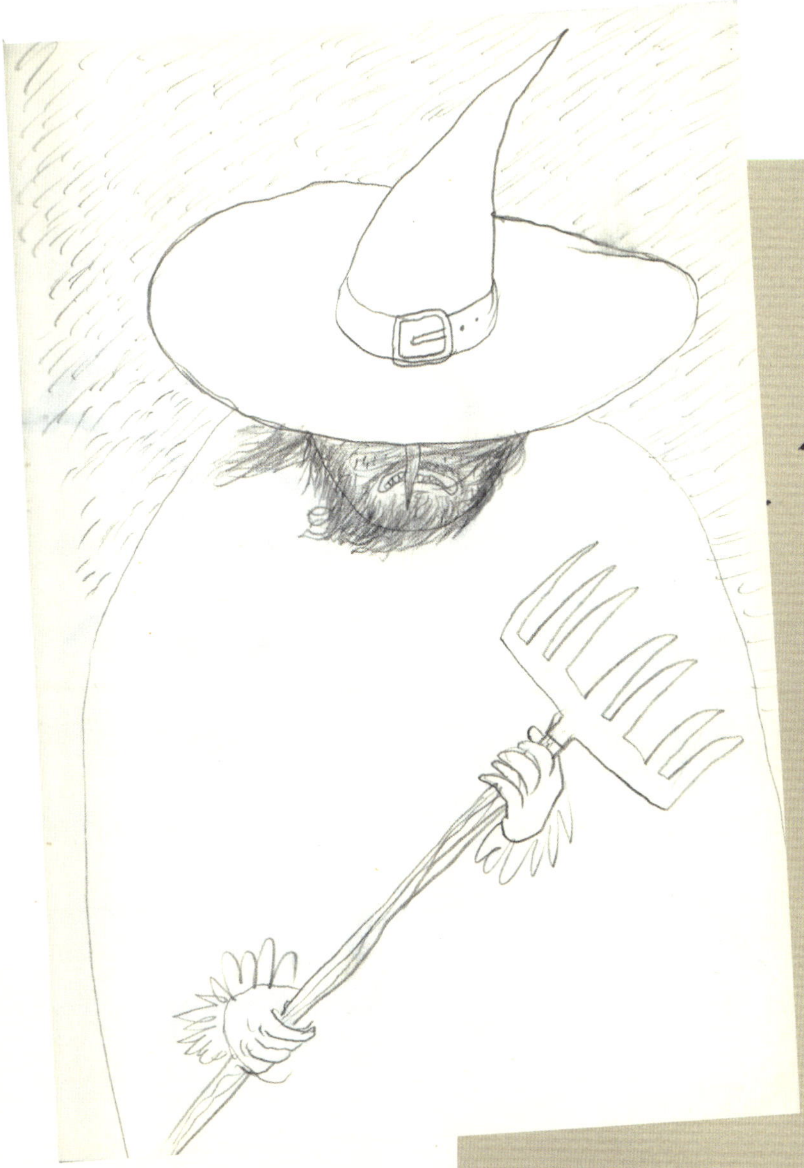

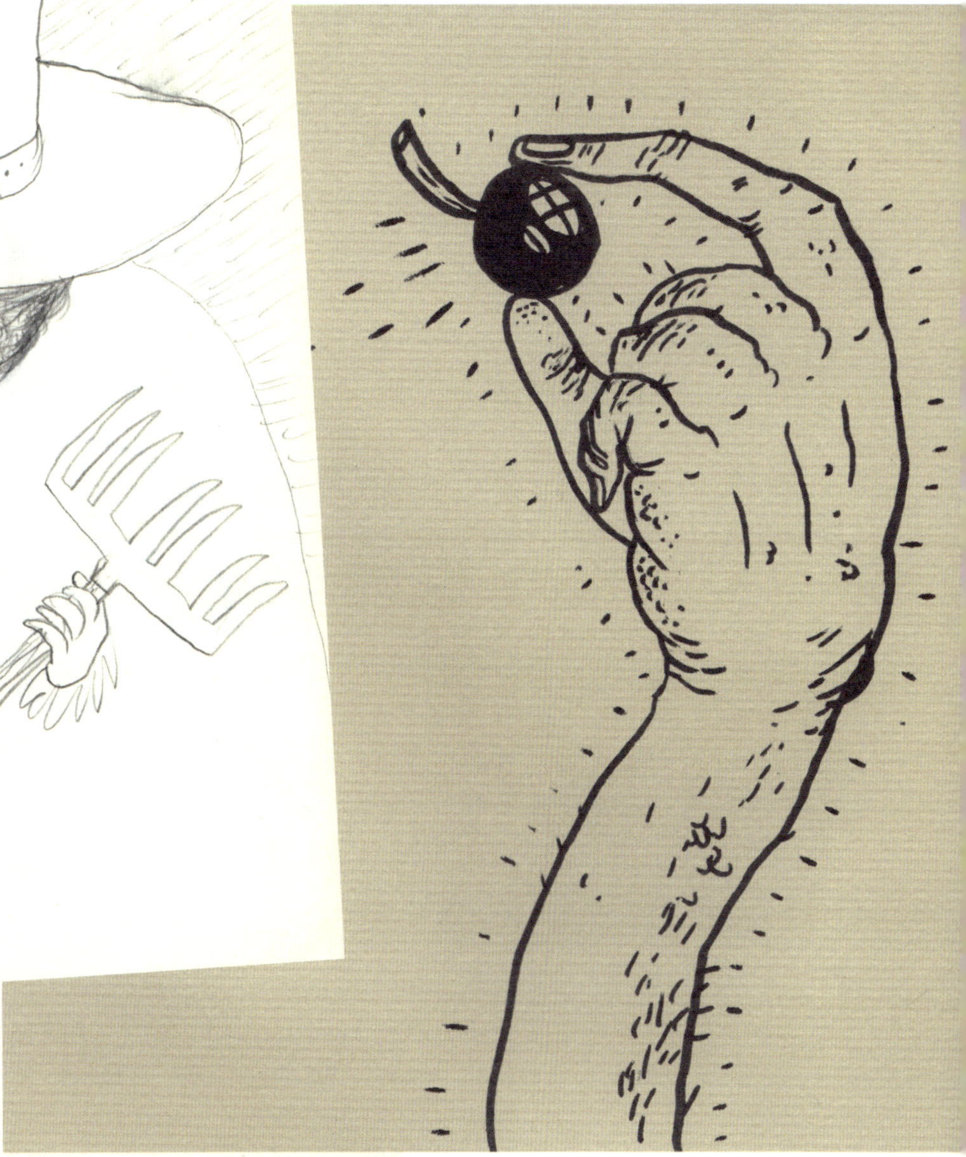

ON TRAIN
TO PARIS.

· FEB 22 ·

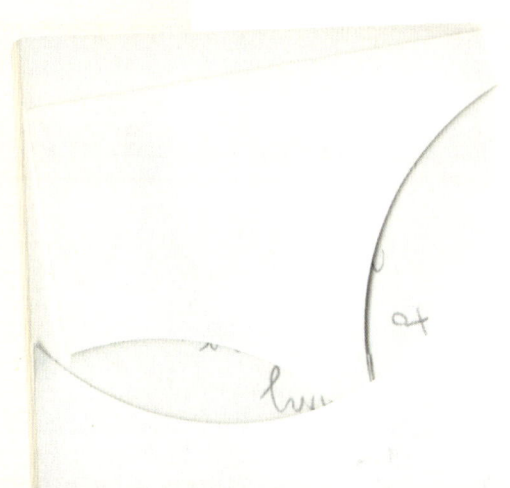

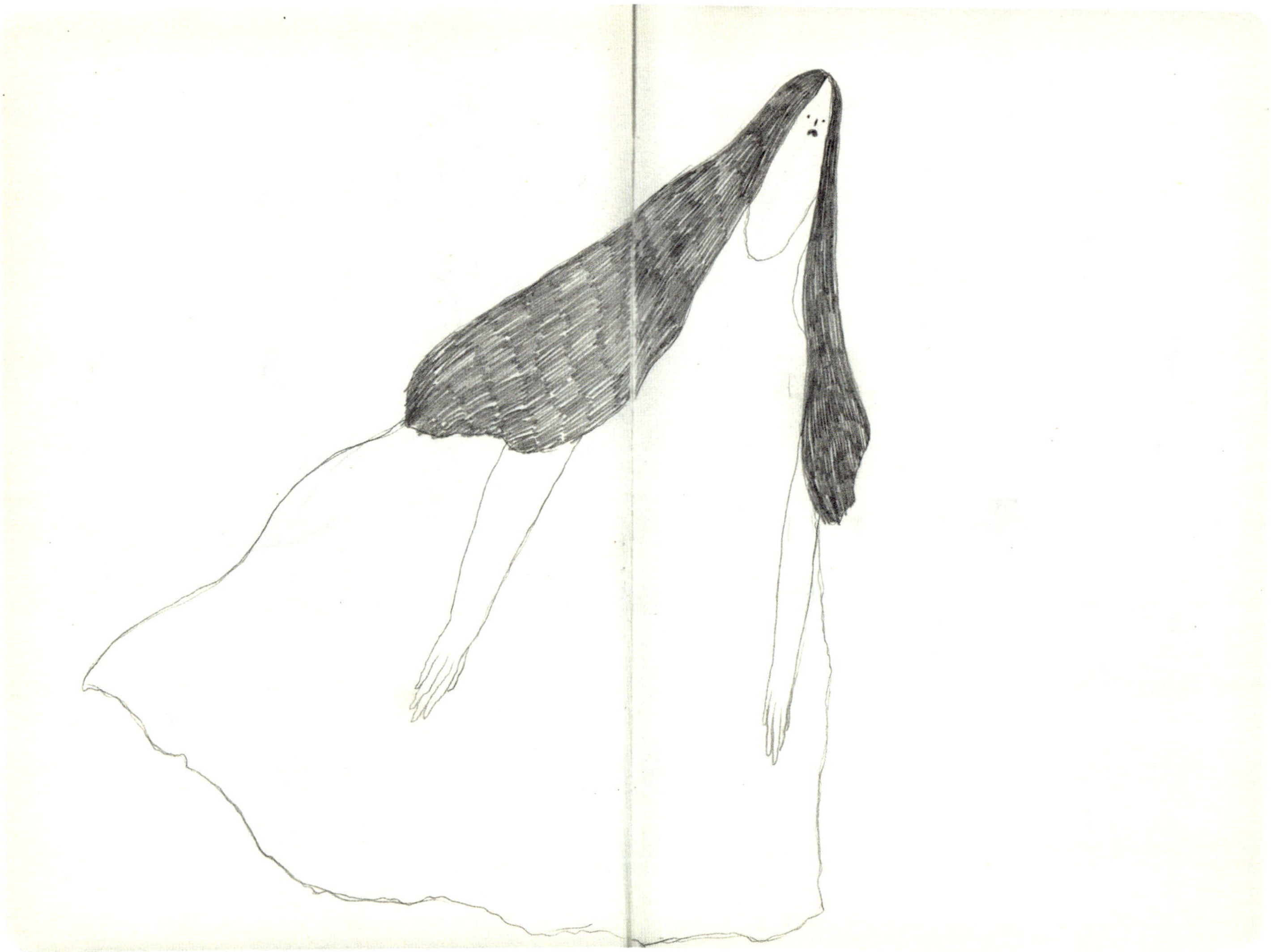

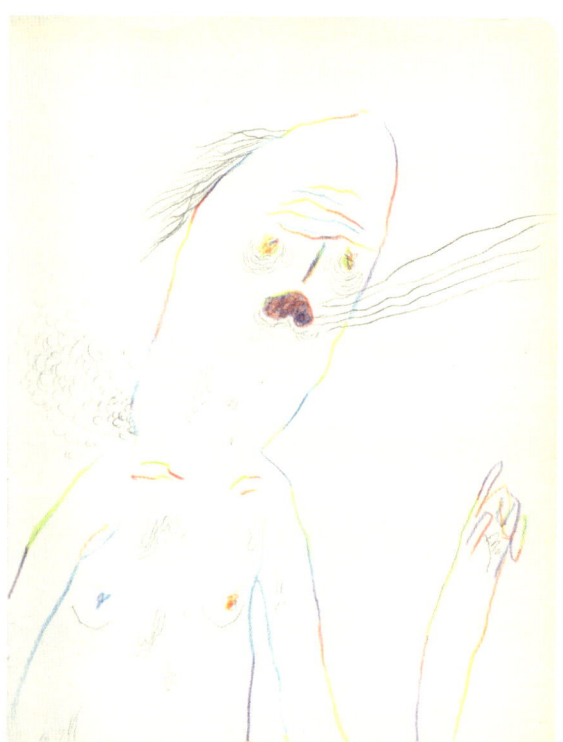

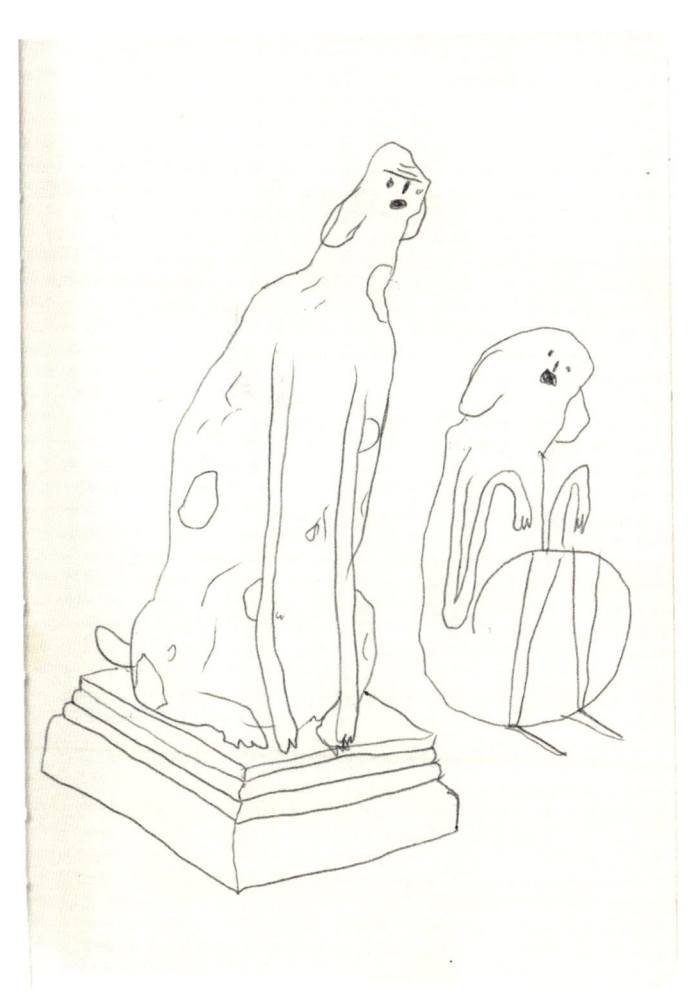
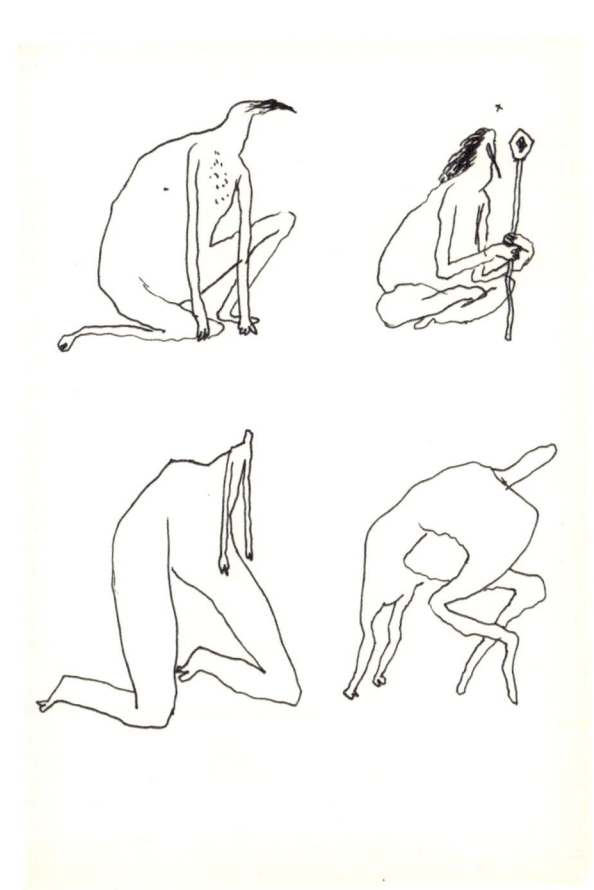
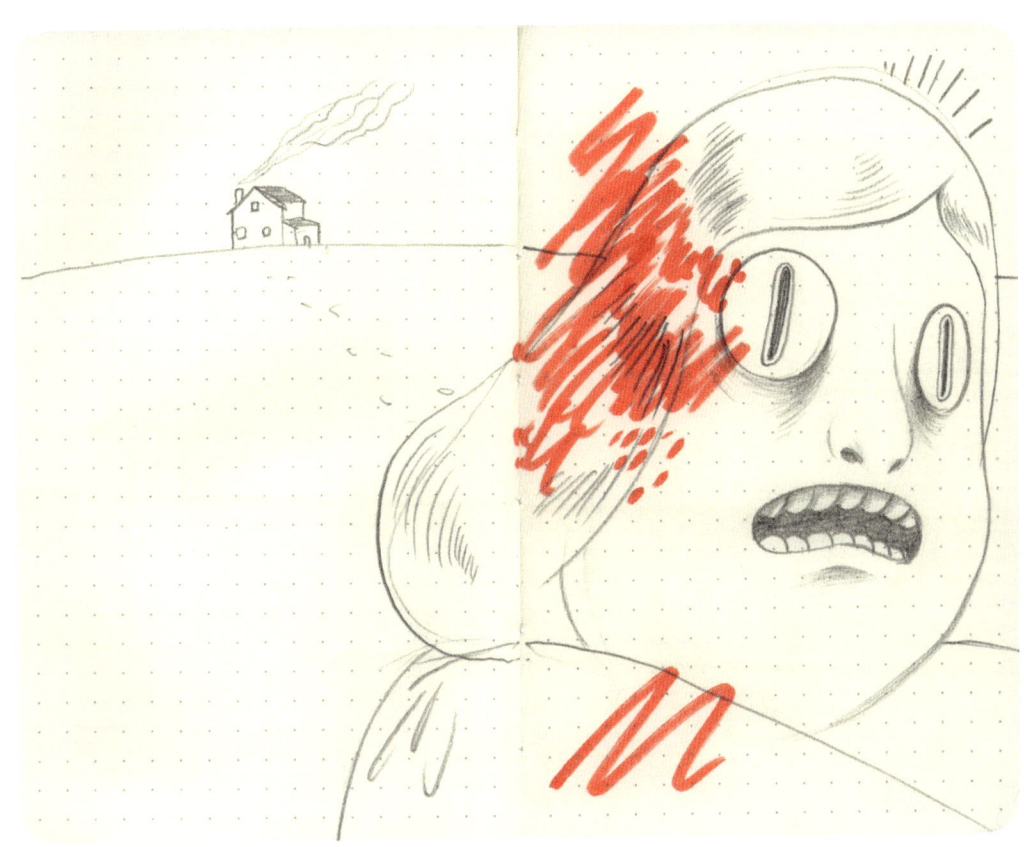

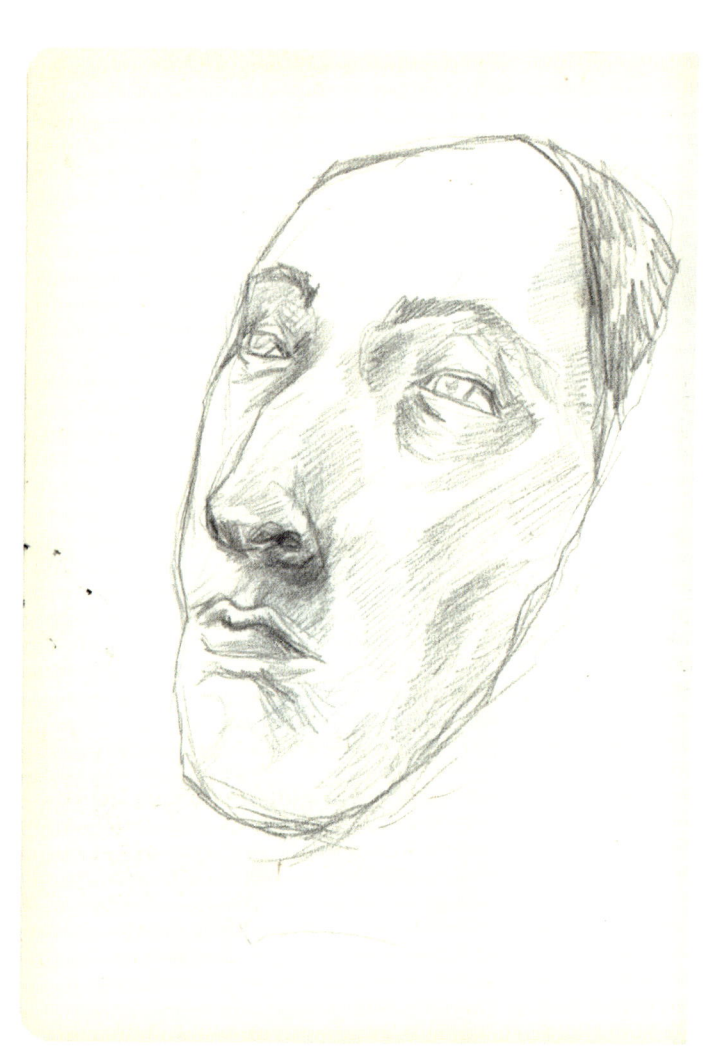
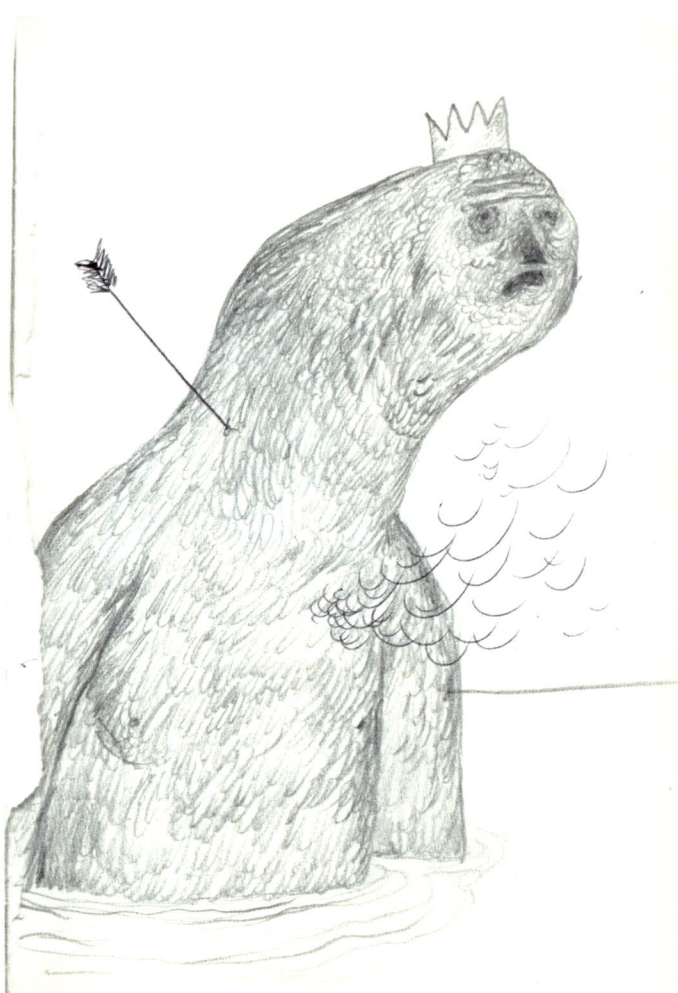

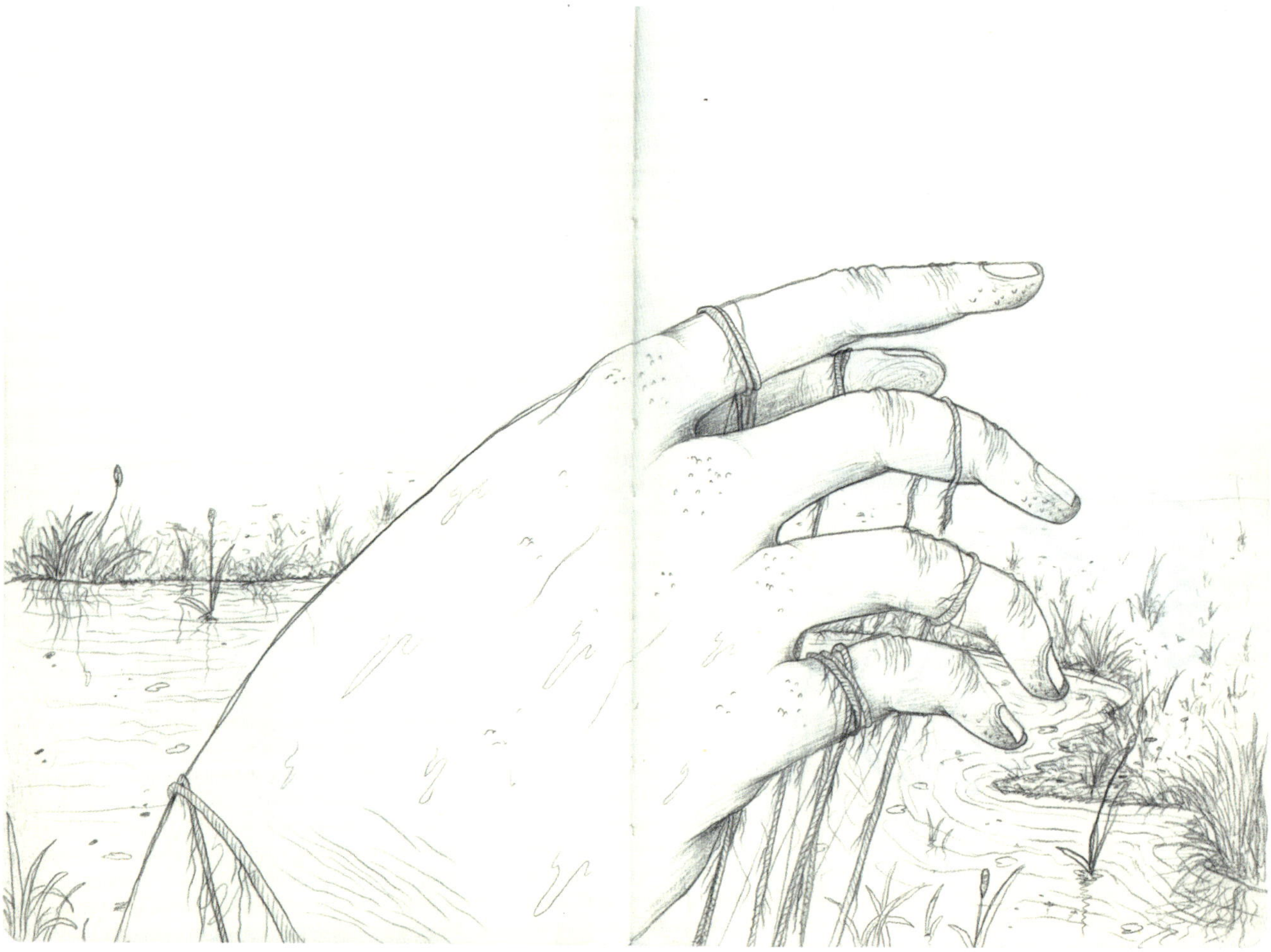

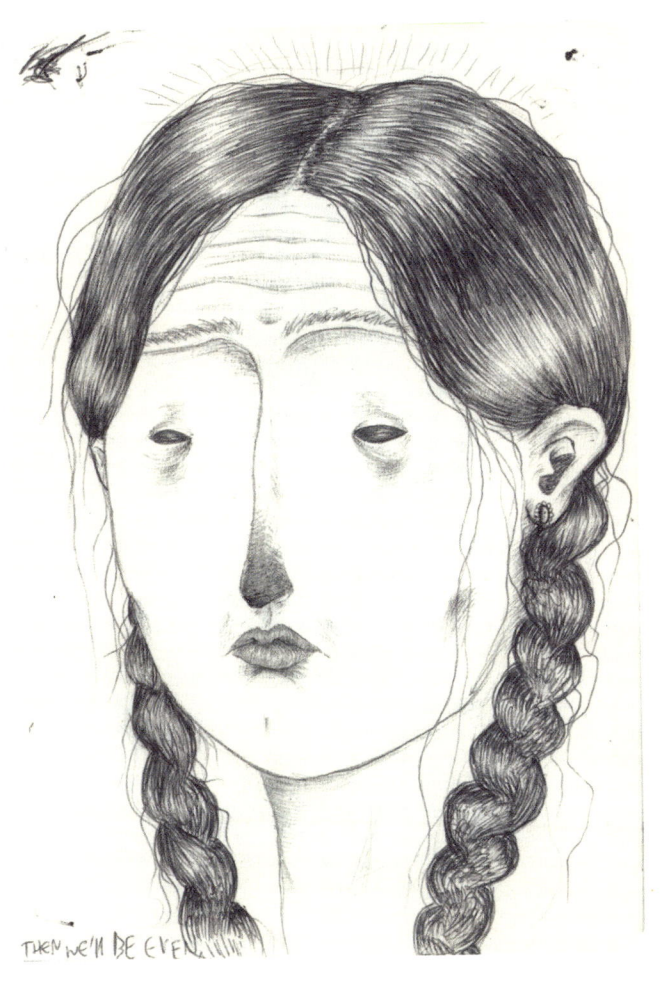
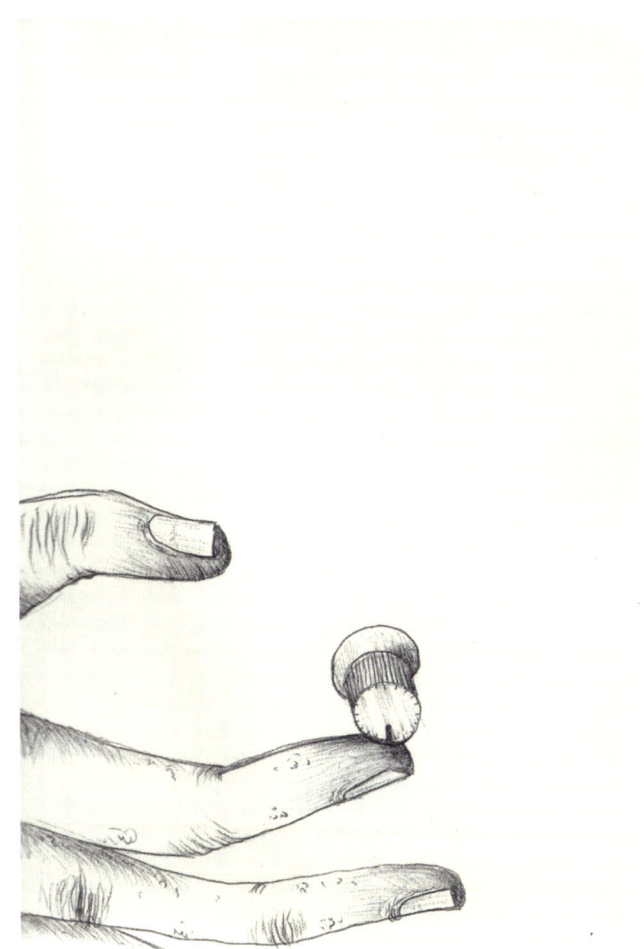
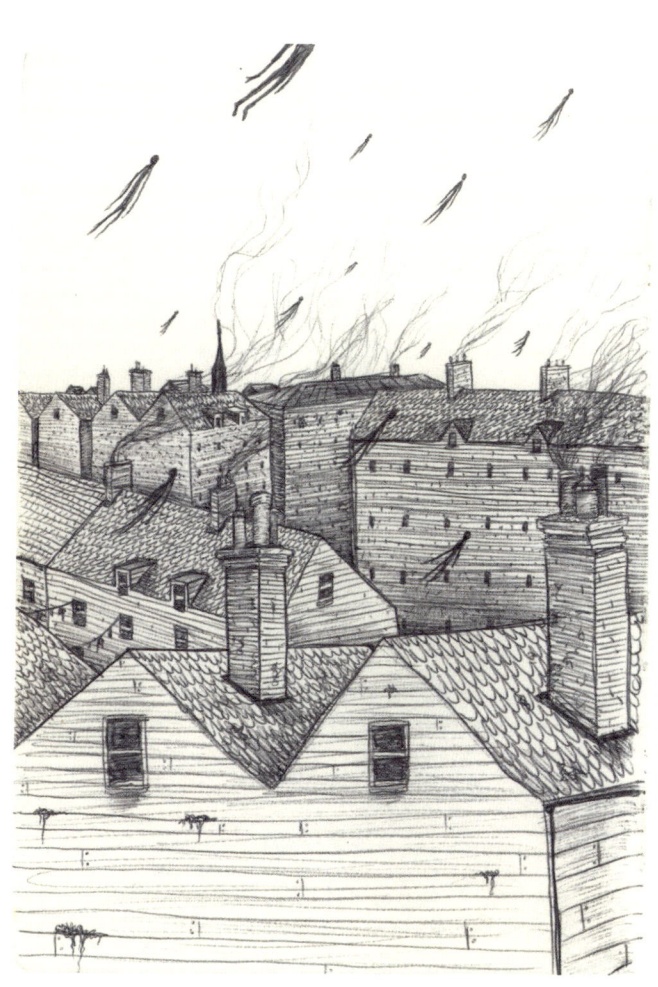
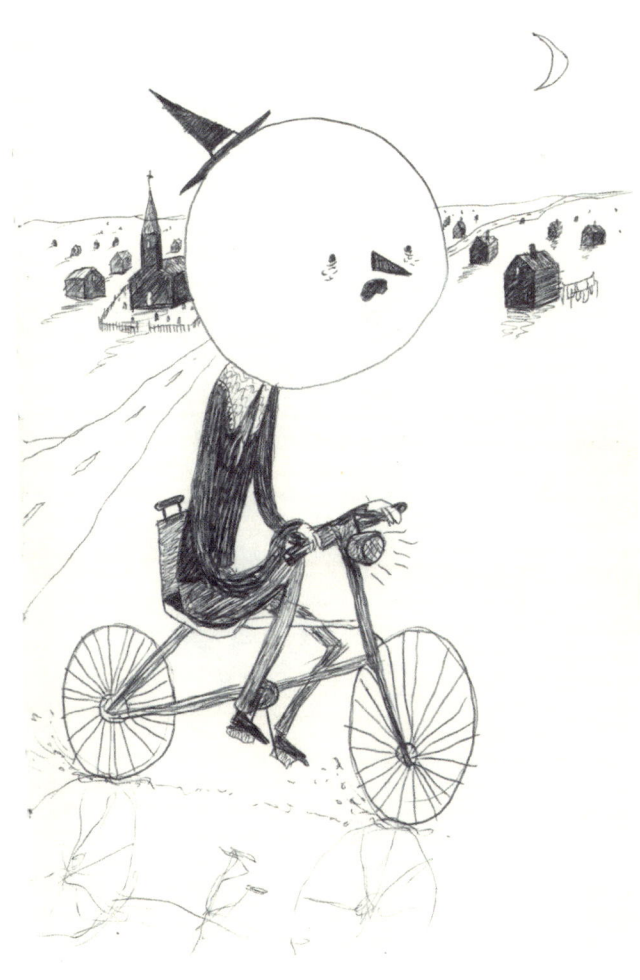

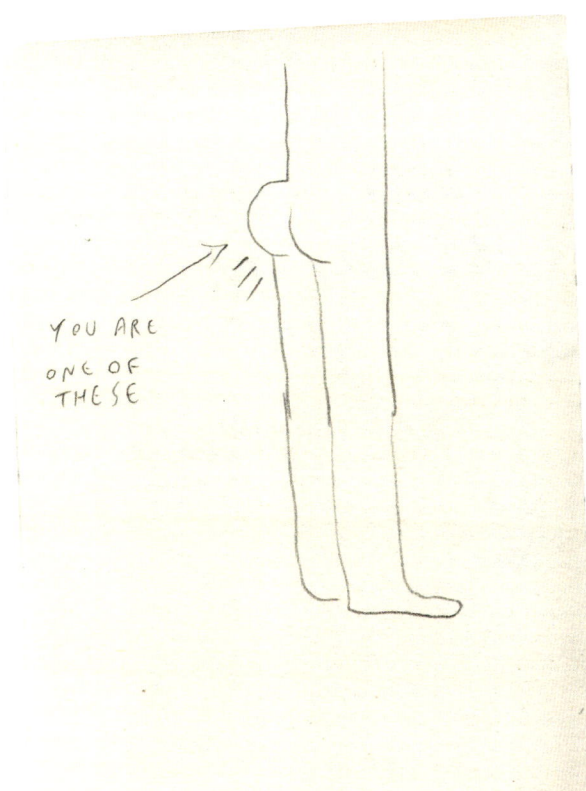

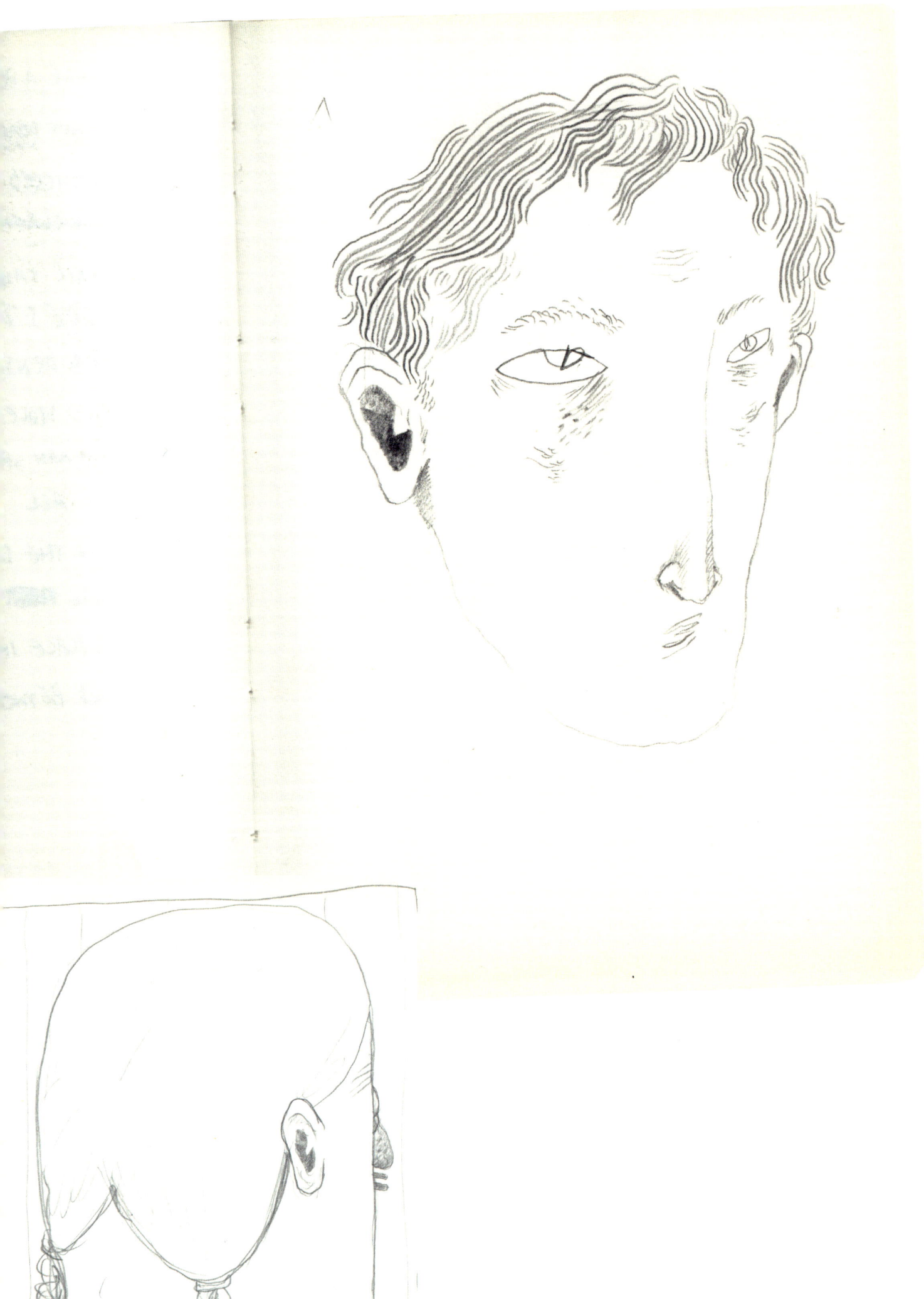

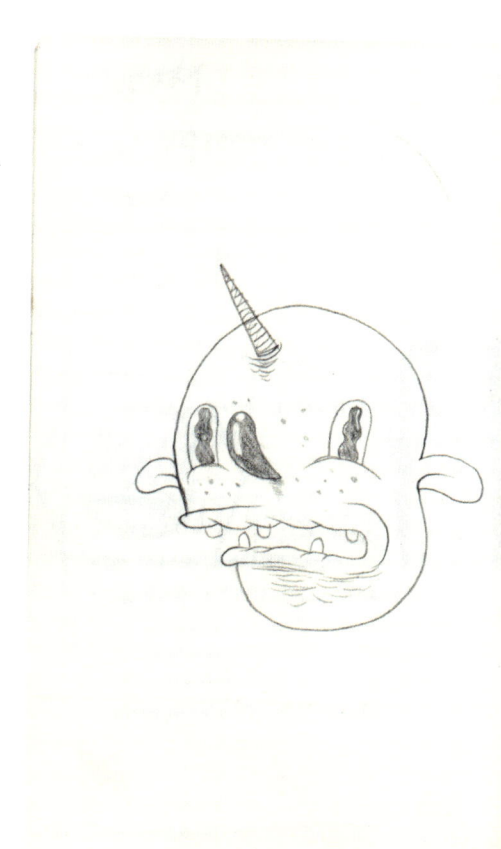
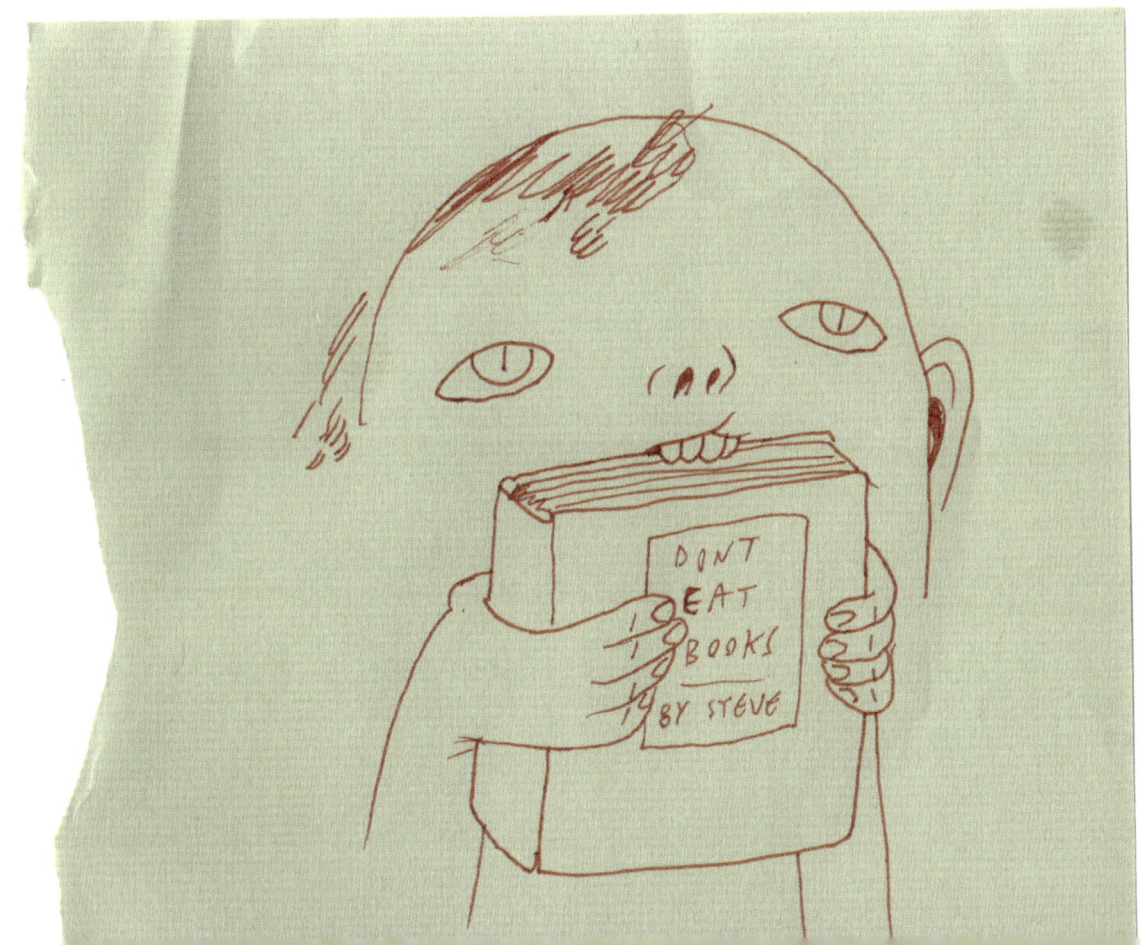

IN THE COUNTRY NOW
SITTING BY FIRE.
LOUISES HOUSE

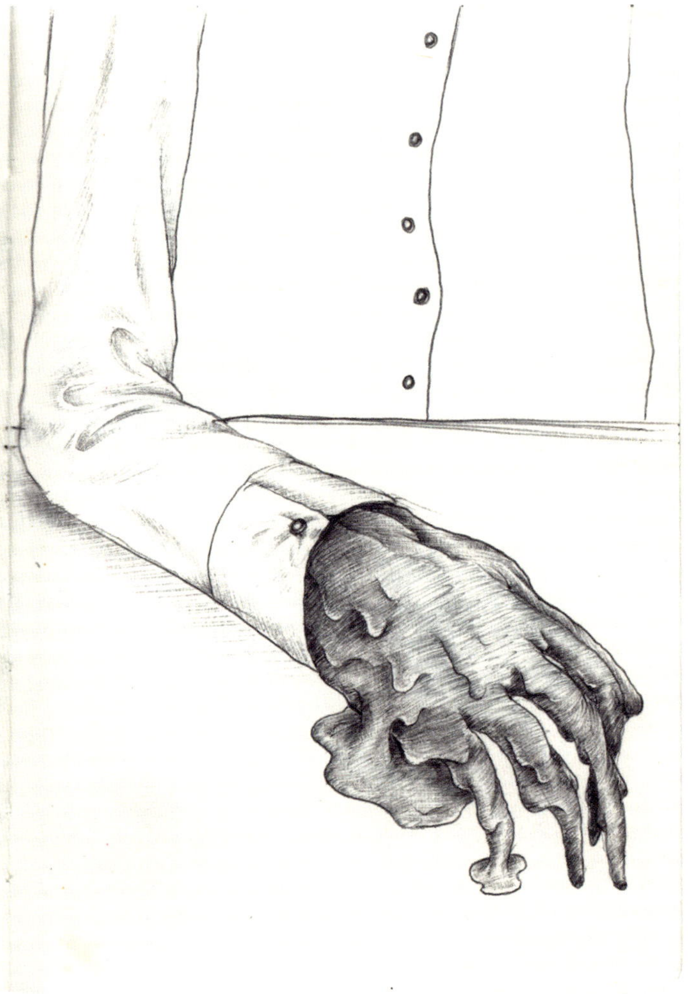

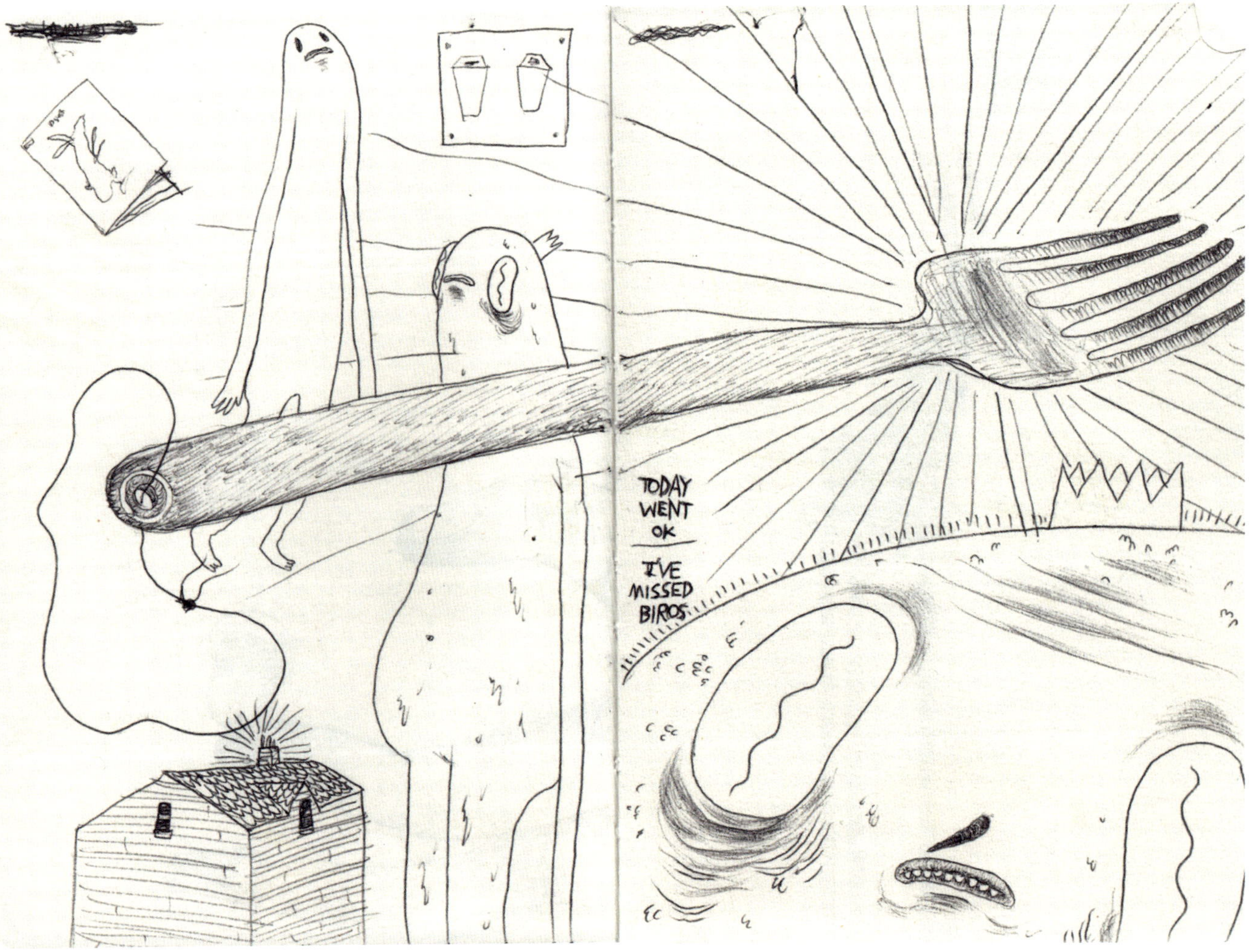

TODAY WENT OK

I'VE MISSED BIROS.

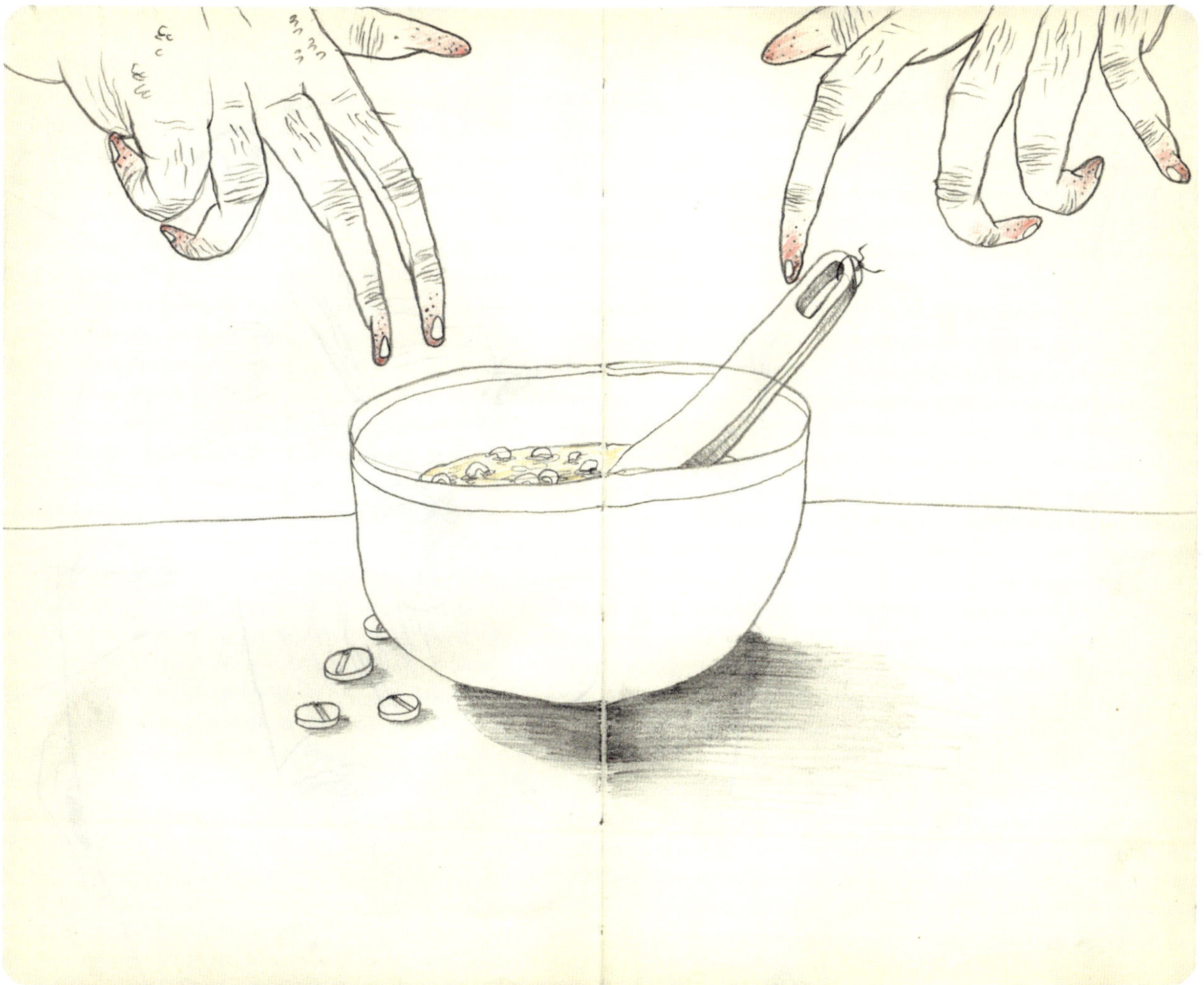

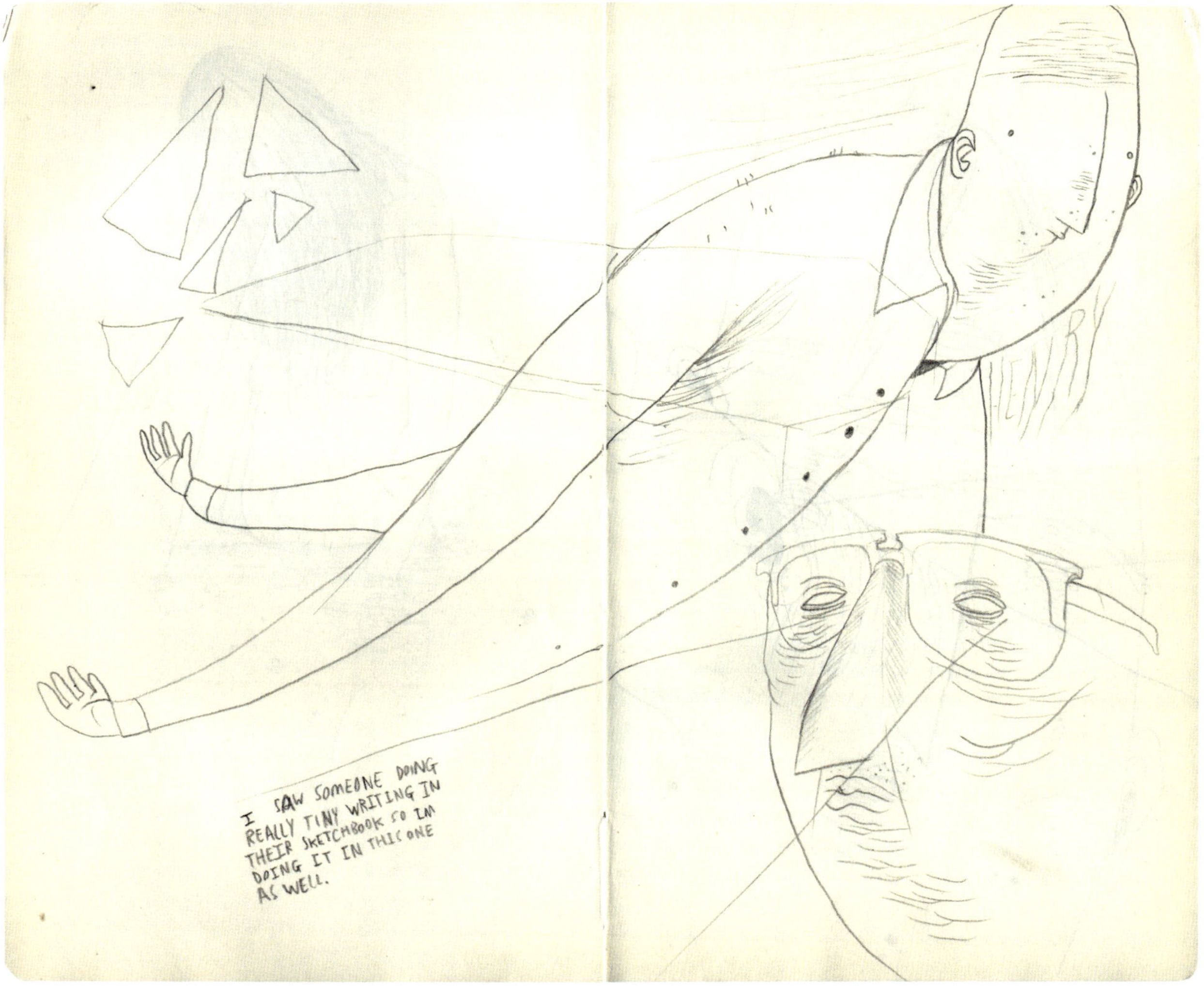

I SAW SOMEONE DOING REALLY TINY WRITING IN THEIR SKETCHBOOK SO I'M DOING IT IN THIS ONE AS WELL.

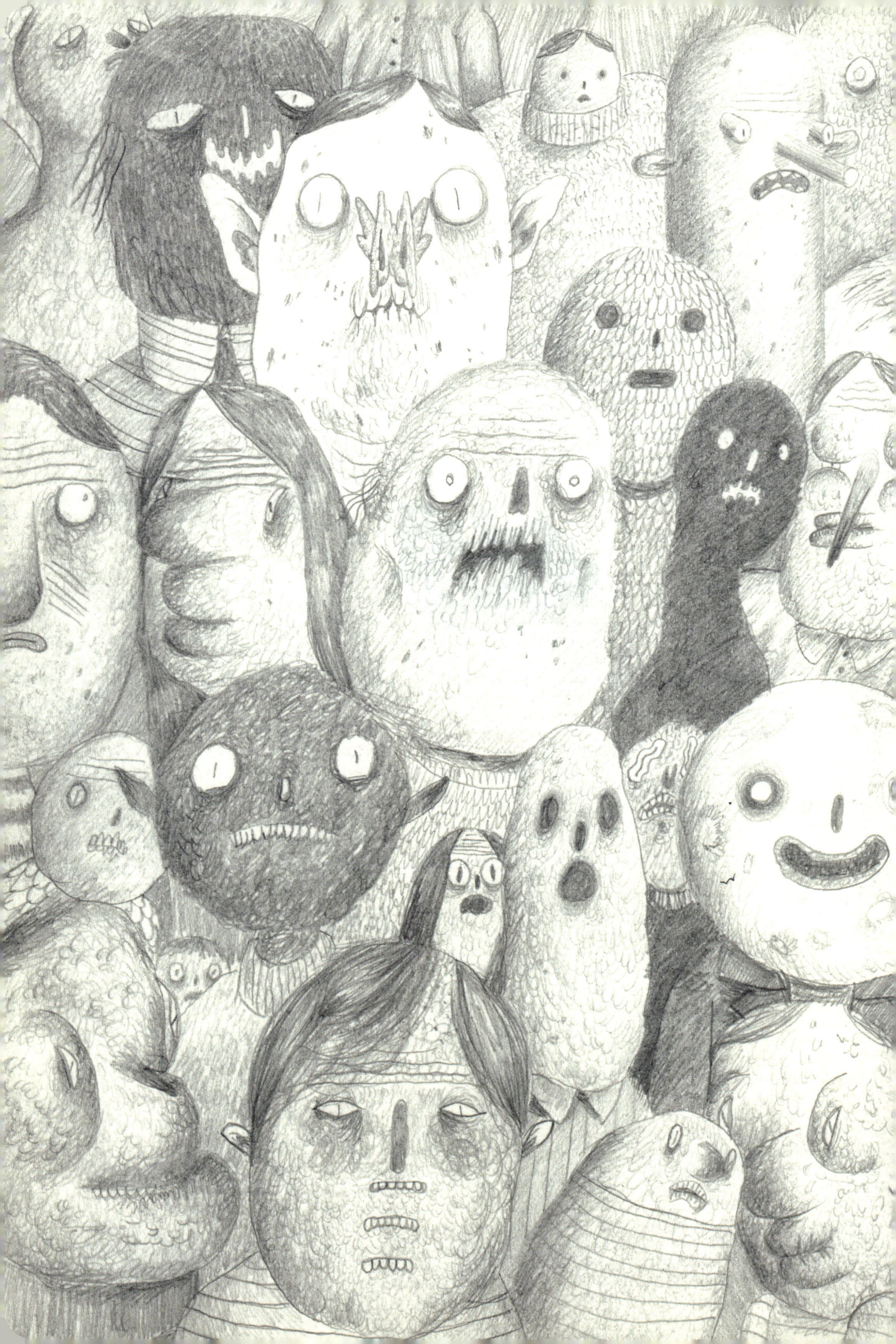

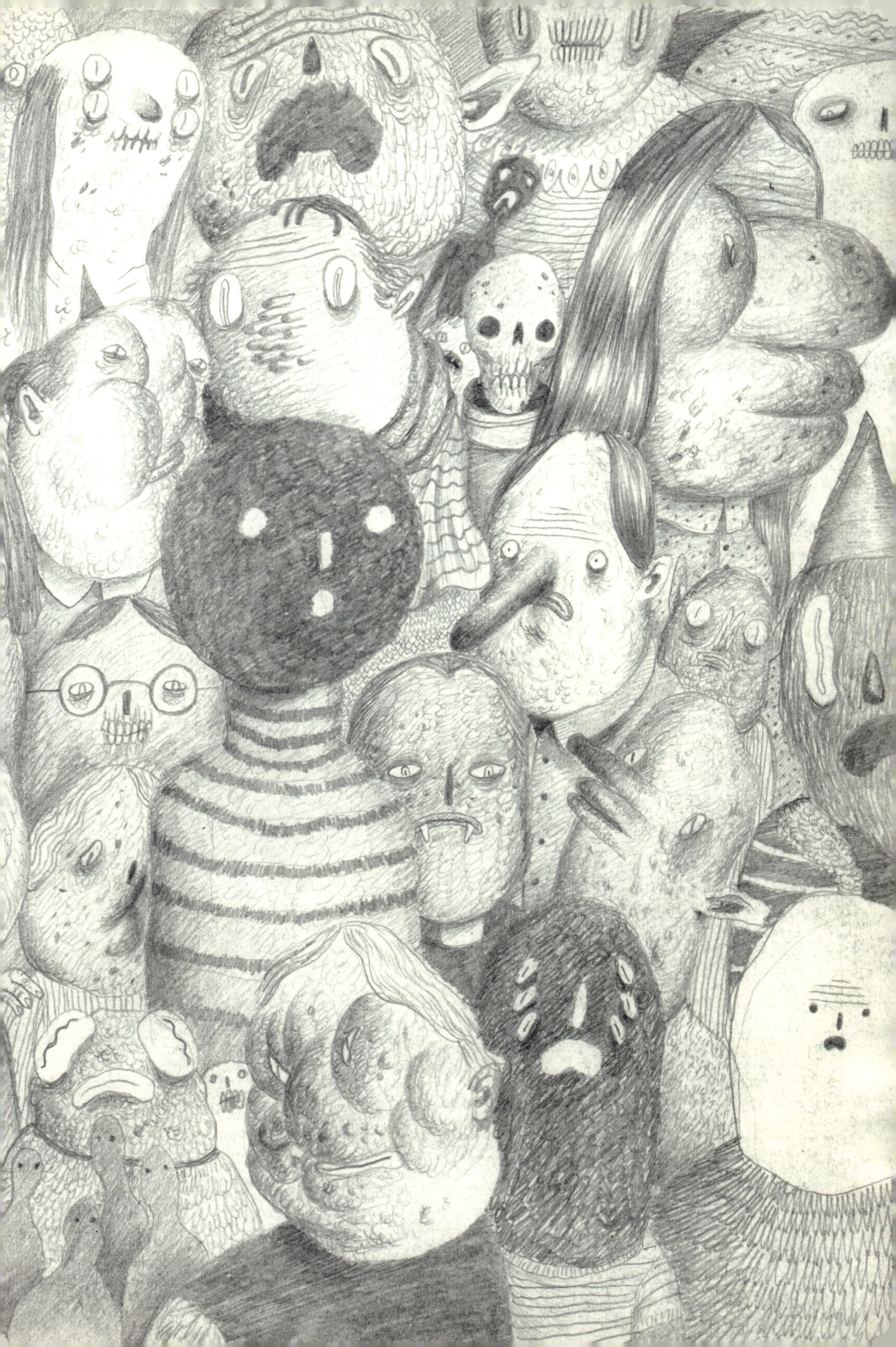

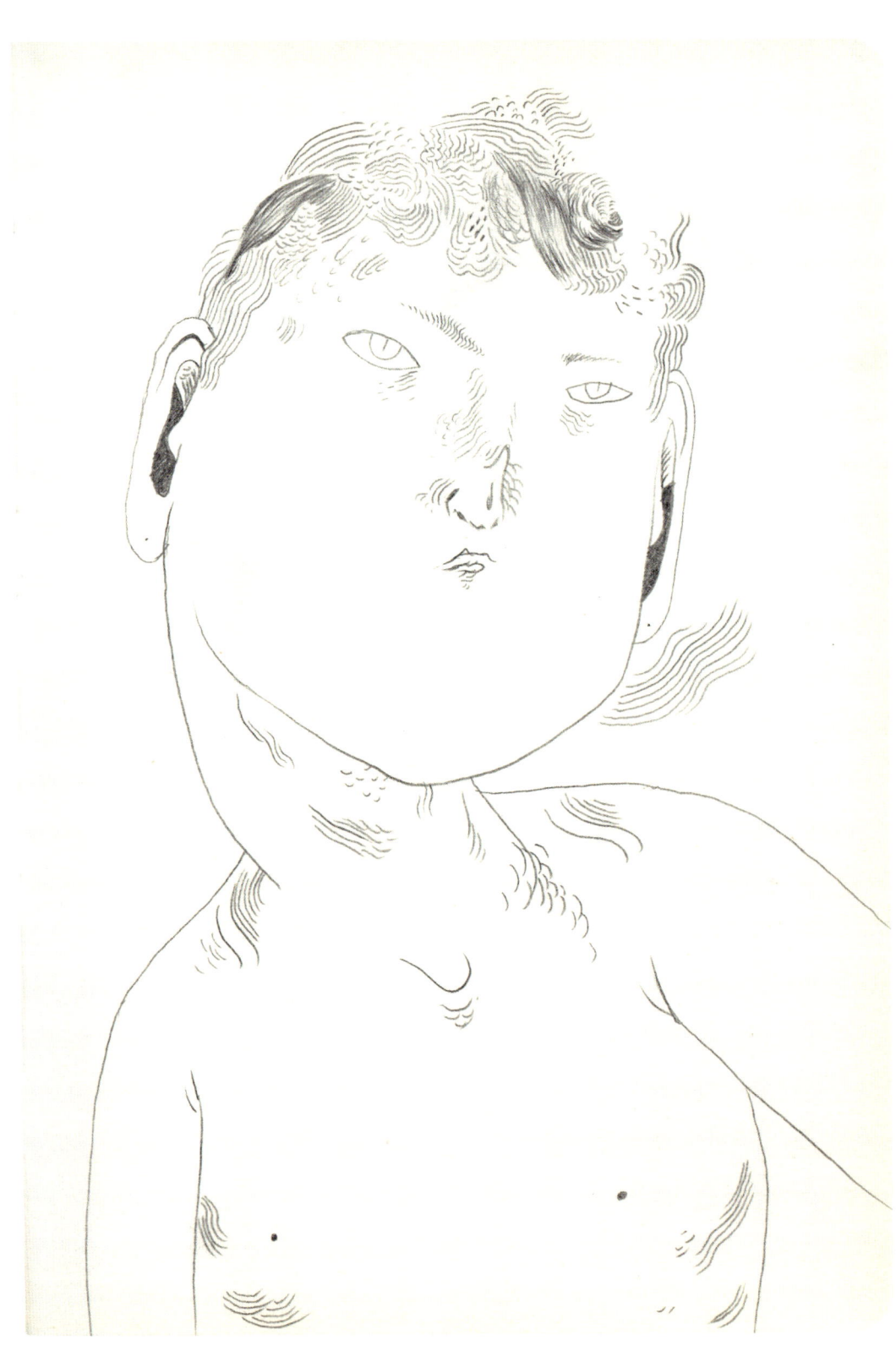

YOUNG MEN – SCENE LIST

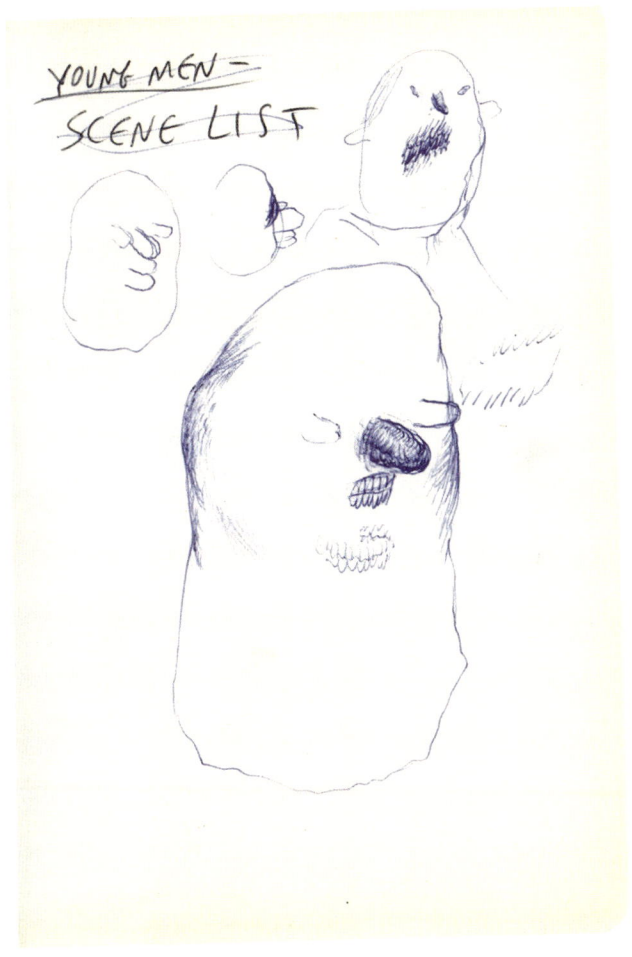

1. mic + valve
2. mic stand
3. interface
4. whiteboard + pen
5. <u>all</u> leads + cables
6. mac
7. acoustic
8. electric
9. capo
10. food
11. thimbles
12. super 8 mic
13. fags

<u>Buy</u>
- HARDDRIVE
- whiteboard
- strings

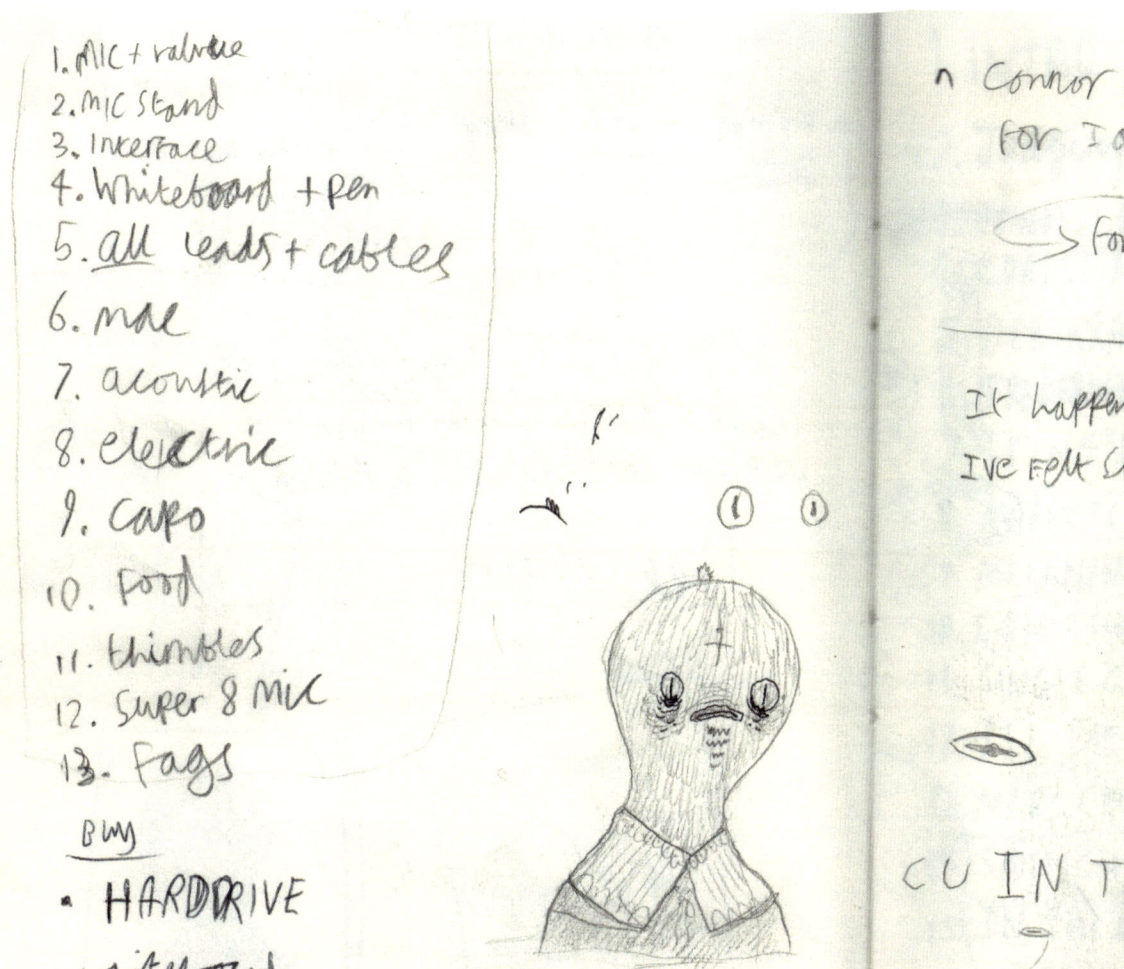

Connor was rig
for I am

→ for I tal

It happened
I've felt sick ev

CU IN THE M

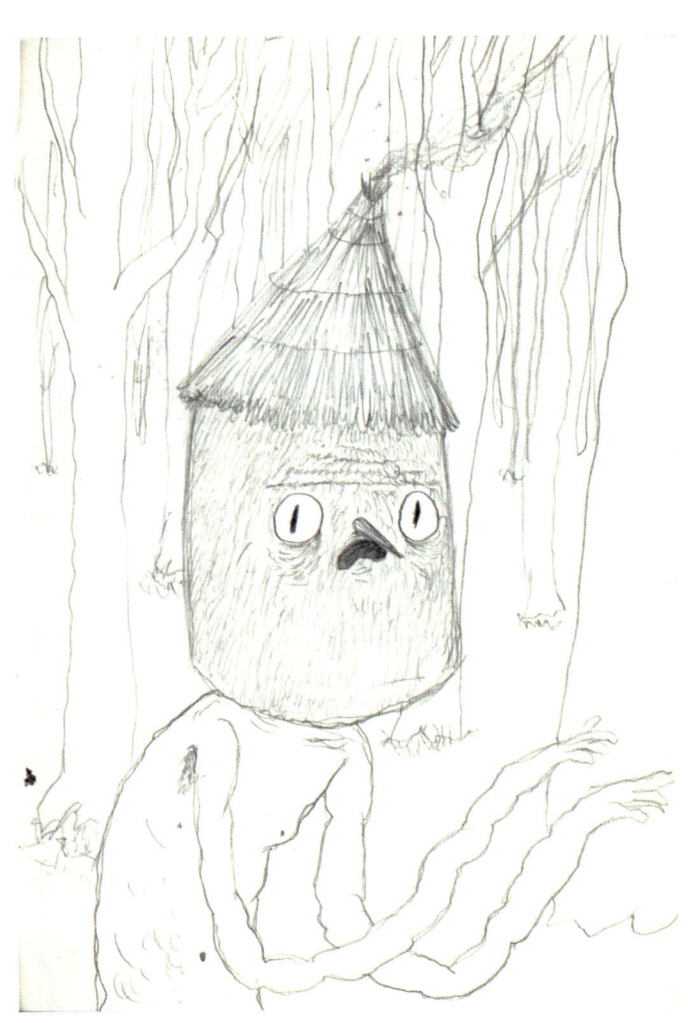

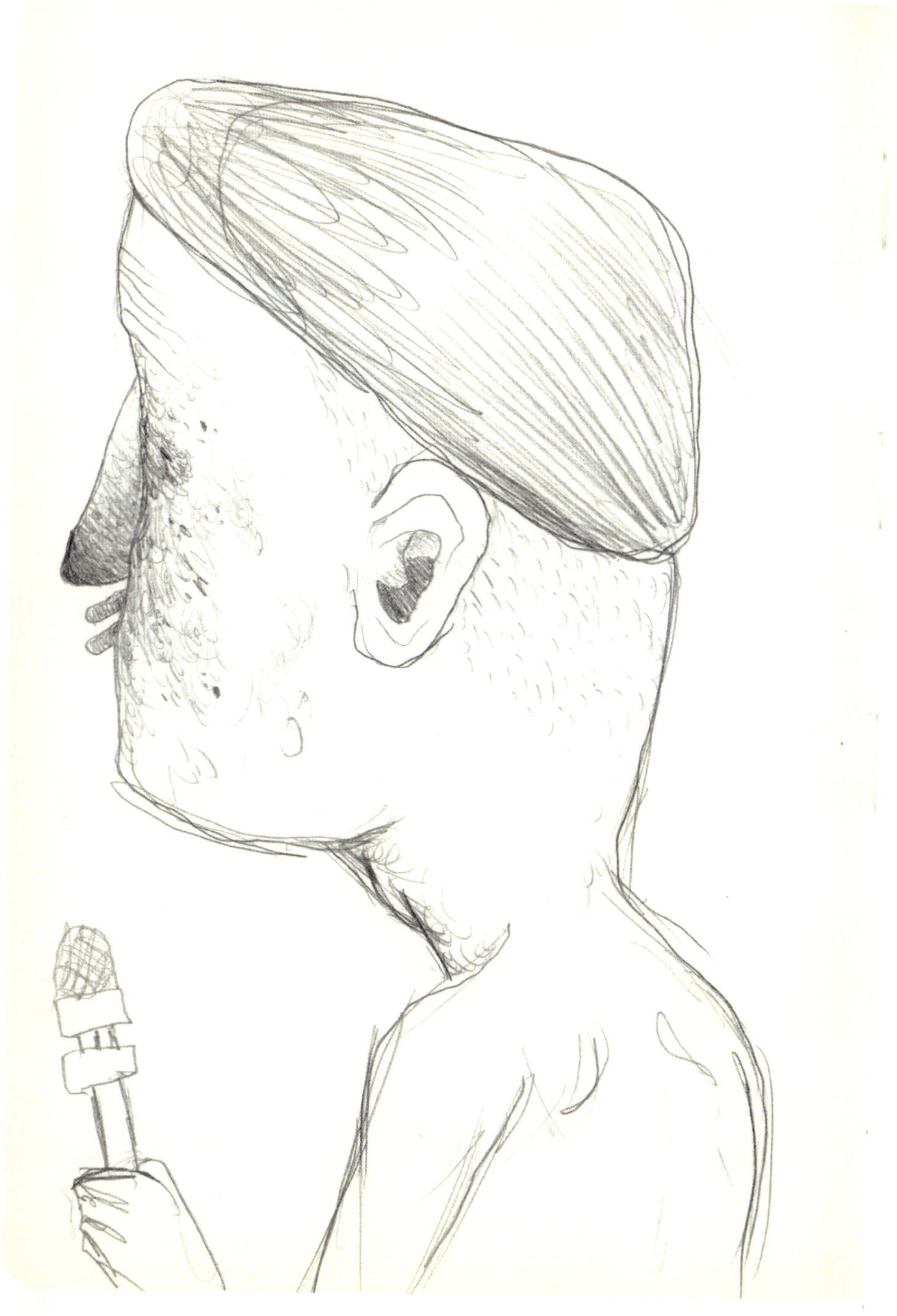

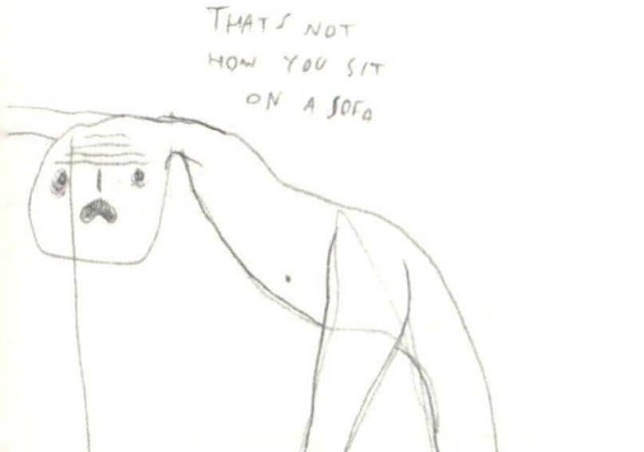

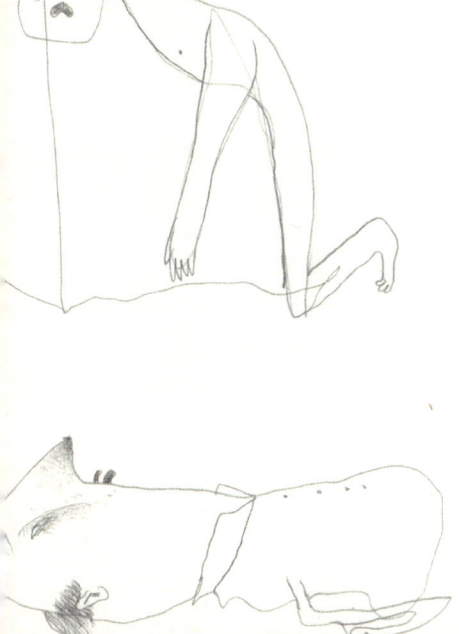

THATS NOT
HOW YOU SIT
ON A SOFA

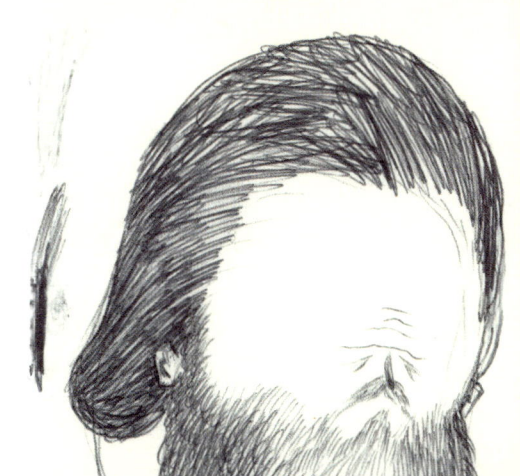

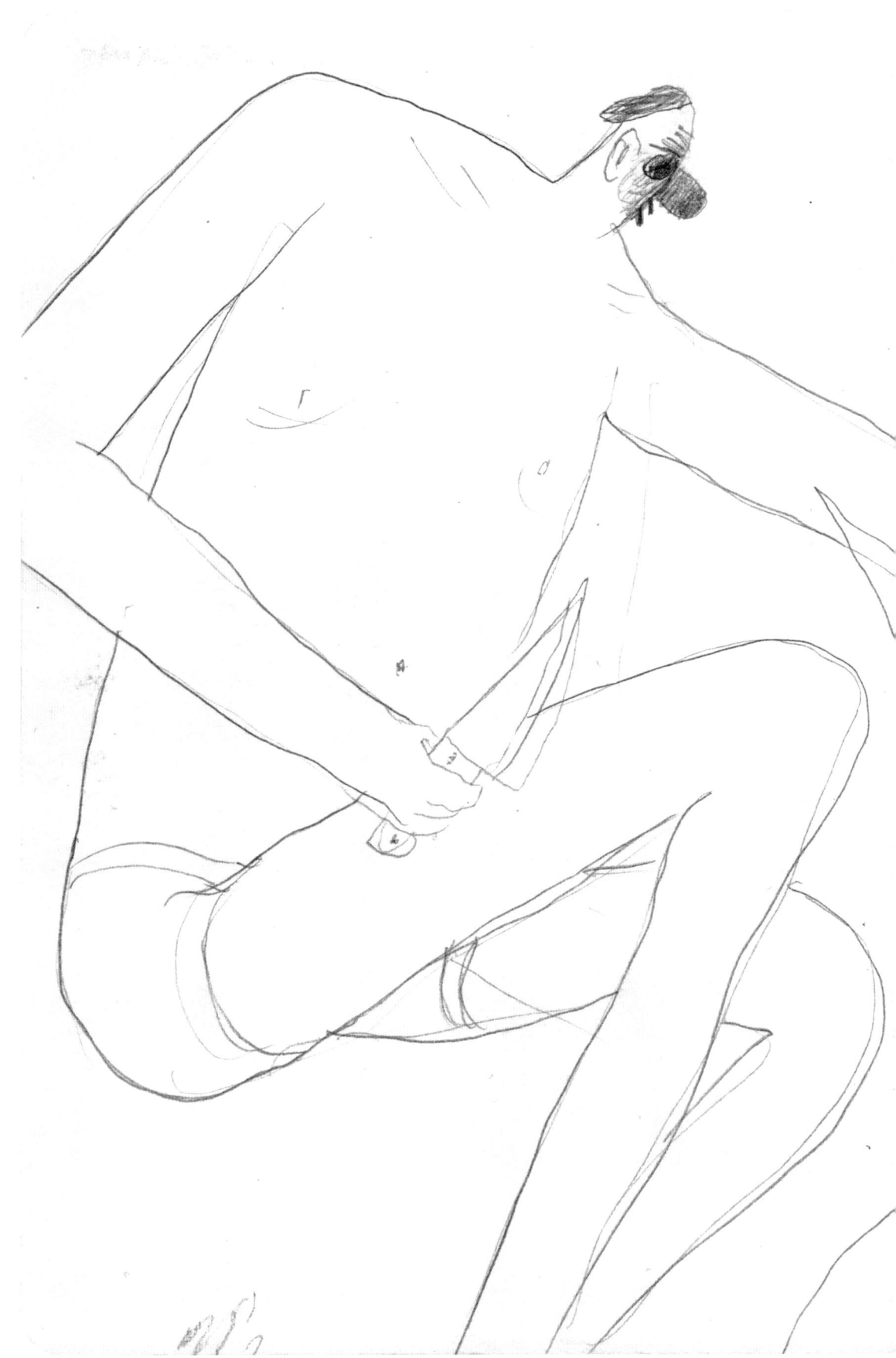

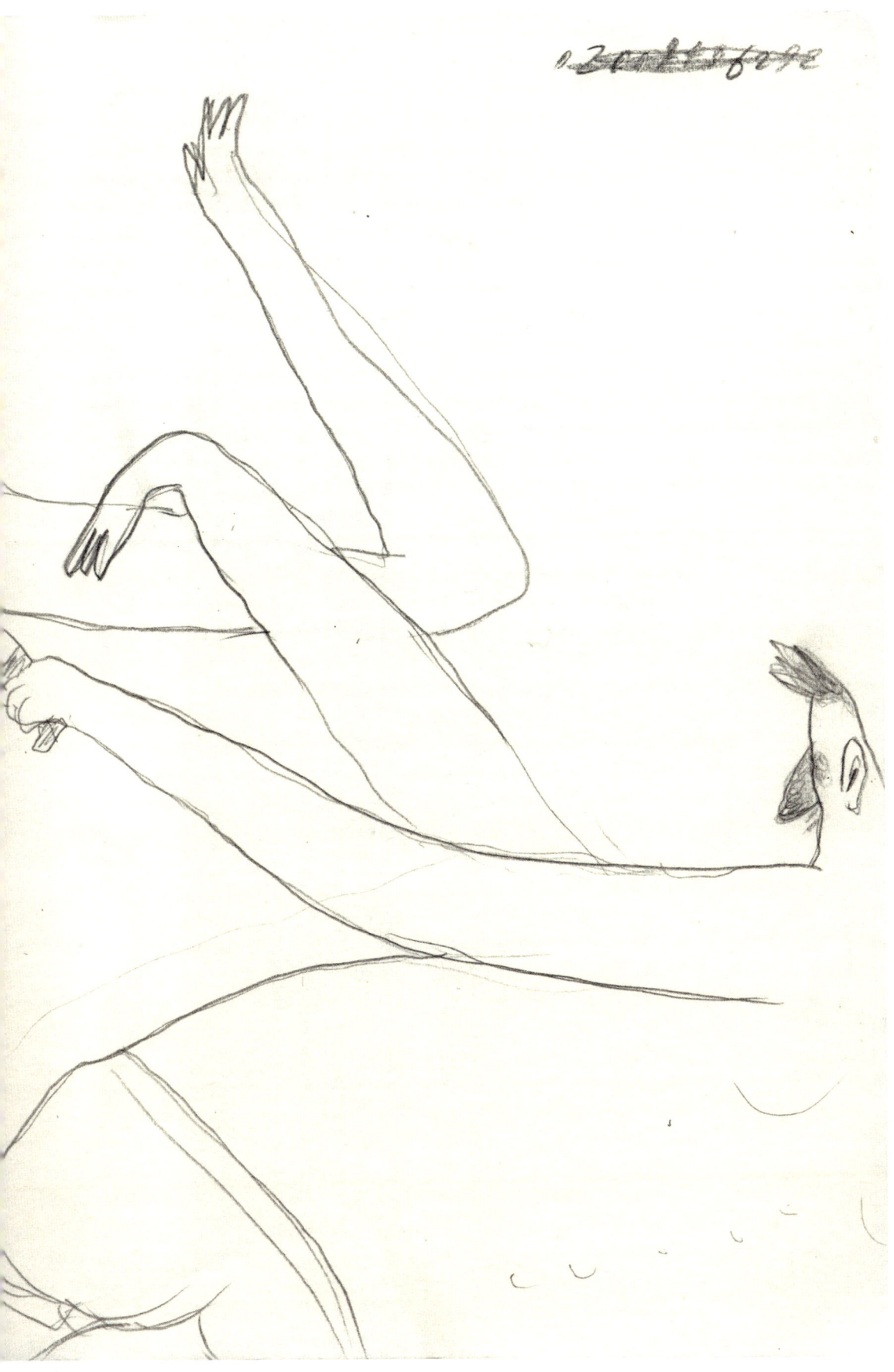

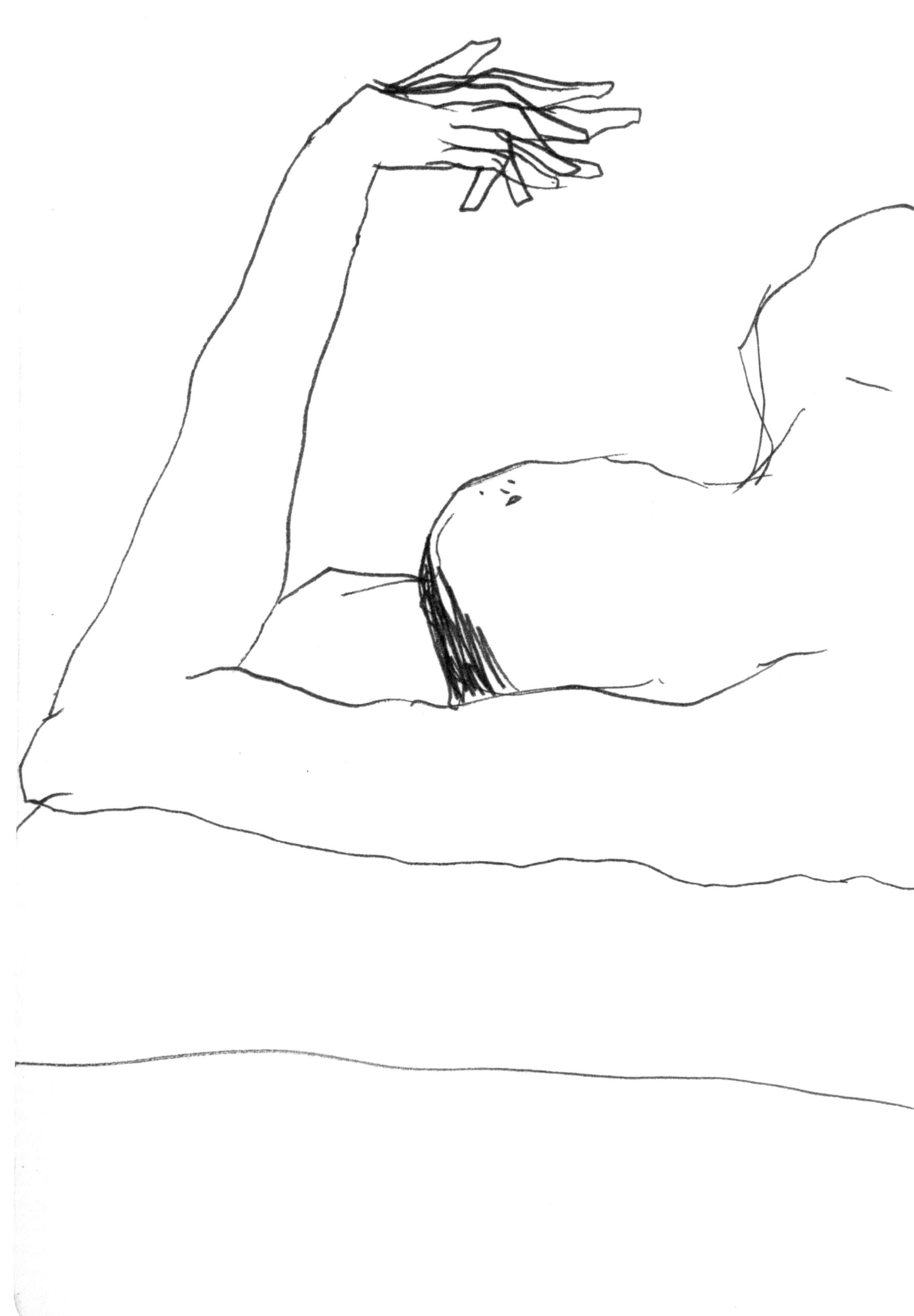

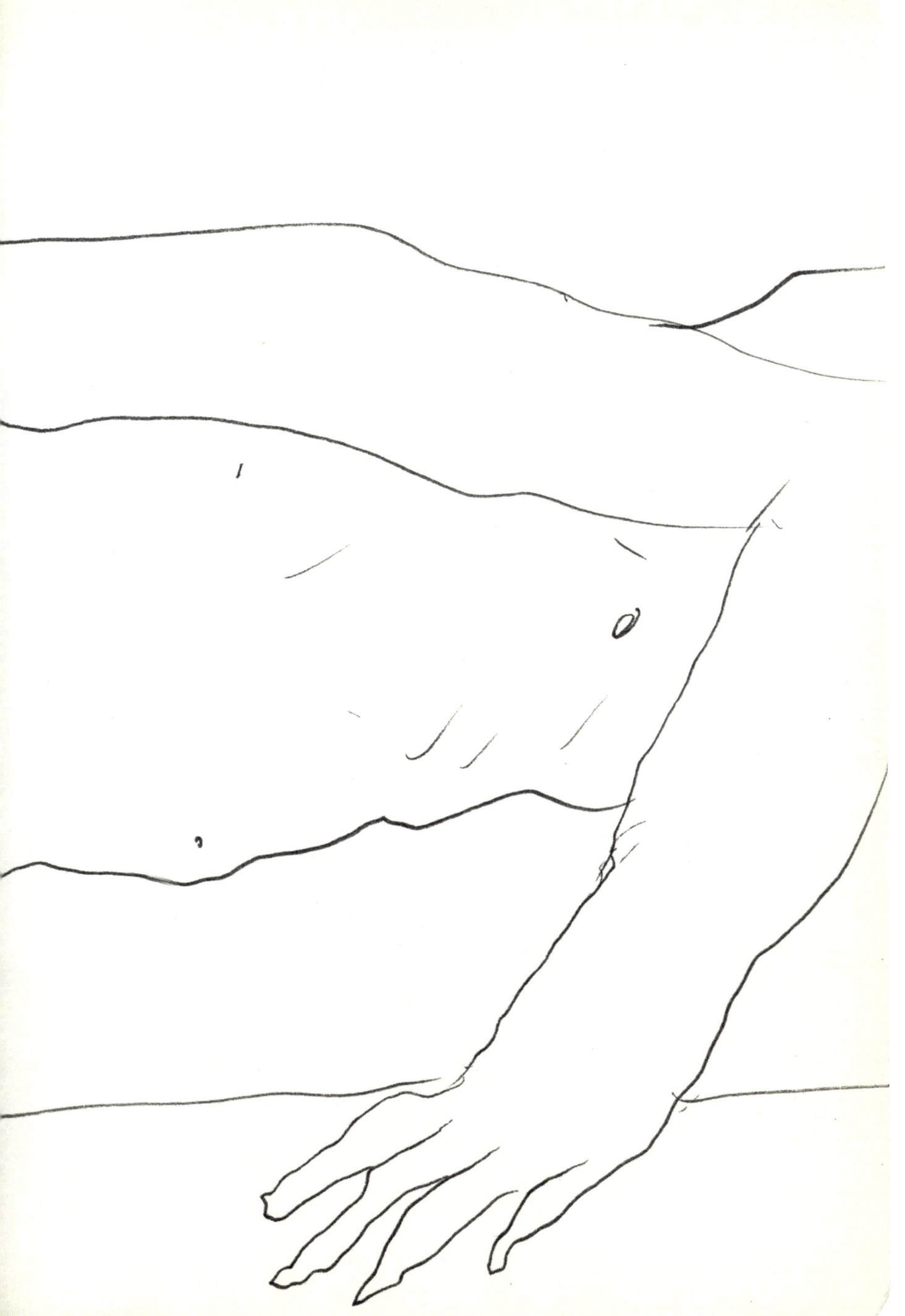

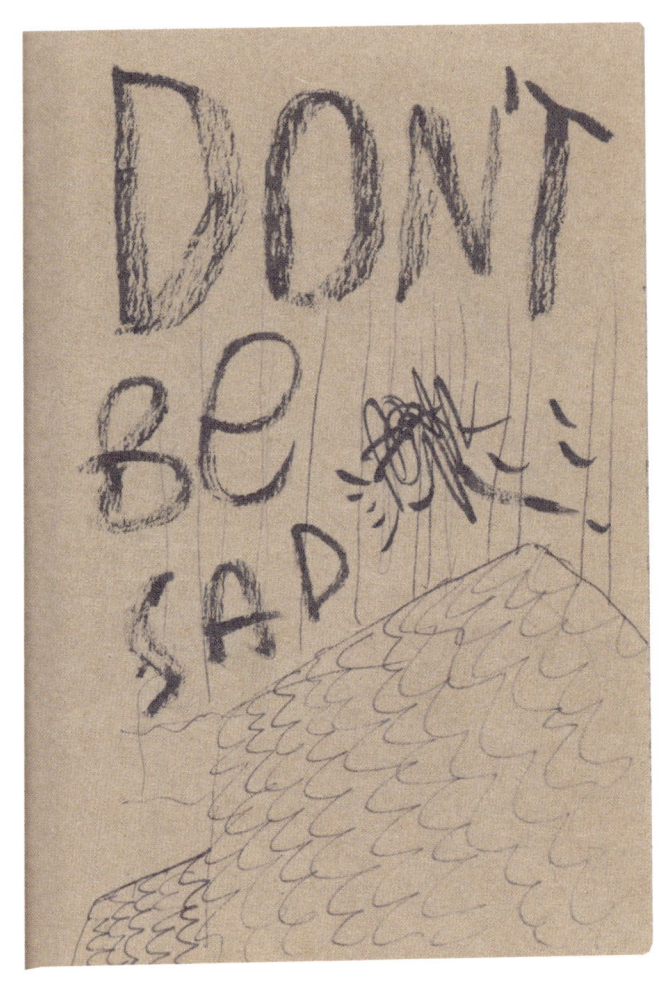

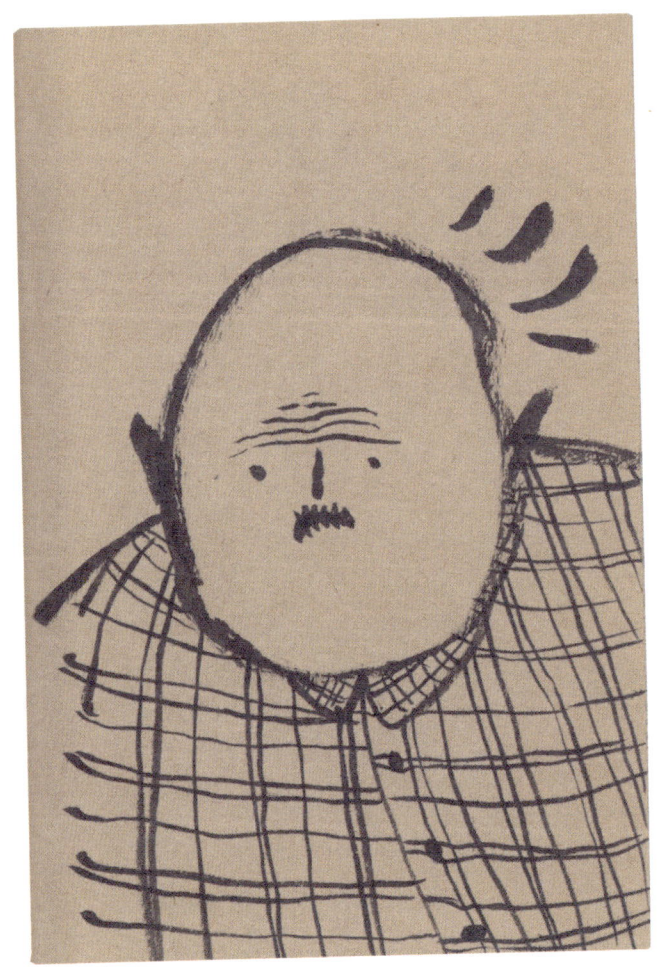

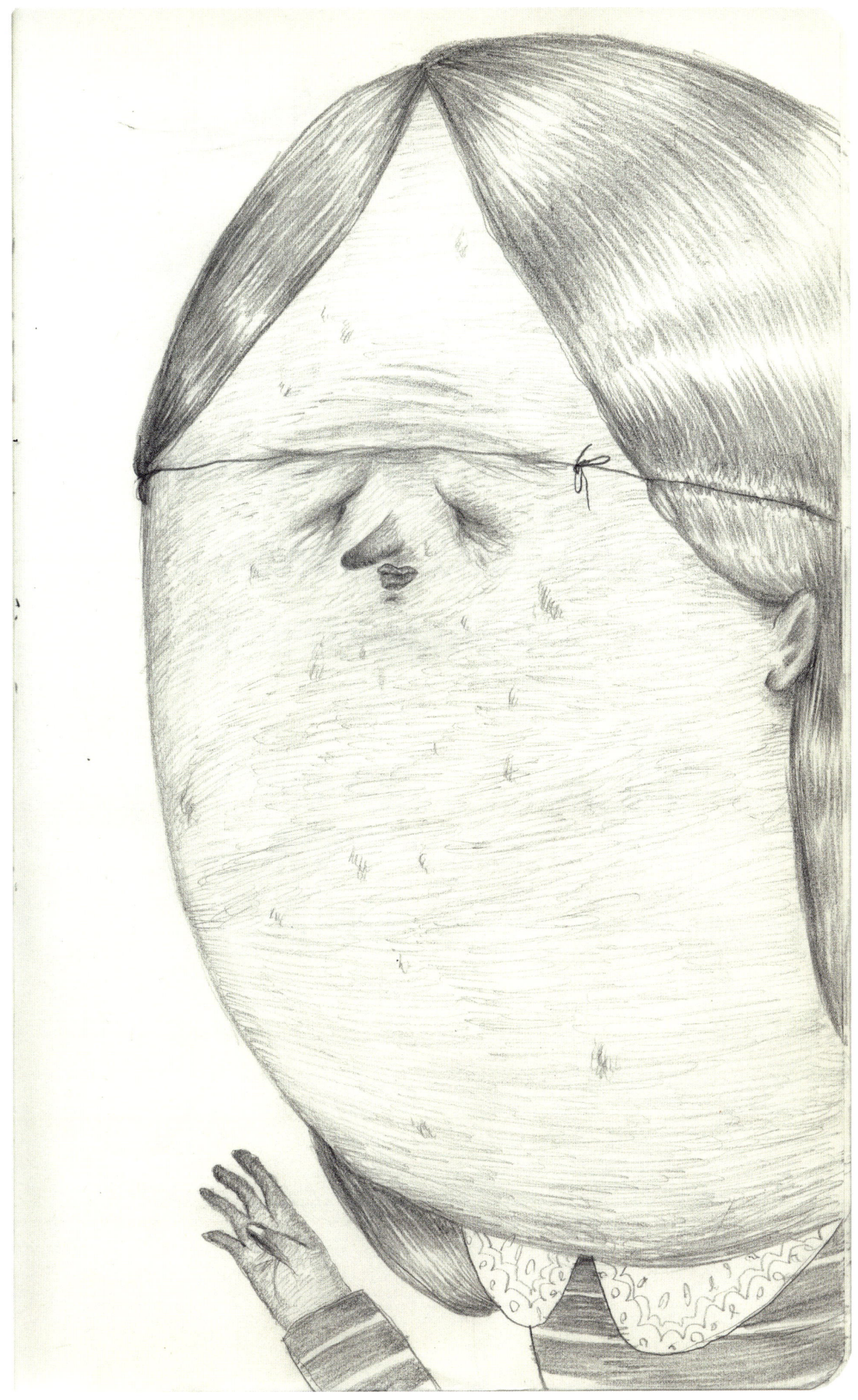

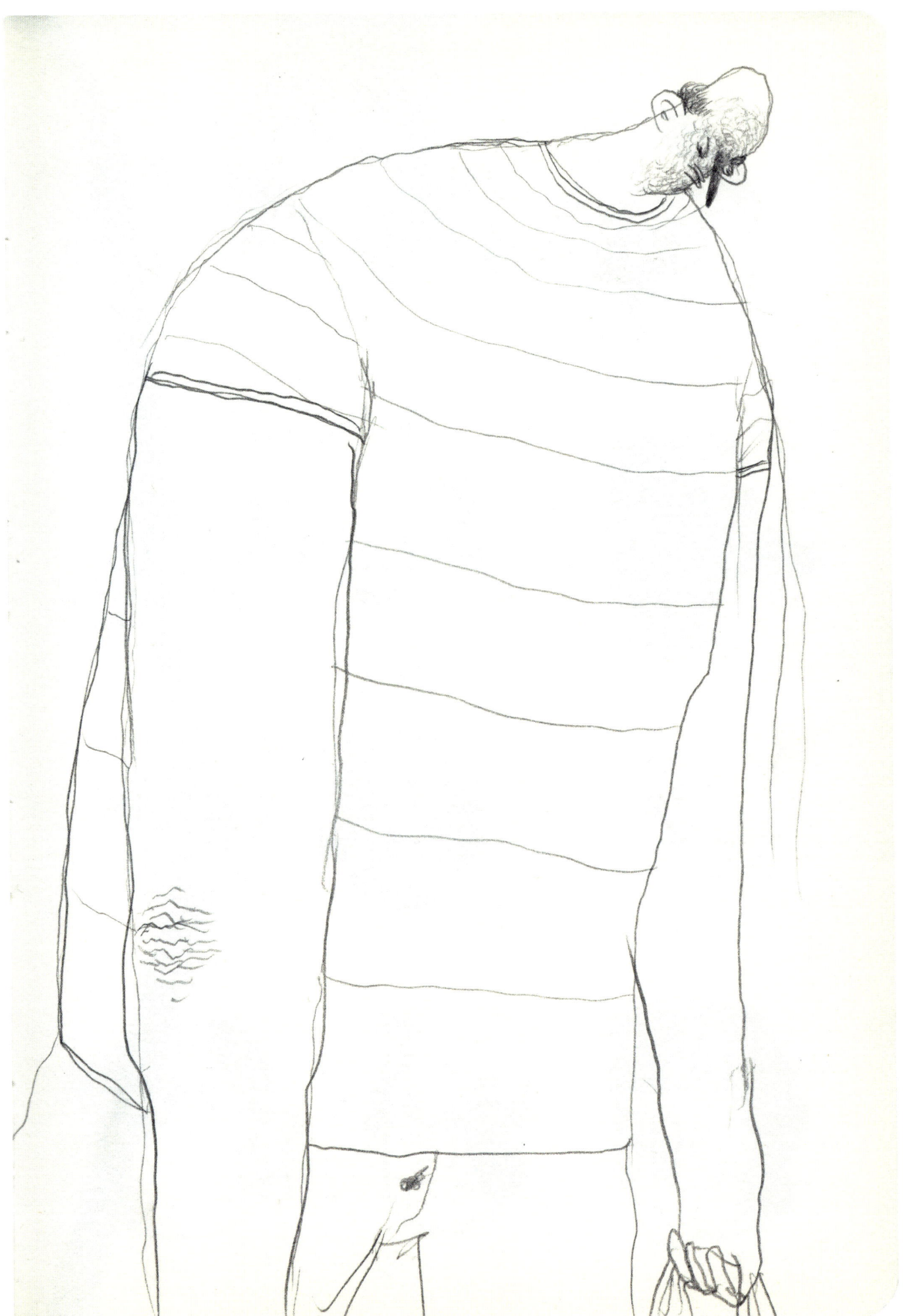

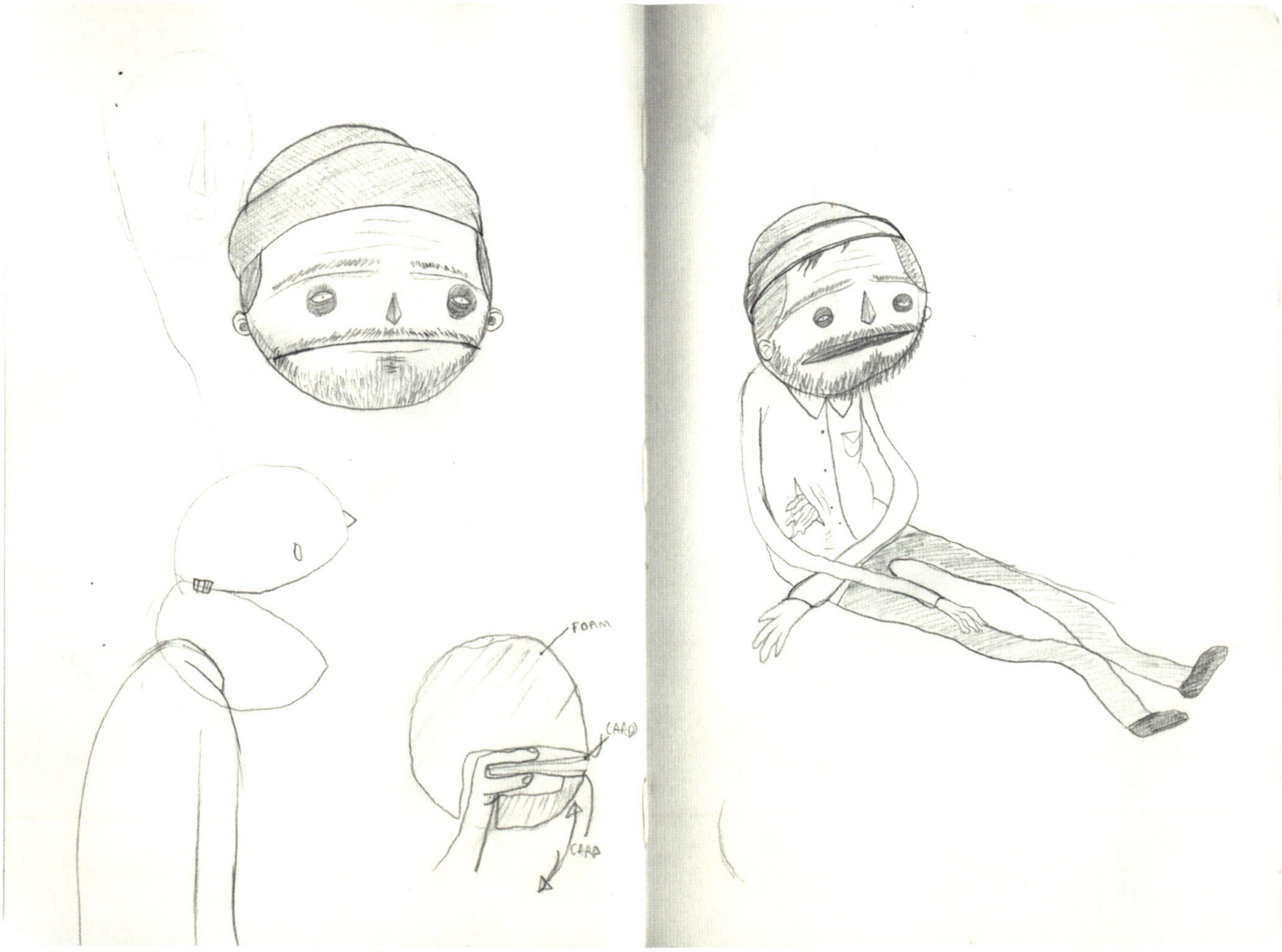

FORM
(CARD)
CARD

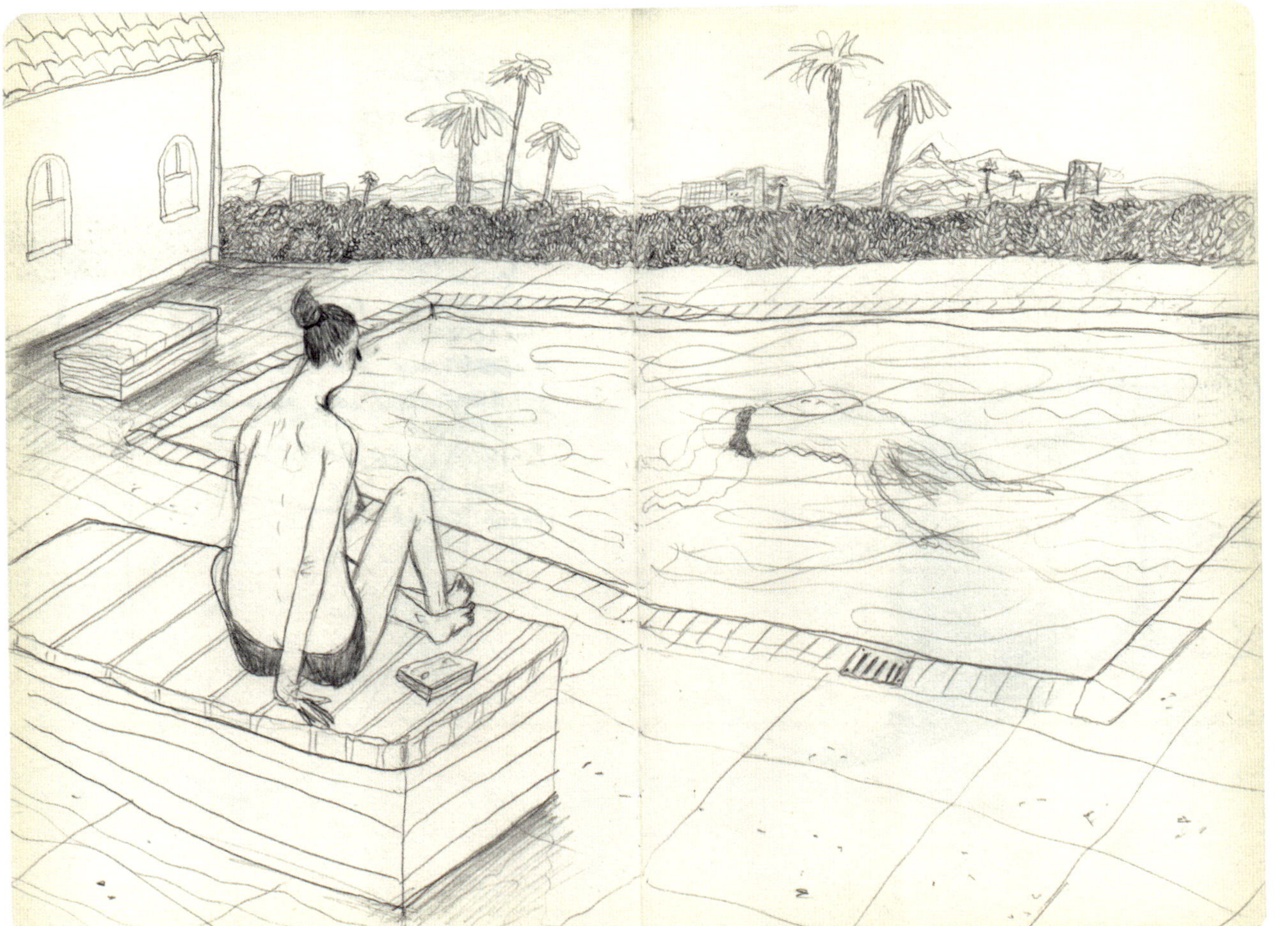

THE URGENT WEARY

A WHAT IS HATE WITHOUT

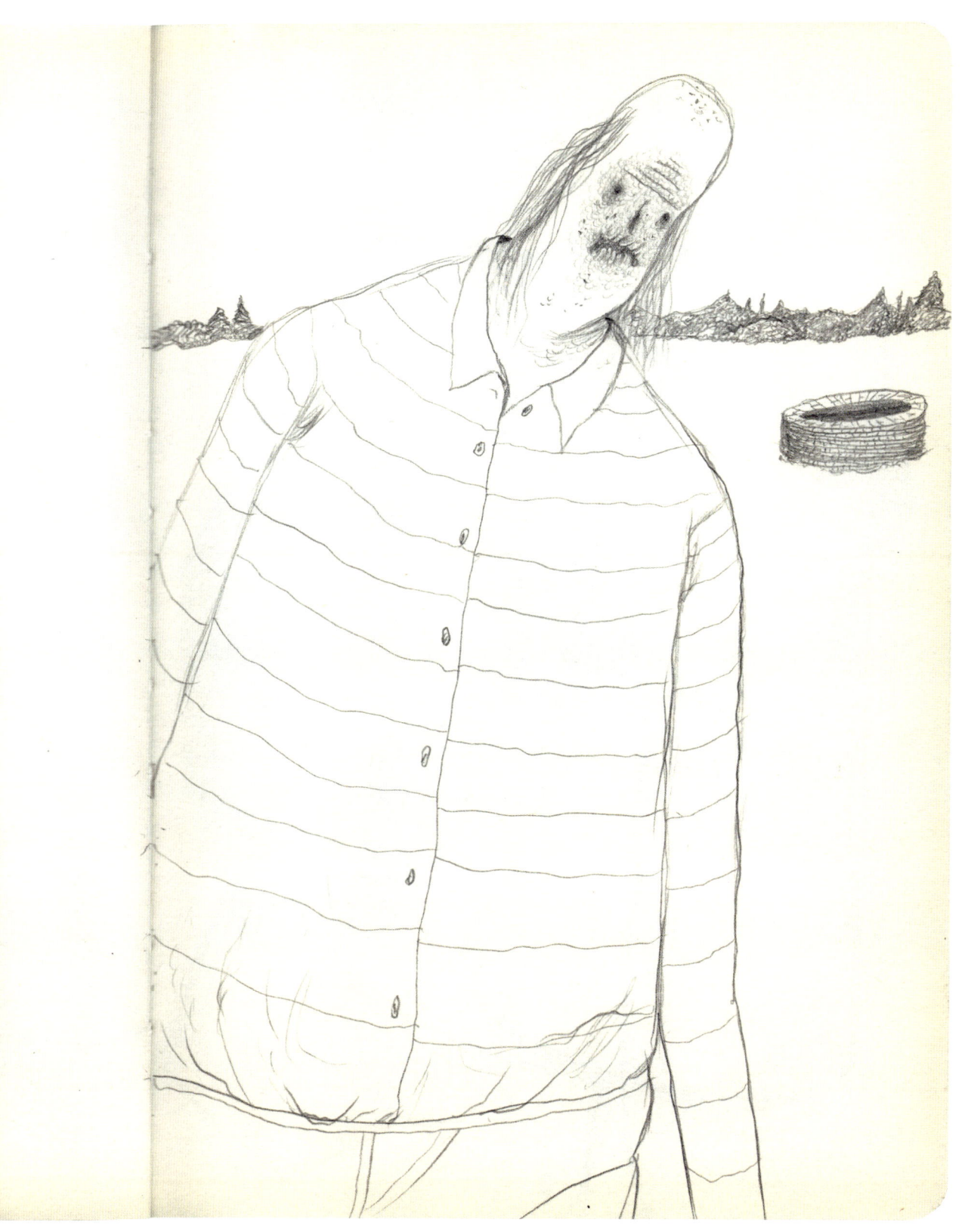

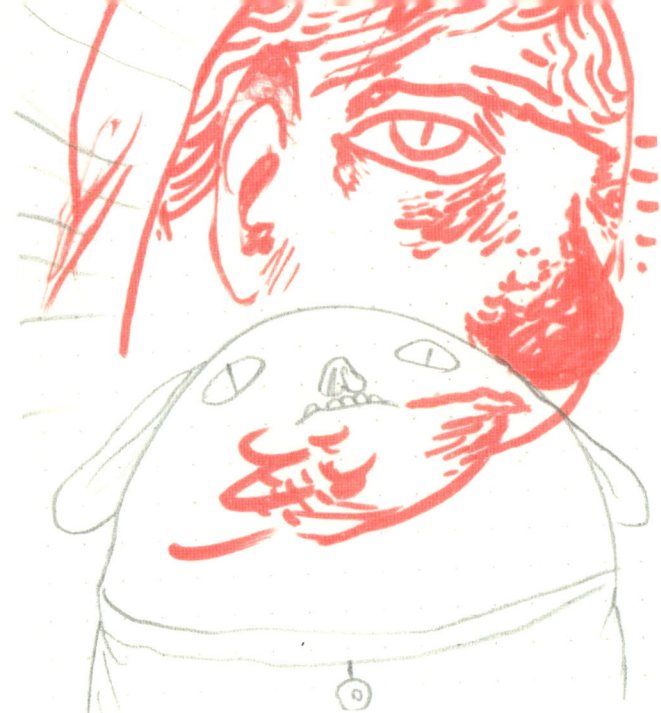
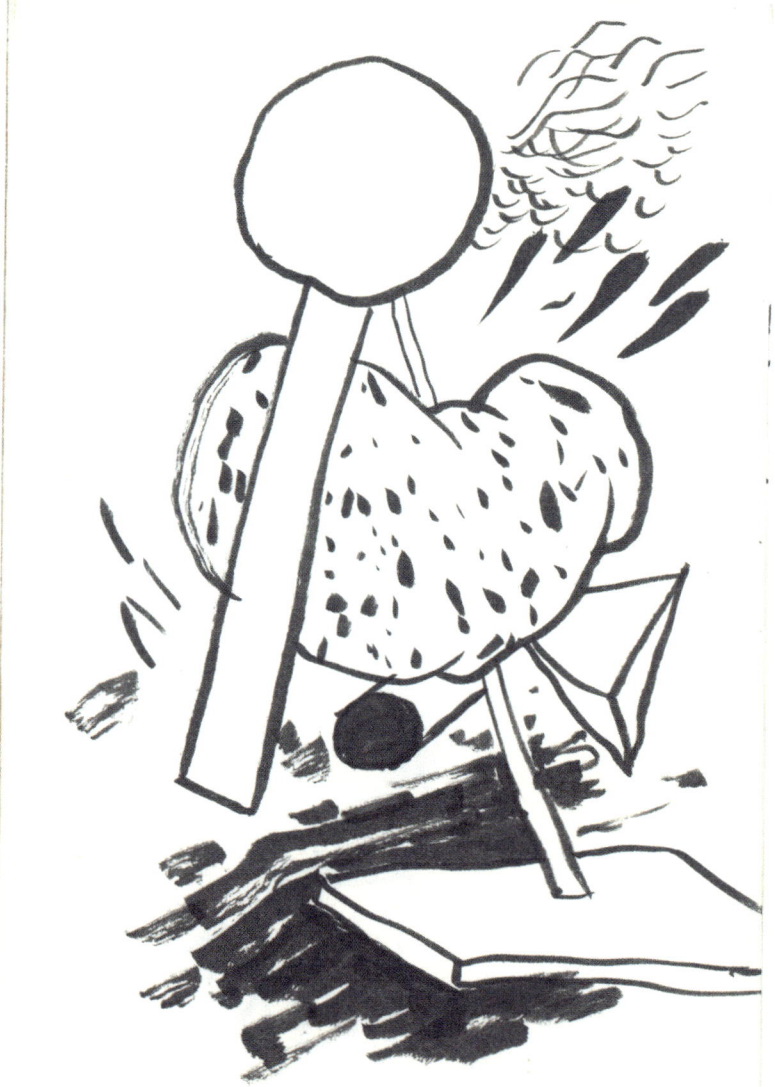
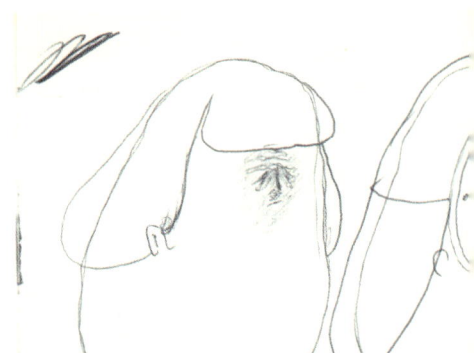

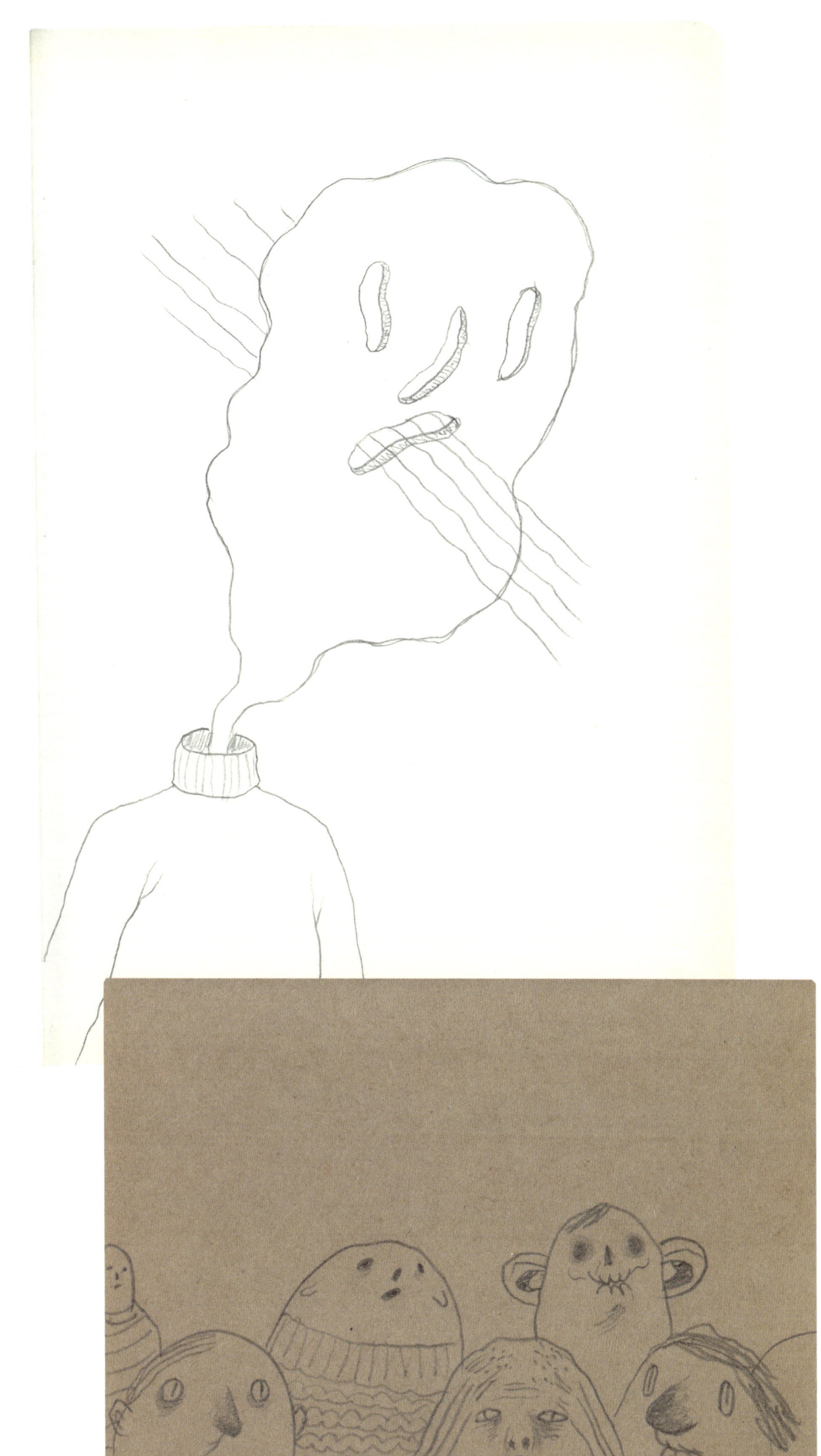

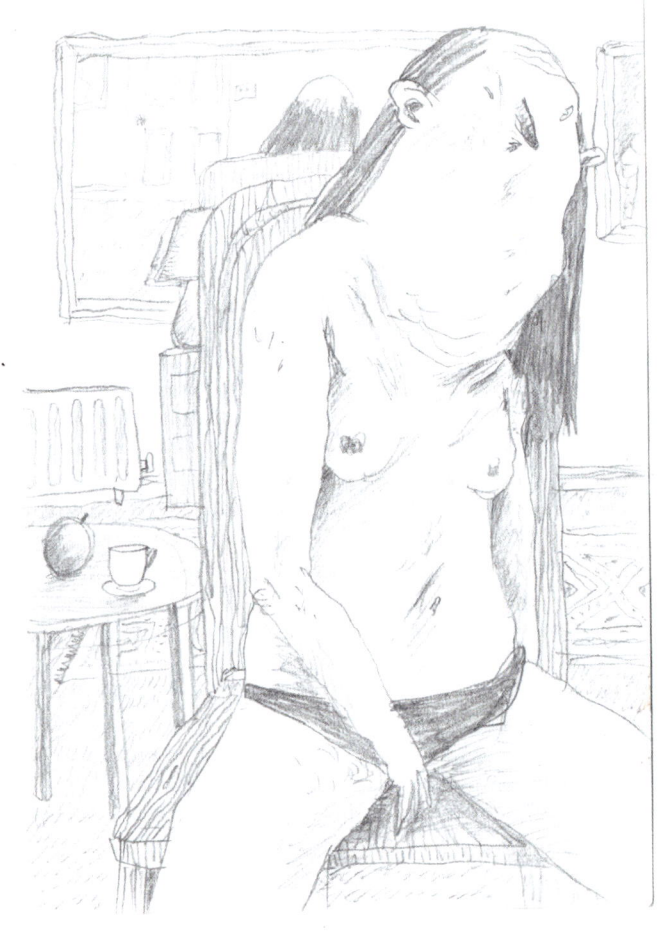
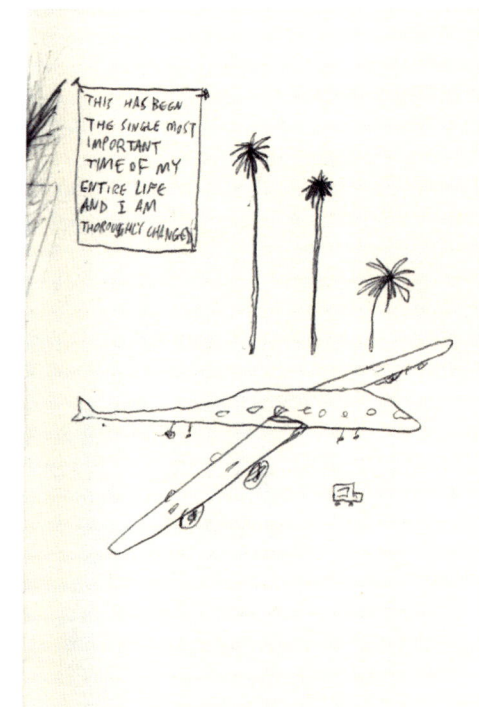

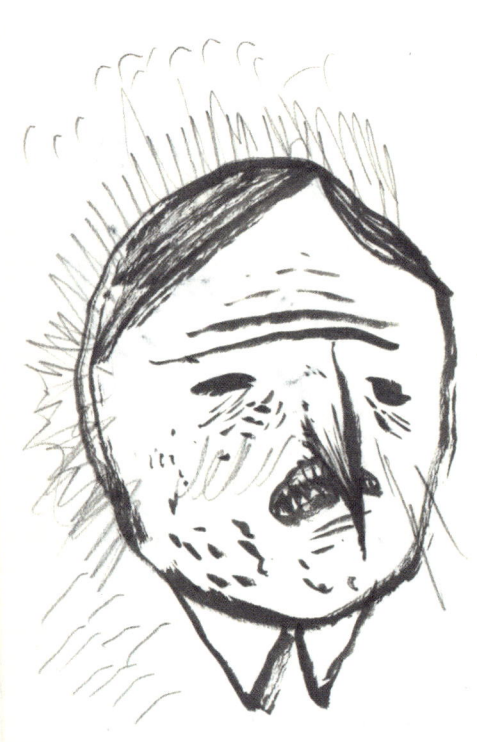

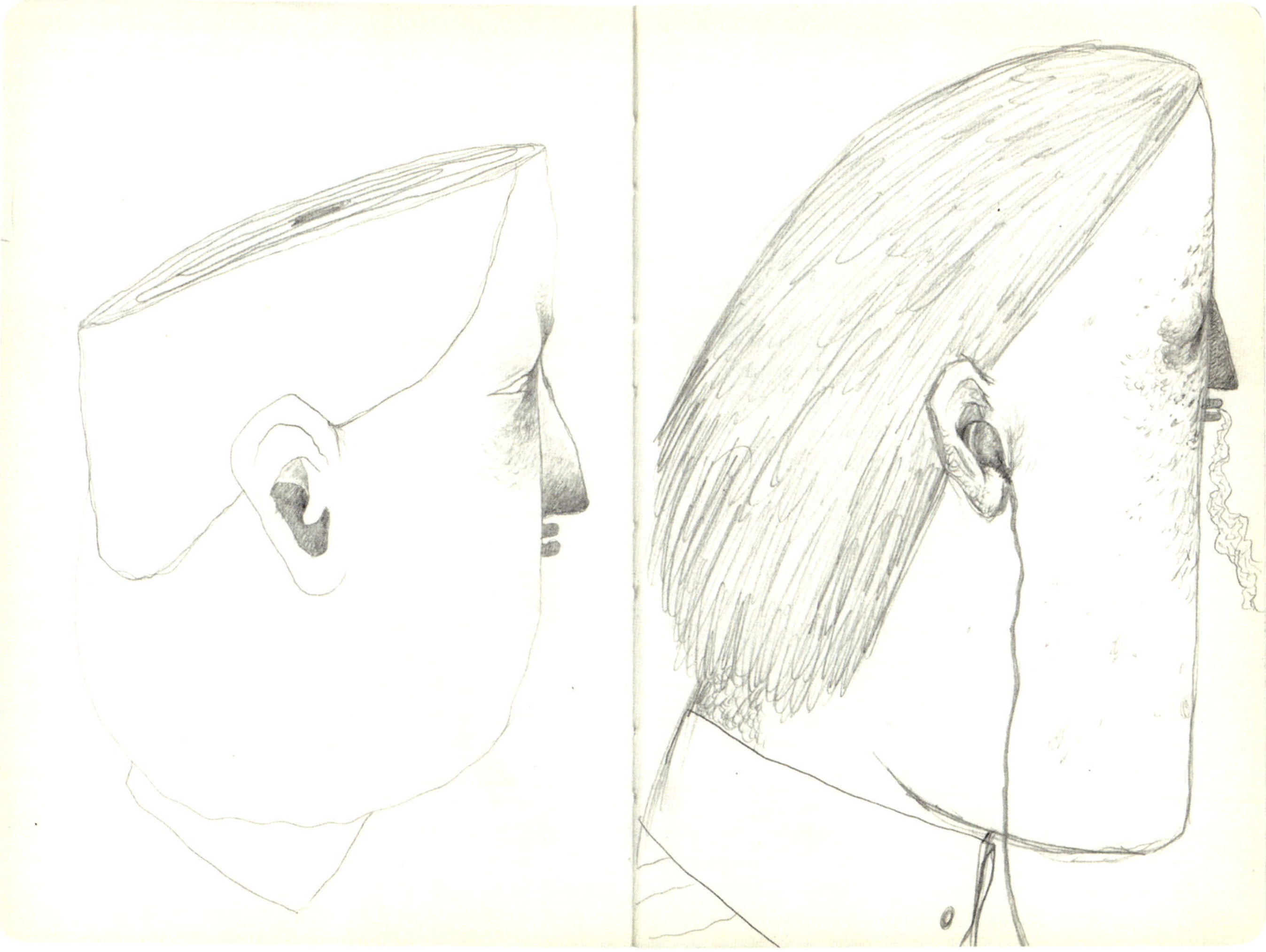

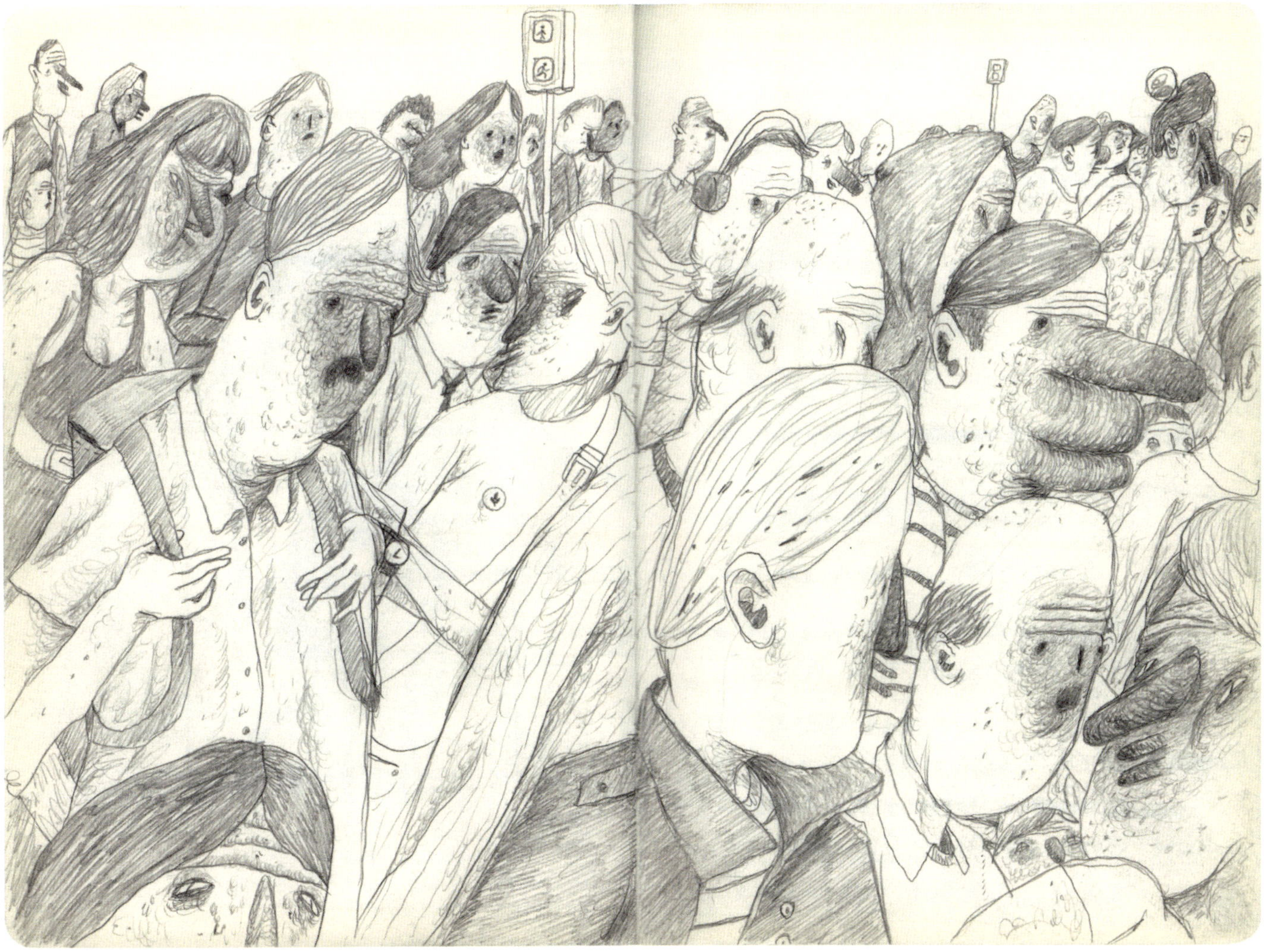

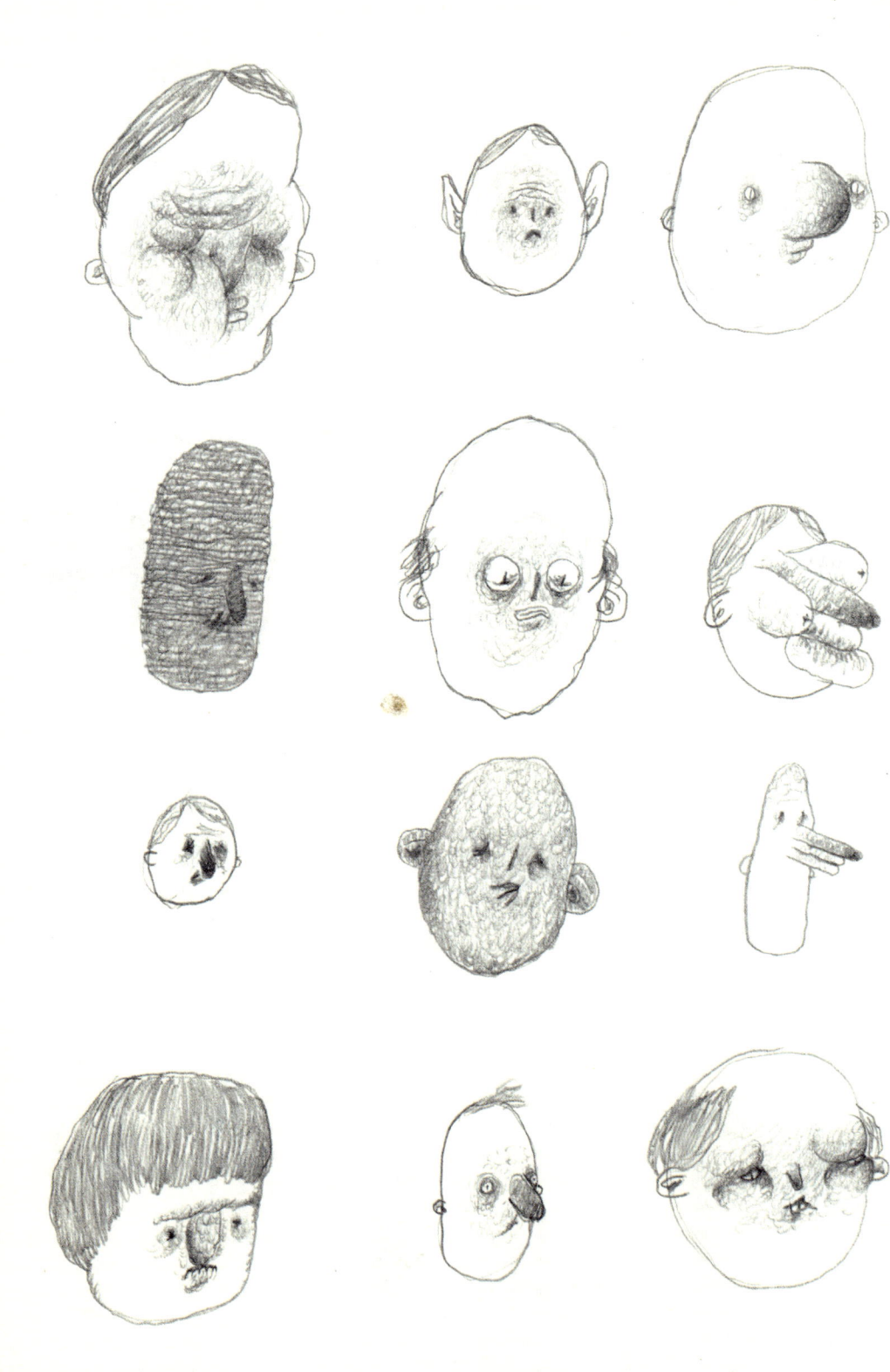

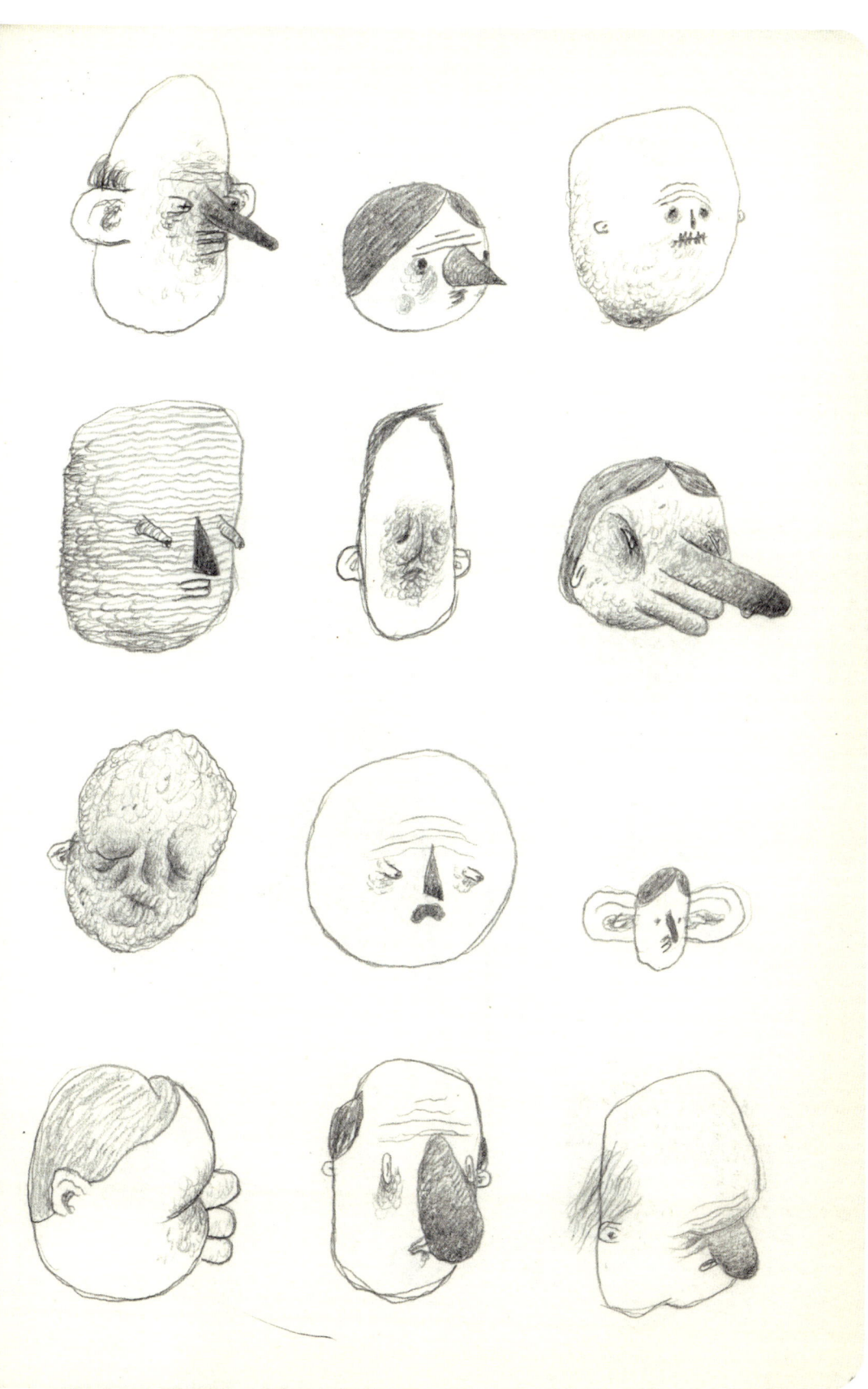

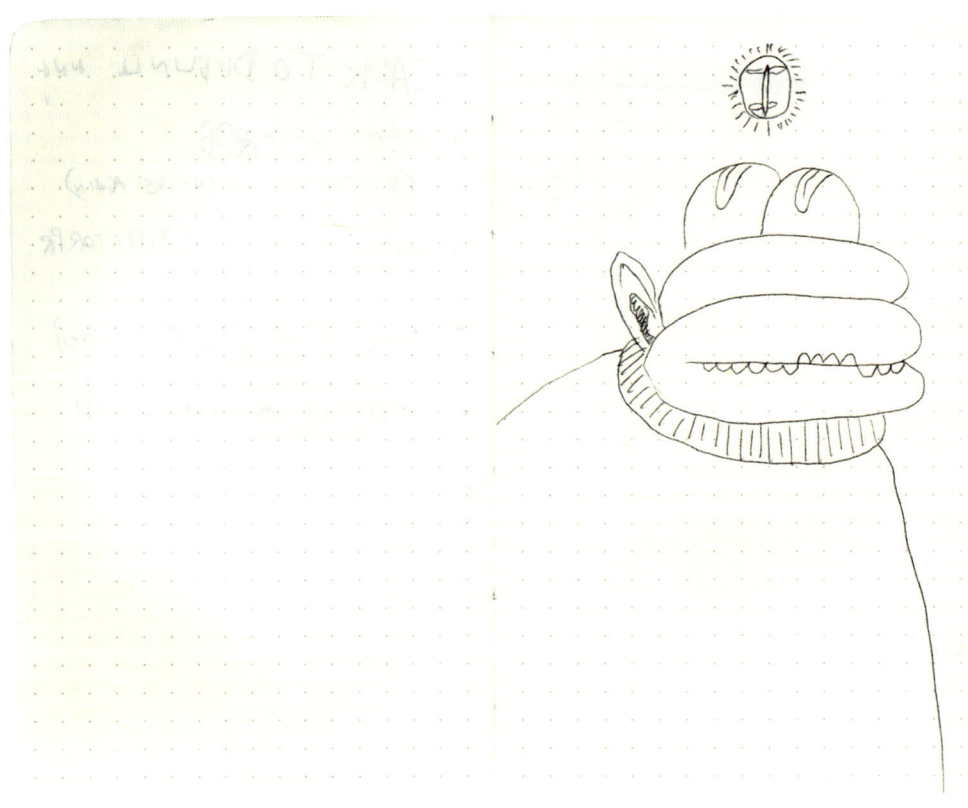
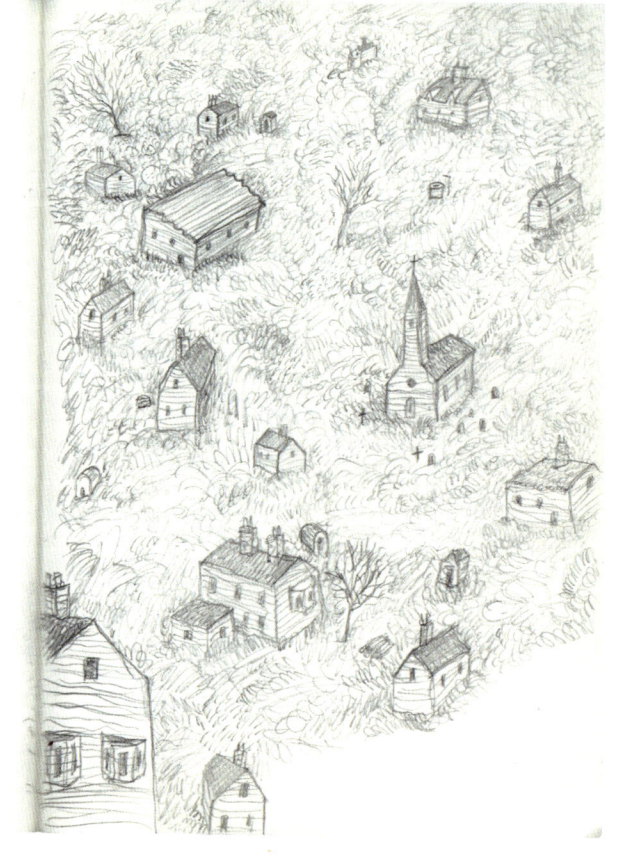

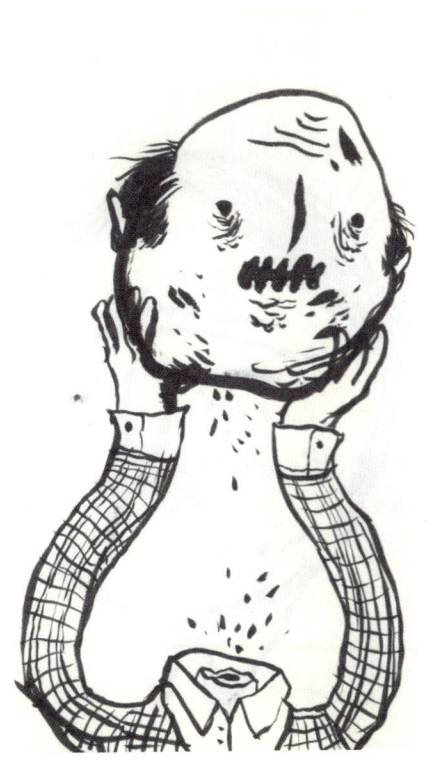

some of these houses are closed
for business
others are open wide
the winter air is whisper thin

and the scariest time of all is
~~in silent~~
in the silent film town of Malbrose
where everyone has a mustache

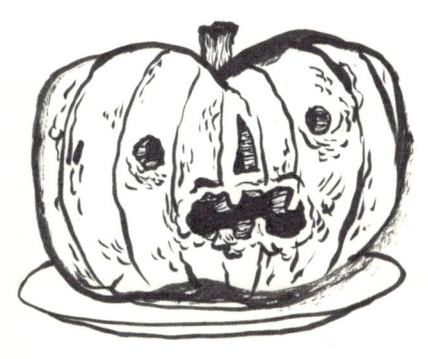

CENTURY OF THE
CHILD

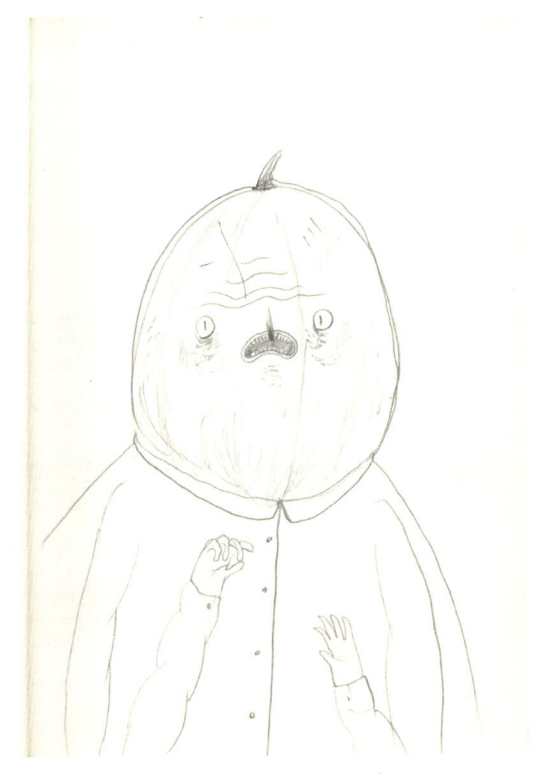

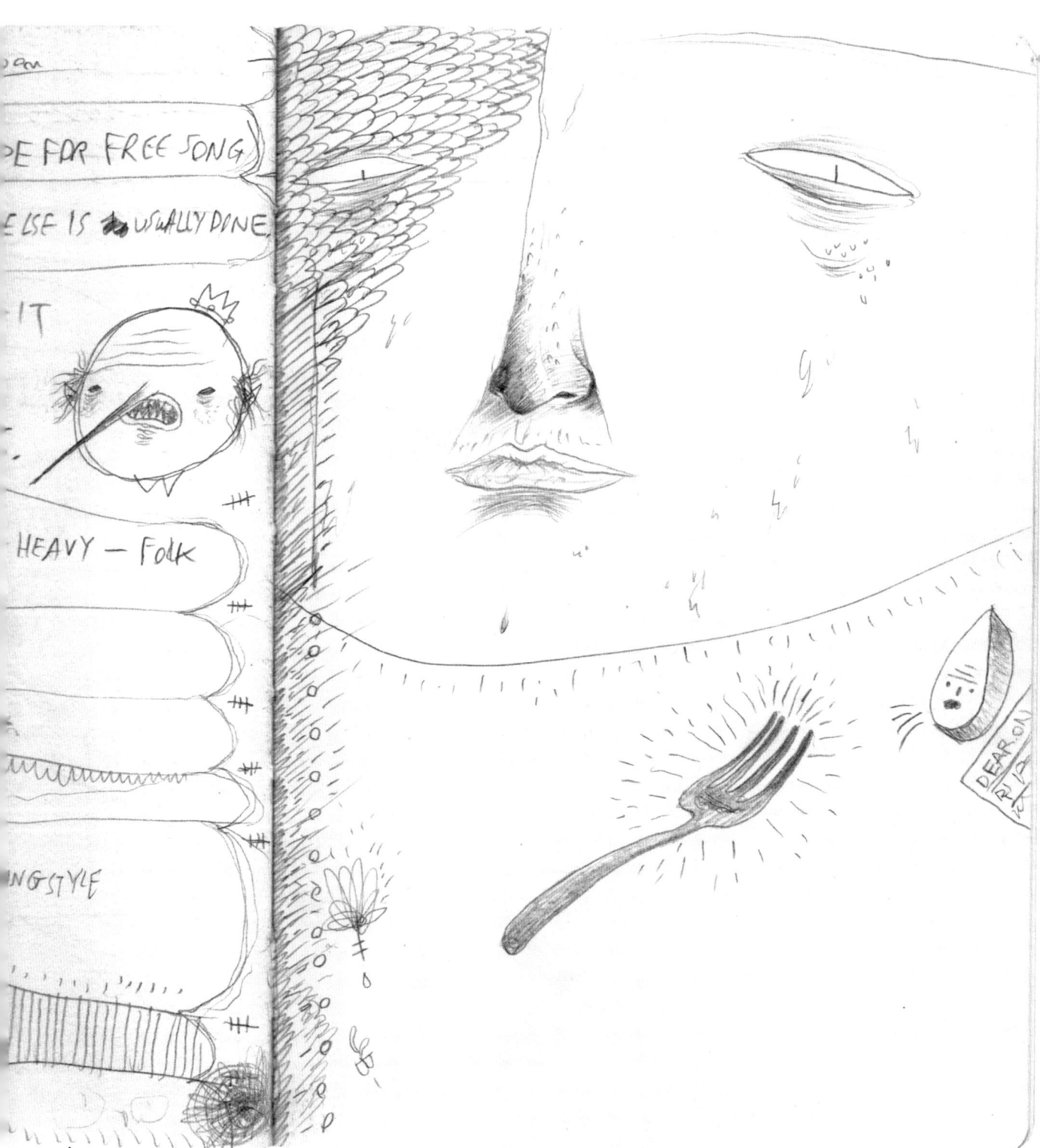

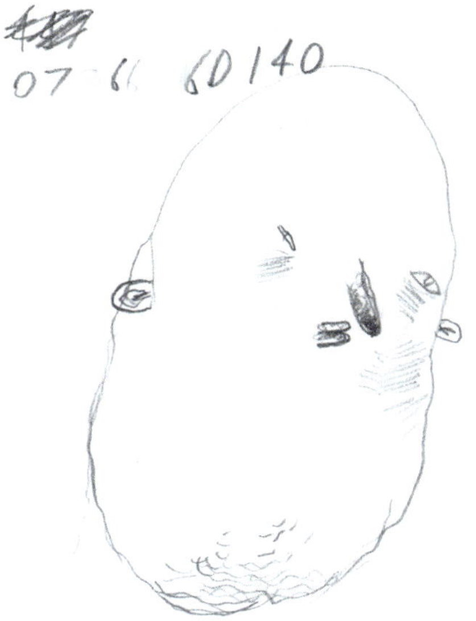

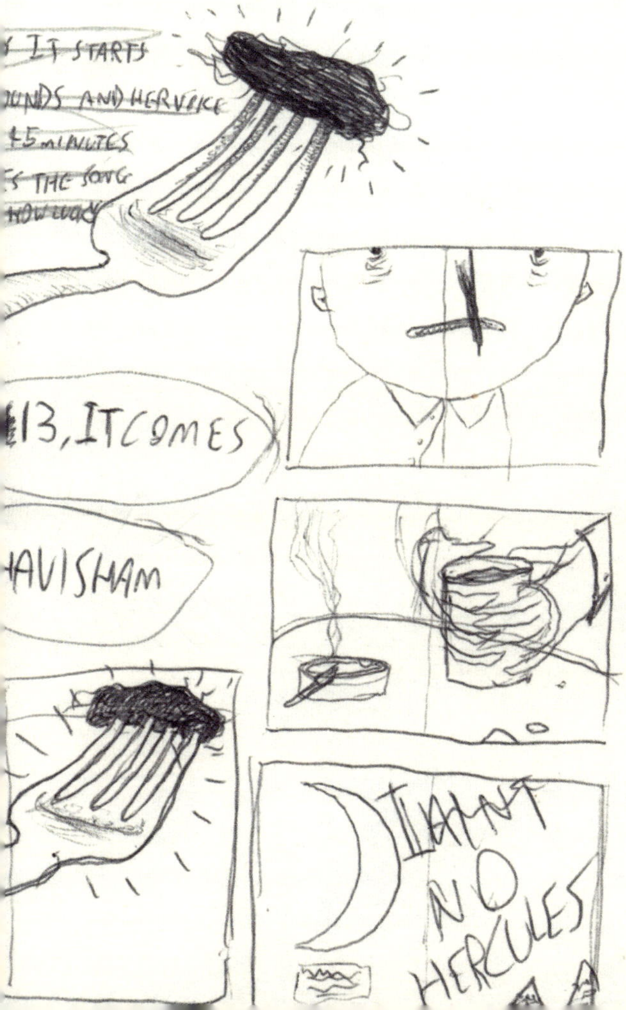

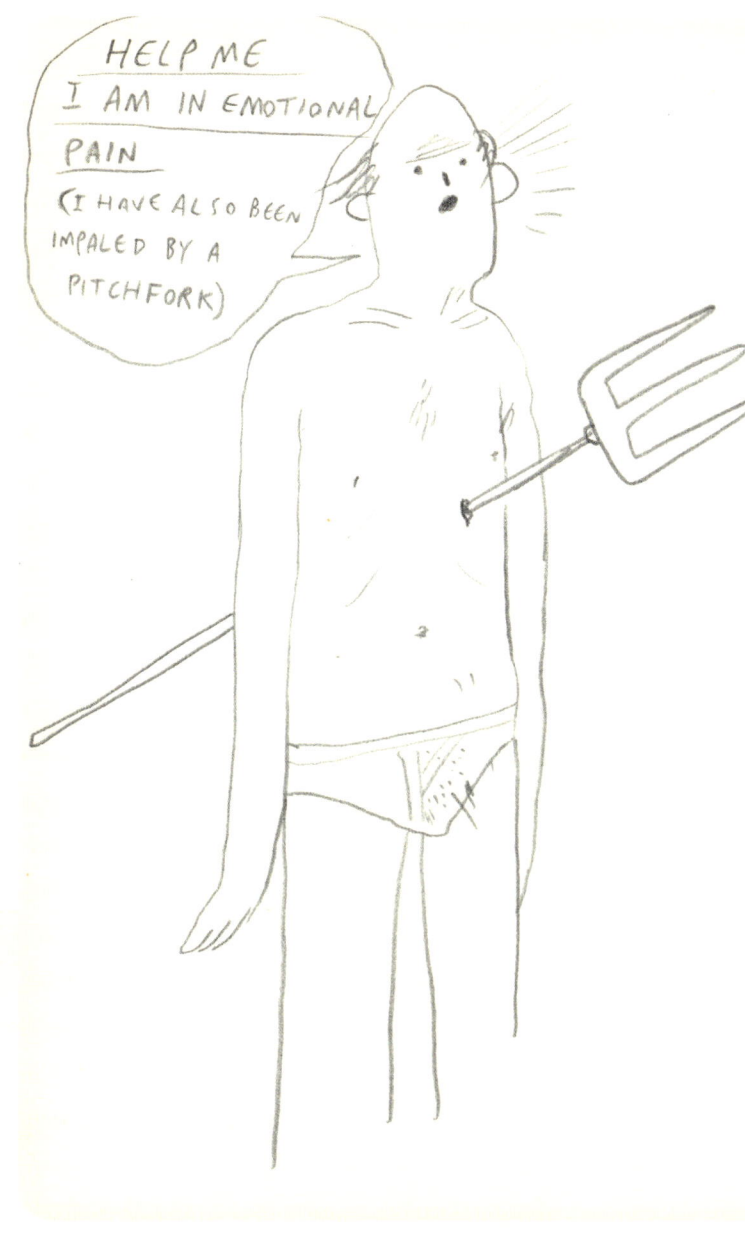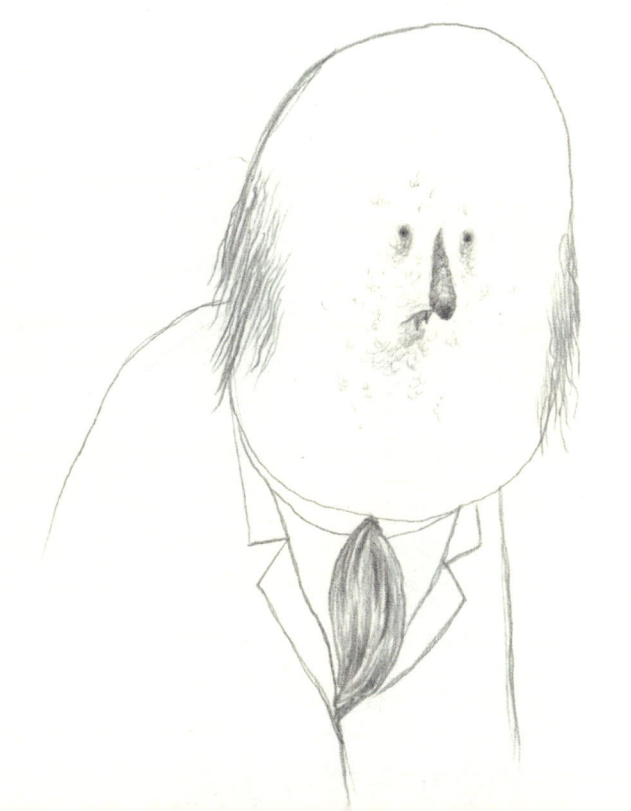

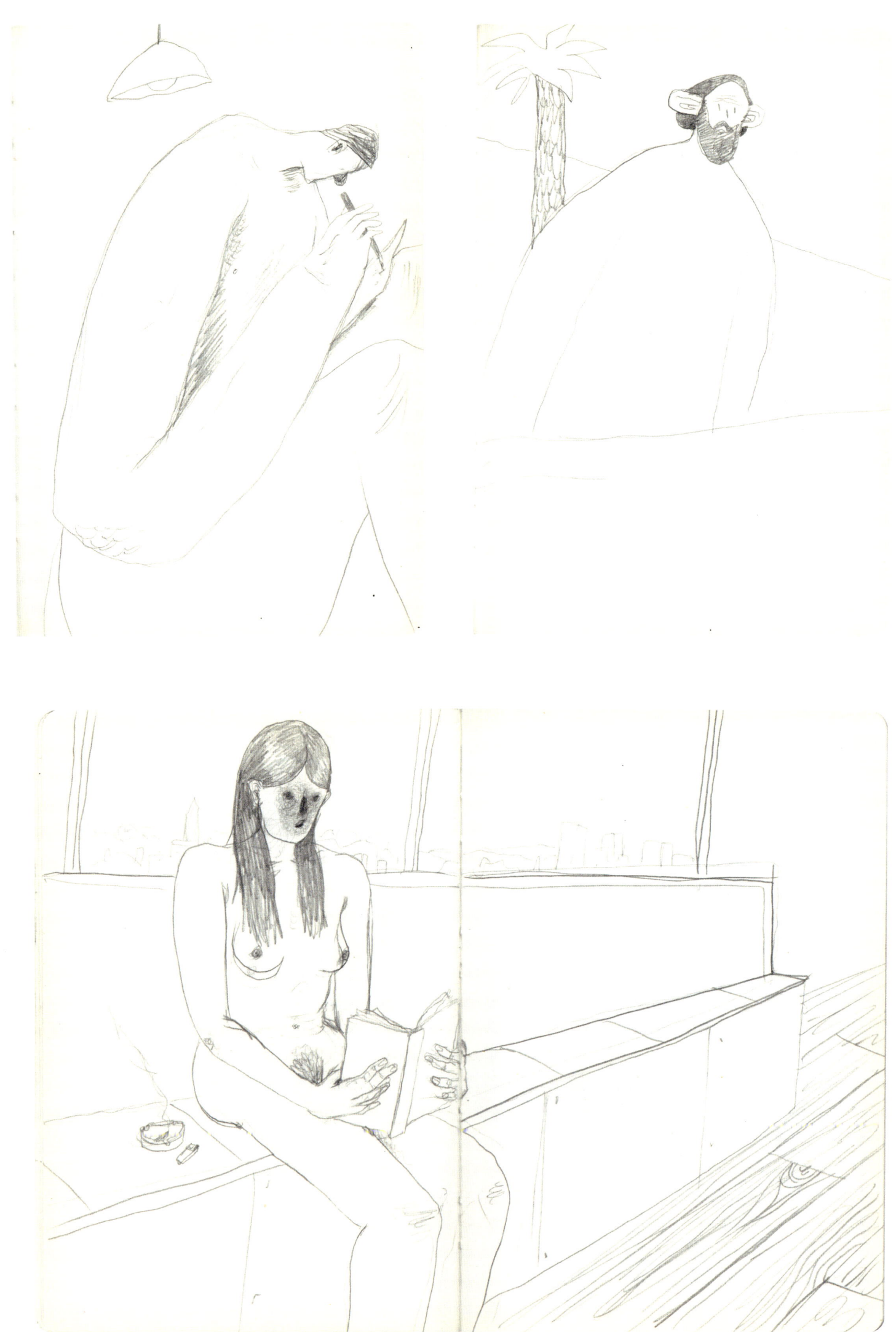

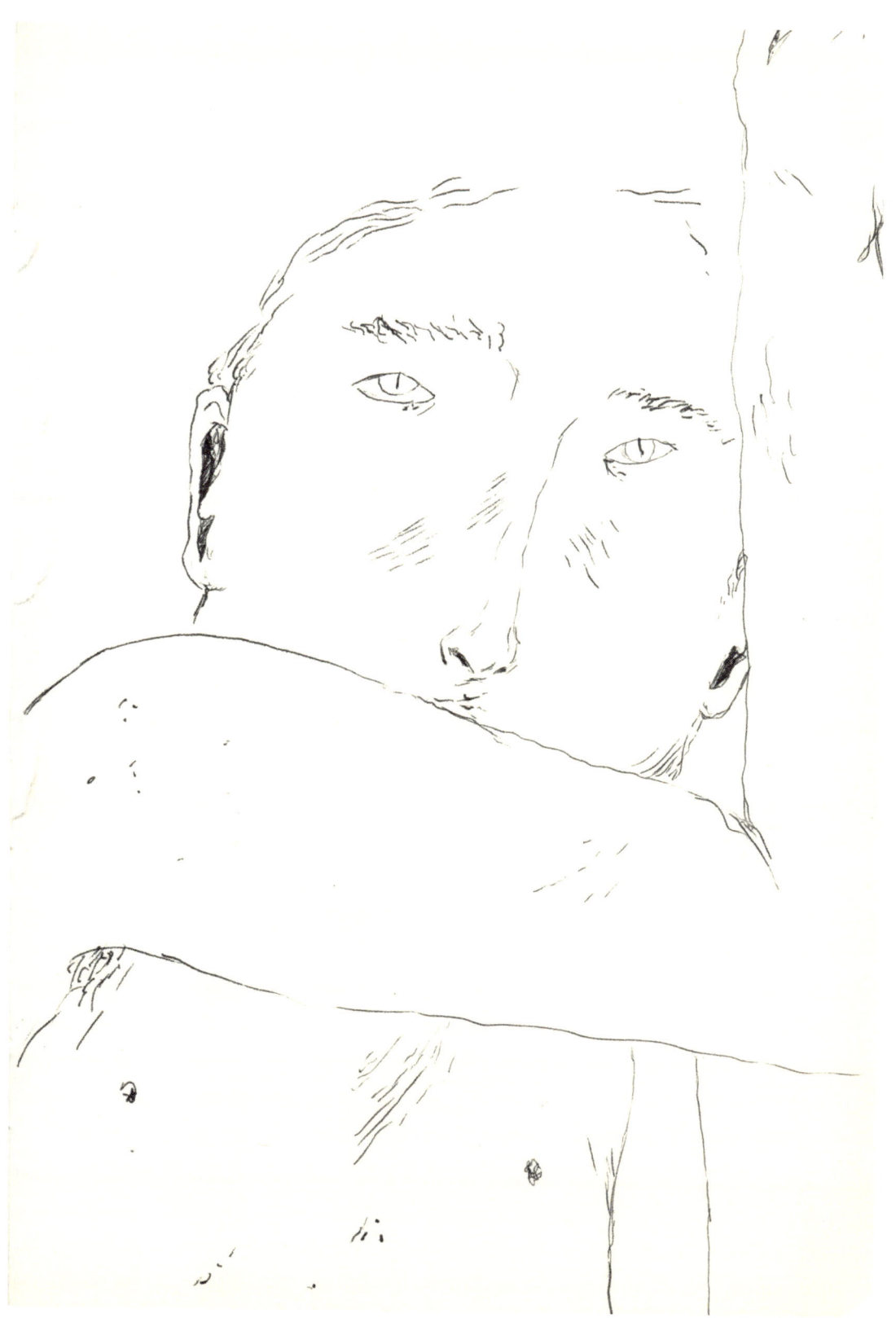

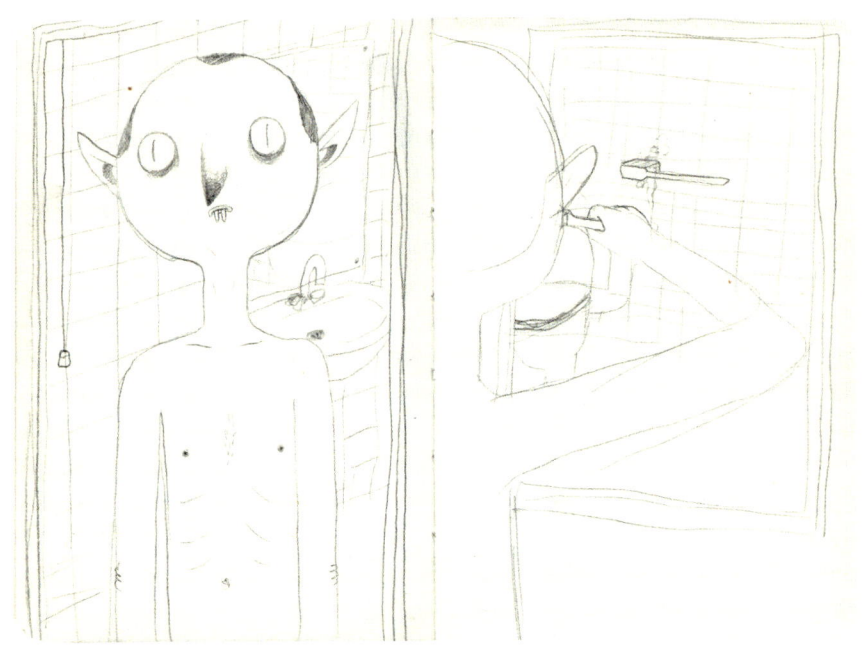

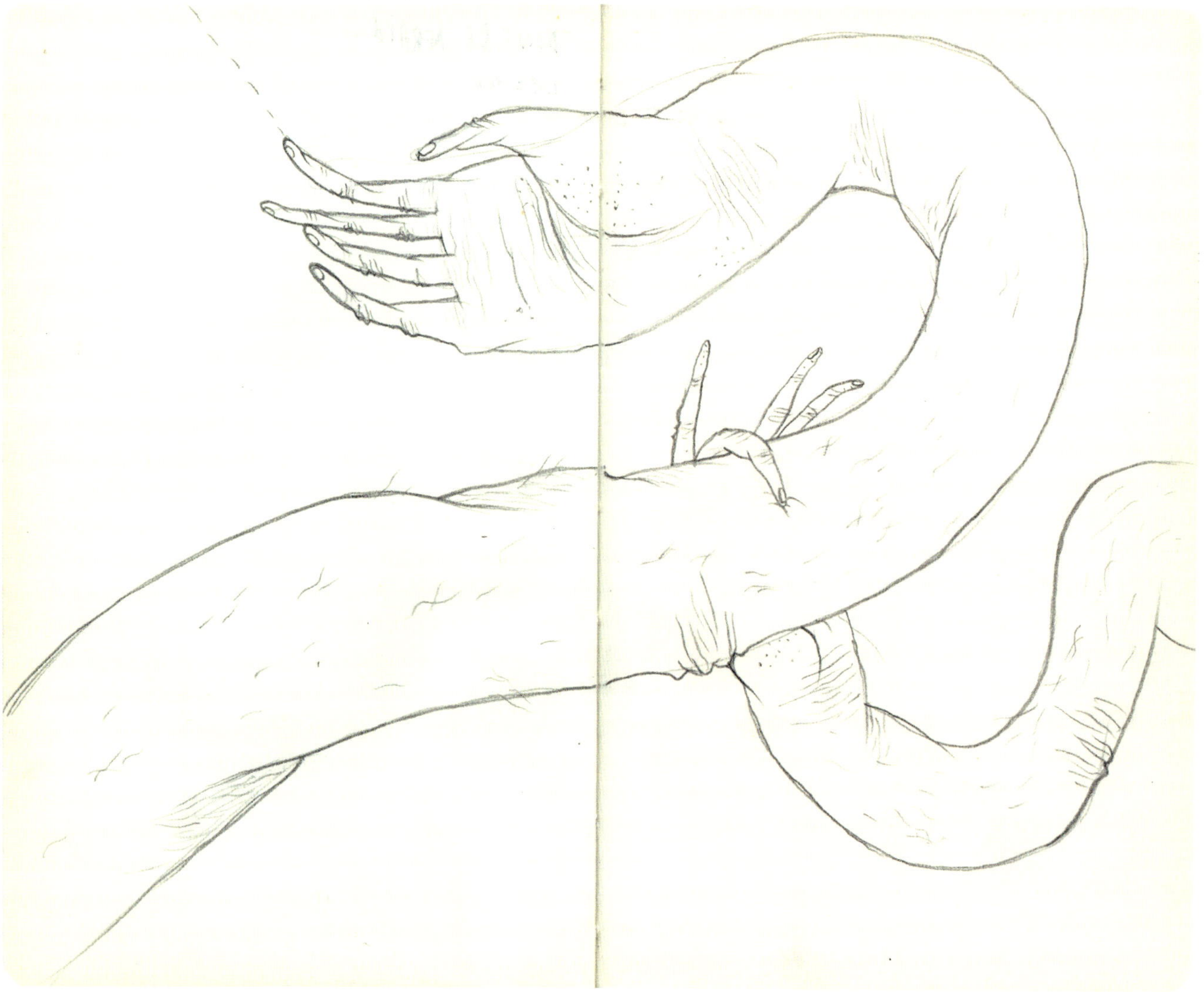

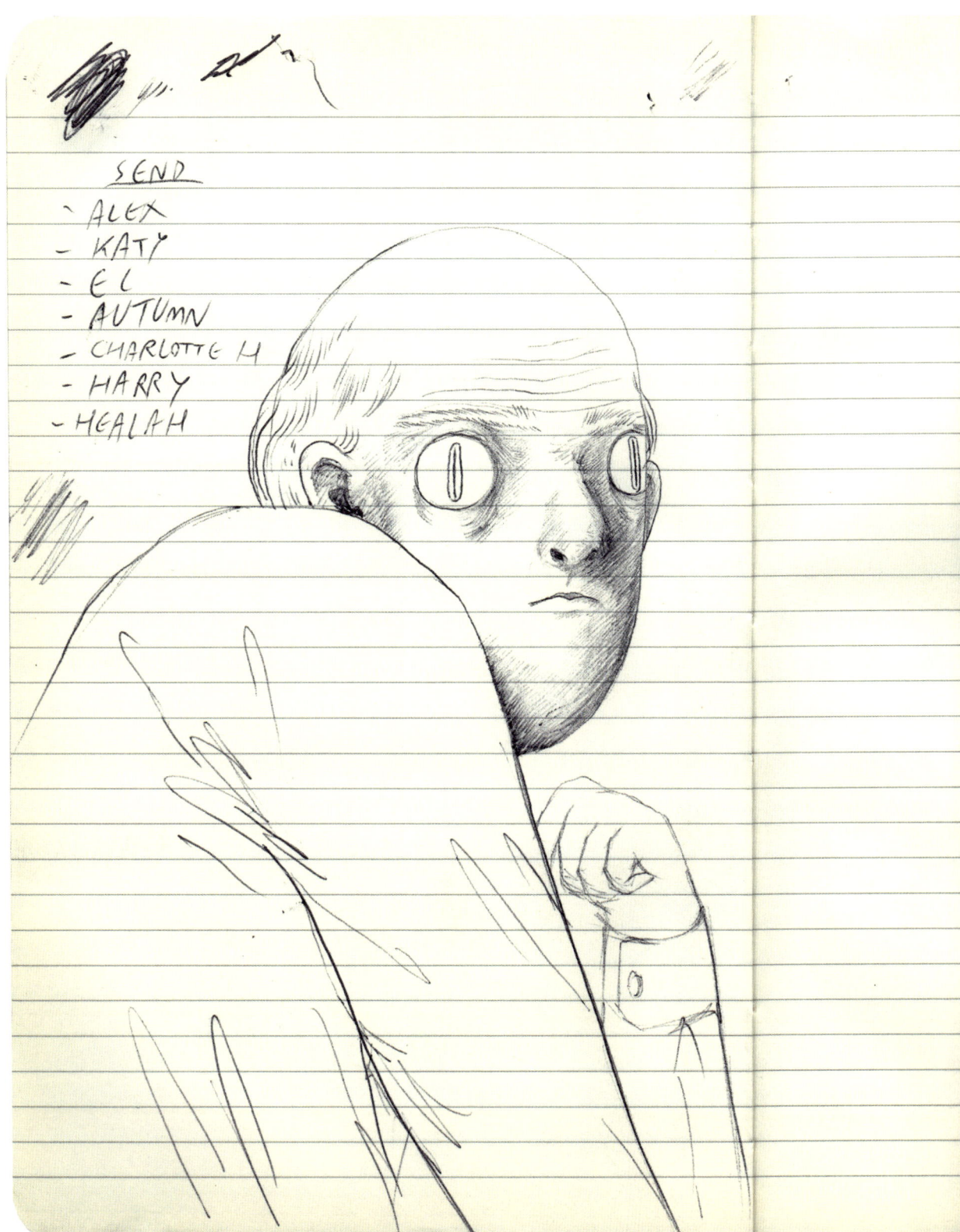

SEND
- ALEX
- KATY
- EL
- AUTUMN
- CHARLOTTE H
- HARRY
- HEALAH

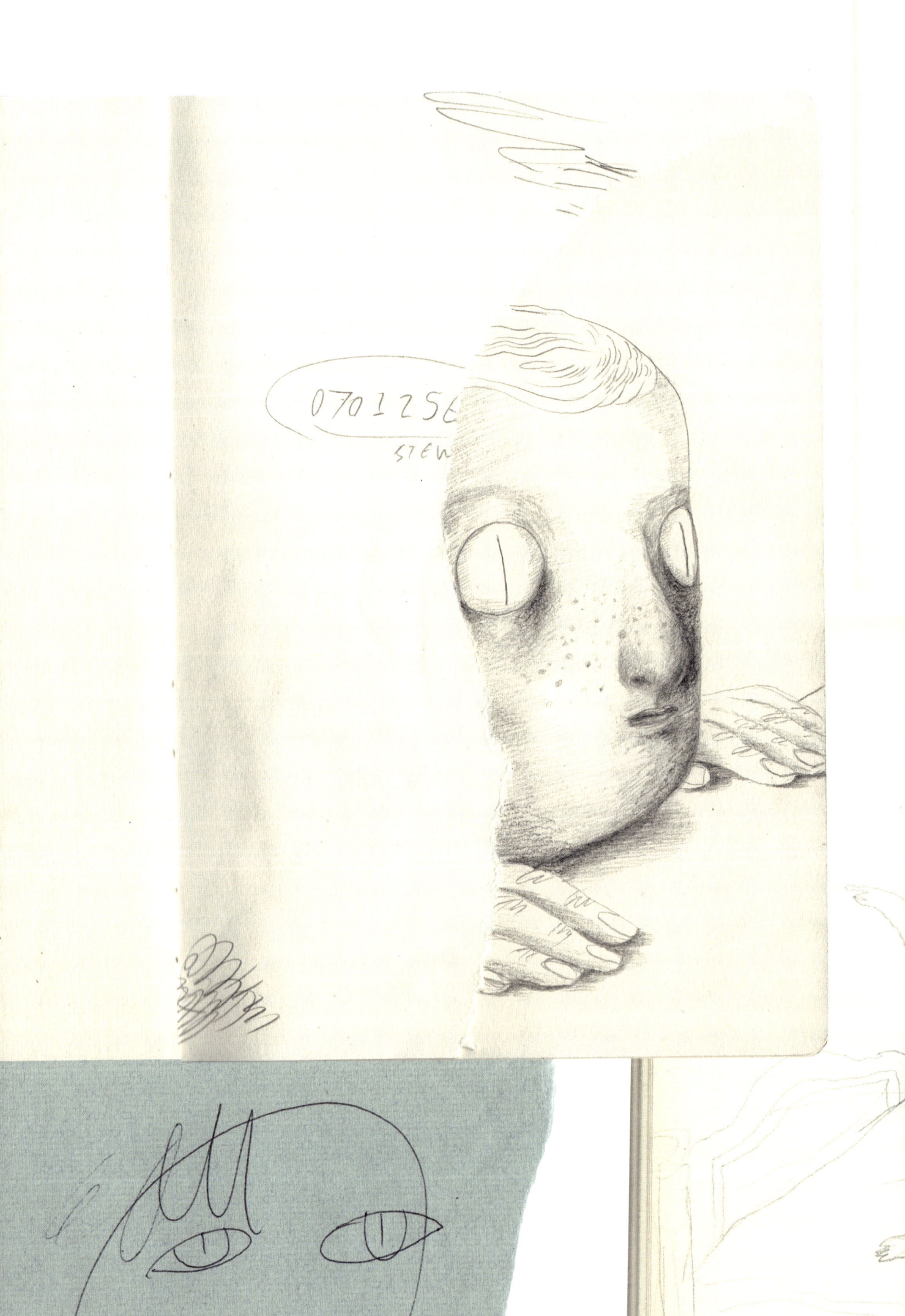

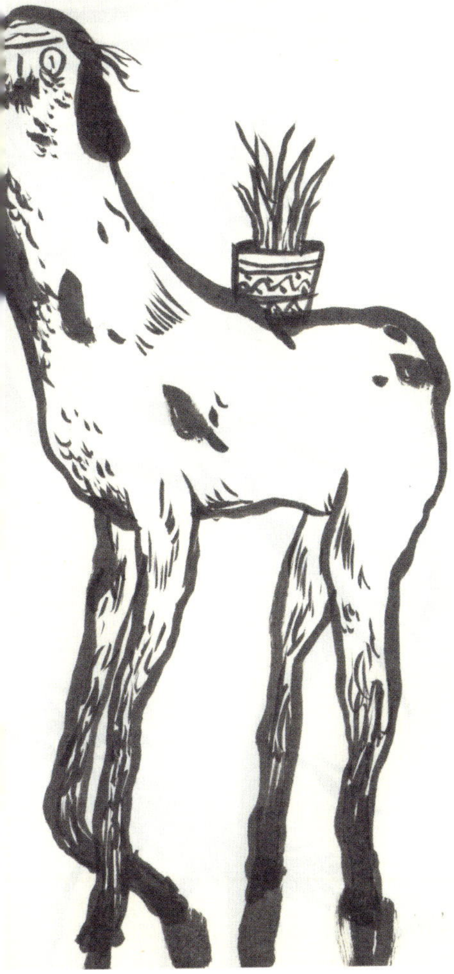

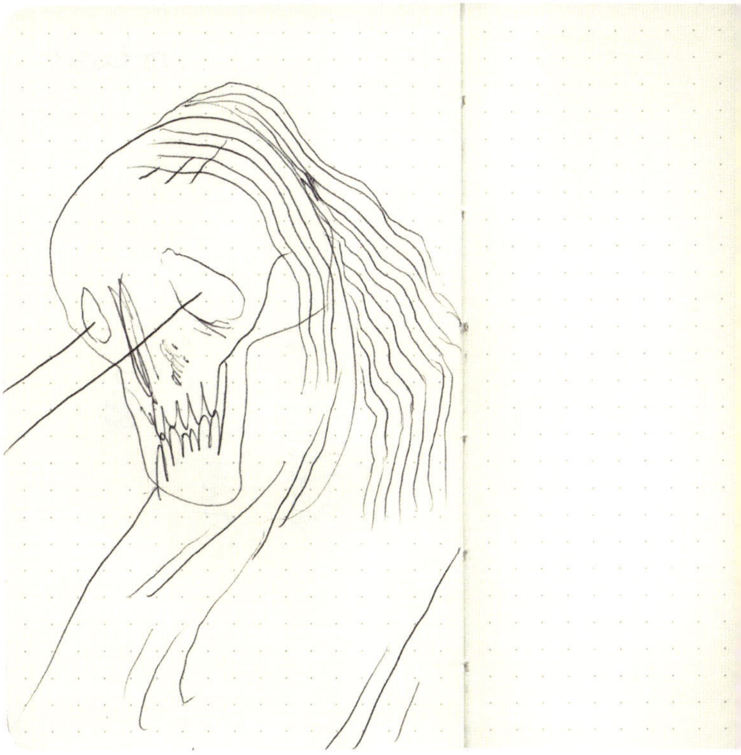

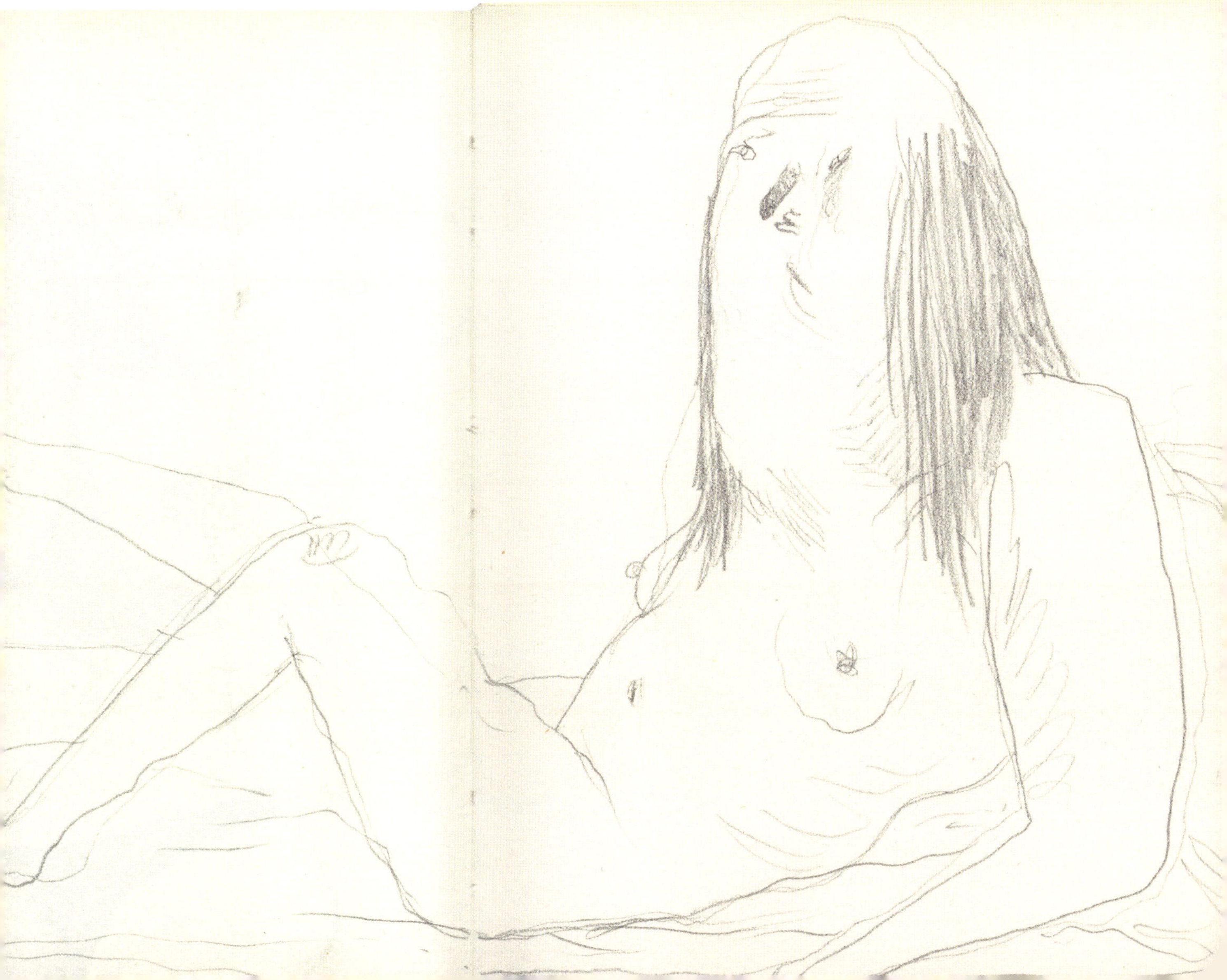

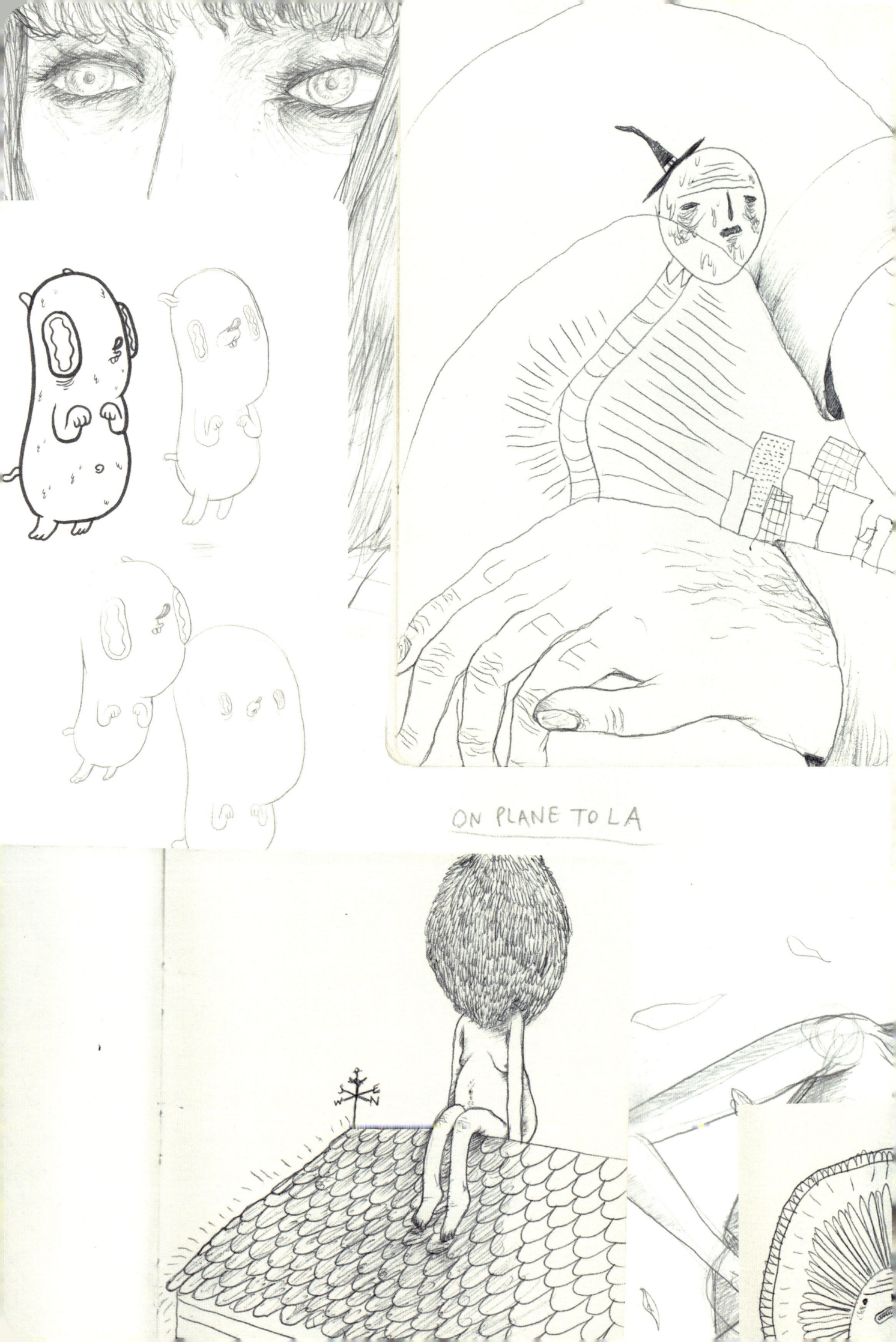

ON PLANE TO LA

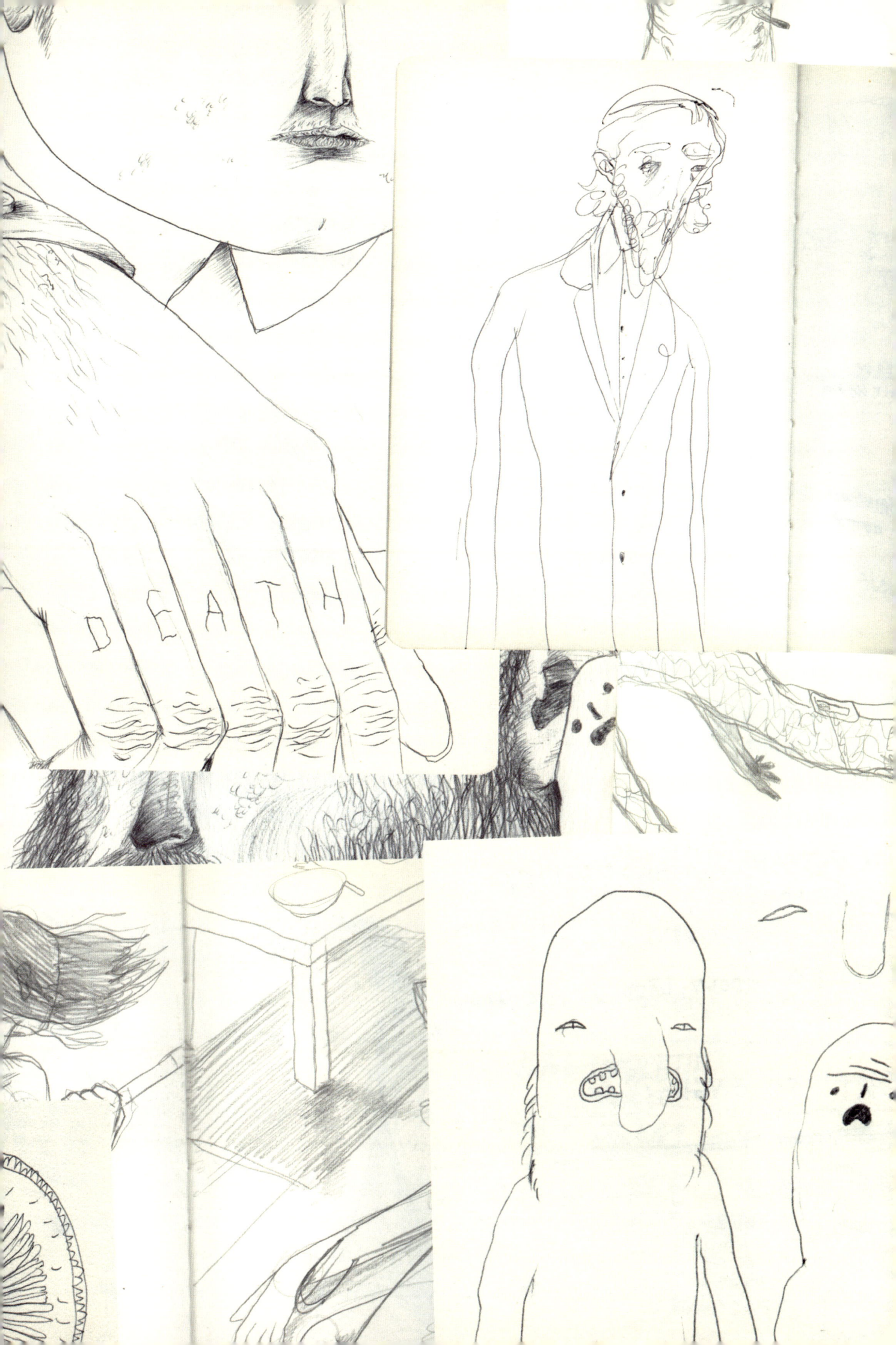

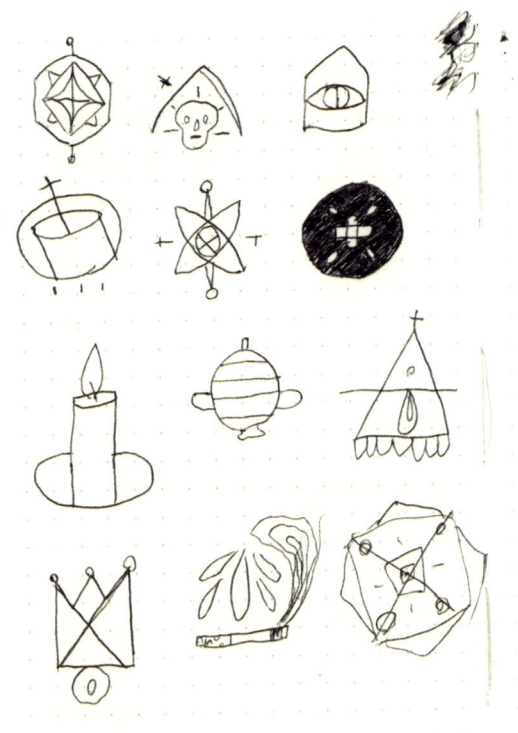
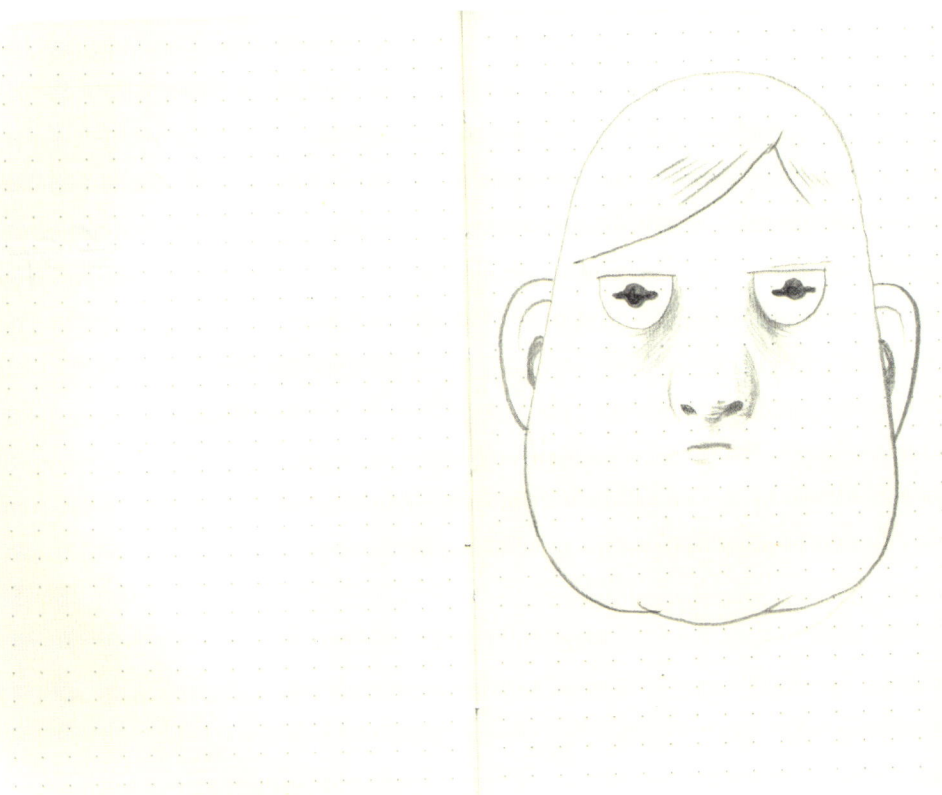

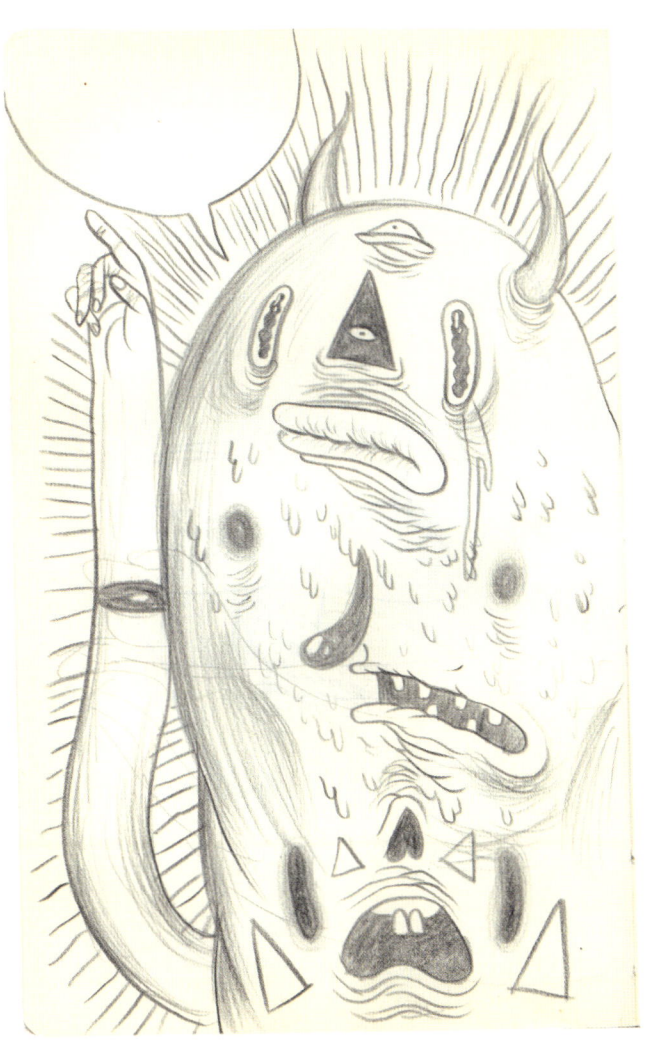
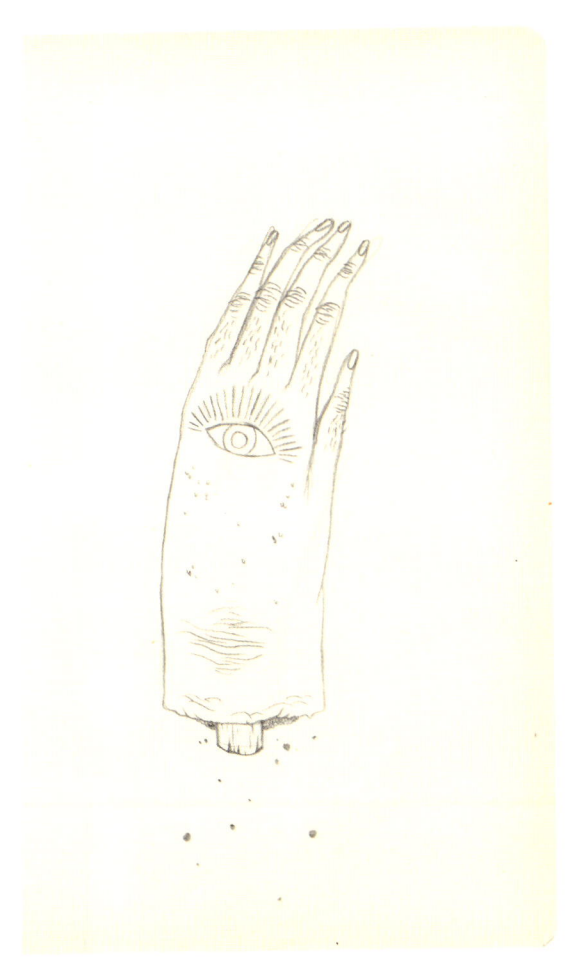

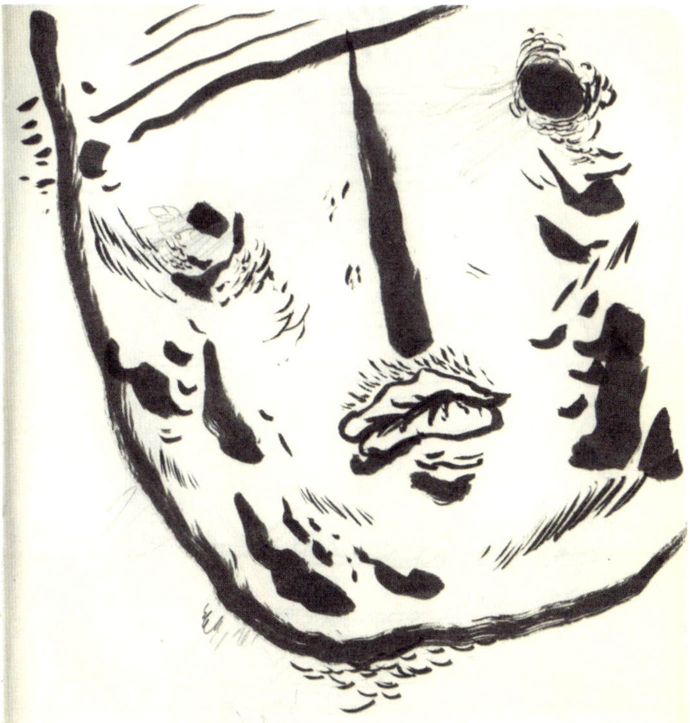

I CAN SEE IN YOUR EYES THAT YOU MEAN IT
I CAN FEEL IN YOUR ARMS THAT IT'S TRUE
AND THOUGH I JUST HEARD MYSELF SAY IT...
BABY I'M LYING TO YOU..

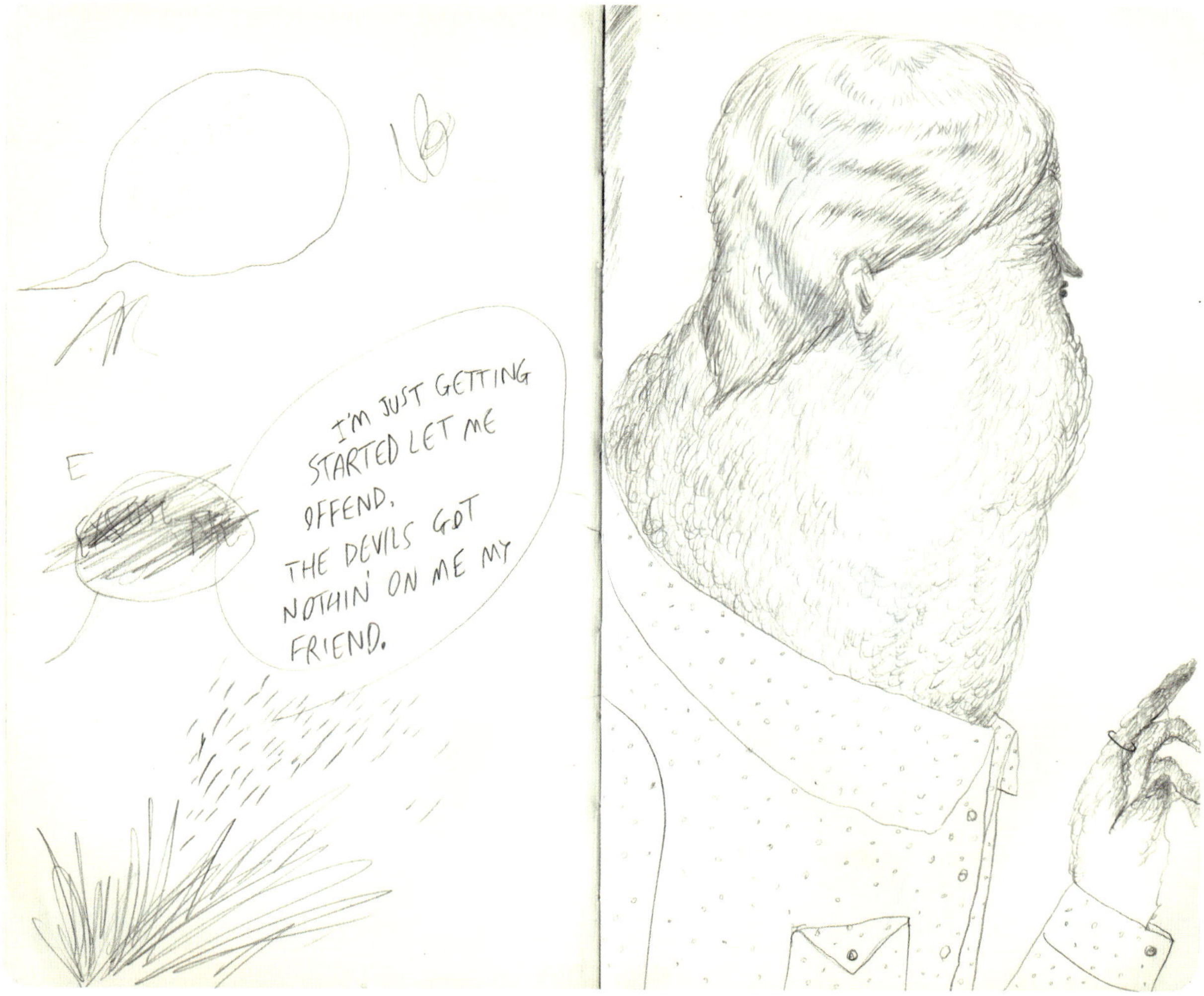

"I'M JUST GETTING STARTED LET ME OFFEND. THE DEVILS GOT NOTHIN' ON ME MY FRIEND."

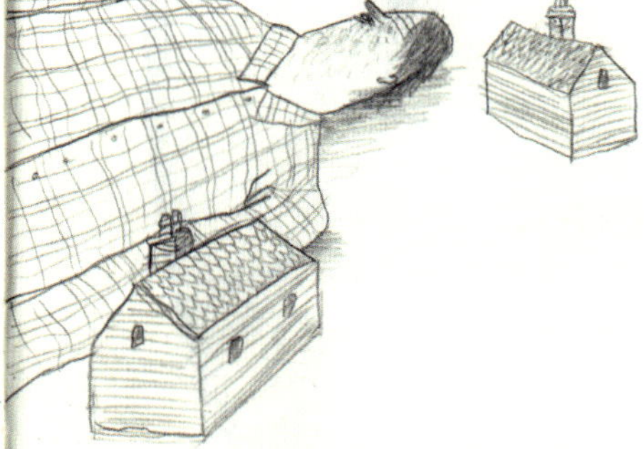

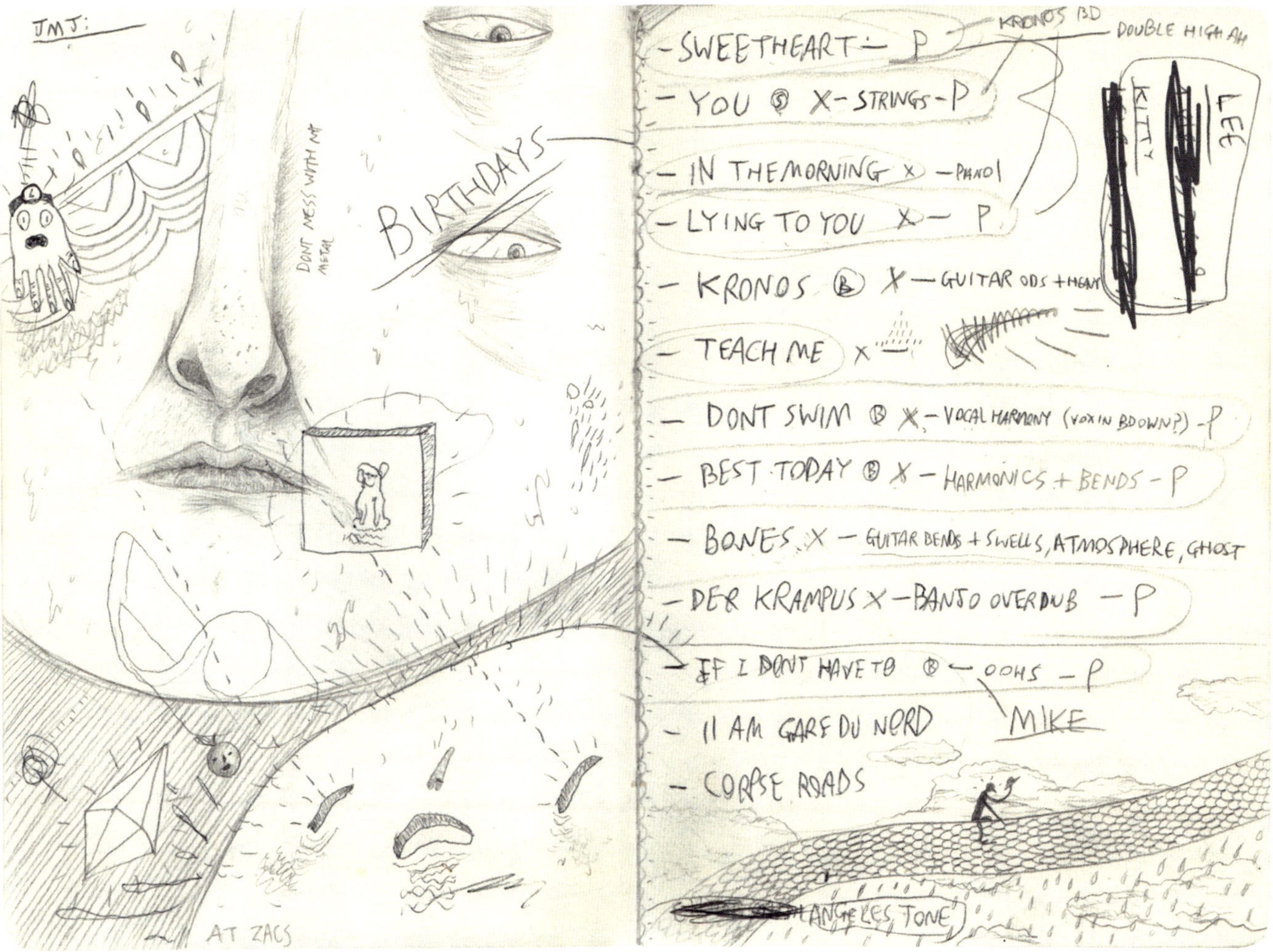

JMJ:

BIRTHDAYS

- SWEETHEART — P
- YOU & X-STRINGS — P   KRONOS BD   DOUBLE HIGH A#
- IN THE MORNING X — PIANO   KITTY LEE
- LYING TO YOU X — P
- KRONOS Ⓑ X — GUITAR ODS + HEAVY
- TEACH ME X
- DONT SWIM Ⓑ X — VOCAL HARMONY (VOX IN B DOWN?) — P
- BEST TODAY Ⓑ X — HARMONICS + BENDS — P
- BONES X — GUITAR BENDS + SWELLS, ATMOSPHERE, GHOST
- DER KRAMPUS X — BANJO OVERDUB — P
- IF I DONT HAVE TO Ⓑ — OOHS — P
- I AM GARE DU NORD — MIKE
- CORPSE ROADS

AT ZACS

LANGELES TONE

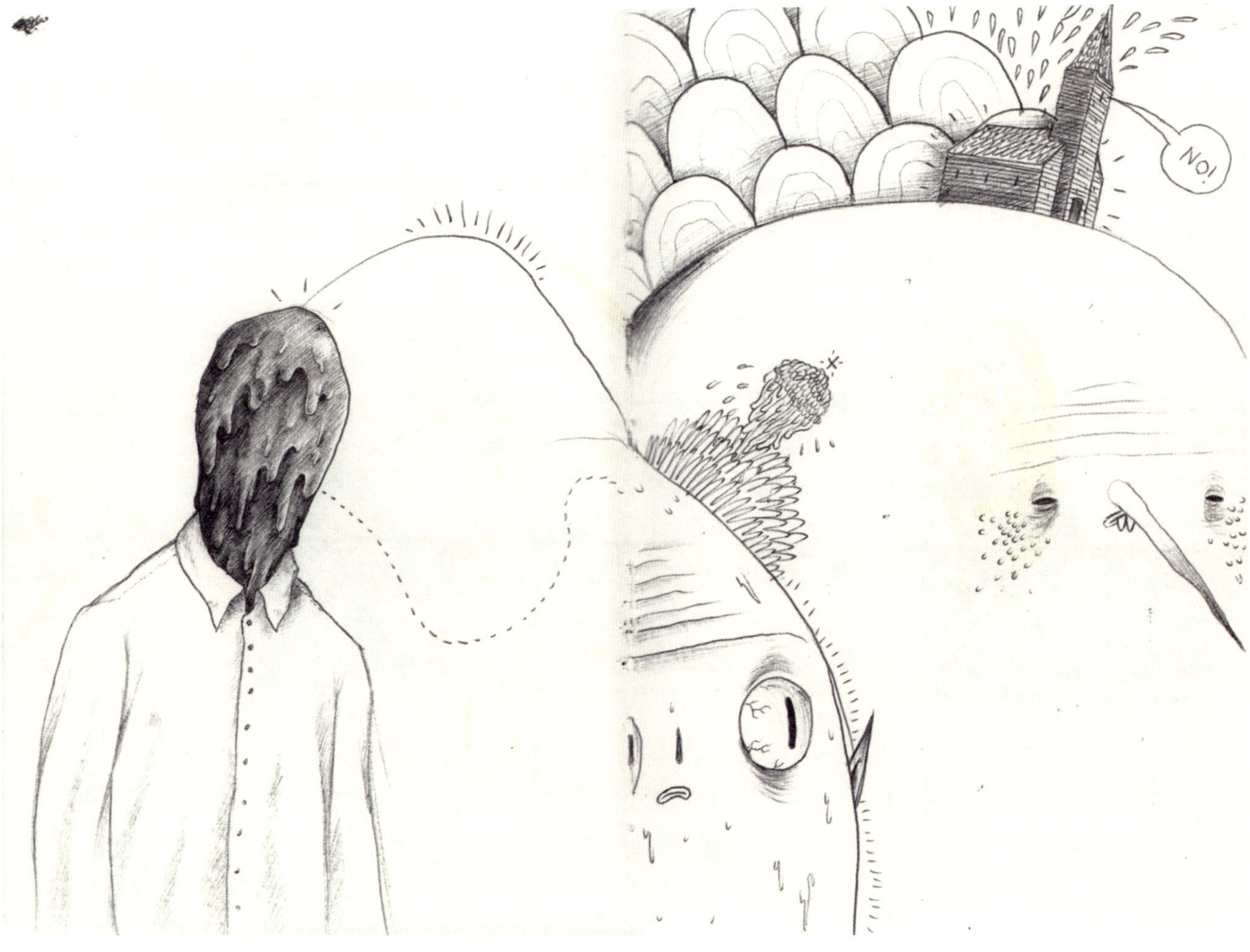

NO!

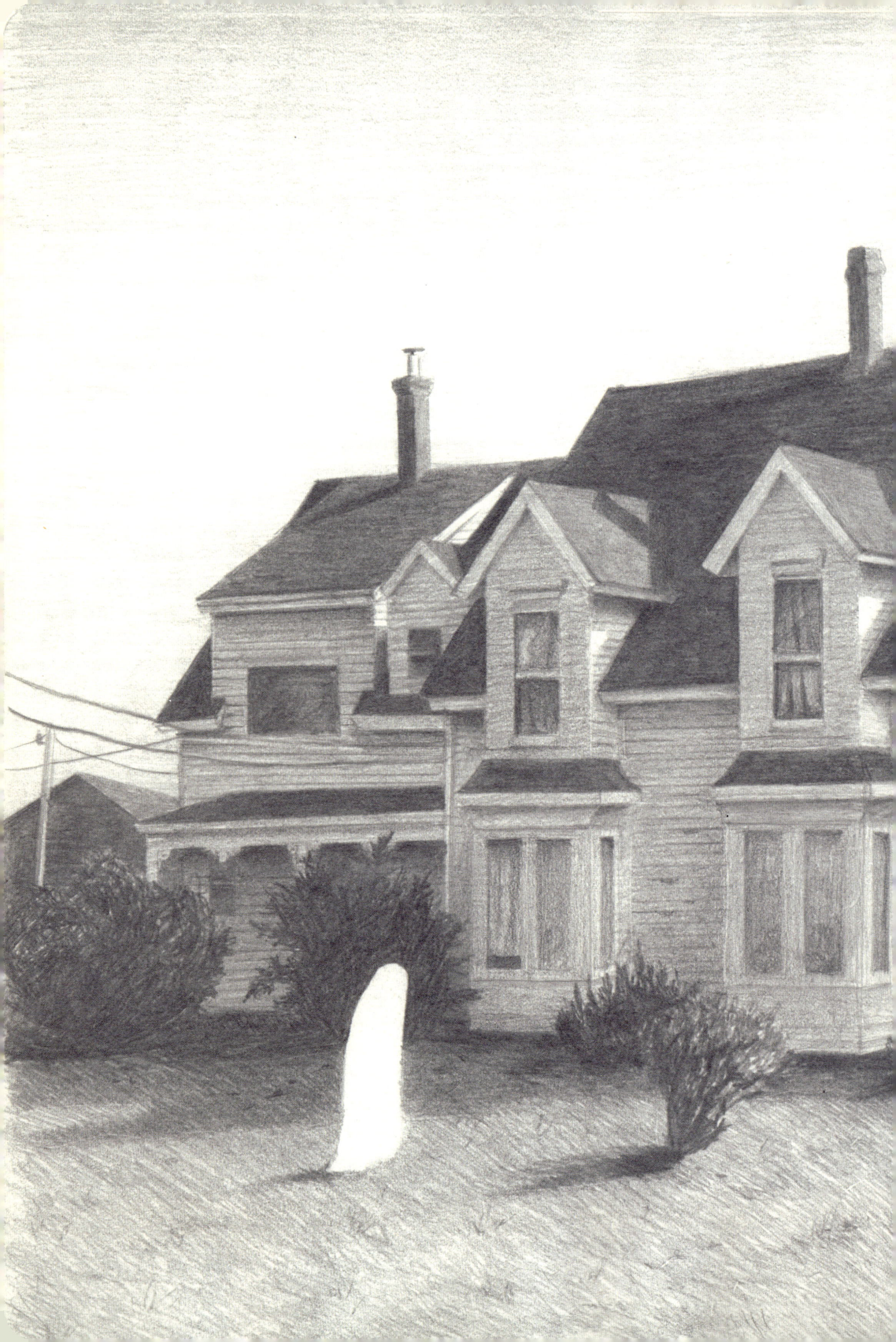

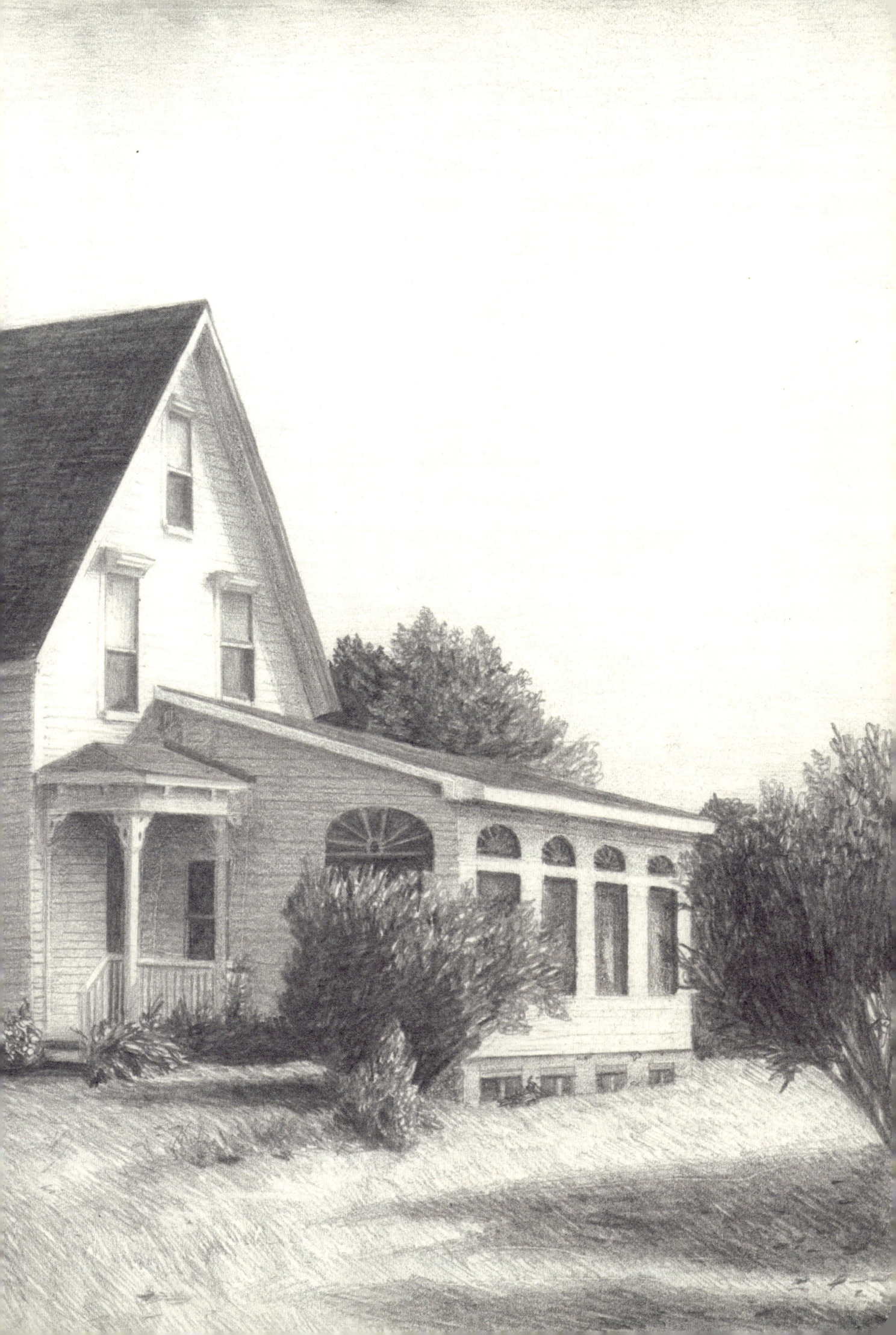

ARE WE NOT BETTER THAN LIQUID & BONE

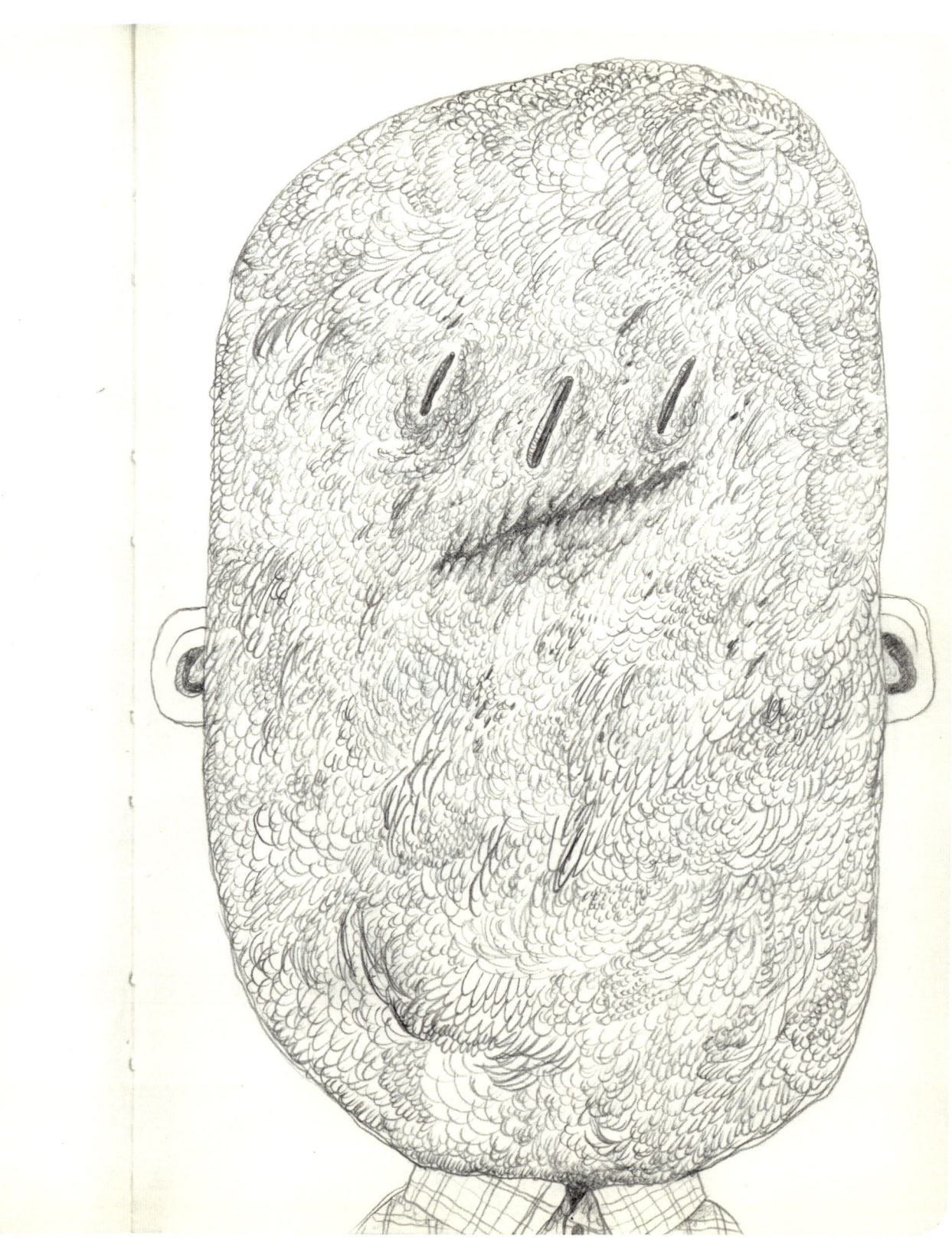

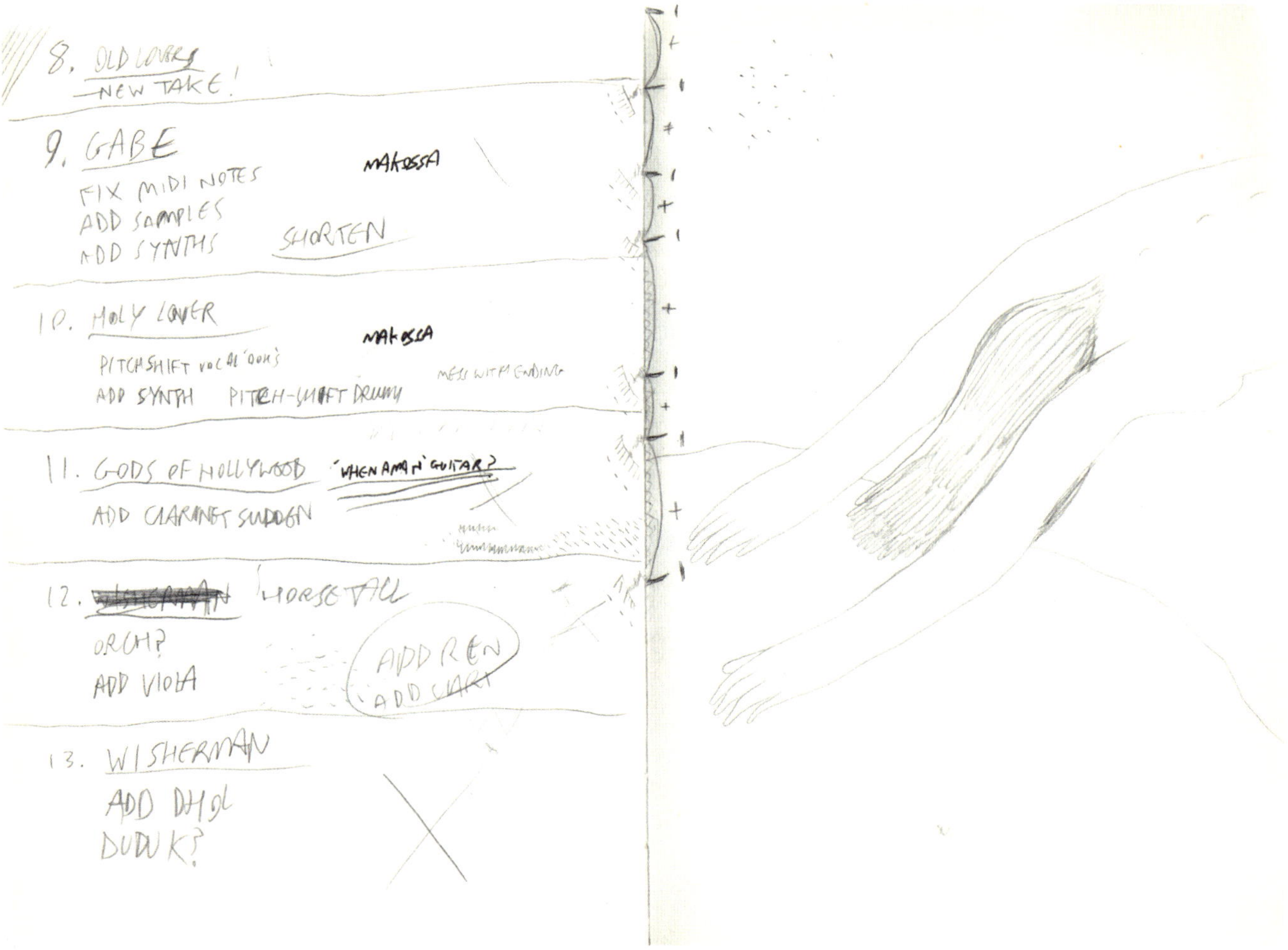

8. OLD LOVERS
   NEW TAKE!

9. GABE
   FIX MIDI NOTES   MAKOSSA
   ADD SAMPLES
   ADD SYNTHS   SHORTEN

10. HOLY LOVER   MAKOSSA
    PITCHSHIFT VOCAL 'OOH'S   MESS WITH ENDING
    ADD SYNTH   PITCH-SHIFT DRUMS

11. GODS OF HOLLYWOOD 'WHEN AM I N' GUITAR?'
    ADD CLARINET SUDDEN

12. ~~LILIAN~~ HORSETAIL
    ORCH?
    ADD VIOLA   ADD REN
                      ADD CLART

13. WISHERMAN
    ADD DHOL
    DUDUK?

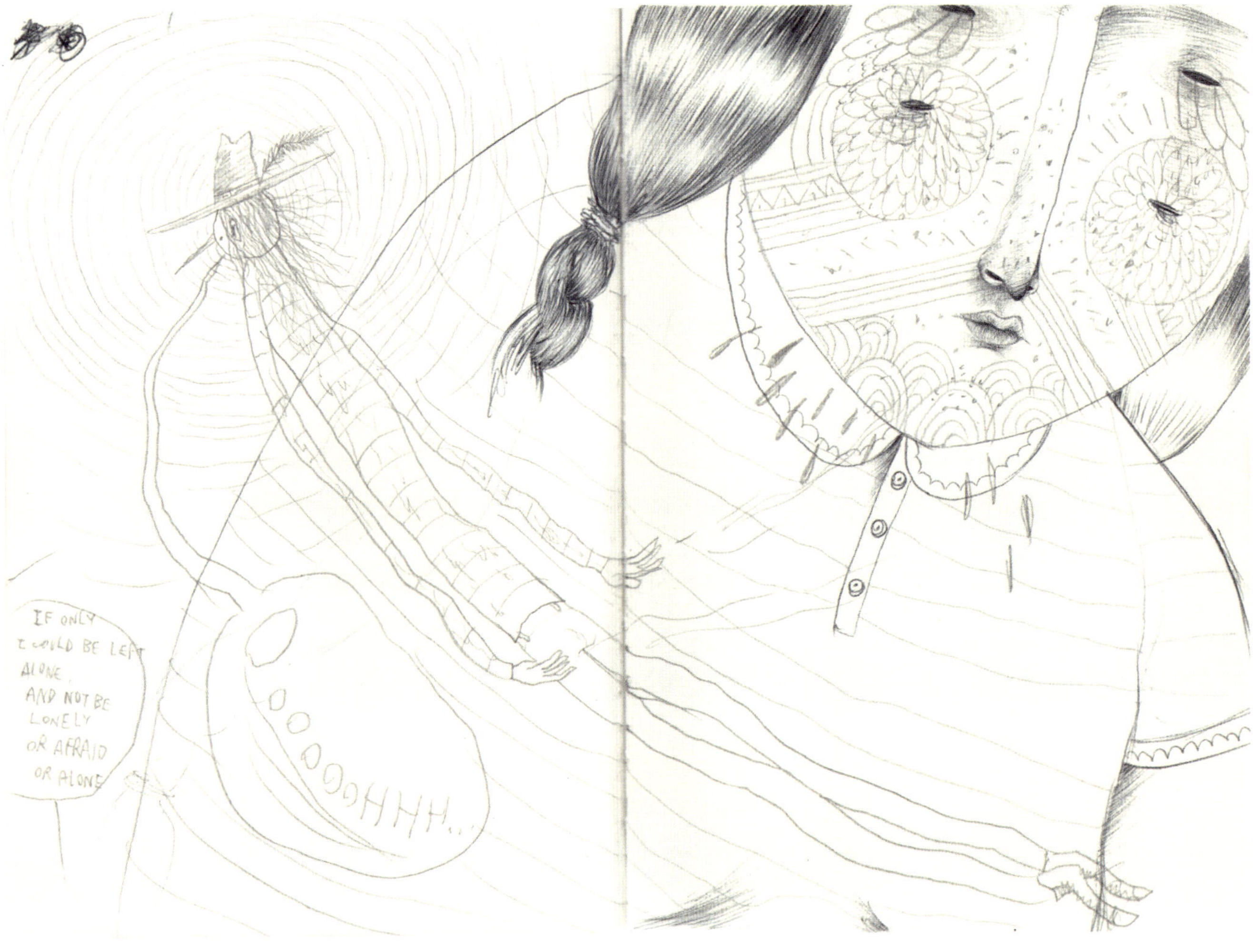

If only I could be left alone. And not be lonely or afraid or alone.

OOOOOHHH...

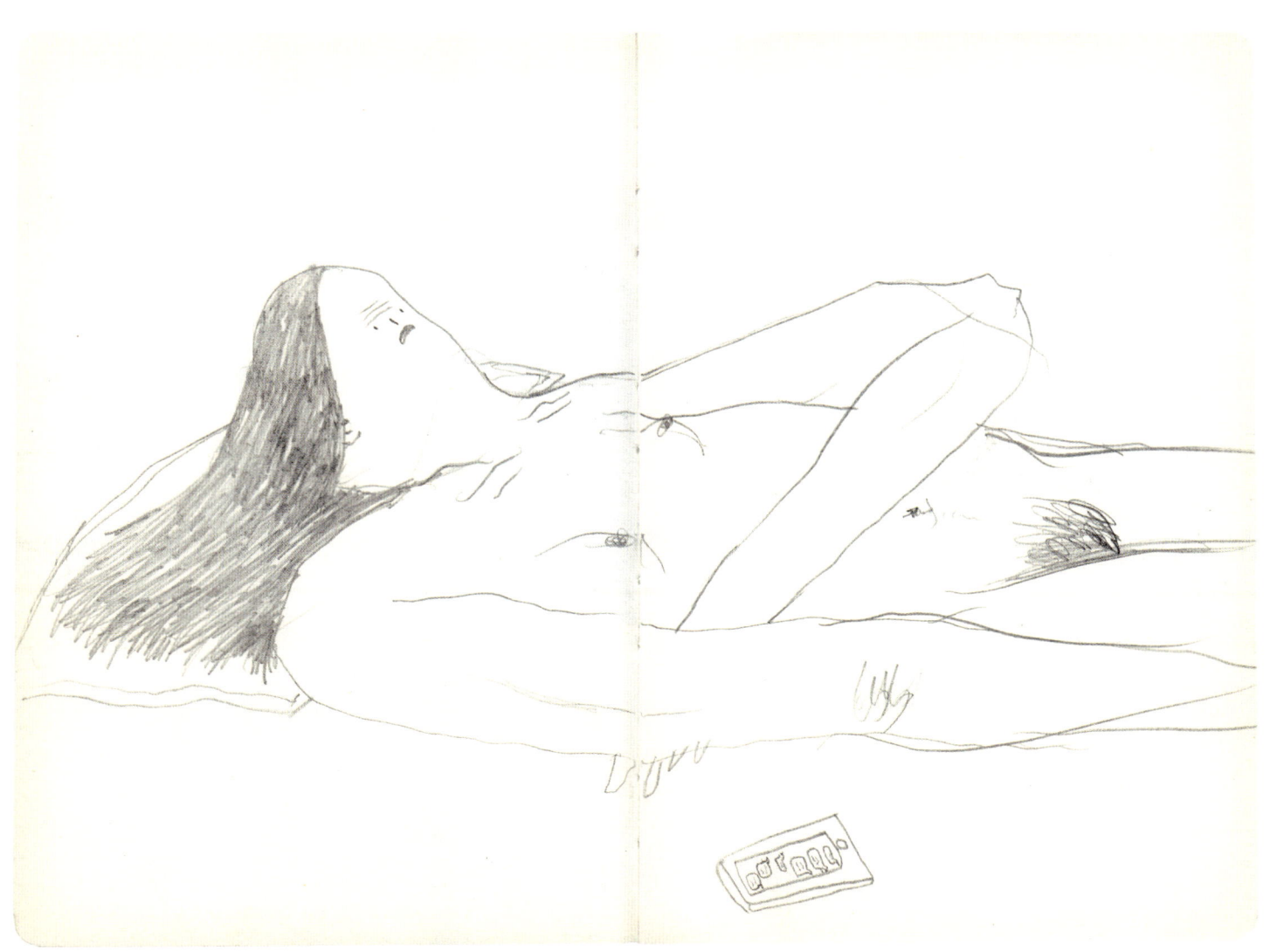

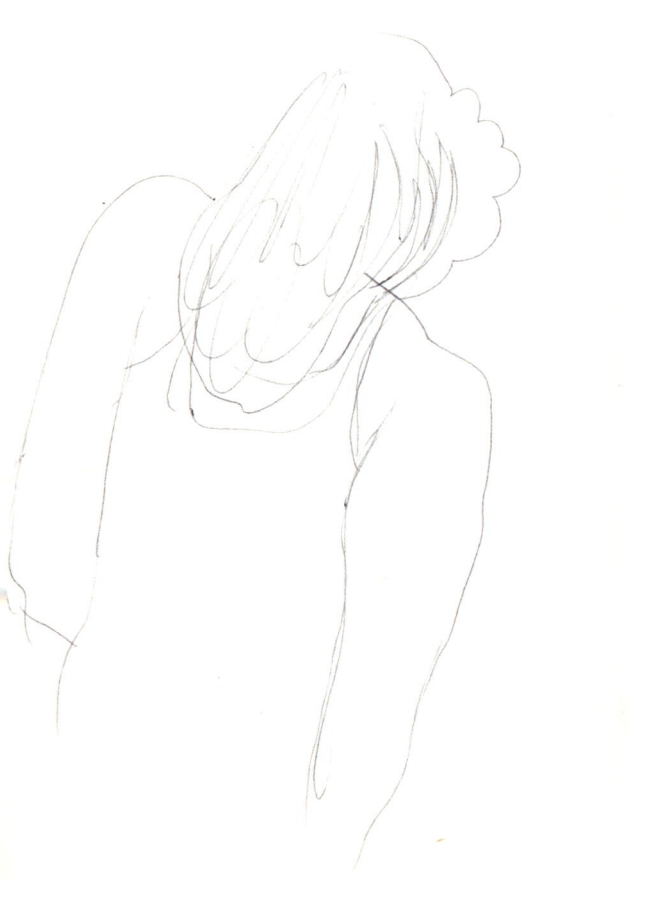
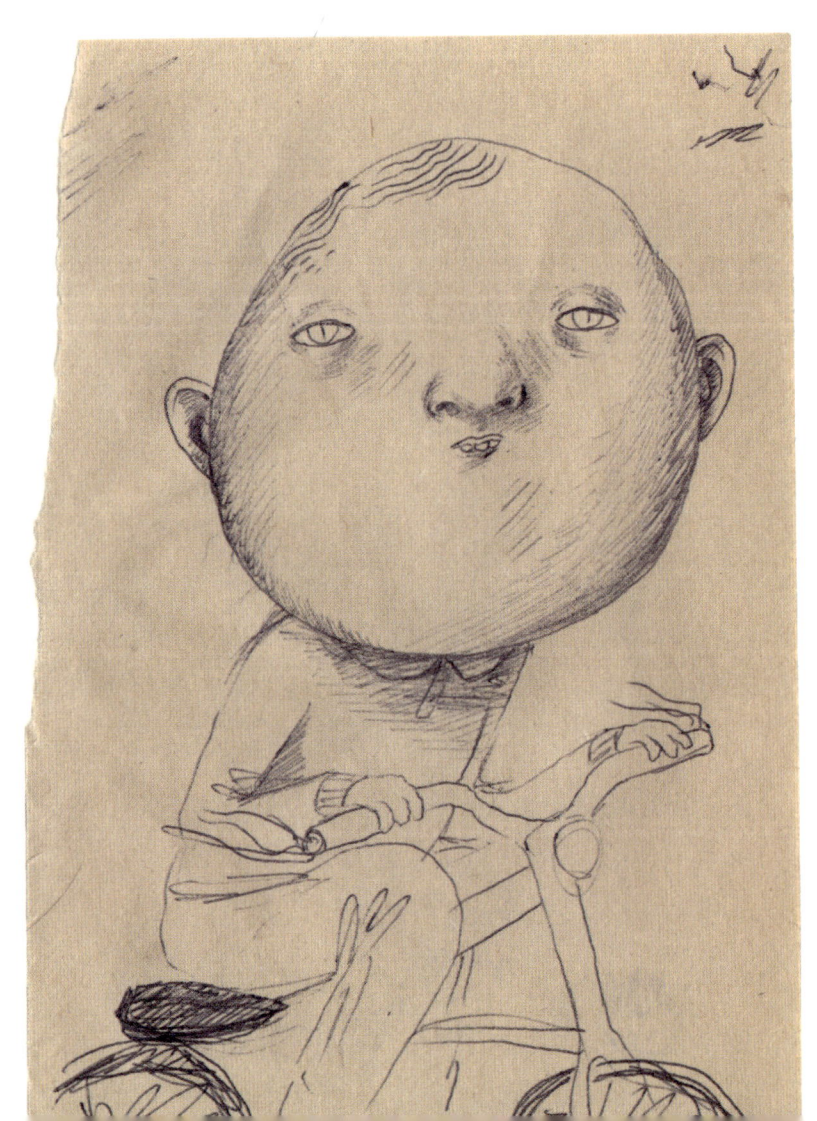

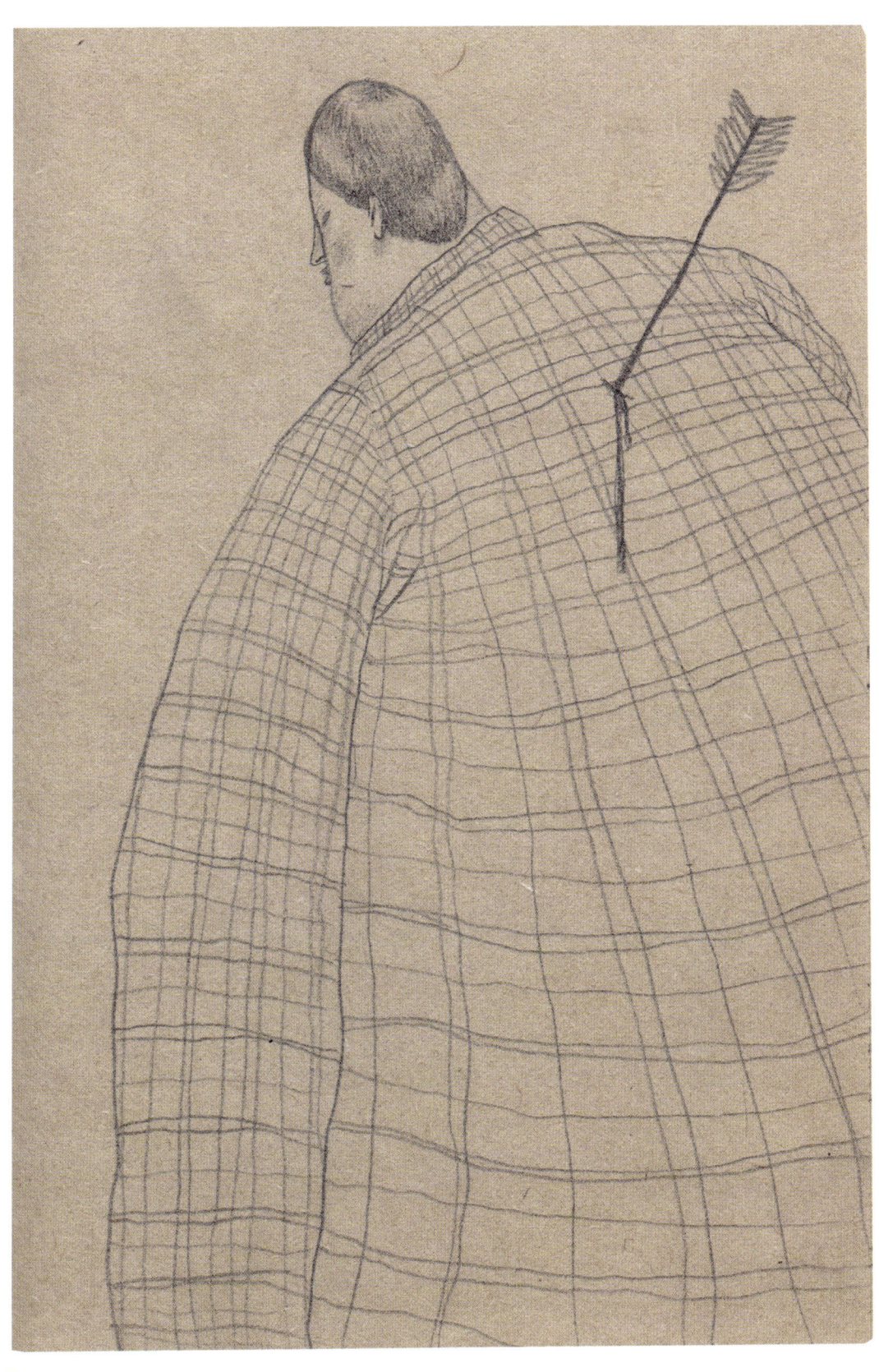

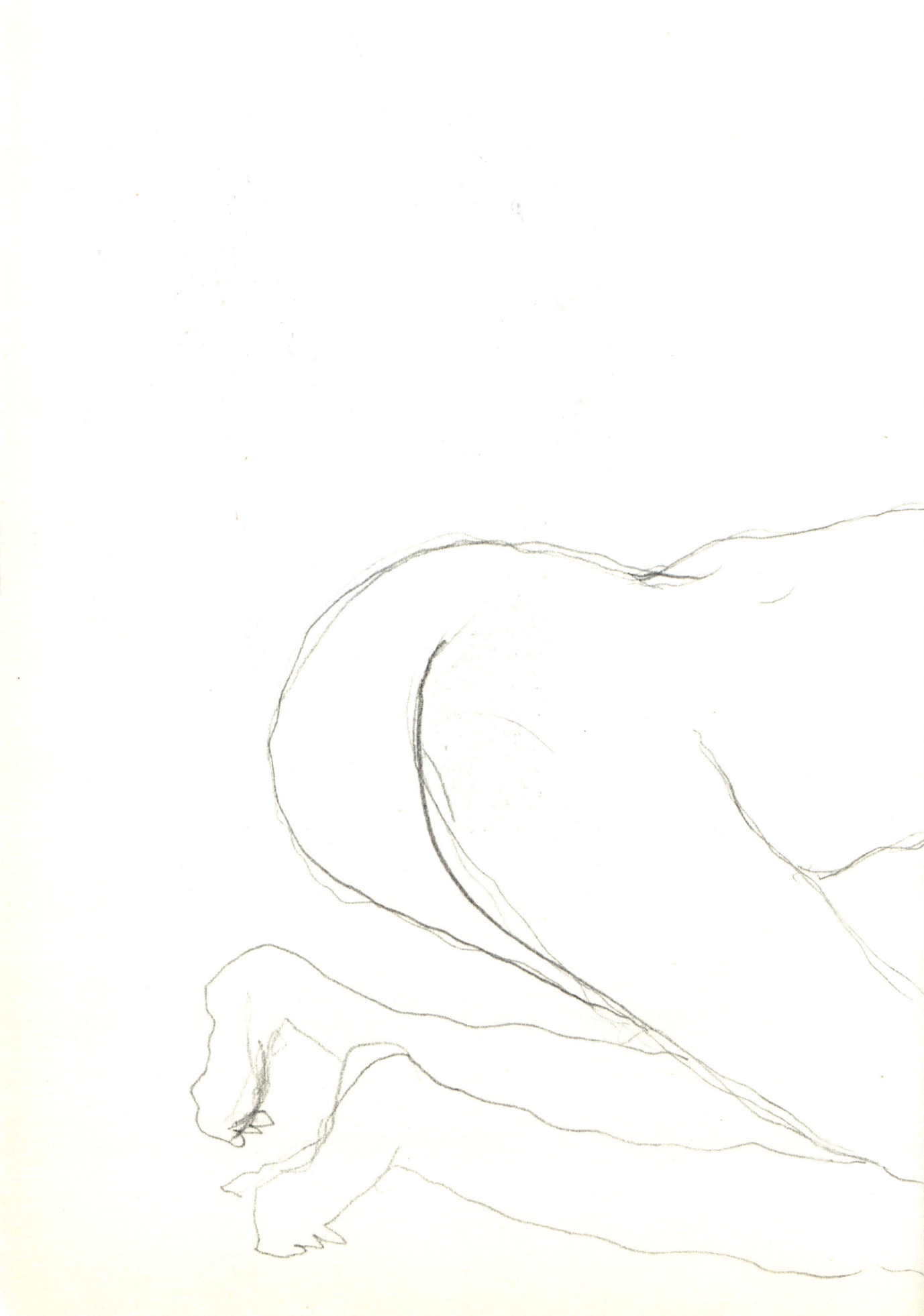

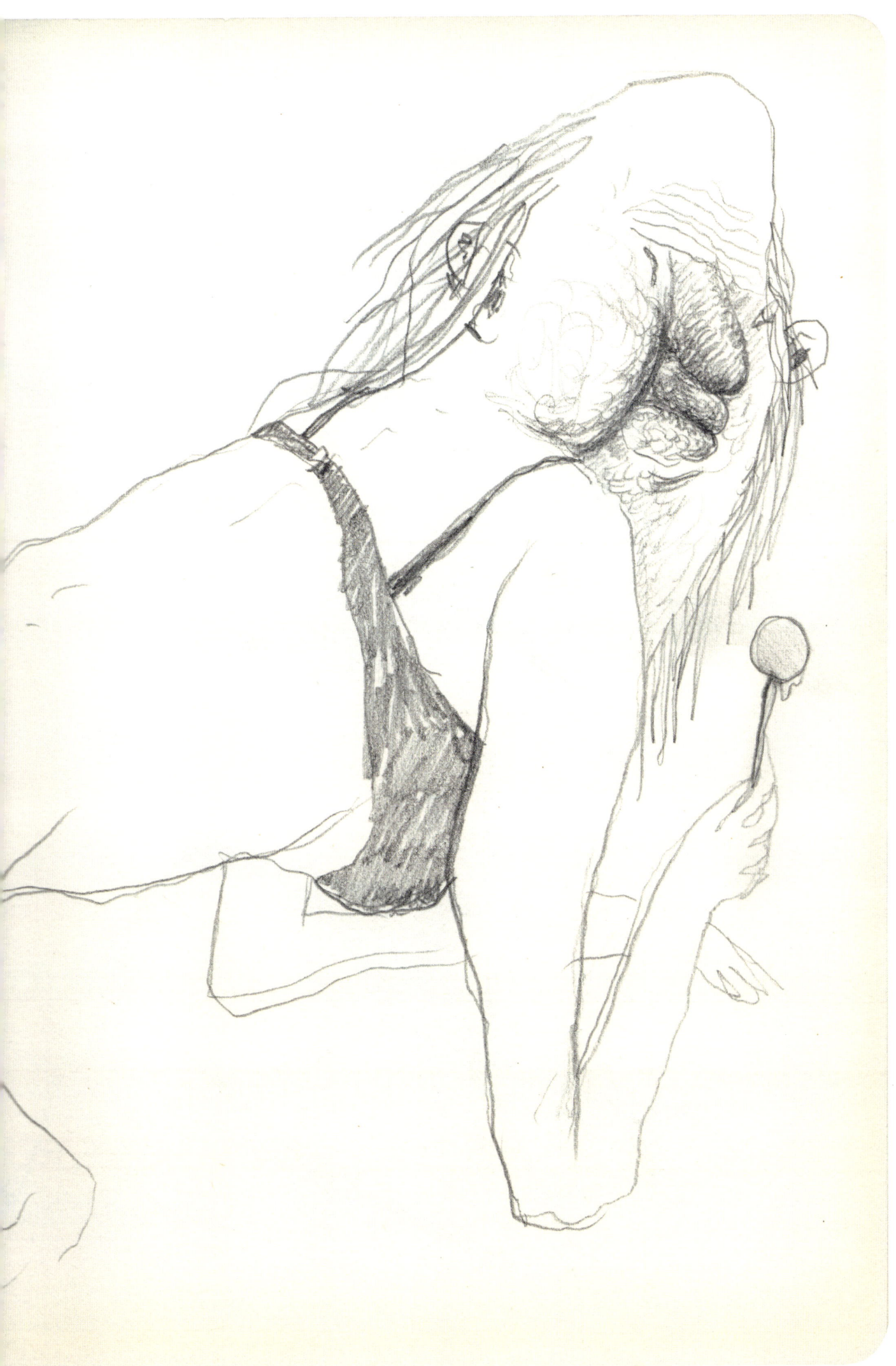

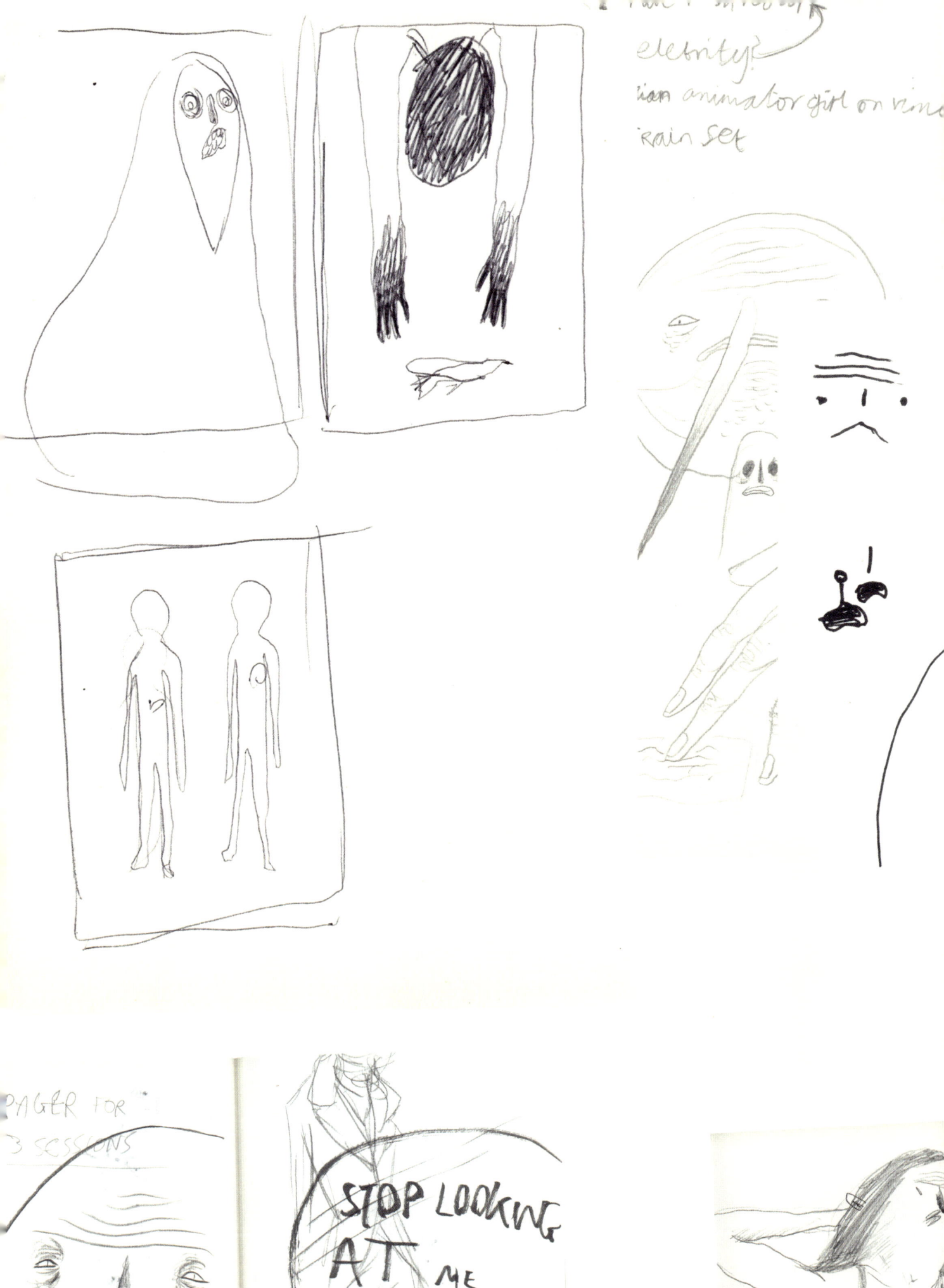

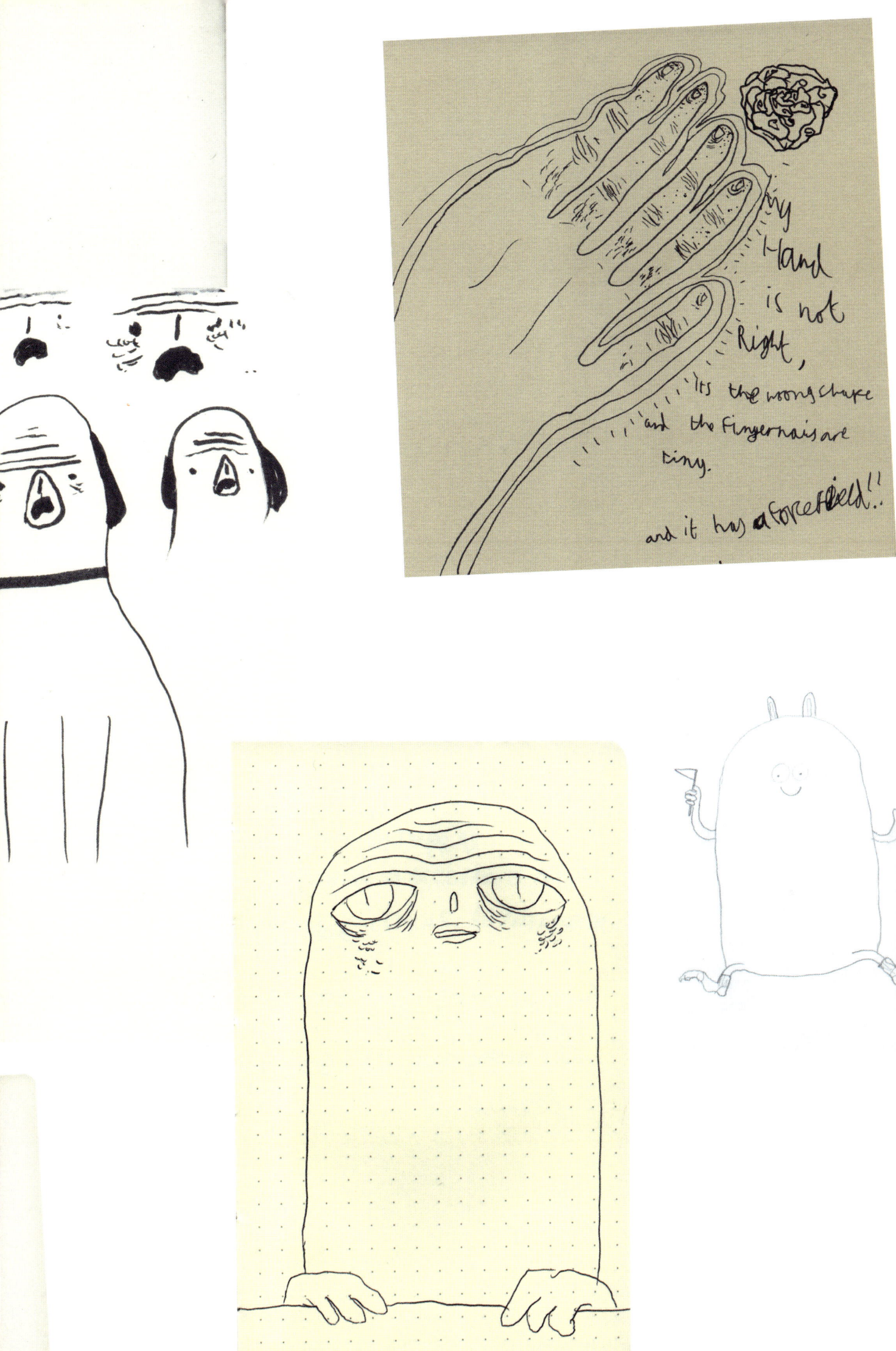

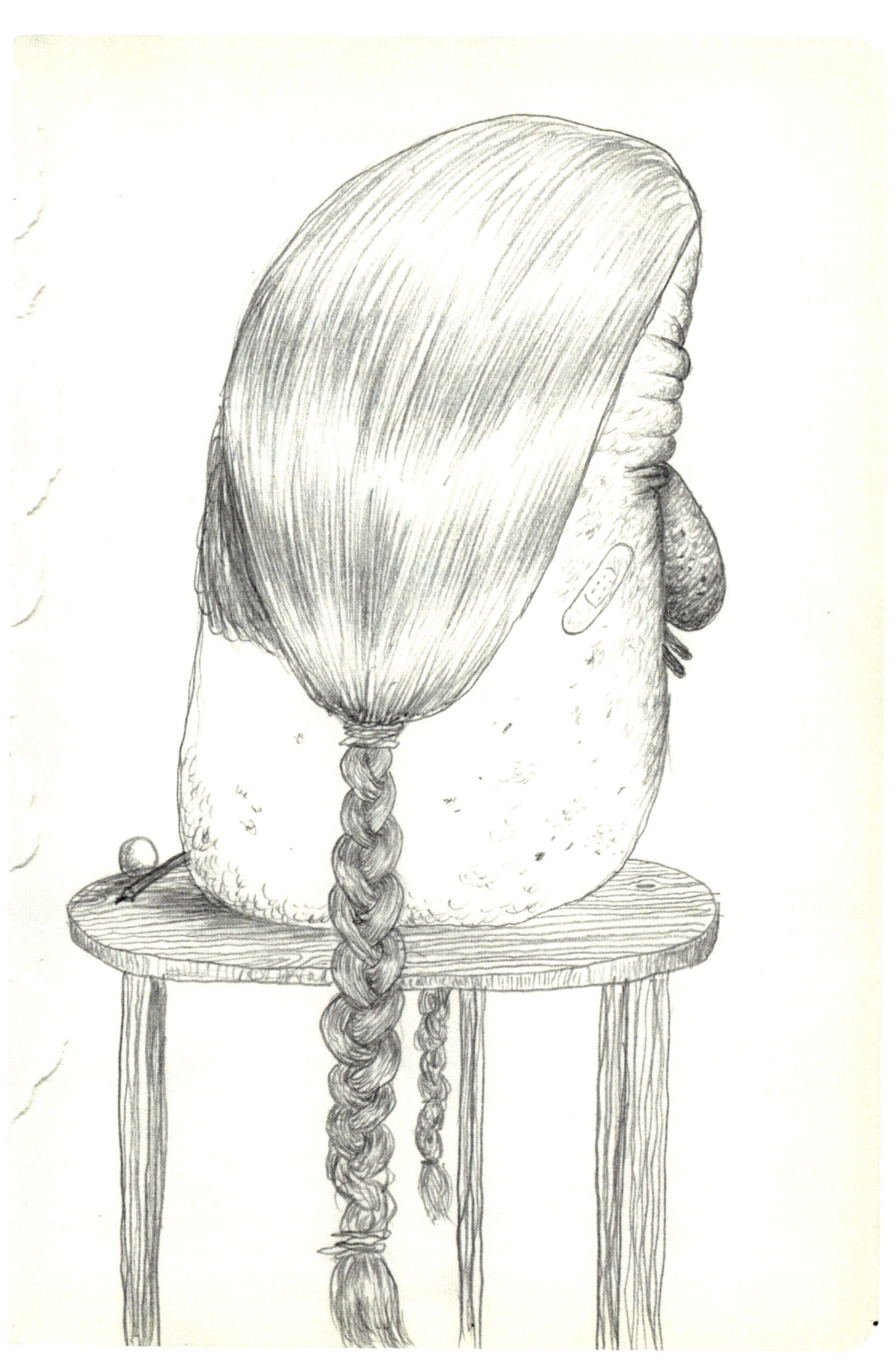

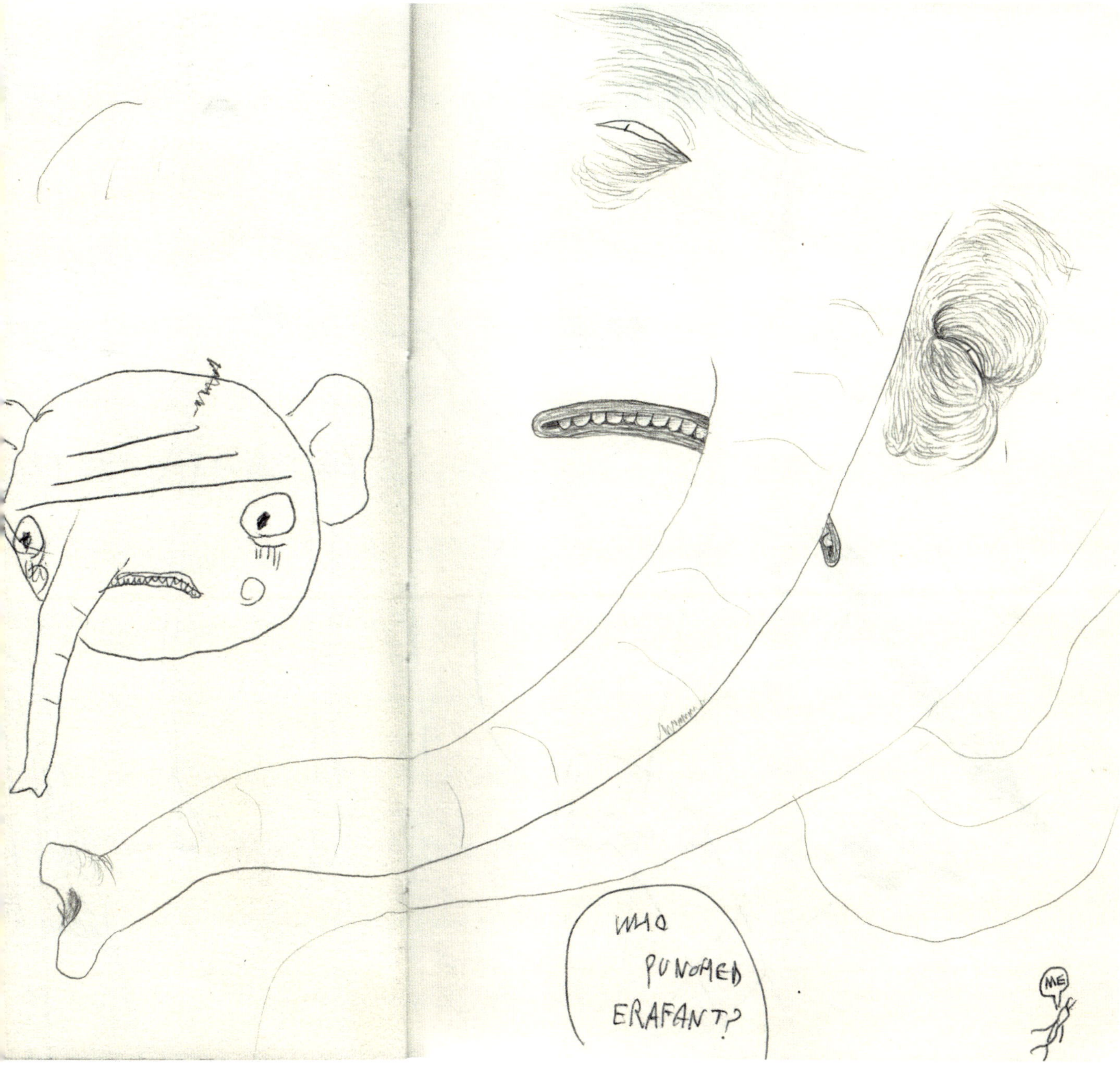

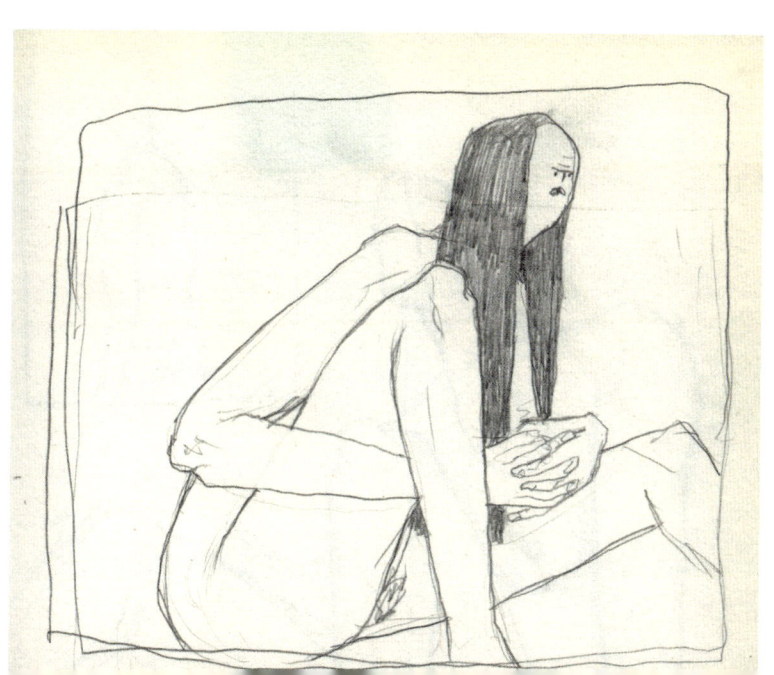

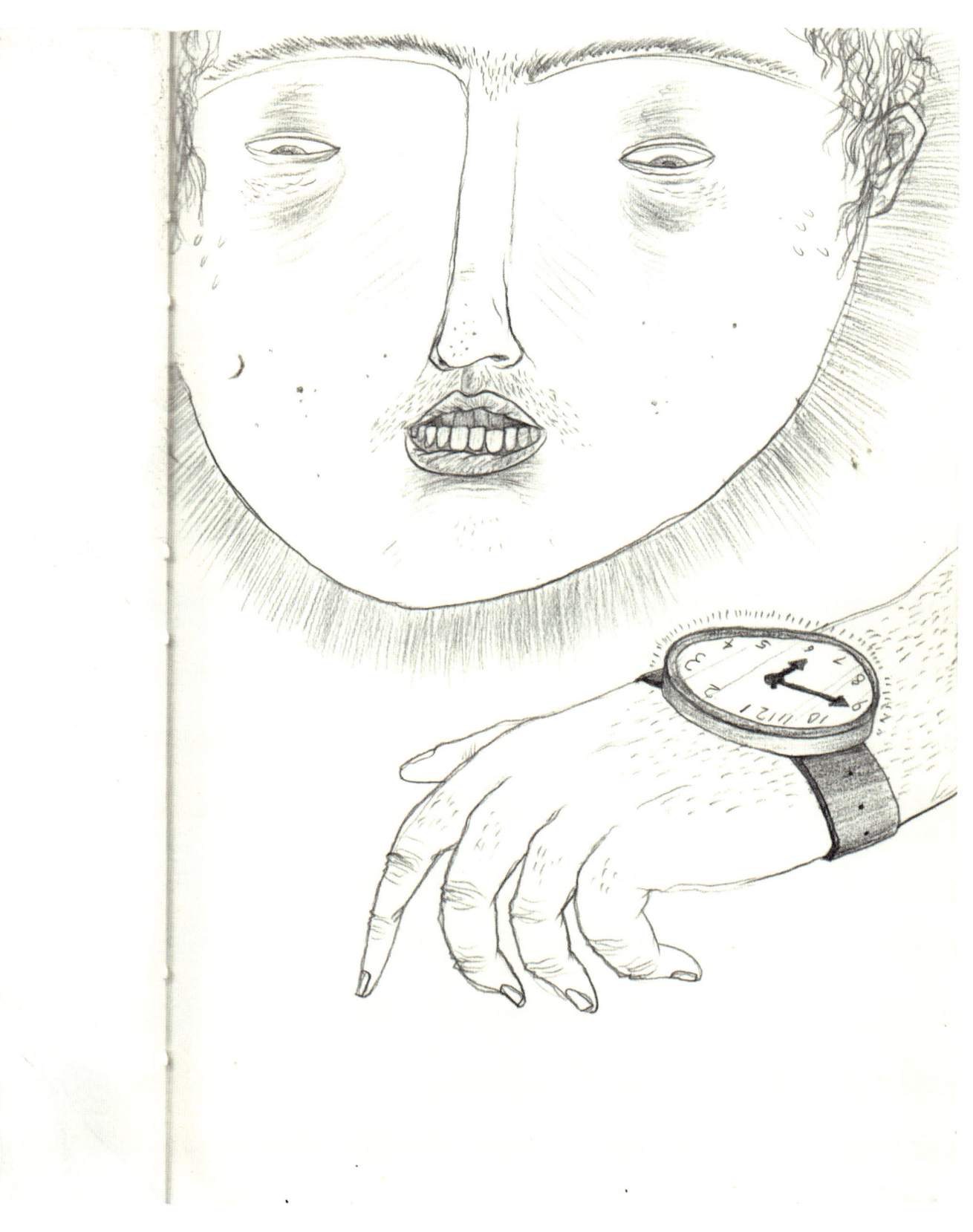

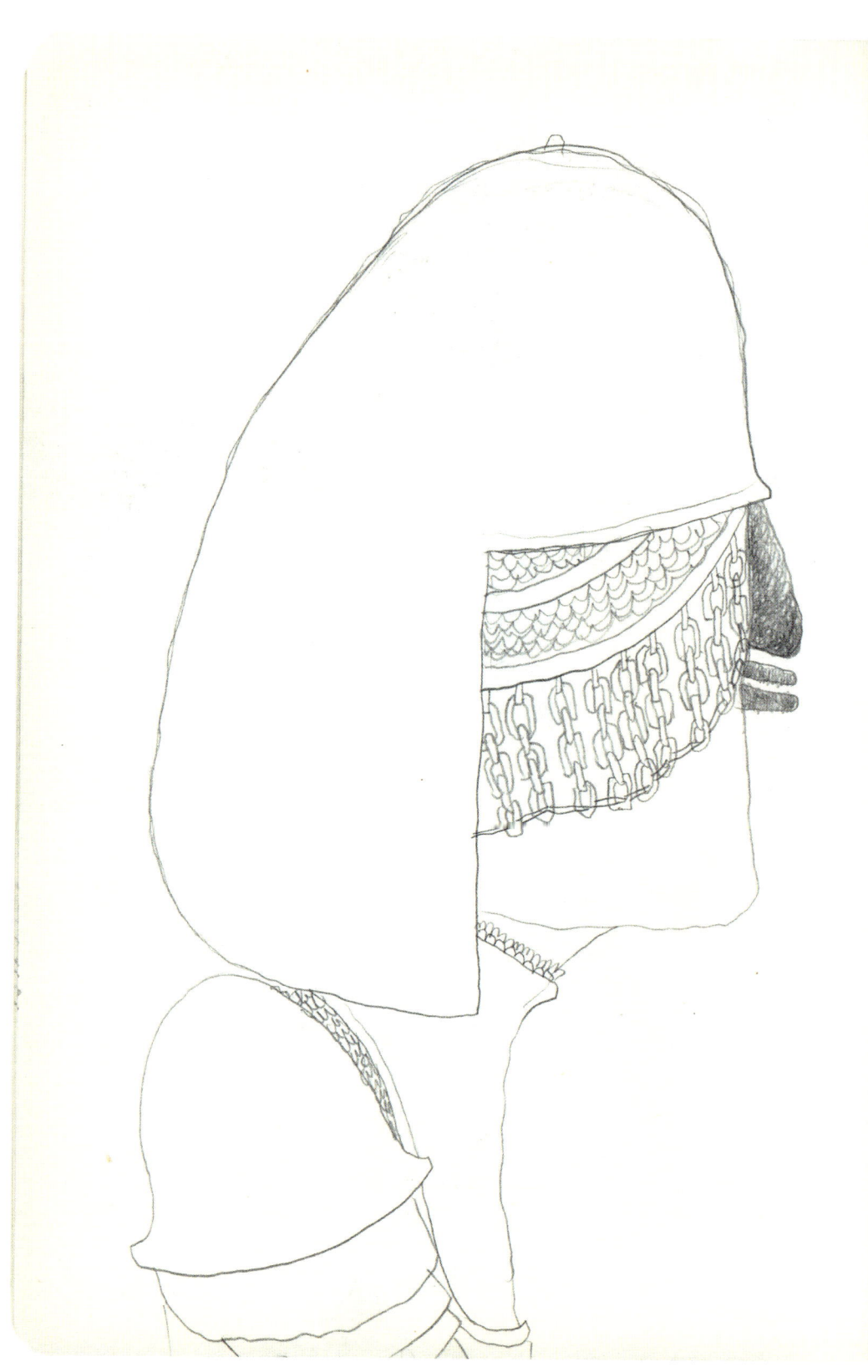

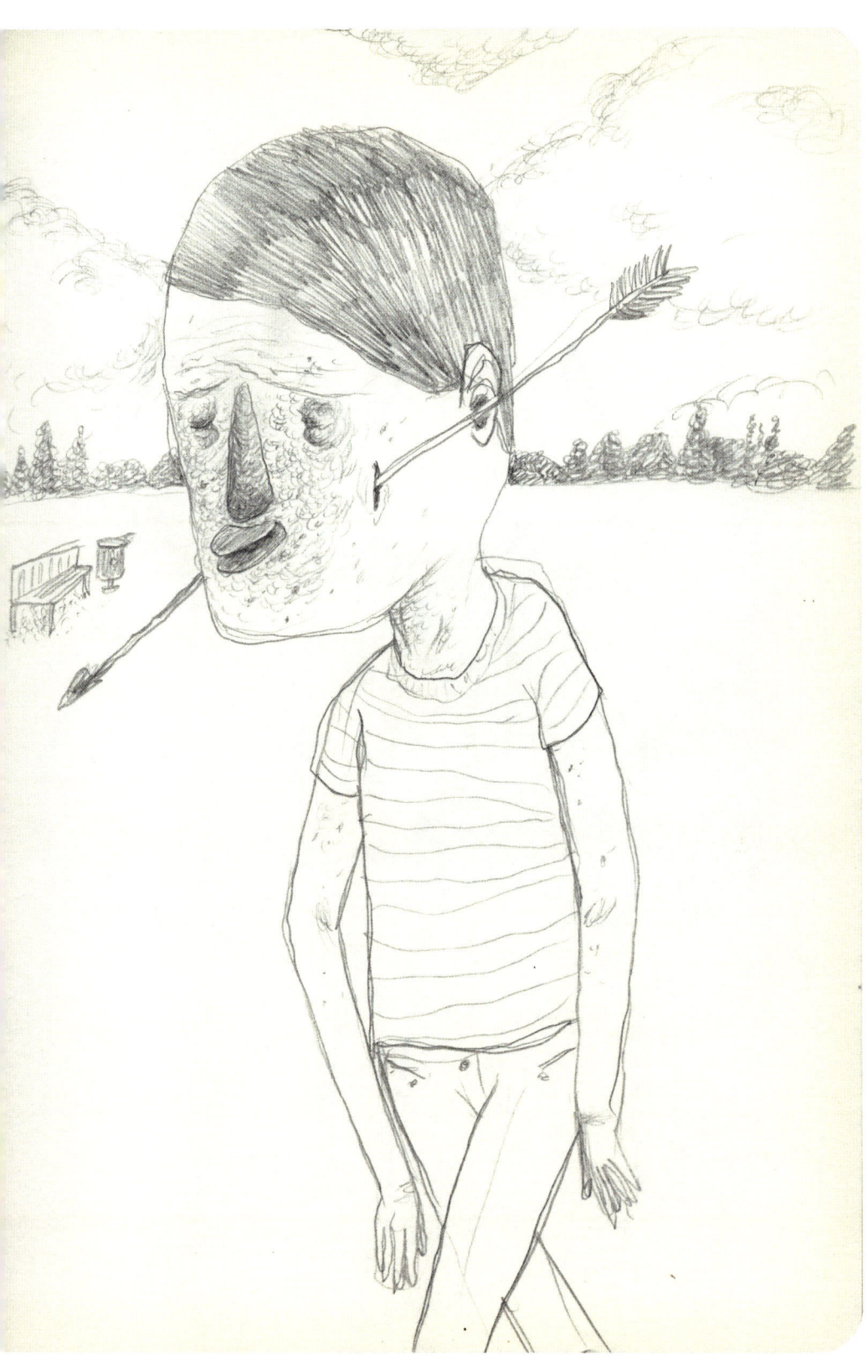

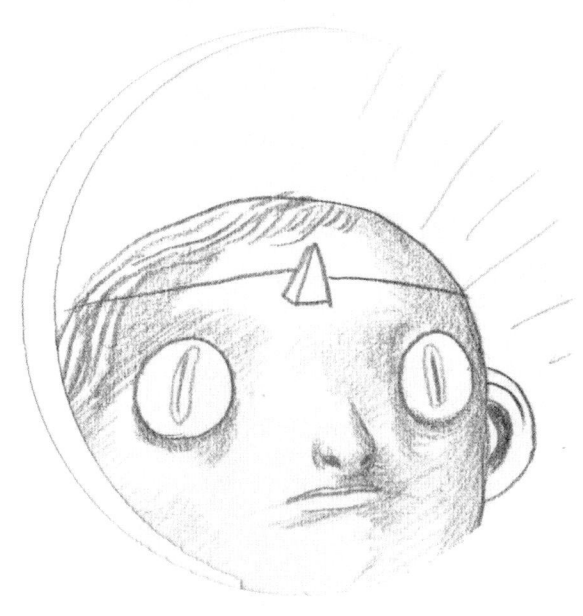

HONEY, YOU LOOK RIDICULOUS IN THAT HAT.

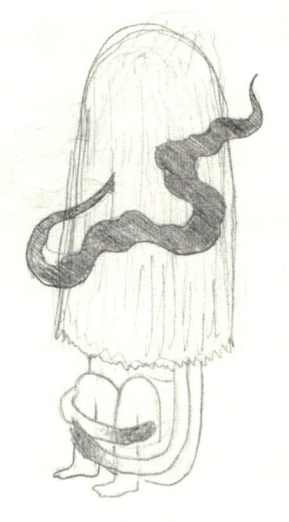
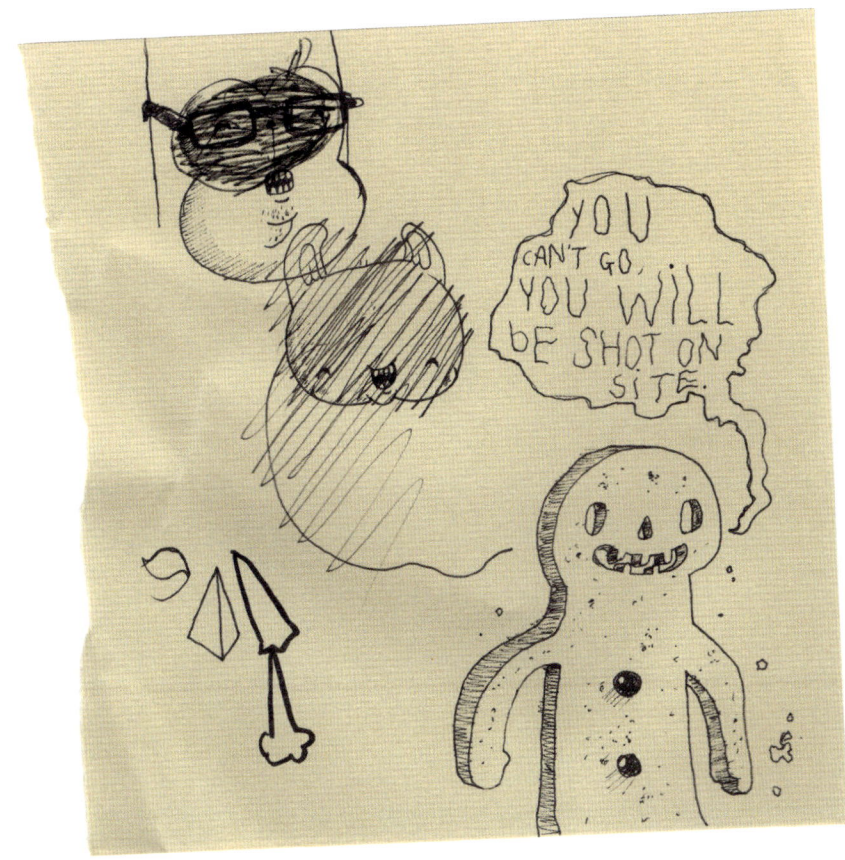

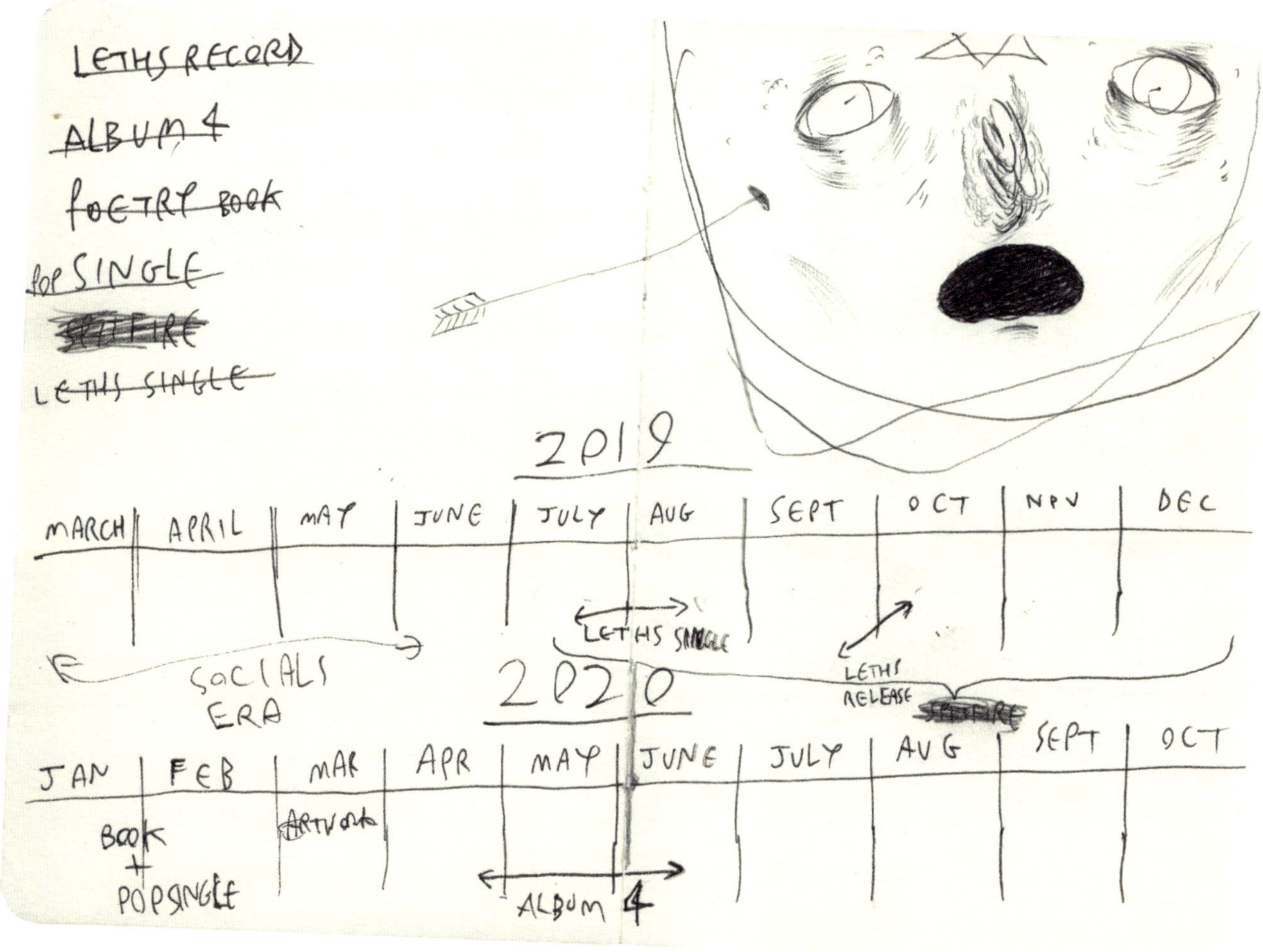

LETHS RECORD
~~ALBUM 4~~
~~POETRY BOOK~~
~~POP SINGLE~~
~~SPITFIRE~~
LETHS SINGLE

				2019					
MARCH	APRIL	MAY	JUNE	JULY	AUG	SEPT	OCT	NOV	DEC
	SOCIALS ERA			LETHS SINGLE		LETHS RELEASE ~~SPITFIRE~~			

				2020					
JAN	FEB	MAR	APR	MAY	JUNE	JULY	AUG	SEPT	OCT
BOOK + POP SINGLE		~~ARTWORK~~		ALBUM 4					

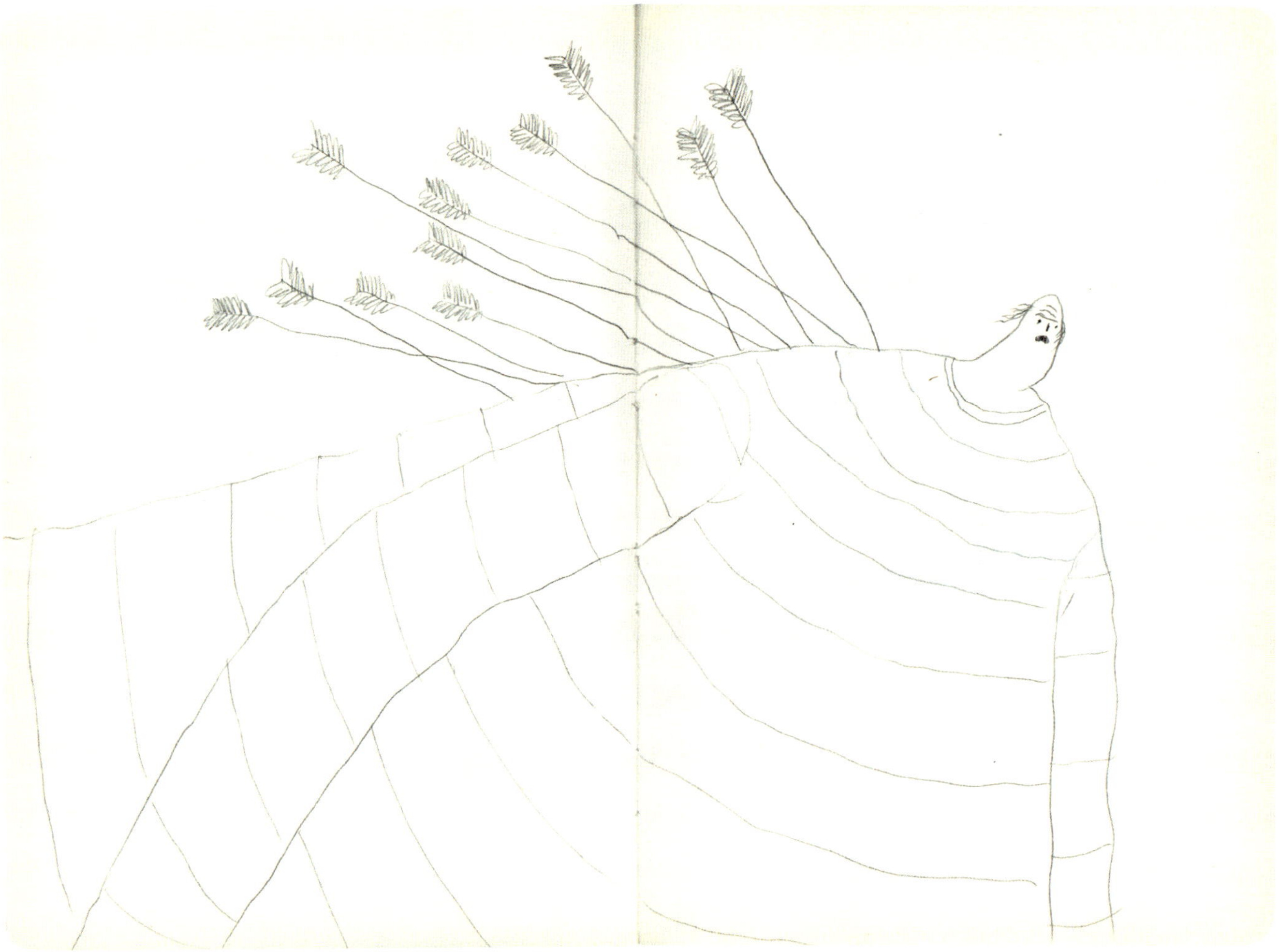

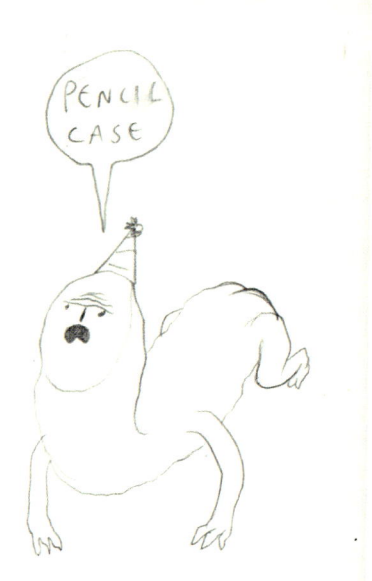

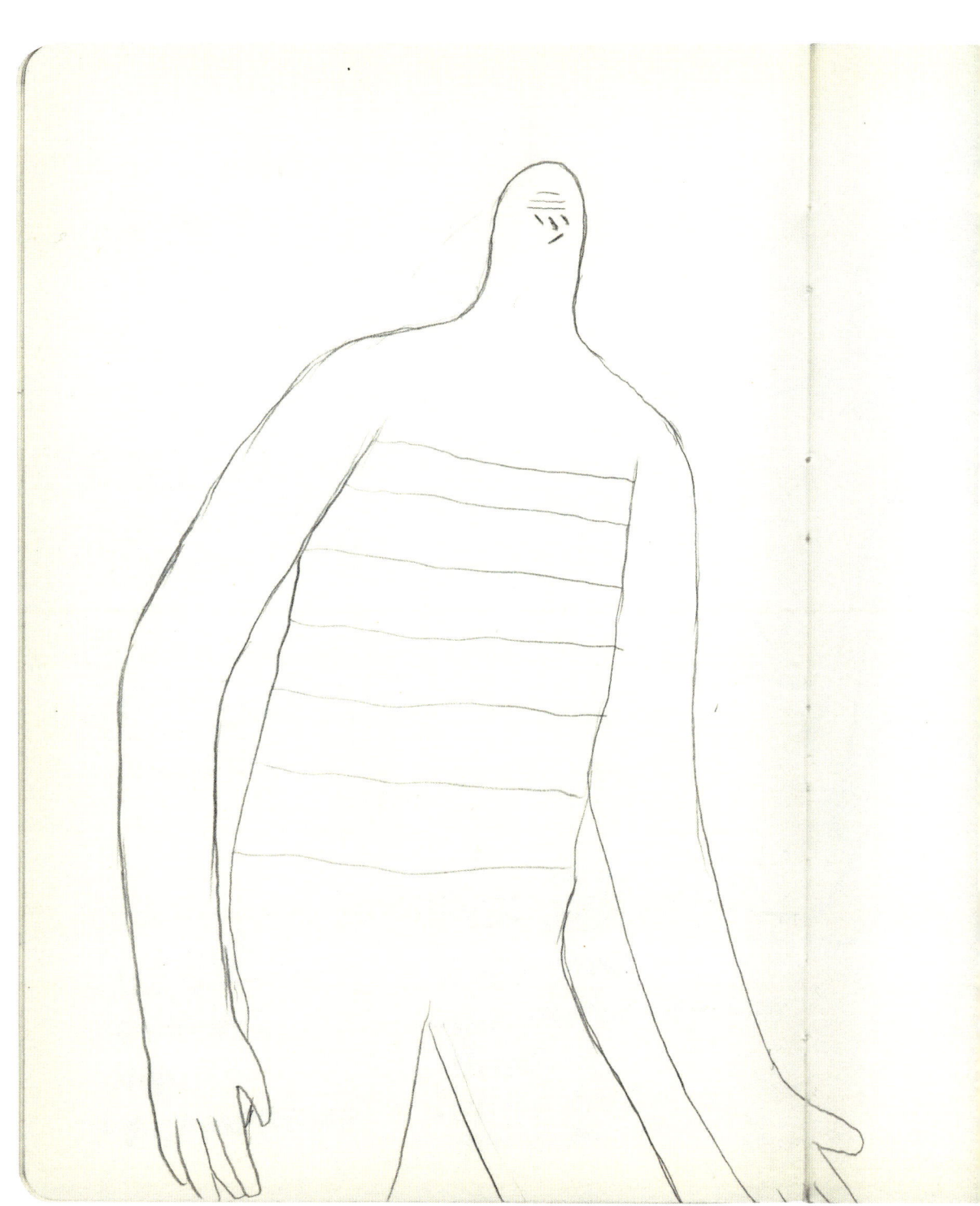

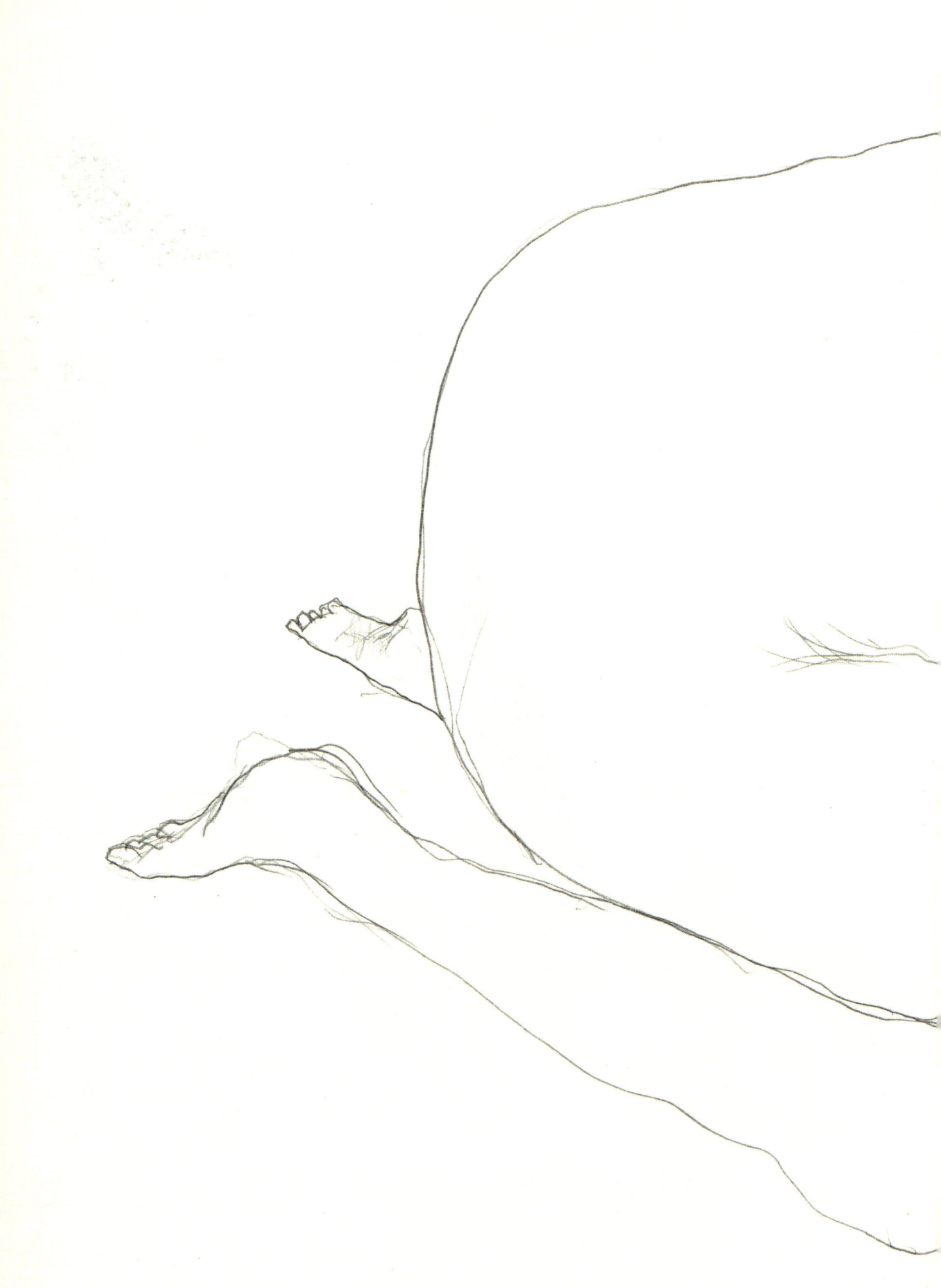

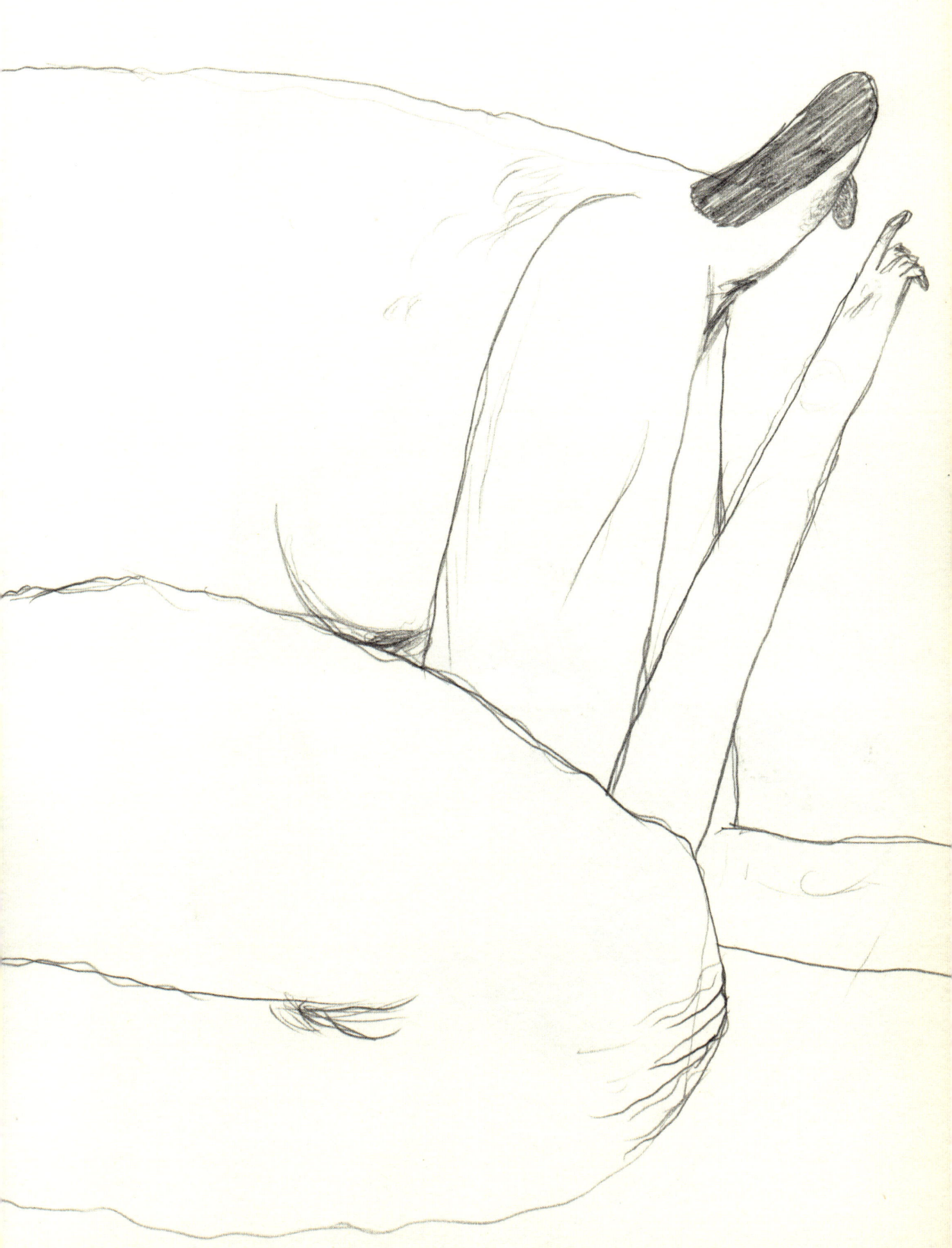

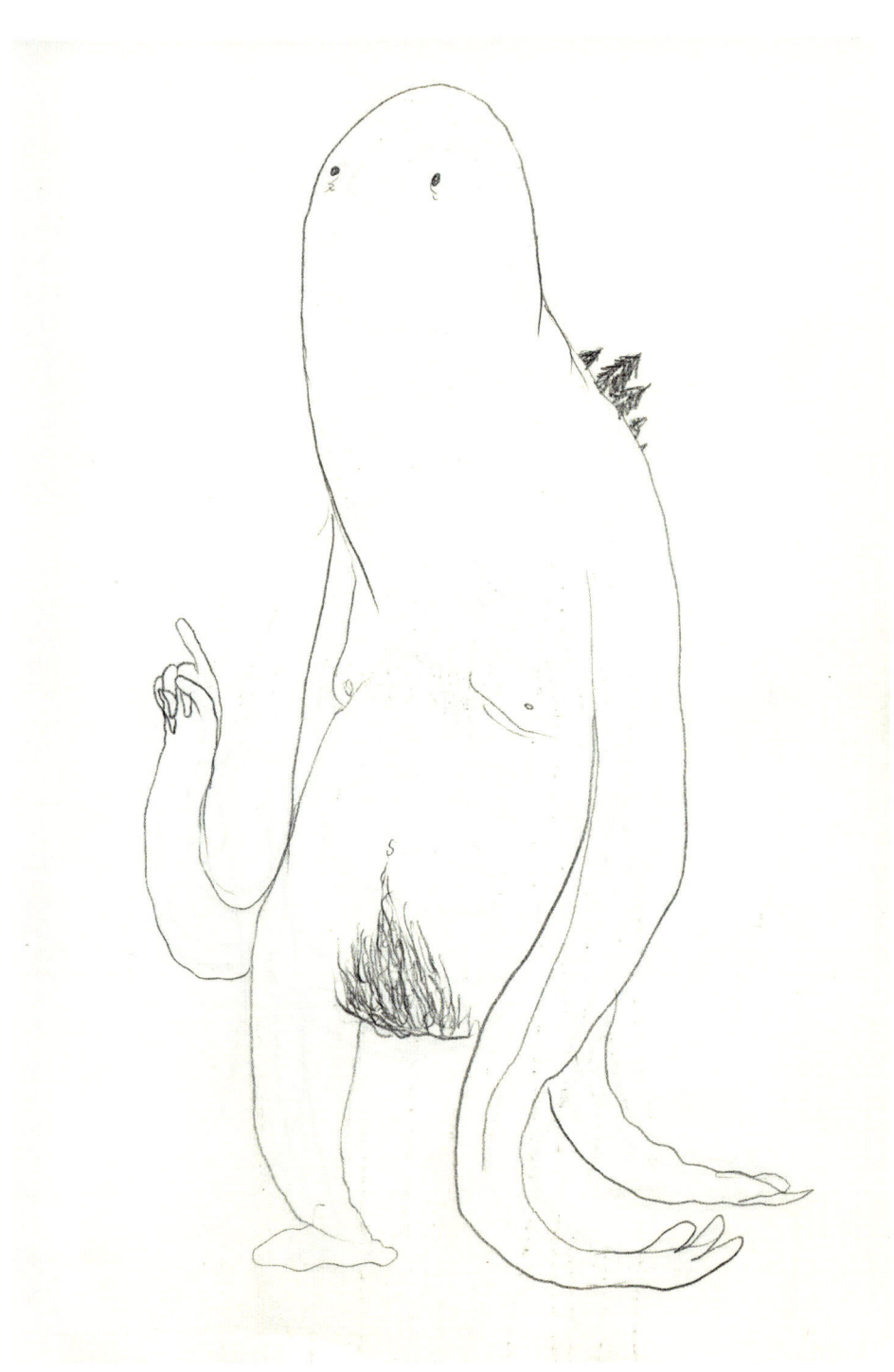

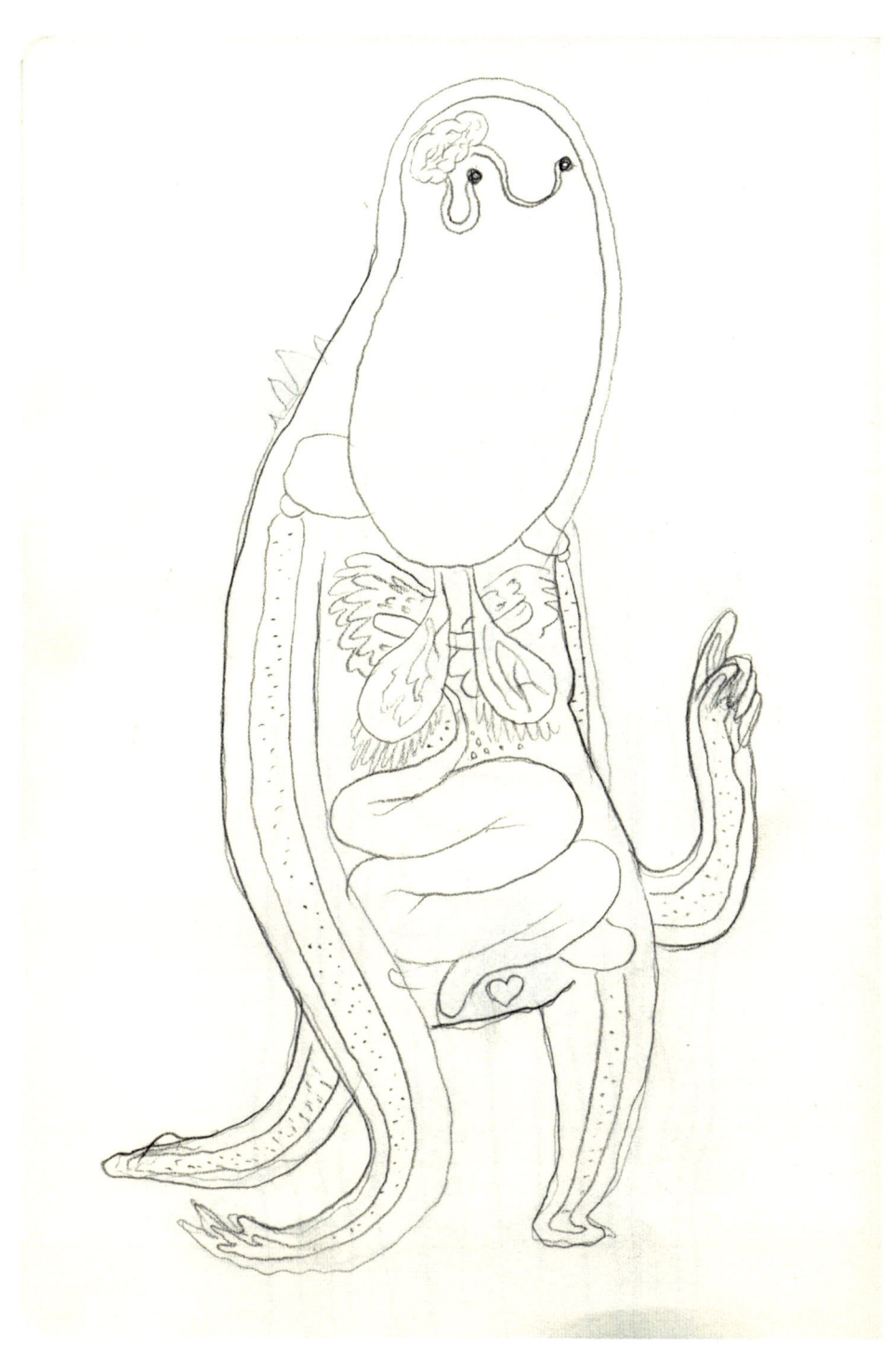

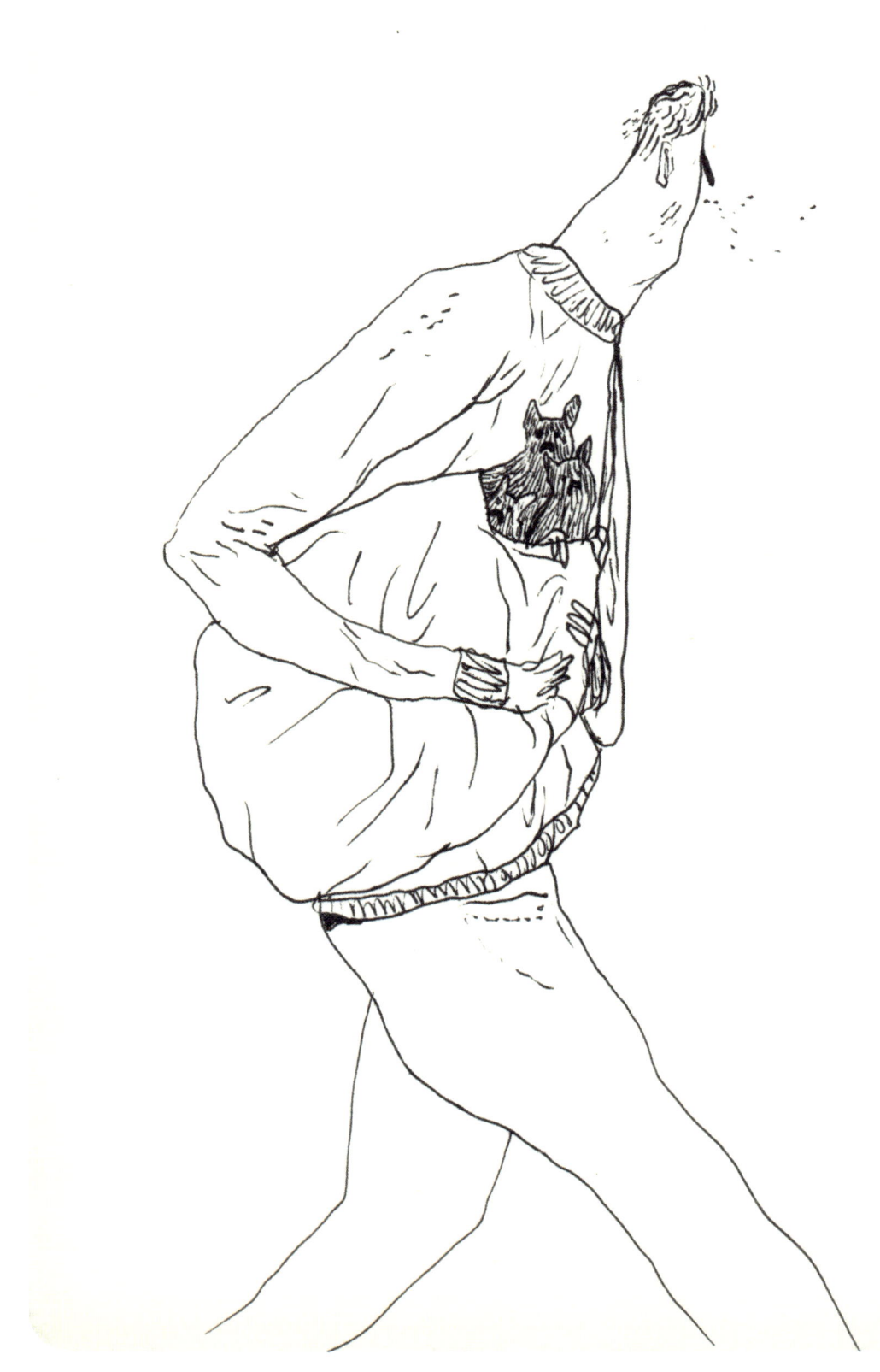

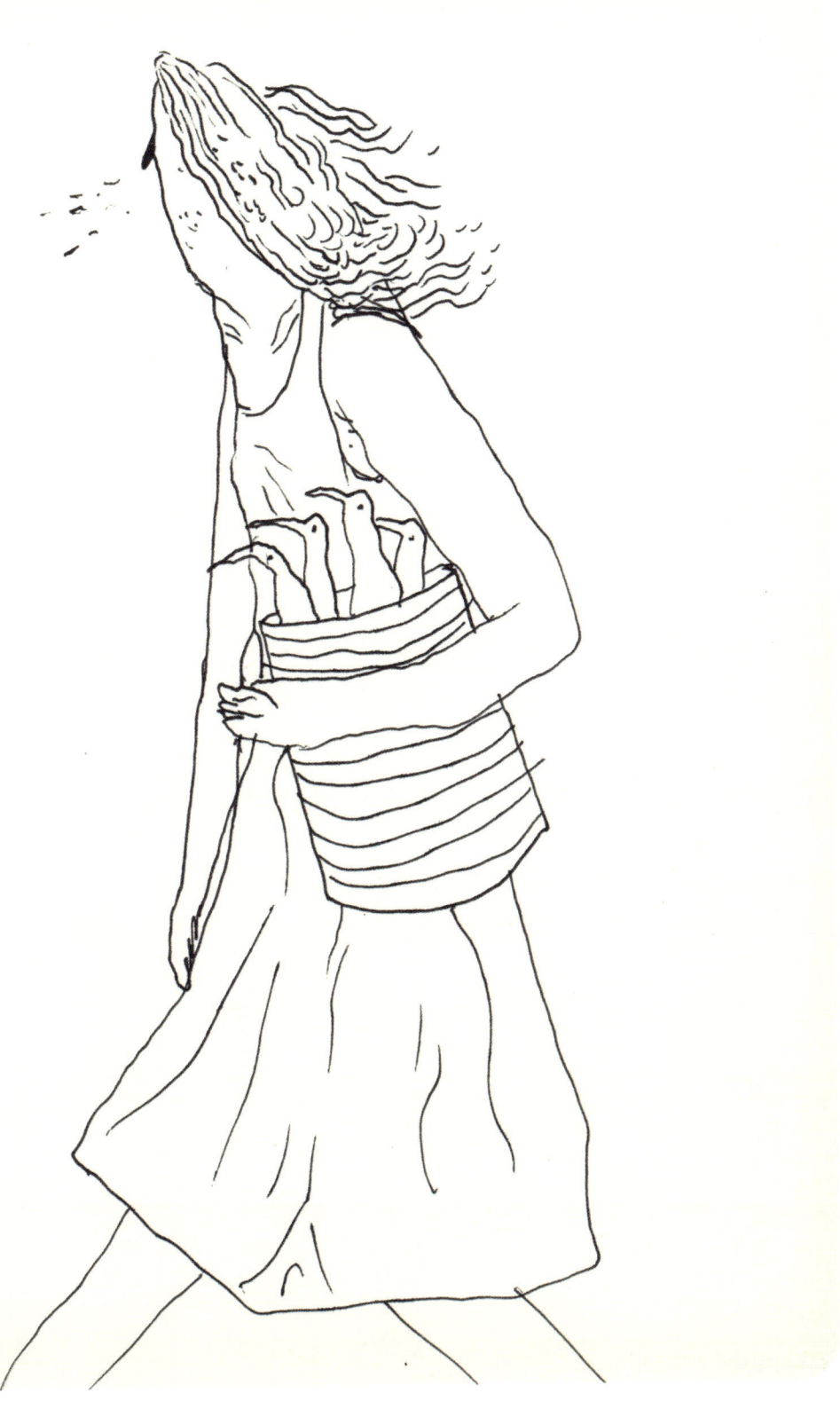

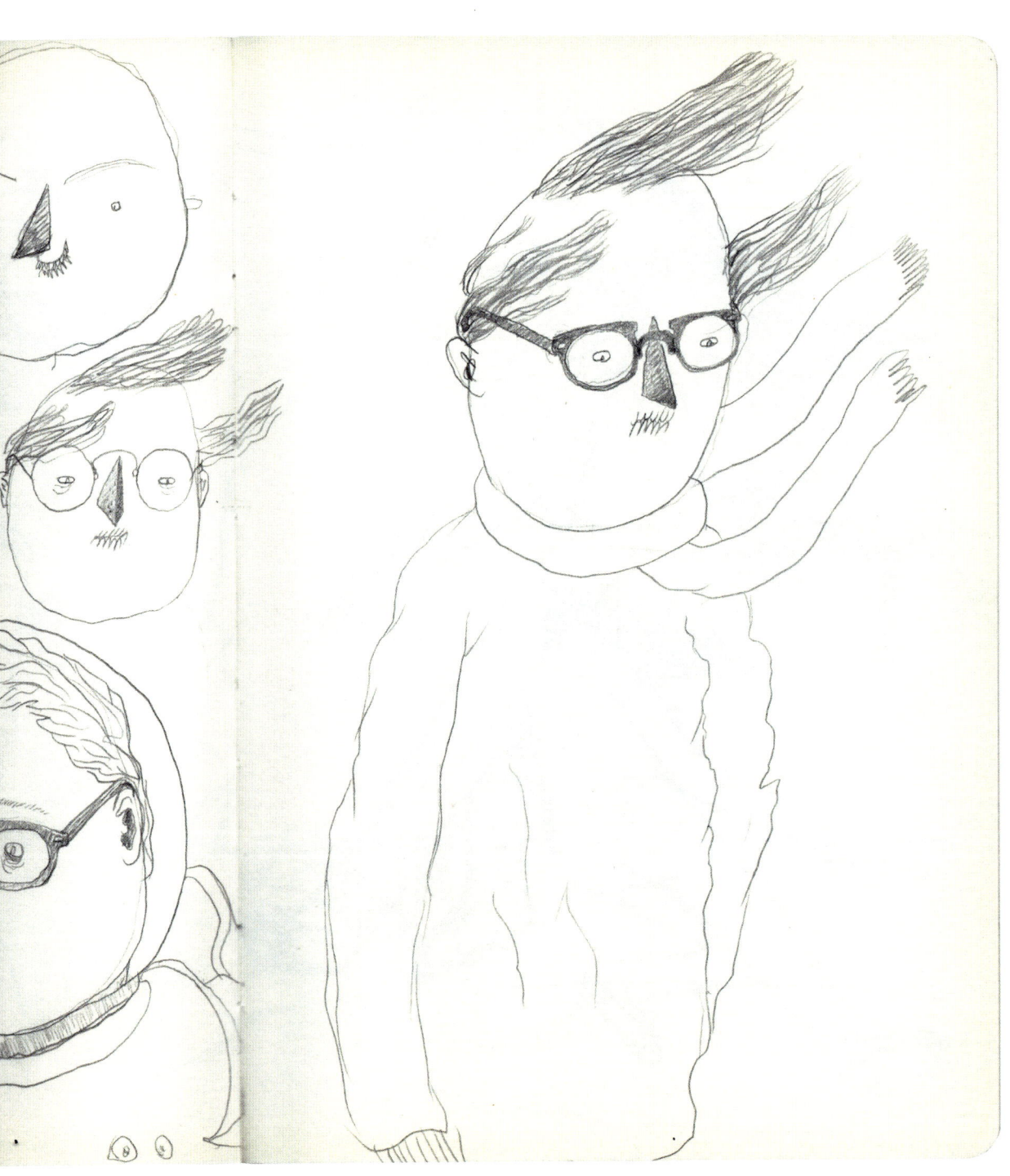

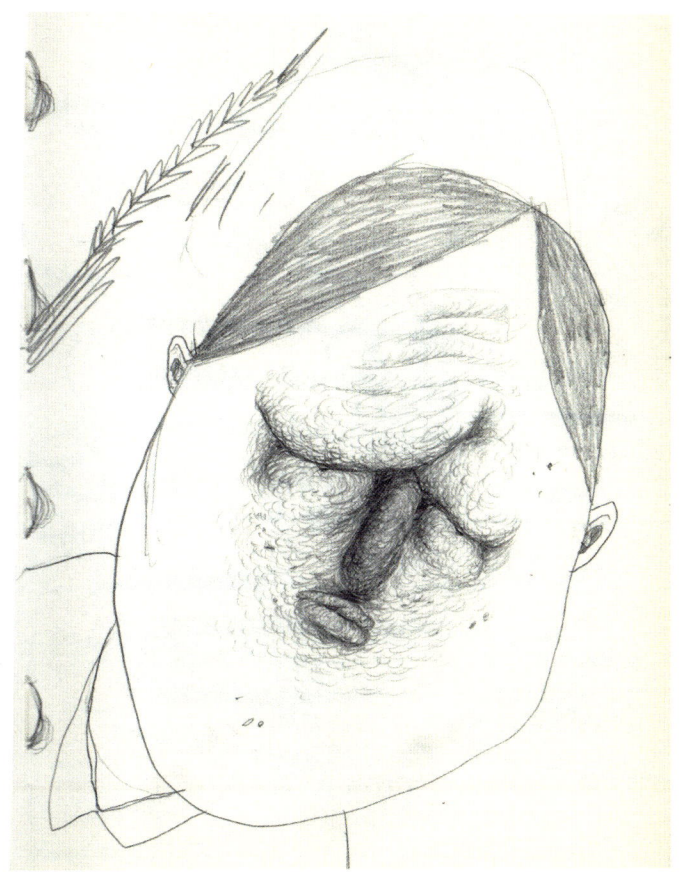

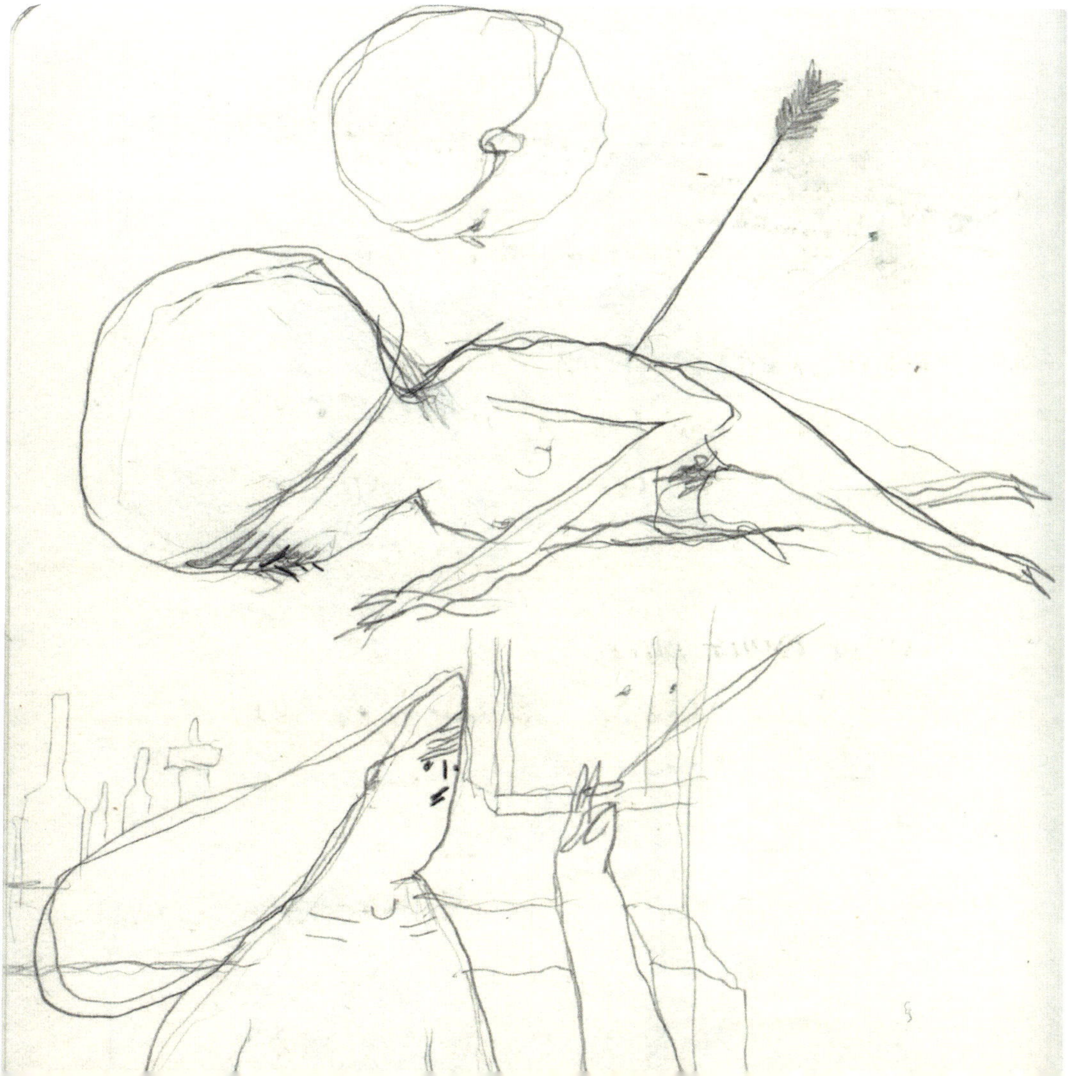

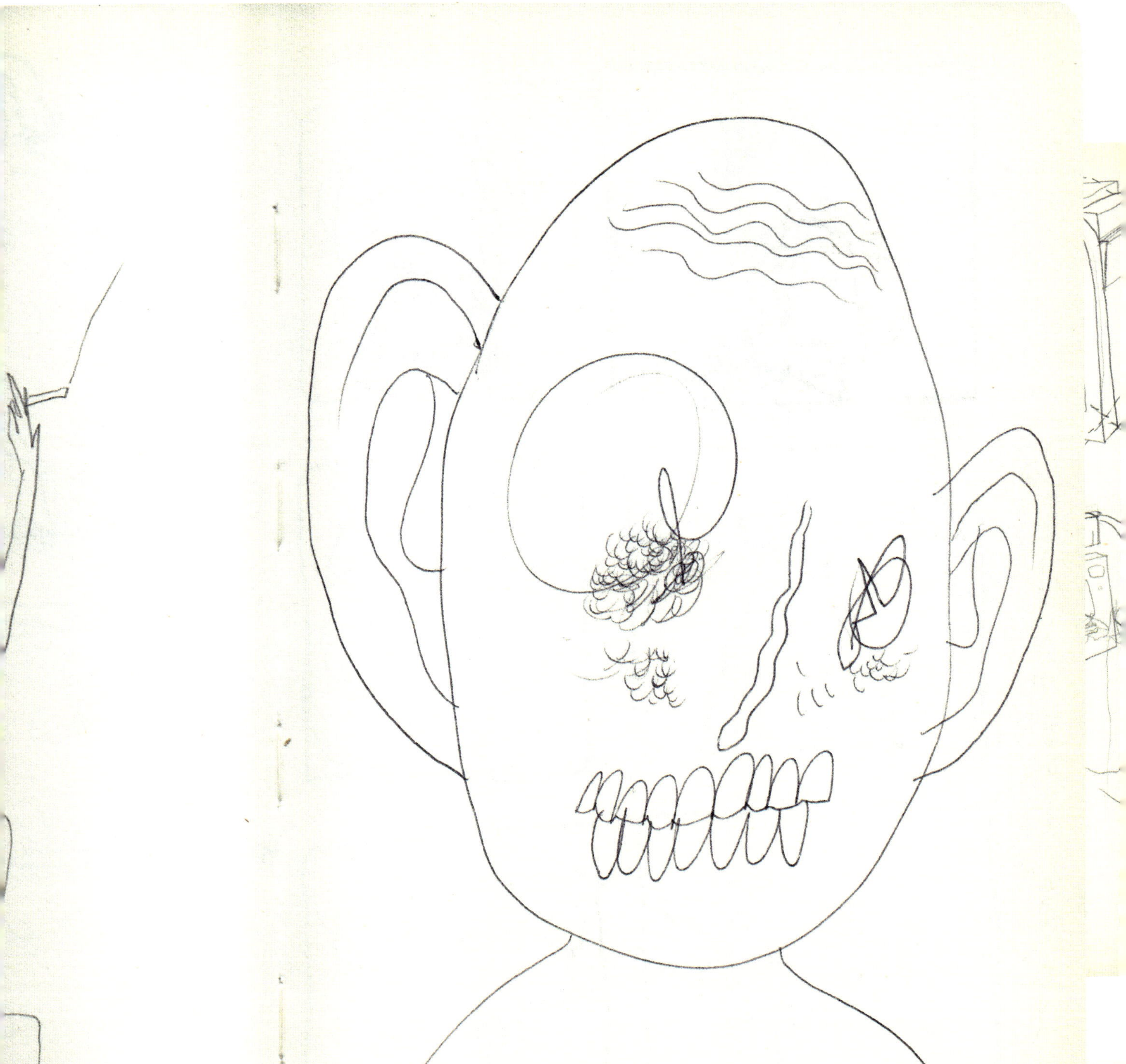

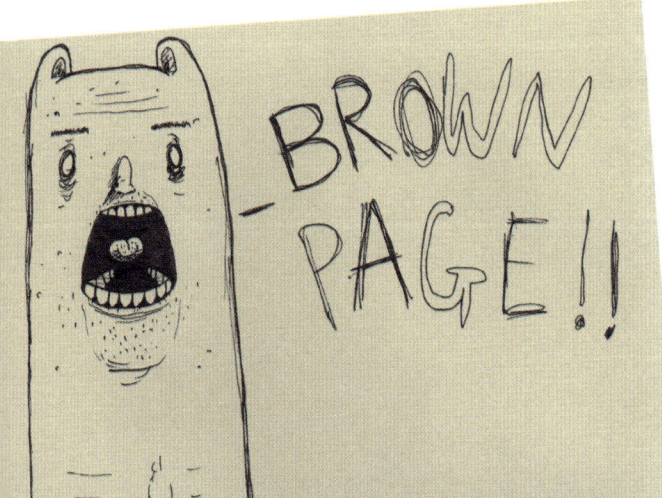
BROWN PAGE!!
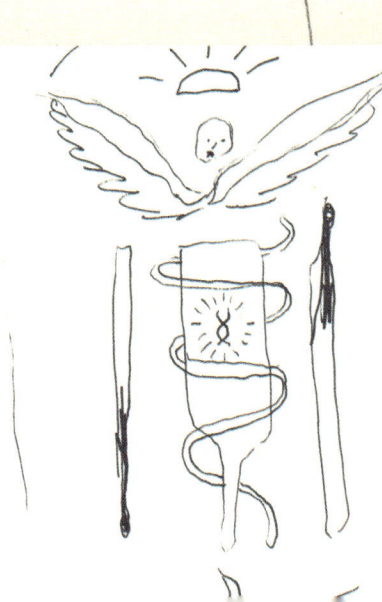

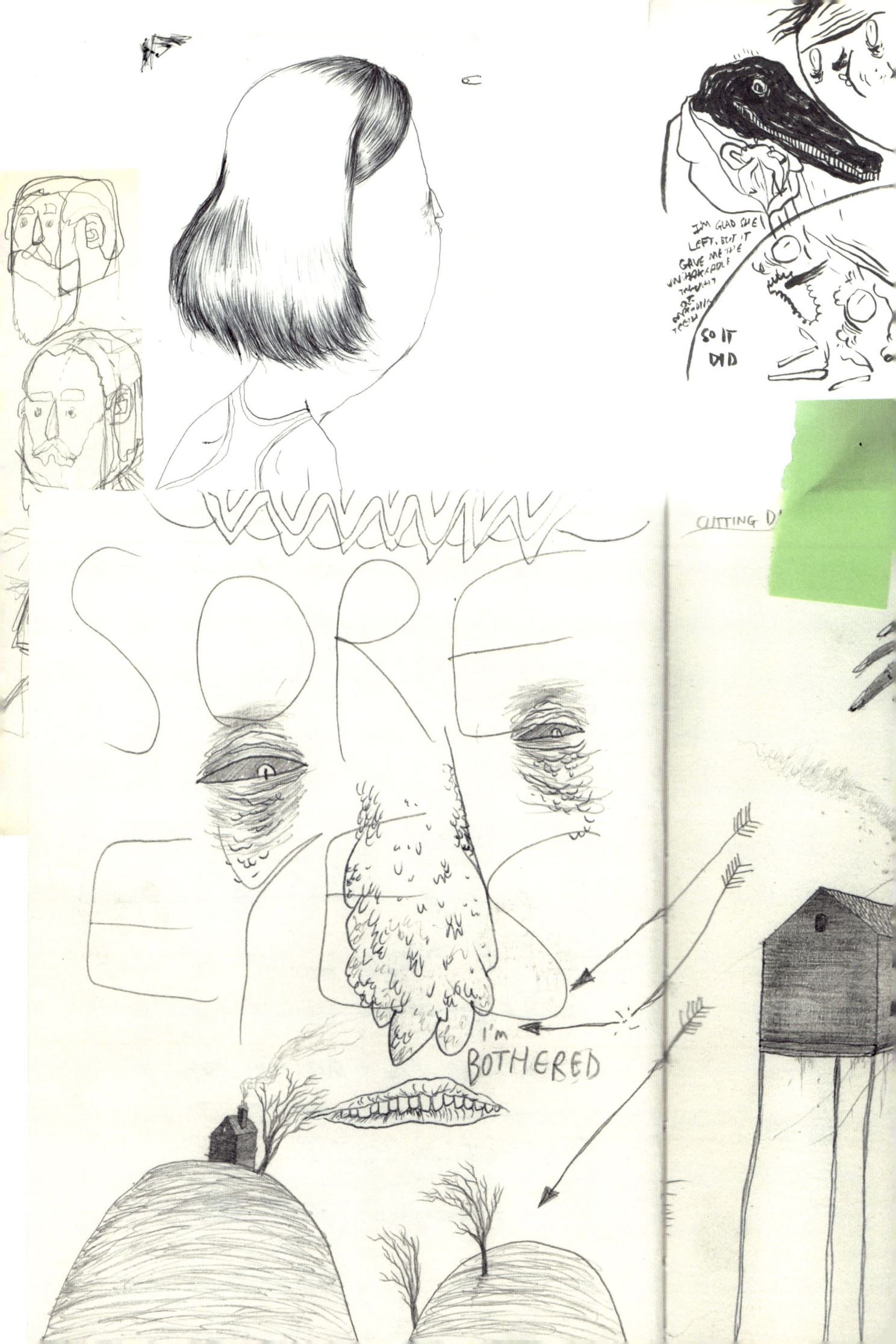

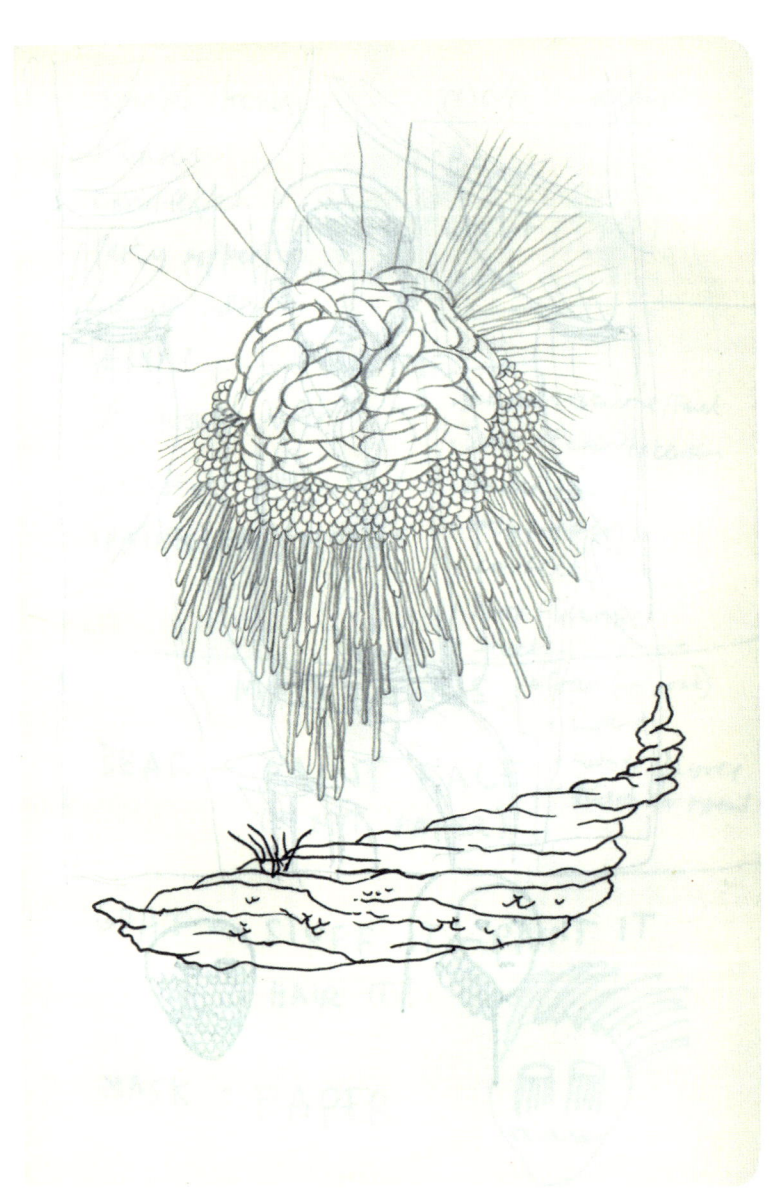

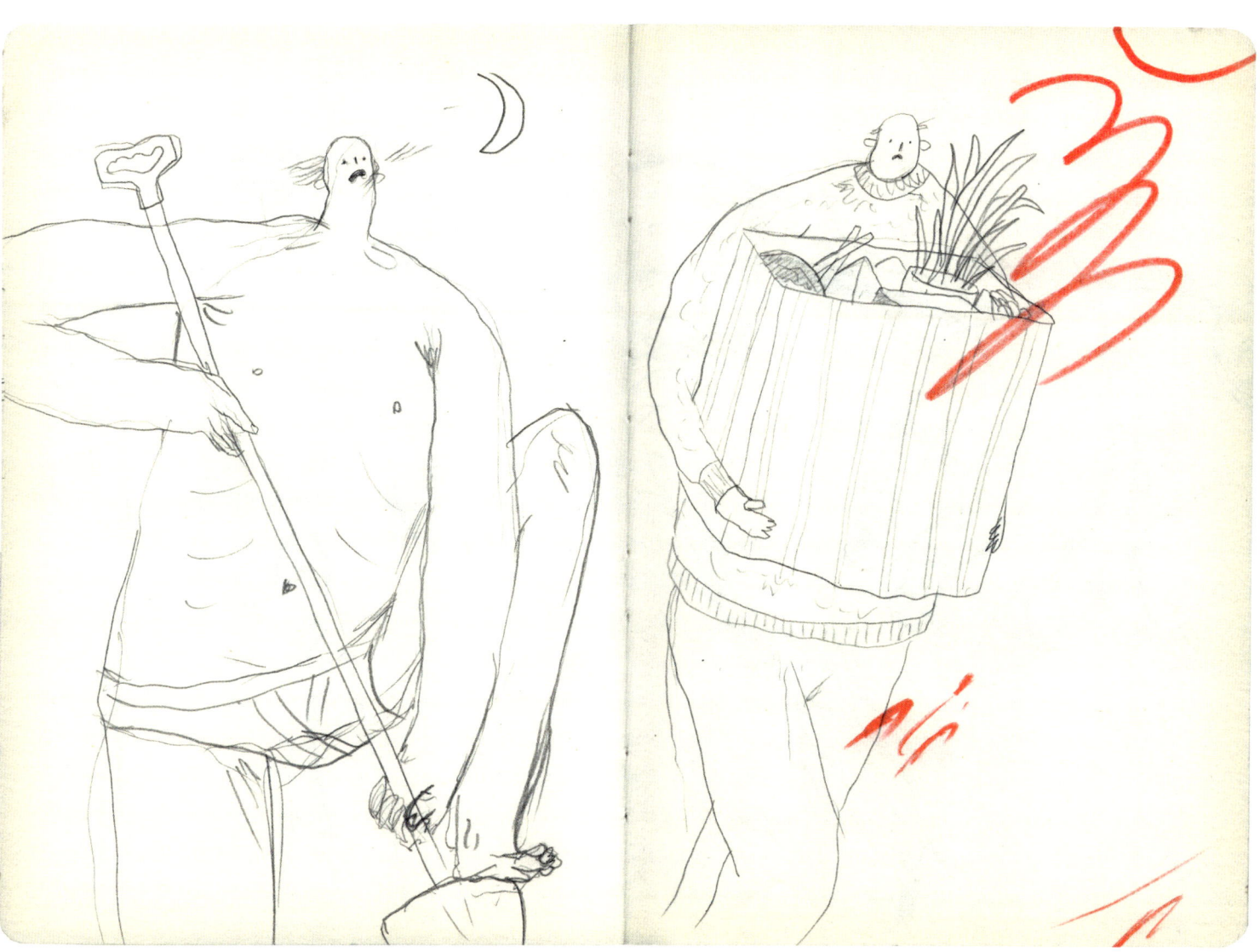

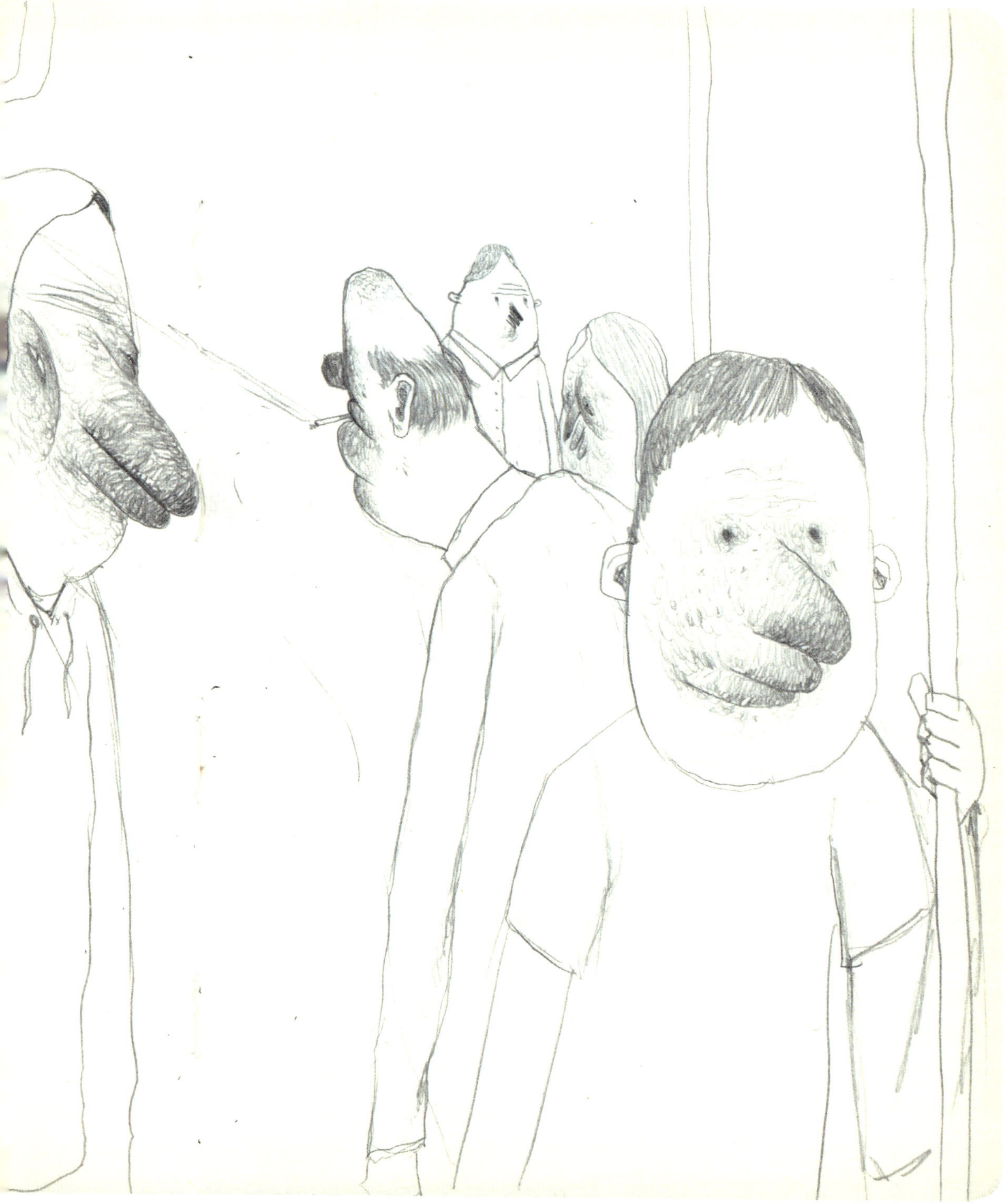

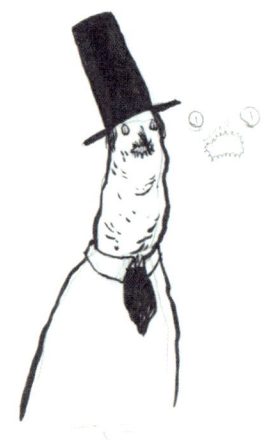

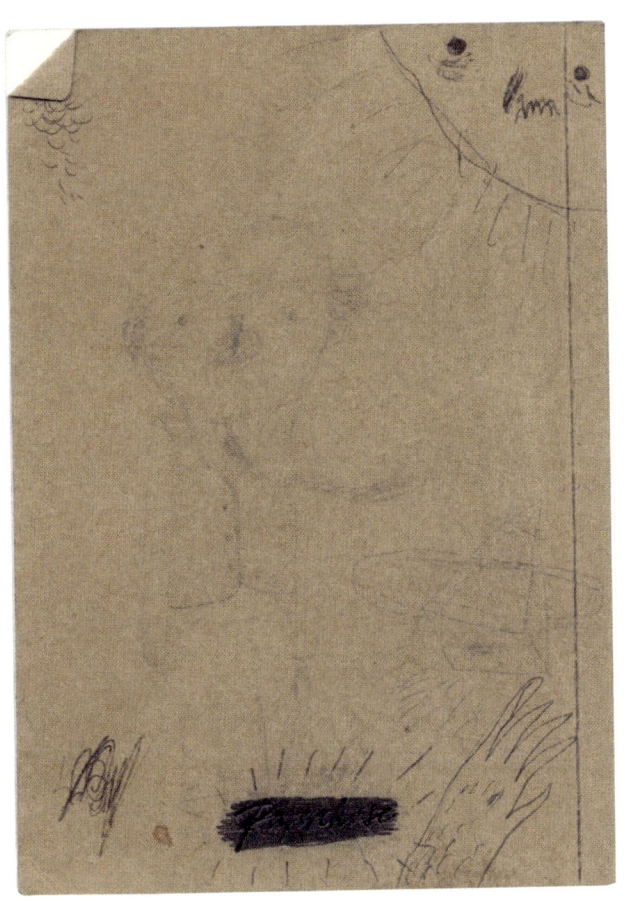

BOOK

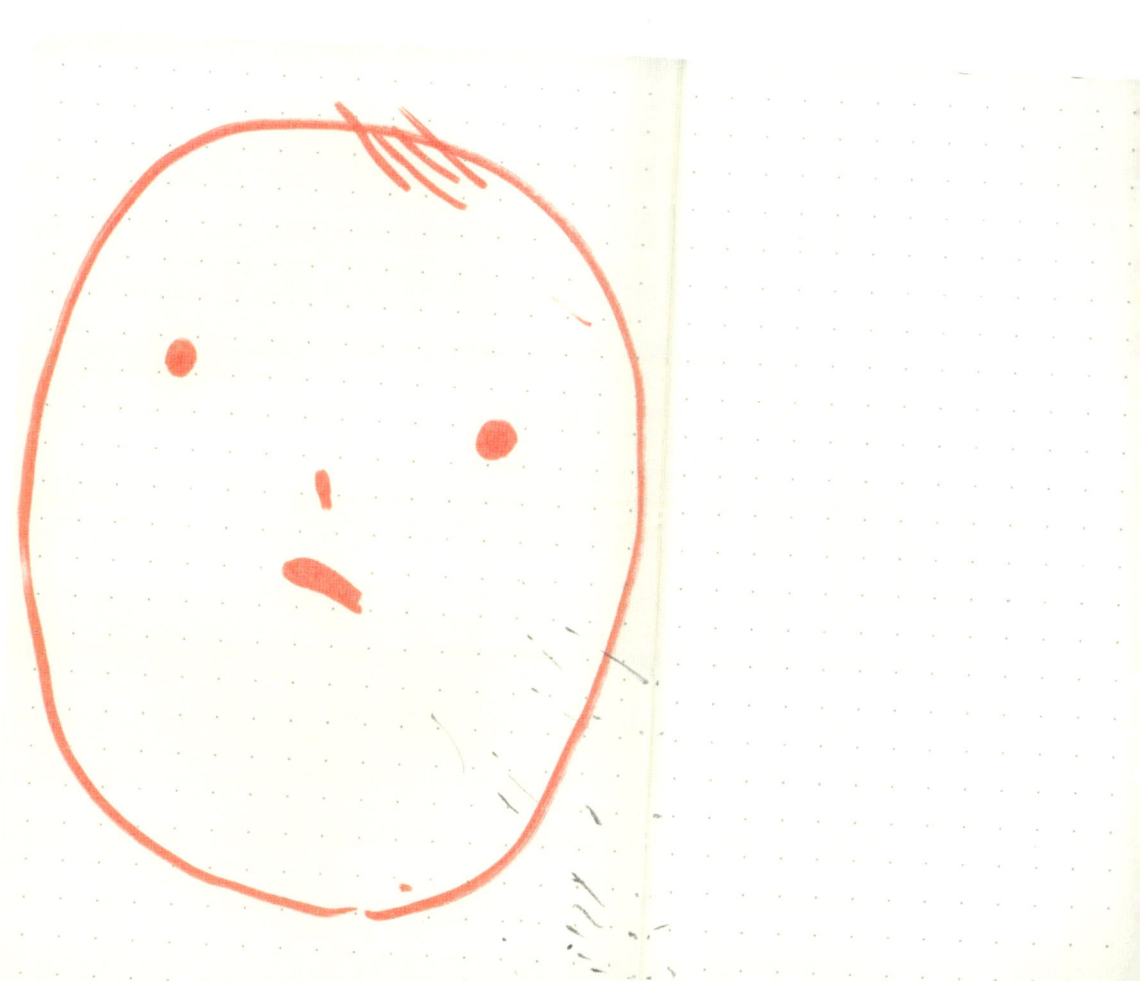

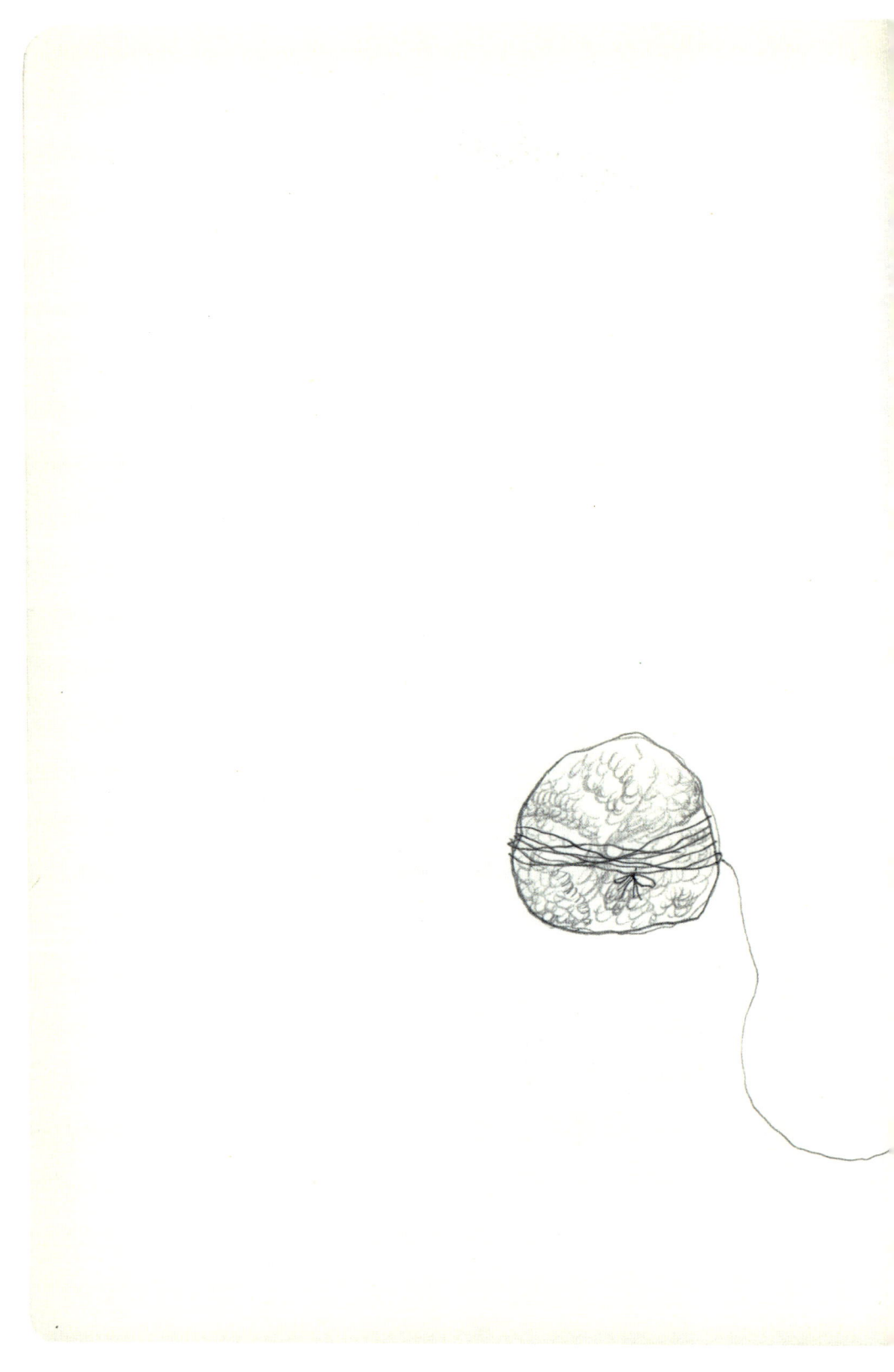

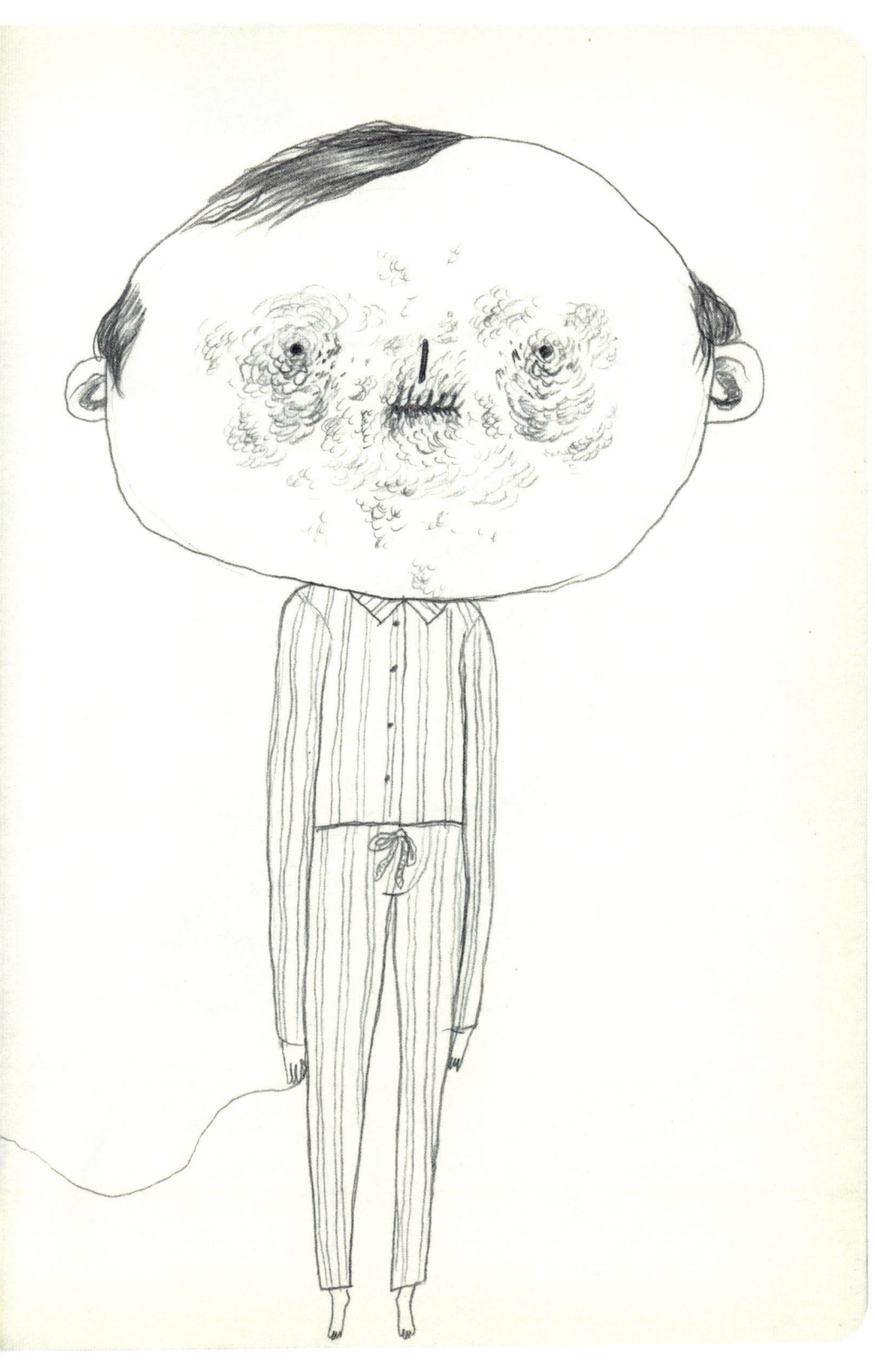

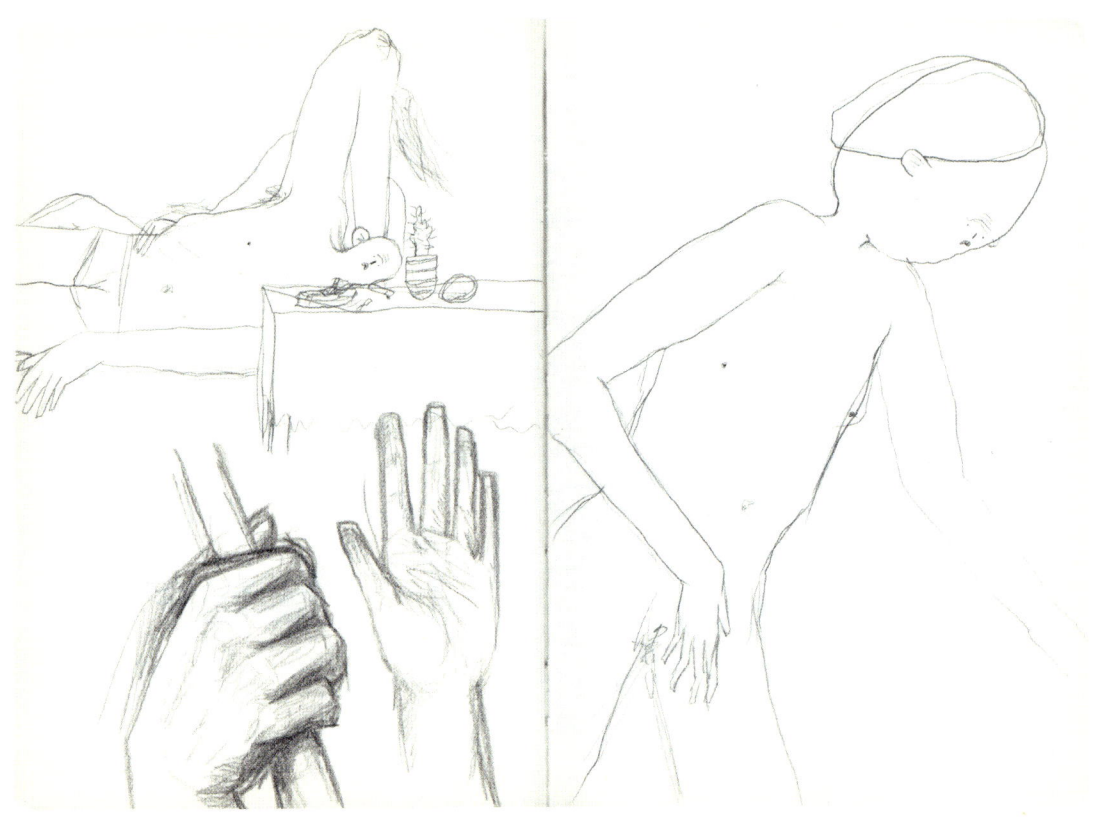
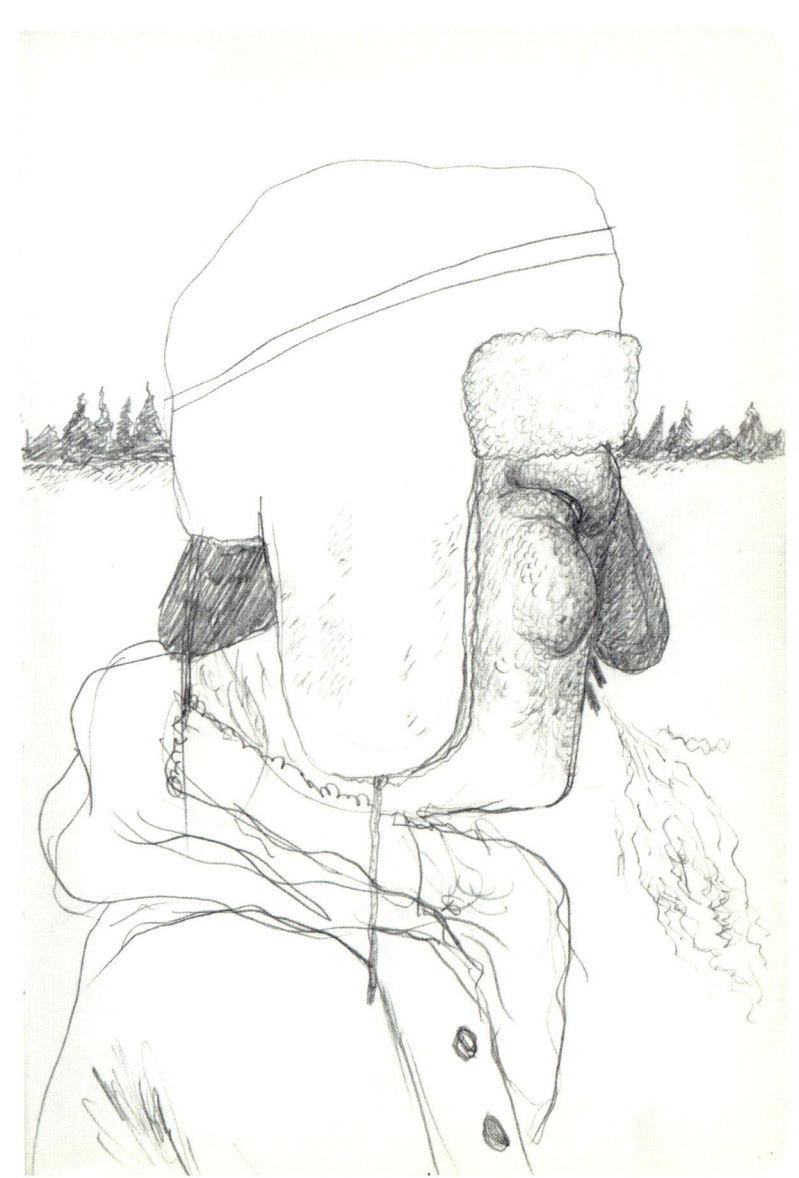

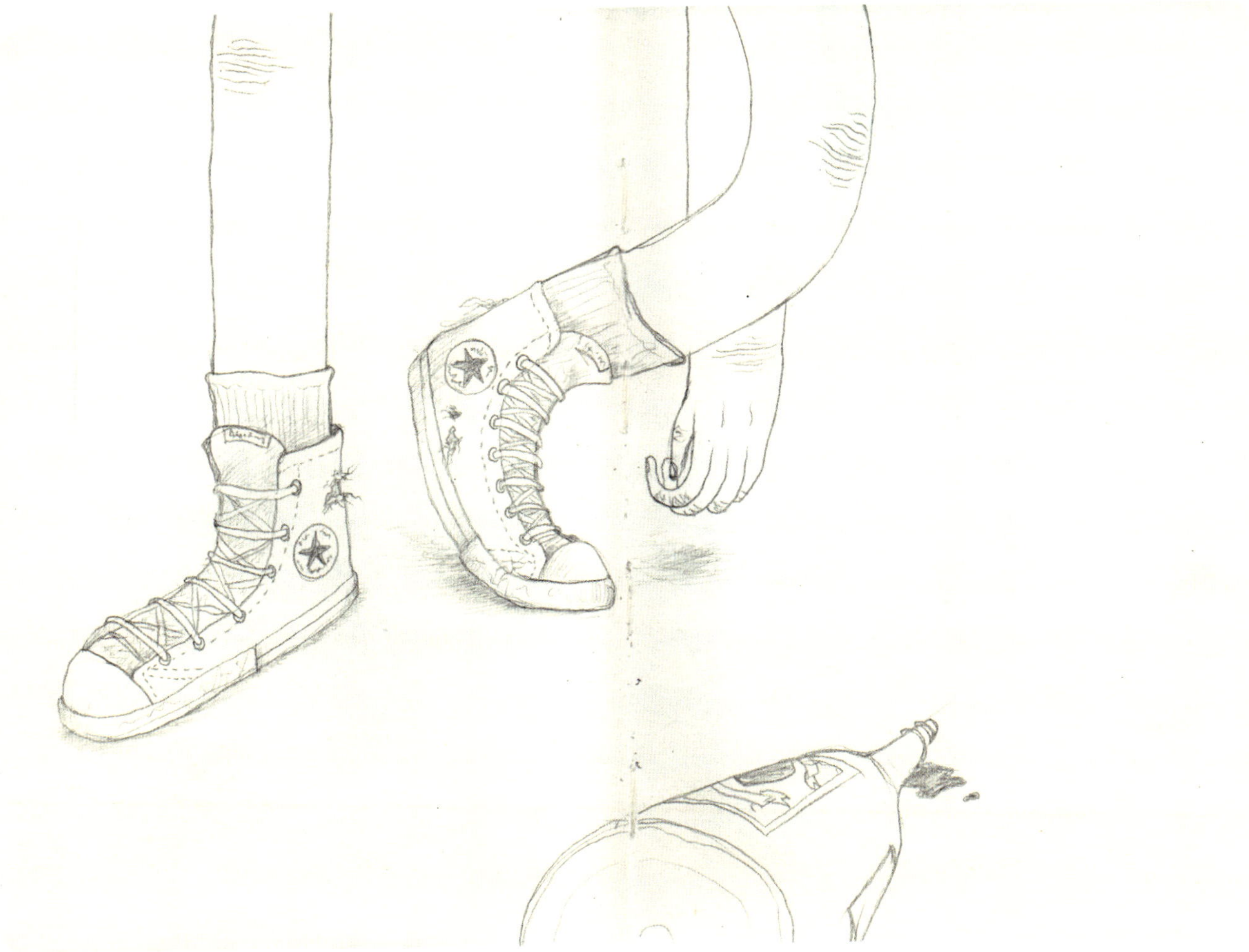

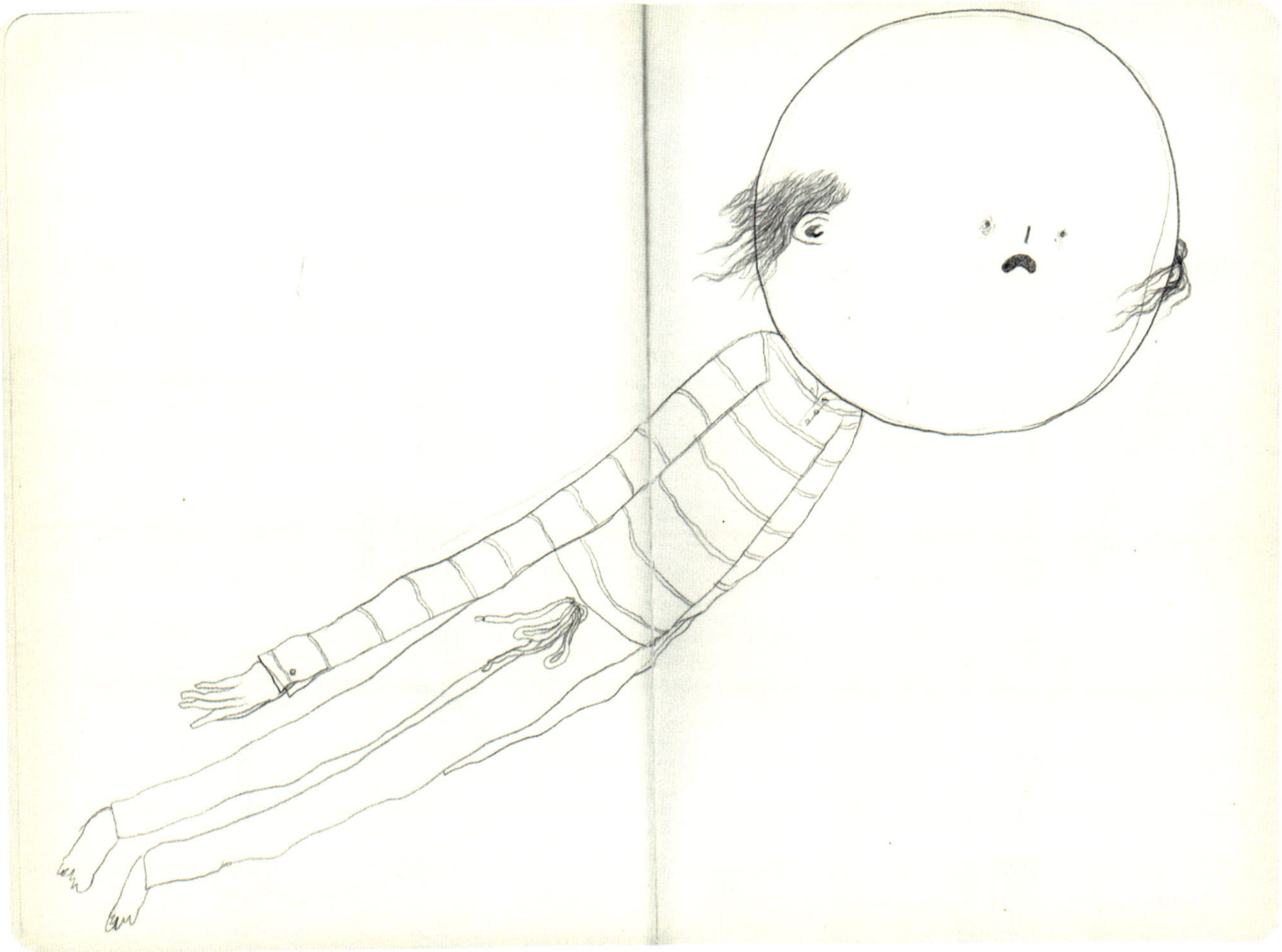

SEND DRIVE TO LUCY!

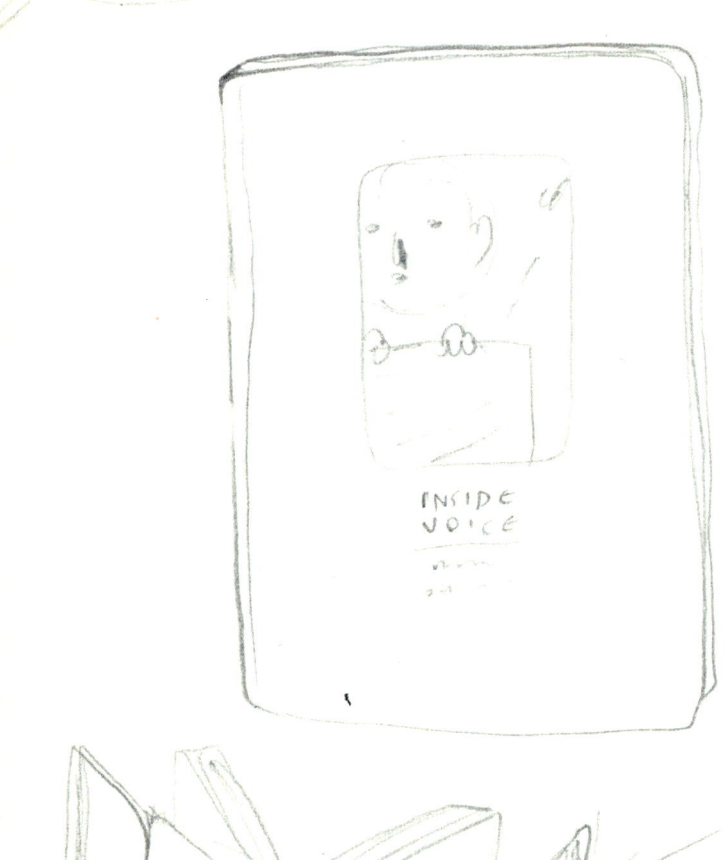

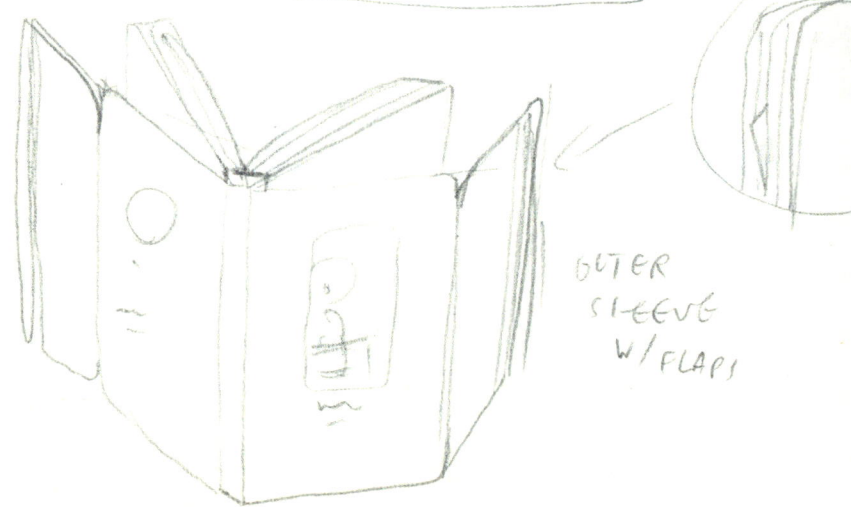

OUTER SLEEVE W/ FLAPS

Copyright © Keaton Henson, 2022
First published by Faber Music Ltd in 2022
Bloomsbury House
74–77 Great Russell Street
London WC1B 3DA

Cover design and drawings by Keaton Henson
Edited by Lucy Holliday
Printed and bound in Turkey by Imago on Munken paper

ISBN: 0-571-54248-4
EAN: 978-0-571-54248-2

Reproducing this book in any form is illegal and forbidden
by the Copyright, Designs and Patents Act, 1988

To buy Faber Music publications or to find out about the full range of titles
available please contact your local retailer or Faber Music sales enquiries:

Faber Music Limited, Burnt Mill, Elizabeth Way, Harlow, CM20 2HX, England
Tel: +44 (0) 1279 82 89 82
fabermusic.com

In case of loss, please return to:

ME

As a reward: $ A SENSE OF MORAL SUPERIORITY

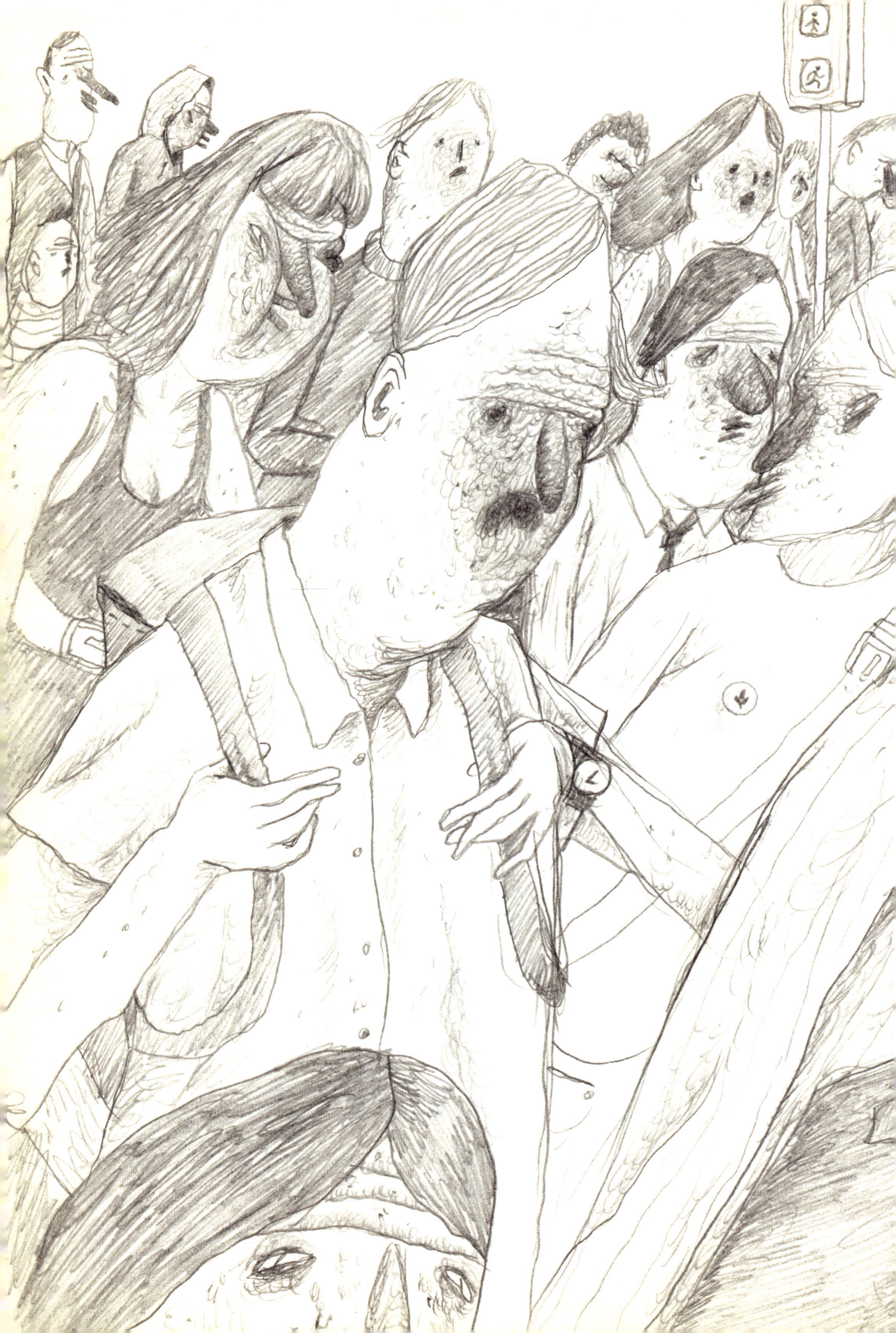